Multicultural Teaching

EIGHT EDITION

Multicultural Teaching

*A Handbook of
Activities, Information,
and Resources*

Pamela L. Tiedt
University of California, Berkeley

Iris M. Tiedt
Minnesota State University at Moorhead

Allyn & Bacon

Boston • New York • San Francisco
Mexico City • Montreal • Toronto • London • Madrid • Munich • Paris
Hong Kong • Singapore • Tokyo • Cape Town • Sydney

Series Editor: Kelly Villella Canton
Series Editorial Assistant: Annalea Manalli
Vice President, Marketing and Sales Strategies: Emily Williams Knight
Vice President, Director of Marketing: Quinn Perkson
Marketing Manager: Darcy Betts Prybella
Production Editor: Cynthia Parsons
Editorial Production Service: NK Graphics
Composition Buyer: Linda Cox
Manufacturing Buyer: Megan Cochran
Electronic Composition: NK Graphics
Interior Design: NK Graphics
Cover Designer: Linda Knowles

For related titles and support materials, visit our online catalog at www.pearsonhighered.com.

Between the time website information is gathered and then published, it is not unusual for some sites to have closed. Also, the transcription of URLs can result in typographical errors. The publisher would appreciate notification where these errors occur.

Library of Congress Cataloging-in-Publication Data
Tiedt, Pamela L.
  Mutlicultural teaching : a handbook of activities, information, and resources /
Pamela L. Tiedt, Iris M. Tiedt. —8th ed.
      p. cm.
  Includes bibliographical references and index.
  ISBN-13: 978-0-13-701101-8
  ISBN-10: 0-13-701101-6
  1. Multicultural education--United States.   2. Cross-cultural orientation--United States.
3. Teaching--United States.   4. Education, Elementary--Activity programs--United States.
5. Teachers--Training of--United States. I. Tiedt, Iris M. II. Title.

  LC1099.3.T54 2009
  370.1170973--dc22   2009019844

Printed in the United States of America
10 9 8 7 6 5 4 3 2   RRDVA   13 12 11 10 09

www.pearsonhighered.com

ISBN-10: 0137011016
ISBN-13: 9780137011018

About the Authors

Pamela Tiedt is a linguist and researcher/teacher educator in literacy and language arts. Her lifelong interest in language led to degrees in linguistics, specializing in the topics of language and the mind, child language acquisition, second language learning, and the social context of language use. Her publications in the area of sex differences in language use deepened her involvement in multicultural issues, drawing her into the field of education, where she incorporated literacy development, language diversity, and multicultural principles into teacher training. Her experience includes teaching English and training teachers in several countries as well as working with students at all levels, from children to adults. Her publications include *Multicultural Teaching* and *The Language Arts Activities for the Classroom.*

Born in Dayton, Ohio, Iris Tiedt obtained her BA in Education at Northwestern University, her MA in Interdisciplinary Studies at the University of Oregon, and her Ph.D in Curriculum and Instruction at Stanford University.

Dr.. Tiedt taught elementary and middle school grades beginning in an all-black school in Chicago and followed by years in Anchorage, and Eugene, Oregon, Later, she taught teacher education courses at the University of Santa Clara, University of Washington, Northern Kentucky University, and the Minnesota State University at Moorhead where she was Dean of Education and Regional Services.

In addition to *Multicultural Teaching*, her publications include: *Elementary Teacher's Complete Ideas Handbook, Contemporary English in the Elementary School, Readings on Contemporary English in the Elementary School, The Language Arts Activities for the Classroom,* and *Exploring Books with Children.*

Brief Contents

Contents

PART II

Integrating Multiculturalism Across the Curriculum   111

CHAPTER 4

Multicultural Language Arts/Reading   113

Preface

This eighth edition of *Multicultural Teaching* is dedicated once again to the teachers of the future, those who are preparing to teach in the school system, from kindergarten to grade 12, as well as to those already engaged in teaching who recognize that the process of learning to teach never ends. We need teachers who are inspired to give their best to teaching, to build bridges of caring among themselves, their students, and the community, and to create engaged, motivated learning communities in which students know that they are valued. In this way, we enable students to reach their full potential in their country and their world.

Although planning for multicultural education has long been an issue of concern for educators, the twenty-first century brings added pressures. The world is knocking at our door, the global village surrounds us, and we cannot ignore the multiple impacts on our classrooms. Any changes in society must be incorporated into our thinking as we struggle to redefine the goals of education—what students will need to know (skills, attitudes, and beliefs) to participate effectively as citizens of a multicultural world.

In the thirty years since this book was first published, every new edition has been substantially rewritten to reflect the shifting national conversation about the meaning of multiculturalism in our lives. As we prepare the eighth edition for 2010, we acknowledge the presence of new concerns and perspectives even as we pose new questions and issues.

We offer the model of *Esteem, Empathy,* and *Equity* to incorporate into every aspect of the curriculum while at the same time address current topics such as the rights of immigrants and standardized testing for educational reform.

❖ New to This Edition

In this edition we:

- emphasize a definition of Multicultural Education that integrates process (teaching/learning strategies) and content (critical concepts such as racism and diversity) to create the curriculum of the future;
- expand coverage to address teaching in grades PreK–12 more completely;
- continue to support the presence of multiple languages in the classroom;
- continue to weave our *Esteem/Empathy/Equity* model into all teaching;
- recognize the importance of Math and Science teaching by dividing our discussions of them into separate chapters (ch. 6 and 7);
- elaborate on the need for cross-curricular planning and development;
- offer additional alternatives for student-centered assessment;

- illustrate the importance of high expectations for students by incorporating higher-level critical thinking skills as well as creative and open-ended thinking;
- include historical events, recent legislation, and legal decisions that affect teaching and learning in diverse settings;
- introduce topics of current concern such as human trafficking and global climate change and their implications for multicultural education;
- provide background information for teaching about anti-Arab prejudice;
- include a variety of sample lesson plans to adapt to different levels or student abilities;
- outline plans for thematic studies on varied topics;
- clarify the significance of "white privilege" and how to recognize its impact on teaching;
- define key terms such as marginalization, social class, indentity group, and heterosexism;
- support teachers of students who speak different languages;
- increase recognition of "mixed race" indentities;
- discuss the external socioeconomic factors that affect student achievement; and
- plan for continued growth as a multiculturally competent teacher.

❖ Instructor Supplement to the Text

To help you get the most out of using *Multicultural Teaching: A Handbook of Activities, Information, and Resources, 8/e* with your students, we have written the instructor resource below. The following instructor supplement is available for download on the Pearson Instructor Resource Center (IRC) at www.pearsonhighered.com. You may contact your local Pearson representative if you need assistance accessing IRC.

Instructor's Manual with Test Bank offers a variety of chapter-by-chapter resources, ready-to-use classroom activities, and test questions.

❖ Acknowledgments

We would like to thank the following reviewers of the previous edition for their thoughtful and detailed input: H. Prentice Baptiste, New Mexico State University; Wendy Brandon, Rollins College; Lorie Hunn, Chadron State College; Kathleen Kaminski, Wilson College; and Rebecca Todd, Highland Elementary School.

We hope that you will join with us in reaching out to all learners to help them become the informed citizens and responsible leaders who will be needed to make critical decisions for the future. We must prepare them now to develop the strengths they will need to confront problems that we cannot yet imagine.

Multicultural Teaching

Multicultural Teaching and Learning

This book is divided into three parts. The first part is comprised of three chapters in which we set up a foundation for multicultural teaching and learning. The second part demonstrates how we build multicultural programs and incorporate multicultural goals into each specific curricular area. In the last section we explore the larger world of social, political, and economic issues which impact multicultural teaching and discuss how we can develop and maintain our cultural competency as multicultural teachers.

We begin with Chapter 1 which describes the development of multicultural thinking and establishes the framework within which we present key concepts for definition. We discuss the nature of diversity as well as the way that differences are used to signal and enforce the dominance of specific groups. We look at the different models of multicultural education that have been developed and explain the assumptions on which we base this book, a model that we call *Esteem/Empathy/Equity*. In Chapter 2, we investigate the role of the teacher as a learner empowered to create an environment that fosters engagement, caring, and growing. We show how teachers can make their classrooms welcoming and inclusive of all students. Chapter 3 looks at multicultural teaching and learning from the perspective of strategies for planning, organizing, and assessing that support diverse students in diverse settings. We include examples of how teachers can adapt these instructional stategies to accommodate the strengths and interests of all students from PreK–12.

Multicultural education concerns all of us. All teachers need to be teaching multiculturally, and multicultural teaching is intended for all students. It won't keep students from dropping out of school or solve poverty in America, but it can prepare them to be active participants in the world, to raise their voices and be heard. Yo Yo Ma, renowned cellist and cultural ambassador, has conceived a project to create international connections between music and identity, based on the model of the "Great Silk Road," the ancient trade route that spread knowledge, culture, and skills throughout Asia and Europe. In the following comment, he explains what this connection means to him today.

If you love some instrument, if you like the sound of it, it's like no other sound. It's really yours. It comes from deep within, and it's something you can always connect with inside. How good can that be? Your music, your sound—it's your friend for life. You can express how you feel, send your self into the larger world. You will always have that voice. That's a pretty powerful thing.

CHAPTER 1

The Changing Face of Multicultural Thinking

If I am not for myself, then who will be for me?

And if I am only for myself, then, what am I?

And if not now, when?

~ HILLEL

Humans are vulnerable beings living in a fragile, increasingly complex world. The many different threats to life around us, such as interethnic violence (genocide in Darfur), global climate change (floods in India), and environmental degradation (deforestation in the Amazon), require us to unite in our common humanity to deal with the consequences. No one can remain unaffected; we are inevitably interdependent. Any event that occurs anywhere on this small planet, even halfway around the world from us, will have an impact on us, as we see in the rising cost of gasoline, the chemicals in the food we grow or import, and the pollution of the air we breathe and the water we drink. The ripples of change reach everywhere, stoking fears about aspects of life we used to take for granted and heightening hostility toward others struggling over limited resources.

On a national level, the political climate in this country has created controversy among educators as they debate the implications of standardized testing, measuring school and teacher accountability, and setting performance levels that all students must achieve in order to graduate. Related topics such as charter schools, vouchers, a set curriculum, and nationalized teacher testing combine for an increased focus on teaching "the basics," resulting in less funding for subject areas such as art and music that don't fit easily into standard tests, and reduced classroom time spent on critical thinking or creative activities. In order to survive, schools are adopting a "one size fits all" approach.

Despite this restricted environment, teachers can still make choices to provide the best education possible for all students. When teachers promote high expectations for everyone, project care for each student as an individual with different strengths and weaknesses, provide content that acknowledges the diversity in the classroom, and adapt their teaching to take into account the knowledge and experiences that every student can contribute to the class, they are teaching "multiculturally." In this chapter, we will talk about the great diversity of this country, what we call our unique "multiculture," challenge the assumptions of how we define an "American," and explain the development of multicultural thinking.

We build multicultural education on a shared goal: to create an educational system that will educate *all* children in our society, to permit them to develop to the greatest extent of their potential, so they can participate fully in what the world has to offer, to contribute to the world, and to benefit from the best resources of the world.

> *When you see Earth from the moon, you realize how fragile it is and just how limited the resources are. We're all astronauts on this spaceship Earth—about six or seven billion of us—and we have to work and live together.*
> ~ CAPTAIN JAMES LOVELL, NASA astronaut

❖ Diversity in America

The United States has always been a country of great diversity. The poet Ishmael Reed calls America the place "where the cultures of the world crisscross." However, when so many different languages, religions, ethnicities, abilities, and values coexist, just getting along becomes an everyday struggle, too often accompanied by violence and hostility. Multicultural education involves recognizing the complex historical reality that shadows us as well as the distant and difficult-to-measure goal toward which we strive. It requires constant attention and self-reflection to make this diversity work. As teachers, we are dedicated to creating a community in our classrooms, a place where diversity is not just tolerated but *celebrated*. We recognize the unique experiences and different perspectives that each person can contribute to the whole as a valuable asset that benefits everyone and, therefore, we build our instruction around this diversity.

The Great Multiculture

The United States has been known around the world as "a nation of immigrants," "the land of opportunity," and "Gold Mountain," always promising a place to make a new identity, to become a "self-made man," to go from "rags to riches." Contrast that with the reality faced by the hordes of nineteenth-century immigrants: they were crammed into processing stations at Ellis Island and Angel Island and laws were passed excluding Chinese.

Irish, Italian, German, Jew—they all landed in a country where they faced unremitting hostility, prejudice, and violence from the groups that preceded them.

Today's immigrants still encounter many of the same conditions. Intense debates over immigration have always arisen when people fear the possibility of changes in their world and begin asking whether it is "time to close the gate." For example, current arguments over the treatment of "illegal" immigrants and related issues such as providing access to schooling, issuing driver's licenses, and granting amnesty are driven by recent dramatic demographic changes. In a region such as Minnesota, Mexicans once migrated through as seasonal workers, but now they are beginning to stay, raise families, put their children in school, and consequently have a visible impact on the community. Negative stereotypes and prejudices immediately flourish as people interpret these new cultural differences in their lives through a lens that tells them to "fear the other." This attitude is often expressed through anxiety over how they and their community will be expected to accommodate these differences. Clearly, many people prefer that evidence of differences disappear, despite the historical reality that Latinos have been present in this country, as Americans, for many generations.

America's promise of welcome to all people was tellingly expressed in 1909, in the play *The Melting Pot* by Israel Zangwill:

> America is God's Crucible, the great Melting Pot where all the races of Europe are melting and reforming! Here you stand, good folk, think I, when I see them at Ellis Island, here you stand in your fifty hatreds and rivalries, but you won't be long like that, brothers, for these are the fires of God. A fig for your feuds and vendettas! Germans and Frenchmen, Irishmen and Englishmen, Jews and Russians—into the Crucible with you all! God is making the American . . . The real American has not yet arrived. He is only in the Crucible, I tell you—he will be the fusion of all races, the coming superman.

Thus, the "melting pot" became the symbol for assumptions about Americanization for many decades, as we wrestled with what it meant to create an "American." Zangwill's words painted a powerful and comforting image. In a time of upheaval in Europe, he claimed that sectarianism could fall away and a new kind of person could be born. His references to the crucible reinforced the necessity of eradicating all prior distinctions. Americanization meant *assimilation,* so generations of immigrants and their descendants jumped into the *melting pot* to eliminate any foreign accents, unusual clothing, or distinctive customs that would betray their (non-American) origins. The children of the next generation wanted to be just like the others they went to school with, to fit in with the "Americans" and not be laughed at.

The metaphor of the "melting pot" began to lose its allure in the last century as people asked questions about where they came from and searched for their "roots" to find out who they were. When people looked back, they found that assimilation had not erased all traces of their language, their cultural heritage, and their ethnic identity. From the beginning, many groups of immigrants had instead struggled to maintain some elements of their heritage: they supported "Saturday" schools that passed the language and traditions on to the next generations (Chinese communities), they published newspapers and books in their language to maintain literacy in it (Yiddish speakers), and they settled near others like themselves and sought comfort in the familiar by joining in ethnic-based social clubs (like many Scandinavians). In fact, the "melting pot" image did not describe how people really lived, nor did it encompass their goals for their families. Although it frequently occurs in common conversation, we feel that the continued use of the "melting pot" is thoughtless; it unfairly distorts the "narrative" of our history and denigrates the lived experience of the diverse groups that came together in the United States at different times and now form what we call the American multiculture.

We need to break the hold of this assimilationist ideology, the uncritical references to "melting pot," and replace it with a metaphor that creates an image more appropriate to the diverse America we celebrate. After all, we are proud that people took many different paths to becoming Americans, holding on to elements of the familiar (food, language, and traditions) while reaching out to the new (public education and increased economic opportunities). The image that we suggest for today's conversation is that of a *tossed salad*.

A tossed salad is a combination of different ingredients that, when mixed, create a special flavor all their own, without any element losing its special qualities.

When applied to groups of people, the *tossed salad* metaphor implies that everyone can add something special without eradicating any part of their unique identity. Other metaphors have been suggested, such as a *rainbow,* a *quilt,* or a *mosaic.* Each metaphor carries

America Is a Tossed Salad!

with it different images and implications for diversity. For example, Robert F. Kennedy, in the 1968 presidential primary, reached out to many when he said:

> Let us begin to see the true promise of our country and community, not just as a melting pot, but as a kaleidoscope. It takes each of us to make a difference for all of us.

What other metaphors have you heard people use? Which metaphor feels most comfortable to you, and why?

If we are going to celebrate the diversity of our population, we will have to look at this concept from a different perspective, as a strength rather than a creation of divisions. Too often, in newspaper reports of increasing minority populations, "diversity" is meant to evoke the specter of the American union falling apart. On the other hand, when "diversity" is part of a description of a place to visit, such as Vancouver, Canada, it is intended to create a positive impression of a desirable asset. Our best illustration of recognizing the contributions of diversity comes from President Abraham Lincoln, who upon his election, two centuries ago, appointed several of his political opponents to be his advisors. He recognized the benefit of surrounding himself with people who would challenge him with their own opinions. Barack Obama reached out for a memorable connection with his predecessor when he took the oath of office as 44th president with his hand on Lincoln's bible.

To be able to live well in this multiculture, we have to keep asking ourselves the following questions:

- From whom can I learn?
- How can I grow?
- What will strengthen my abilities to work effectively with people who come from different backgrounds?
- What skills will I need to be a competent citizen of the world?
- How can we build a better world?
- How can we prepare ourselves and our students for an increasingly unpredictable future?

Our country is a giant multiculture, and in a multiculture there must always be more than one acceptable way to live, think, and be oneself. Such an understanding is fundamental to our planning for multicultural education, to prepare students, as philosopher-educator John Dewey advocated, to reach their fullest potential.

Who Is an American?

Thinking multiculturally means recognizing truths that have always been present; we just need to learn how to look at the familiar through new eyes. One place to start is to think of the history of the United States as a clash of cultures. When we look at the story of the land that eventually became our fifty states, we begin to recognize the constant presence of diversity. Typically, when we begin to study our country, we learn about Jamestown and Plymouth Rock, the early English settlements, but not about the Spanish presence in Florida or the Russians and Spanish on the West Coast. By 1810, New Orleans was the seventh-largest city in the area that would become the United States but only a small percentage of its population was Anglo American. The rest of its inhabitants included

French, Spanish, Portuguese, German, Italian, Irish, free people of color (usually freed slaves), enslaved Africans, and Haitians of mixed White/Black heritage. The language of communication in this diverse community was French. However, once New Orleans joined the Union, all these people of varying backgrounds suddenly turned into Americans.

Colonists from Spain had settled a large area, from California and the Southwest to Texas, and these settlements were ruled first by Spain, then Mexico, and finally some became independent. When that region was gradually made part of the Union, Spanish was suddenly the native language of a large proportion of Americans. Not surprisingly, many of these Americans passed along Spanish as a part of their heritage for generations. Are these people not considered real Americans because they are "hyphenated"? How can we define who is a *true* American? Many non-White people, born in the United States and native speakers of English, report being complimented on the quality of their speech or asked what country they come from, under the assumption that only Whites are American. Many people still carry a single, simplistic vision of what an "American" is and refuse to recognize the diversity of the Americans with whom they share this country.

From Alaska to Florida, Hawai'i to Maine, each region has been influenced throughout its history by a variety of distinct racial, ethnic, linguistic, religious, and cultural groups, and thus each region contributed its complex diversity to the United States. For illustration, look at the range of languages other than English that are spoken in the following states. (As you peruse the list, remember that many of these people also speak English.)

Alaska: Inuit, Inupiaq (Eskimo), Yupik (Native American), Aleut, Spanish
Florida: Spanish, French Creole, German
Hawai'i: Hawai'ian, other Pacific Island languages, Tagalog, Japanese, Chinese
Maine: French, Spanish, German, Italian, Chinese

When a school district such as Cupertino, in California, experiences an explosion of Asian student enrollment, from 42 percent to 70 percent in ten years, some accommodation must be made. Schools, once the overt agents of assimilation, now have to take on new roles: supporting the students as they learn English without letting them fall behind in content areas, nurturing their development of new identities as Asian Americans, for example, and modeling how each group (those new to school culture and those who are experienced in negotiating it) can learn from each other. Both groups, the new students and the veterans, have stories they can share and valuable knowledge they can communicate to help the new students confront the dilemma of figuring out how to be an American. Schools are instrumental in bridging that gap.

The latest population statistics make it plain that increasing diversity is a reality we will all have to face. U.S. Census demographers project, based on today's trends, that the population will rise from about 302 million (in 2008) to 439 million by 2050. Minority groups, currently about one-third of the total population, are expected to become a majority by around 2042 and to constitute 54 percent by 2050. The nation's population of children is also predicted to show major changes (see Table 1.1).

By 2050, the Hispanic population is expected to triple from one in six to one in three, its growth significantly outpacing that of all other minority groups (African American, Asian Pacific Islander, and American Indian/Alaska Native). The White population currently shows a small increase and is expected to begin decreasing by about 2050 (see Table 1.2).

TABLE 1.1

Children	2008	2050
All minorities	44%	62%
Hispanic	22%	39%
Non-Hispanic White	56%	38%

Source: www.census.gov.

TABLE 1.2

Race/Ethnicity	2008 (in millions)		2050 (in millions)	
White, non-Hispanic	199.8	66.0%	203.3	46.0%
Hispanic	46.7	15.0	132.8	30.0
Black	41.1	14.0	65.7	15.0
Asian	15.5	5.1	40.6	9.2
American Indian/Native Alaskan	4.9	1.6	8.6	2.0
Native Hawai'ian/Pacific Islander	1.1		2.6	
More than two races checked	5.2		16.2	4.0
All Minorities			235.7	54.0
Total Population	302		439	

Source: www.census.gov.

Already several regions are experiencing a balancing of the racial/ethnic makeup of their residents, especially in California. In 2007, Santa Clara County, California, had the unique position of an approximately equal distribution of racial/ethnic groups, including Whites. Said one resident, "You kind of work together or you don't work here." Estimates from 2006 (Table 1.3) showed four similar states as having "a majority of minorities."

TABLE 1.3   Minority Population

State	Percent
Texas	52
Hawai'i	75
New Mexico	57
California	57

Source: www.census.gov.

Five more states already had estimated minority populations of about 40 percent at that time. The media and the general population tend to focus on some groups, particularly Latinos, as potential problems for schools as their representation in the population increases more rapidly than others. For example, in 2005 (see Table 1.4) one in five children over eight years old was of Hispanic origin, and Hispanic children accounted for approximately 80 percent of English language learners.

TABLE 1.4   Hispanic Children

Country of origin	Percentage from each country (2005)
Mexico	65
Puerto Rico	9
Central America	7
South America	6
Cuba	2
Dominican Republic	3

Source: www.census.gov. Eighty to 90 percent of these children are American citizens who have been born in the United States to immigrant parents, in addition to the children from Puerto Rico, which is already part of the United States.

English is still the only language spoken in 80.3 percent of households, but the percentage of other languages is rising. In 1990, 13.8 percent of individuals surveyed reported they spoke another language at home, and by 2000, that figure had increased to 17.9 percent. By 2007, 19.5 percent of the population over five years old spoke a language other than English at home. In California, one in five residents over five years old reported they spoke English less than "very well." Arizona, New Mexico, and Texas have similar percentages, while nationally 12.3 percent (35 million people) spoke Spanish at home. There were 38.1 million (12.6 percent) foreign-born residents in 2007. Of these, 12 million, or 31 percent, were born in Mexico.

These figures show our growing overall diversity but cannot reflect the situation at local levels. Counties are more likely to illustrate a patchwork effect, with one group holding a solid majority: Whites in the rural Northeast and Midwest, Latinos in some Texas areas, Blacks in parts of the South, and American Indians in sections of the Southwest.

America has been generous in conferring citizenship. There are three routes to citizenship: 1) being born in the United States, 2) being born to American parents, and 3) naturalization. Countries vary in the criteria used to define citizenship. Many countries, such as Japan and Spain, do not consider birth on their soil to be sufficient; you must prove your blood ties to the country. In America, you can become a citizen through the process called naturalization—by passing tests of reading and writing skills in English and taking the citizenship exam. This test has been considerably redesigned, and the questions asked have changed from trivial and factoid-based to those requiring comprehension and allowing multiple correct answers. The new test is intended to be more challenging and to show that the candidates understand democracy. There are 100 questions on the test. In an oral exam, the applicant is asked ten of these and must respond correctly to at least six. Could you pass this test?

Old Test

Q: Which president is known as the father of his country?
A: George Washington.

Q: What do the stars on the flag mean?
A: They represent the 50 states.

New Test

Q: What does the Constitution do?
Possible answers:
  • It sets up the government.
  • It defines the government.
  • It protects the rights of citizens.

Q: What is one thing Benjamin Franklin is known for?
Possible answers:
  • He was a U.S. diplomat to other countries.
  • He was the first Postmaster General.
  • He set up the system of free public libraries.

You could argue that these naturalized citizens are the true Americans because they have had to demonstrate their desire and knowledge to become citizens. As former Congressman and Japanese American Norman Mineta remarks: "Immigrants leave the country of their birth to come to the country of their heart."

Developing an Identity

Our country has always included many different kinds of groups. In addition to immigrants, there were forced migrants (people who became part of the United States when their territory was conquered), refugees (people who fled their home for political, economic, or religious reasons), border crossers who sought greater opportunities, indigenous people (who were killed off, moved around, and separated from their cultural traditions), and enslaved Africans (who were deliberately kept from forming tribal, cultural, linguistic, or familial bonds).

There are still other examples of diverse groups. We have regional pockets of communities (Basques, Amish, and Cajuns, for example) who have a history specific to their group and a reason to claim that identity, maintained through traditions and other signs of group membership (occupations, food, language). There is great diversity of religious groups in the United States and many have been treated differently from ethnic groups. Among them, some are fairly obscure and fit smoothly in their communities; for example, the Mennonites. Others have experienced considerable historical discrimination and only recently are becoming accepted, such as Mormons. Still others, despite their considerable numbers, such as Muslims, are perceived as foreigners whose religion conflicts with their status as Americans. In addition, there are groups that proudly display their differences and lack of assimilation, such as Hassidim, with distinctive dress and appearance, and Sikhs, whose turbans are less threatening than exotic.

Every human being needs to belong somewhere and to counteract feeling like an outsider. Each individual occupies multiple spaces—human, social, personal—and an individual may have multiple identities. Most people have experienced the pain of being different. It is human to seek out those who are like us in some way, to associate with them as others who can understand us, with whom we can be ourselves. Think about the different groups you belong to, the different identities you assume through the day. Some examples of different types follow:

- Born (deaf, size, gender—though that can change)
- Chosen (religion, area of residence)
- Temporary (cancer patient)
- Invisible (some disabilities, gay/lesbian/bisexual/transgender)
- Optional (good girl, troublemaker)
- Unknown (adopted, don't know family history)
- Relational (parent, sibling)
- Progressive (age)
- Learned (profession)
- Buried (skill you used to have)

The 2000 Census was the first to let respondents check more than one box for racial/ethnic identity, finally recognizing at least partially the messiness of varying ways people define themselves. The mixture of ethnic (Hispanic) and racial (Black) was always problematic, forcing uncomfortable categories labeled White, non-Hispanic. There is no cultural agreement on the meaning of Hispanic: less influenced by Spain, the colonizing power, and more a mixture of indigenous Indians (mestizos) and African Americans (as in Cuba). The African American label is also ambiguous, because for many years "one drop of blood" was enough to be Black. Words once used, like mulatto, quadroon, and octoroon, to indicate specific amounts of Black/White ancestry, suggest the extent to which this heritage was considered socially significant.

Identifying with a racial or ethnic group has advantages and disadvantages. Together, Vietnamese Americans can influence electoral politics, have their interests recognized, and exercise the clout that comes from numbers, all factors demonstrating their acceptance into the community. On the other hand, Barack Obama, the first Black President of the United States, was criticized by some people as "not African American" during his candidacy because he was not the descendant of enslaved Africans. However, people related to him as a Black person and he experienced the pressures of racism, stereotyping, and expectations that applied to all Black people, despite having a White mother from Kansas, a Black father from Kenya, and Asian half-siblings. The champion golfer Tiger Woods, who received much attention for his extraordinary performances, called himself "Cablinasian," in an attempt to acknowledge his mixed heritage of Caucasian, Black, American Indian, and Asian.

An identity is a stable inner sense of who one is, a successful integration of multiple experiences into a coherent whole that is one's self-image. Positive self-esteem and a strong sense of identity are what gives a student the self-confidence to do well in school and find satisfaction in life. The more positive the student's identification with an ethnic/racial identity, the greater his or her sense of well-being. Students who carry negative attitudes about their own groups are more likely to experience depression, emotional distress, and low achievement at school. Many students feel that teachers respond to them differently depending on the group they associate with. They feel that teacher expectations make it difficult for them to cross borders, to be both Hispanic and succeed in academically challenging classes, for example. Yet without a positive identity, one that incorporates their cultural heritage, students have no chance of building an integrated sense of themselves that will allow them to achieve according to their own potential.

❖ Power and Privilege

Our country proclaimed its freedom with a Declaration of Independence that asserted all men were created equal, with equal rights. But even then there was conflict between social classes (landlord/tenant, master/servant). The new government protected the rights of only the few. Enslaved Africans were already present in large numbers in both the North and South but they were too entrenched in the economy to be allowed freedom. Despite frequent revolts, their owners managed to maintain authority by breaking their spirits, tearing apart families, and separating cultural/linguistic groups. Women were politically invisible. Men controlled their wives' property while children labored as hard as adults or starved in the streets. At first, only White men who held land could vote. Rich men's sons received schooling; others were generally illiterate. The indigenous people were decimated by disease, physically and culturally uprooted, and constantly betrayed by the government, their guardians. It has taken a few hundred years to overcome this narrow view of who mattered and to recognize the need to enlarge our picture of the world.

Myth versus Reality

The history of the United States must be seen as the history of all of **us**. There is not just one kind of American, but many, and some of them are hyphenated. When we want to know who we are, we include not just the White landowners, northern and southern, but also the enslaved Africans, their mixed descendants, and the free people of color earning their own living. We include not just the men who met to vote on the Constitution, but also their wives, other women, indentured servants, and artisans whose lives were affected as well. We include not just the English speakers present in the thirteen colonies, but also their Dutch neighbors in New Amsterdam, the French-speaking Acadians forced out of Canada who found refuge in Louisiana, the Spanish of Florida, and the many speakers of long-lost indigenous languages who gave us words for the life found in the strange New World. We include the deists like Thomas Jefferson, who carefully kept religion out of the new government program that was able to unite so many conflicting interests, but also the French Huguenots (Protestants) fleeing mass killing in Catholic France, Mormons who were despised and chased to the desert of Utah, the creation of Rhode Island as a safe haven for those who disagreed with New England religious leaders, and the floods of immigrants who brought with them a multitude of world religions. Because these "others" cannot be separated from "us," we must learn their special stories; how they had to overcome more obstacles to achieve their goals (the Tuskegee airmen), work harder to prove themselves (the Japanese Americans who enlisted to fight while their families were confined to internment camps), receive less recognition for their contributions (Filipinos who never received the pensions and citizenship they were promised for their bravery in World War II), and be treated as worth less than "real" humans (Puerto Rican women on whom medical experiments were performed without their knowledge).

Inequality and dominance by one group have been driven deeply into the social structure since the beginning of this country. Any differences have have been equated with inferiority. As an early example, after some 10,000 Chinese had poured their lives into building the western end of the Transcontinental Railroad, their labor was no longer needed. Racial prejudice was expressed in riots, killings, and burning of the Chinese parts of towns throughout California. The fear of a growing Chinese presence in the country led to the passage of the Chinese Exclusion Act of 1882, cutting off immigration and ensuring that the remaining Chinese could not become citizens.

In a more recent example, Mexican laborers were temporarily imported to work in agriculture in the "bracero" program. As soon as the need for this extra labor force was over, the Mexicans were sent back home. But agricultural work was seasonal, growers were not going to pay for labor year-round, and the Mexican workers began following the crops, serving as a convenient migrant labor force, moving on when not needed, residing in the United States, an invisible part of the population. When the labor camps became permanent structures, these workers brought families, and their children were enrolled in school (at least for part of the year). Social activists then began to organize protests to draw attention to the need for improvement in working and living conditions and, suddenly, the migrant workers were recognized as a group deserving human rights. Changes come slowly, however, and despite inheriting an activist tradition from leaders such as César Chávez and Dolores Huerta, today migrant workers are still fighting for access to basic resources. Fresh drinking water is a critical need, as deaths from dehydration continue to occur when workers spend long hours in the field enduring high temperatures without rest. Agriculture is not the only area that benefits from easy access to cheap labor, and illegal immigrants continue to make the deadly and expensive border crossing in search of jobs that no one else will take.

Access to cheap labor was an important element of the economy in the North as well as in the South as the English colonies grew and the indentured servants were insufficient to fill the need. So the slave trade, already actively supplying the sugar plantations in the Caribbean, began with a small number in the 1600s and became rapidly profitable as Africans were caught, shipped over to the colonies, and sold as slaves. Although freedom for enslaved Africans did not make it into the Constitution, due to the opposition from the southern colonies, six states made the slave trade illegal between 1777 and 1784, and eventually the importation of additional slaves from West Africa was cut off. Unfortunately, that didn't inhibit the southern social structure's treatment of enslaved Africans as if they were farm animals; they were bred, worked hard, and sold as possessions. African Americans didn't find safety even after the Civil War had ended, the Union was restored, and three Constitutional Amendments were introduced promising that they had the rights of free

IDEAS IN ACTION!

The Right to Vote

People of various ages, races, and social groups stand in the early morning daylight, single file. What are they waiting for so patiently? They are waiting for the voting polls to open. The year is 1994 and this is the very first all-race election in the history of the Union of South Africa, so they want to be sure they get a chance to cast their vote. "This is what people died for, so we could achieve this day," said a woman in line. Long loops of people snake around the polling stations, and some will stay open late to be sure to accommodate everyone. Whites wait in line next to Blacks. "The ordinariness of the election shows just how far the country has come," said Archbishop Desmond Tutu, Nobel Peace Prize winner for his work in bringing democracy to South Africa. Until 1994, only the ten percent White minority population could vote. The Black South Africans have not forgotten their history; the right to vote is precious.

In the United States, the attitude toward voting is different. Not everyone eligible registers to vote, and of those registered not many vote in every election. People argue over whether one vote makes any difference. They are skeptical about their ability to influence the government. Talk about voting with your students. Do they know that people died for the right to vote in this country as well? When did women get the right to vote? How old do you have to be to vote? Are people who were convicted of crimes still eligible to vote? After the Civil War, constitutional amendments ended slavery and gave "suffrage," the legal right to vote, to all (male) African Americans, even former slaves. What factors kept African Americans from freely exercising their power as voters until the Civil Rights movement of the 1960s? What conditions continue to constrain the right to vote freely, and for which groups?

Share the picture book *The Day Gogo Went to Vote: South Africa, April 1994,* by Elinor Batezat Sisulu, with students to stimulate discussion of what voting means to different groups in different countries. How did Black South Africans achieve the right to vote? How would you feel if you were voting for the first time in that election?

Challenge older students to develop a plan to get more people to participate in voting. Identify some of the obstacles that keep them from voting, perhaps by interviewing people in your neighborhood. Are people afraid to register to vote? Are there reasons why they might not be able to reach the voting location? Brainstorm strategies to respond to the issues people raise. Organize a committee to include representatives of various political, social, and community groups that share an interest in increasing the percentage of voters. A math class could conduct a survey and present the chart at a public meeting. English and other language classes can arrange for interviews in which people describe their experiences. Social studies classes can invite elected officials to speak about how they got started in politics or set up a debate questioning the need to improve accessibility of voter registration. Other classes could compare the voting turnouts in the United States with those in other countries or research the differences in who is allowed to vote.

people. The period of Reconstruction only strengthened southern hatred of Blacks and solidified structures that kept them in their place. Despite decades of social protests and legislation, many barriers remained to voting freely, to equality under law, and to equal access to quality education, especially in the professions. The civil rights movement (from the 1950s to the 1960s) led to great changes in attitudes, behavior, and awareness of issues such as persistent racism, but these were accomplished at great cost. Three young girls were killed when their church was blown up during Sunday School, voter registration volunteers were beaten and their bodies tossed away, and Blacks who "didn't know their place" were still lynched without penalty.

The fact that urban poverty and racial bigotry continue to persist shows how much the ideals promised by the young United States have been betrayed. Our diversity comes with a price. Examples of inequality abound. Twenty-one percent of our childen live in poverty, compared to 4 percent in Sweden, and we know that poverty is toxic for childen: it limits their brain development, reduces their general health, and accumulates as stress in the body. We have one of the largest gaps between low and high income earners among industrialized nations and that gap has been widening since the 1980s. People continue to debate whether some groups ("races") are more intelligent than others, based on differences in test scores. From childhood to adulthood, whether we know it or not, we act in ways that support and enforce the dominance of certain groups. For example, children can be very focused on enforcing differences between the sexes, despite much discussion of equality and sexual discrimination. They will attach themselves to sex-appropriate roles even when the sex is not specified or become upset when asked to "reverse" roles for a play.

Hate crimes and harassment of individuals because they belong to the "wrong" group is a new category of crimes that are now being tracked separately from the usual crimes against person or property. Members of minority groups can feel uncomfortable, scared, and vulnerable. You may never have heard of it, but African and Latino American men are very familiar with a crime known as "driving while Black (or Latino)." At any moment, and for no reason, the police might pull them over, even hassle them a bit, just because they are Black or Latino. Despite complaints, police continue this practice of racial profiling, and, as a minority male, you never know when it might happen to you. Jewish students may also experience fear of being harassed at any time. For example, in a St. Louis middle school in 2008, a number of sixth-grade students turned Spirit Week pranks into a "Hit a Jew" day. While only a few students actually hit Jewish students, other students taunted Jews or egged on their friends. In addition, these events were witnessed by many students who didn't do anything about it. Another group of vulnerable students includes those who are gay or lesbian. The Gay Lesbian Straight Network, in a 2003 survey, found that 84 percent of those polled reported being verbally harassed and 91.5 percent had heard homophobic attitudes expressed. Again, 82.9 percent of the students said that faculty and staff were present at these incidents and didn't intervene. Not speaking up implies approval of these acts of verbal and physical harassment.

Even the dominance of a majority religion has to be resisted. Conflicts over prayers in schools and the inclusion of the phrase "under God" in the Pledge of Allegiance have occurred because few people understood that these religious customs represented the assumption that only one religion was permitted. In fact, these practices excluded many people and denied them the right to worship according to their beliefs. The Seventh Day

Adventists were one of the religious groups that tried to claim their freedom when members were fired for refusing to work on Saturday, their Sabbath. Although the Supreme Court decided in their favor, many issues remained unresolved. Many schoolteachers think of Christmas as just a popular school holiday and rarely consider the religious implications for non-Christians. As a result, they can't understand why these holidays have to be eliminated from the public schools, except as an example of "political correctness."

One group that has been virtually invisible is the Muslim community. Many people find the relationship between Arabs and Muslims confusing because the media has often treated them as the same. However, not all Muslims are Arabs (some are from Pakistan or Iran), and not all Arabs are Muslims (some are Christian and others follow Zoroaster). Glossing over the differences leads only to more stereotyping and insensitivity toward the special needs of children in the classroom. As Zakia Hyder shows in *I Am an American Too,* a story about an Arab American child, we need to "demarginalize" these diverse groups, bring these communities into the public life of America, and learn more about the history of Arab Americans and the identities of Americans who are Muslim, because they live here, too. It has become even more difficult for people to speak up and identify themselves as practicing Muslims or as coming from an Arab background when their audience barely knows the difference between the cultures of Iran and Iraq.

A different kind of grouping that also poses difficult questions for our society are people with disabilities. In 2002, about 18 percent of Americans reported some kind of disability and 12 percent said they had a severe disability, for a total of more than 50 million people. Children aged between six and fourteen years accounted for 11 percent or 4 million. And this number does not include those who are affected by another's disability: a parent, a spouse, a teacher, or a caregiver. People with disabilities followed the model of the civil rights movement and struggled for many years to be accepted as a group that deserved the accommodations necessary for them to participate freely and publicly in society. Many people initially resented the changes required by the Americans with Disabilities Act and felt discomfort with the increased visibility of people displaying some kind of disability. Despite this resistance, this legislation has enhanced many people's lives by taking them out of institutions or isolated care and showing that they, too, can contribute to society. In addition, the pressure on schools to provide students with "the least restrictive environment" (mainstreaming) has given all students an opportunity to learn about different types of diversity and to expand their idea of community. Students can learn about the Special Olympics and watch "differently abled" people (people with autism, Down syndrome, cerebral palsy, or mobility impairments, for example) performing, acting, and dancing in many contexts.

Deaf culture is a different area. People who are deaf, become deaf, or are born into deaf families consider themselves part of a unique cultural community with its own language (American Sign Language, or ASL), customs, and history. Although they share similar interests with people who have disabilities, they prefer not to identify with a model that labels their language a "deficit." Instead, they want people to see their deafness as part of their identity as a linguistic minority. ASL is not a translation of English but a language with a grammar and vocabulary of its own, which uses hand movements and facial expressions to convey meaning. Activists have been very successful at gaining attention for deafness as just another attribute, for example, by placing a deaf actress

(Marlee Matlin) in a TV series *(The West Wing)* where she played a professional whose deafness was not a factor in her ability to perform her job. Education for deaf children and adults has also become an area of empowerment. After many years of protest, the National Deaf Education Center at Gallaudet University hired its first deaf president. Because deaf culture is not transmitted the way other cultures are, by being passed on through the family, it is particularly important that deaf children be placed in an environment in which they can learn ASL in the same way any child learns a first language. From this base, they can learn to read and write English as a "new" language, because they have no oral foundation on which to build literacy in English. Technology (the telephone, computers) has opened new possibilities for jobs where deafness is not a factor. In addition, the National Theater for the Deaf has brought ASL to large audiences as they tell stories through a mixture of sign and movement.

Although many Native American cultures have been wiped out or lost most of their heritage, there are still groups that have managed to keep their culture alive, not as a frozen historical curiosity but as a way to live today. The Zuni, who live on a reservation in New Mexico, have occupied this area for thousands of years, outlasting drought, famine, and Spanish conquest. The population of the reservation is large enough, and there are enough elders to pass on their knowledge, so that these people (they call themselves A:shiwi) can provide a fully developed ethnic identity for their members. When traditional customs such as their method of painting pottery appeared to be dying out, old crafts were revived, and the people were able to maintain their pride in Zuni identity. Despite the need to switch back and forth to survive in the modern world, the Zuni have remained united by their traditional religion, ceremonies, and kinship network. Like most other surviving Native American cultures, such as the Navajo, the greatest danger they face now is that of losing their language. As one leader says, "If we lose our language, we lose the base of our religion and culture. And if we lose our religion, we lose what binds us together as Zuni." They go to great lengths to preserve their language, from Head Start programs in Zuni, immersion language programs in the schools, to a local radio broadcasting in Zuni and English.

The American myth was assimilation. The American reality is that the answer to the question "Who belongs here?" is always changing. The examples provided above show the many diverse ways people find their own path to being an "American." As people make choices, they are creating the hybrid, complex, conflicting, always-in-flux identity we call American. This is a land of possibilities. Living well in such a world means being flexible, finding riches in diversity, and challenging oneself by working with others in a truly multicultural community.

Racism and White Privilege

When talking with teachers, both prospective and those already in the classroom, about multicultural education, they often respond that they have already covered the subject, that it has been dealt with, or the issues are no longer important. Often teachers will explain that they don't see race (or other differences) when they look at their students; their teaching is "colorblind." However, Whites are the only ones who think that being colorblind is even desirable. The fact that they can make such a statement shows how much they need to dig more deeply into the issues of multicultural teaching. "People of color" already know that we don't live in a colorblind world because they are never allowed to forget that they belong to a group that isn't the norm, that isn't White.

About 85 percent of our teachers in K–12 grades come from White, middle-class backgrounds. In contrast, the students in our classrooms increasingly represent diverse races, cultures, social classes, and experiences. There is a "cultural mismatch" between the teachers and those they teach. Every teacher must be prepared to confront this gap instead of denying that it exists. Many young people preparing to be teachers have spent most of their lives in a "monoculture," living and going to school with others much like themselves, and are comfortable with the school culture. This background separates them from the world their students live in, where such differences as race, ethnicity, religion, culture, and language, permeate every encounter, cause conflicts, and have a major impact on student life at home and at school. In multicultural education courses, it is common for White students to feel uncomfortable discussing racist experiences with students of color. They may respond with "Why am I being judged for what my ancestors did?" or "Am I supposed to apologize or feel guilty for being White?"

In the assimilationist narrative of White America, White people don't have to think about whether they have a culture, belong to a racial group, or possess stereotypes about others. For this reason, simple exposure to the ideas of multiculturalism may not be enough to lead them through the difficult processes required to rethink their assumptions, confront their biases, and learn how it feels to be an outsider. It is still possible for White people to refuse to recognize the racism that surrounds them because for them, being White is the norm, the standard against which others are measured and defined as "different." We call this assumption "White privilege," and learning to live in a multicultural world requires that all of us examine critically exactly what that means: the benefits that accrue to those who are White, the privileges that only White people, as members of the dominant group, can take for granted.

The following are some examples of these assumptions:

- You can walk into a store and ask for water or to use the restroom.
- If someone drops something and you call out to them, they will appreciate it, and they won't think you are going to rob them.
- When you go into a restaurant, you expect to be served politely, within a reasonable time; otherwise, you would feel comfortable asking to see the manager to complain.
- If you bump into someone in a crowd, you apologize and the other person accepts it without thinking you're trying to steal something.
- You can walk through your neighborhood at night without being stopped by a police car, headlights glaring, and being asked for your ID.
- If police officers come to the door, you might think it's bad news but you won't think they are there with an illegal warrant to plant drugs.
- If you're involved in the legal system, you expect fair treatment and a jury of your peers.
- If you happen to be in an identity line-up for a suspect who is short, with red hair, wearing glasses, and you are tall with black hair and no glasses, you can be certain that the eyewitness won't pick you out for resembling the suspect.

Discuss these examples. Do these assumptions feel familiar to you? How might you feel if you didn't live with this umbrella of security always sheltering you?

The position you occupy at the table of power determines how you see the world and how others see you. Systems of privilege and preference create exclusionary enclaves in which certain demographic groups are well-served while others vanish between the cracks. The world divides easily into "Us" and "the Other." Special programs are needed to benefit "them," "they" experience difficulties fitting into communities, "they" are less interested in how their children are doing at school, and "their children" are the ones we focus on when we talk about the achievement gap. It becomes very difficult to "unlearn" our unseen biases and "relearn" how to work as partners with others to improve education for all our children. Empathy for others can take us only so far. We can learn about the lives of others who have succeeded, but keep them at a distance when we have to acknowledge our own part in maintaining the structural inequities.

Critical pedagogy has provided us with a means of analyzing this system and coming to grips with the need to make changes in our own way of thinking. Once we recognize how much we rely on a White, middle-class framework through which to see the world, we can gain a better understanding of how possession of these privileges affects our expectations and interactions with people with other cultures or points of view. There is no more pretense of a level playing field; the positions of power are not distributed equally. A White man views the world from a different position than a White woman and, in turn, her position in society gives her a perspective that differs from a Black woman's view. Although we may occupy different positions as we take on different roles, we must become more aware of the ways our position affects what we think of as reality. We call this the "lens." Many factors are involved in creating our lens and how we see the world. Some are relatively obvious, such as professional training, generation, experiences living in different places. Other aspects of our lens are less apparent. Look for examples of the hierarchies of power in your world. What group has the most power at your school or in the district? Who do you see exercising power in the media? Based on the faces that look back at you from television programming and advertising, what group represents the unstated norm against which others are measured?

Relative positions of power are well-maintained by the social structure. People from lower social classes are much more likely to have heart problems, high blood pressure, diabetes, and other serious health conditions, compared to people in the upper range of social class. In addition, there are many "gatekeepers" that restrict access to whatever society values highly ("social capital"). Teacher expectations of student success, for example, are often based on their students' social class.

Programs to help teachers acquire the skills and knowledge needed to operate in a multicultural world have to be evaluated according to the extent they can actually change teachers' practices, attitudes, and perspectives at the deepest level. At the beginning, teachers are likely to be uncomfortable when anger or other emotions are brought out in discussion. They are often frustrated and overwhelmed. More personal experiences with different ways of looking at the world and how many different ways people have solved the problems of living can help teachers change their belief from "there's only one right answer" to understanding the importance of seeking out diverse perspectives. Teachers who reach this level can recognize, critique, and act on issues of social injustice while opening their hearts to let others into a world that they share.

❖ Models of Multicultural Education

For the roots of multicultural thinking, it is important to look back at the history of various oppressed groups and discover the social base for the development of this type of thinking. The coexistence of many groups has led to the focus on getting along with others. From the start, ideas about diversity and race were involved but increasingly people became aware of the complexity of the relationships. Gradually, interest groups coalesced around a shared identity and the need to fight for their rights, from access to services to inclusion in the school curriculum. Discussions of multicultural diversity turned into organized critiques of how to go about dealing with the issues raised.

History of Multicultural Thinking

The origins of today's multicultural thinking can be found in the social and political turmoil of the 1960s. Before that time, the context for discourse was intergroup relations and cultural pluralism (in sociology) and the belief that increased contact between groups reduced prejudice and led to everyone getting along (in social psychology). As the civil rights movement grew rapidly, following the Supreme Court decision on school segregation in 1955, everyone could see non-violent demonstrators being beaten in their struggle for human rights and the degree of hatred that hindered children's attempts to go to school. People's growing awareness of the abysmal position of African Americans and broken promises of racial equality brought out uncomfortable truths of racism, discrimination, and the power that communities wielded to maintain the status quo of White supremacy.

Other protest movements benefited from these examples. The nonviolent philosophy espoused by such leaders as Dr. Martin Luther King, Jr., stemming from Mahatma Gandhi's success at winning Indian independence from Great Britain, took hold among antiwar activists. Women active in that movement began to develop a feminist consciousness of the many factors that also maintained their inferior position. As the country moved out of the conformist 1950s, more and more people were questioning authority (free speech), attacking the patriarchal structure of society (university protests), and demanding to be treated as individuals (not as IBM cards). Other social forces were involved, such as immigration from non-European countries and changing thought about the need for bilingual education. Major American industries, such as steel and manufacturing, moved out of the United States, leaving workers without their traditional lifetime guaranteed job incomes.

On the other hand, the cold war had left us with an extensive "military industrial complex" that reacted to social/political changes as "un-American" and destructive to the unity of the country. Many people resented what they saw as increasing "identity politics," which they thought would lead to "Balkanization" by putting special interests ahead of the national identity, thereby, nibbling at the notion of a single "America."

New ideas were pushing their way through from the grassroots. In the meantime, legal remedies sometimes led, sometimes followed the pressure for change. Once laws were passed, civil rights protestors still had to push the federal government into enforcing them. It became obvious that the inequities being uncovered were structural and entrenched, not superficial conditions easily coped with by legislation. How could we explain the gaps between high school graduation rates for Whites and African Americans, the different rates for college attendance, the lack of representation of minorities at the highest levels of power, once the law had made everyone "equal," had granted the right to attend the same schools, the right to vote in all elections?

Questions about the racial makeup of the power structure, the lack of social mobility, and the academic achievement gap generated new ways of looking at our history and led to a new field of academic research broadly called Ethnic Studies. Instead of a single historical narrative, this approach advocated examining familiar events from multiple perspectives. "U.S. History" began to include the experiences of the losers as well as the winners, the working class as well as the ruling class, and the voices of women as well as the voices of men, among others. This multiplicity of conflicting voices had to be brought forward and woven together, creating a novel picture of a Multicultural America.

As the movement for change gathered momentum, other groups recognized that they were also treated as inferior. The elderly, the disabled, gays and lesbians were just a few of the groups who wanted recognition of their contributions and advocated for equal access to services. The definition of diversity expanded enormously and became a major factor to be considered when thinking about multiculturalism. A new vocabulary entered the discourse to represent discrimination: in addition to racism and sexism, we added ageism, classism, and heterosexism, for example. The critical thinking that we were applying to social structure turned into "critical pedagogy," including the implications of differences in access to resources and the influence of cultural capital as educators were pressed to recognize the reality of our multicultural society and incorporate the new thinking into the school curriculum.

Comparing Models for Multicultural Education

A multicultural perspective requires a different framework for thinking about education. The earliest approaches involved adding new courses to teacher training programs and ethnic studies programs to the secondary curriculum. The values promoted were primarily tolerating and accepting differences, and the emphasis was directed at understanding others. We began to include new heroes and cultural holidays, for example, with Black History Week (which grew into Black History Month). Such activities may have communicated "I see you," but they did little to actively support the extensive cultural and linguistic diversity encountered regularly in our classrooms. Students from diverse backgrounds needed to see themselves as equal participants in school and that meant acknowledging the diversity in everyone, not just those who looked different (according to whose standard?) and spoke different languages (not necessarily a disability). Education would require the inclusion of multiple perspectives and the negotiating of cultural conflicts. Change might be uncomfortable and create resentment. School systems had to stumble their way through defining multicultural education and developing programs to meet their goals. The following descriptions of types of multicultural programs, based on discrete approaches identified originally by Carl Grant and Christine Sleeter, illustrate some of the paths that were chosen by schools.

Assimilation
Assimilation theory, which dominated the thinking of the early United States, assumes that all persons living in the United States should be acculturated to become *Americans*.

According to this view, everyone should be culturally similar as in the "melting pot" metaphor discussed previously. The problem is that those who espouse assimilation may equate *difference* with *deficiency*. This stance can scarcely be termed multicultural, but it is a viewpoint that still appears in newspapers and is clearly lodged in the minds of many Americans who were educated to perceive assimilation and the melting pot concept positively.

People still complain when they hear others speak languages they can't understand or see signs in languages they can't read. Misunderstanding of the advantages of multilingualism turns to fears of the loss of English and motivate irrelevant and ineffectual "English only" legislation. Other people cling to negative stereotypes about ethnic groups despite personal positive experiences with individuals. The discomfort that these people feel (out of place "in their own country") leads them to revert to a mythic ideal of a time when everyone was expected to assimilate, of course.

Human Relations
The human relations movement in education, with its emphasis on valuing the individual, nurturing self-esteem, and helping everyone succeed provided another base for multicultural programs. As early as 1972, the American Association of Colleges for Teacher Education recognized multicultural education as follows:

> Education which values cultural pluralism. Multicultural education rejects the view that schools should seek to melt away cultural differences or the view that schools should merely tolerate cultural pluralism. Instead, multicultural education affirms that schools should be oriented toward the cultural enrichment of all children and youth through programs rooted in the presentation and extension of cultural alternatives. Multicultural education recognizes cultural diversity as a fact of life in American society, and it affirms that this cultural diversity is a valuable resource that should be preserved and extended. It affirms that major education institutions should strive to preserve and enhance cultural pluralism. Multicultural education programs for teachers are more than special courses or special learning experiences grafted onto the standard program. The commitment to cultural pluralism must permeate all areas of the educational experience provided for prospective teachers.

These programs also stressed interpersonal communication skills. Human relations programs remain an important tool for teaching how to get along in a culturally diverse society.

Focused Group Studies
These programs were instrumental in uncovering information about different groups—their history, values, and culture—and making it possible for the "voiceless" to be heard. This approach led in a different direction, focusing on content and developing pride in one's distinct heritage, rather than working with young students to overcome negative attitudes and beliefs about others or examine the prejudices they carried inside themselves. Women's Studies, Afro-American Studies, and Queer Studies were examples of bringing new perspectives into the mainstream where they could no longer be ignored. Their analysis of persistent structural inequities was valuable to developing a critical approach to multicultural teaching.

Integrated Multicultural Education

The broader term *multicultural education* was not widely used in the earliest discussions in the educational literature. It appeared for the first time as a subject heading in *Education Index* in 1978, about the same time that the National Council of Accreditation of Teacher Education rewrote its standards to include multicultural education. This text, *Multicultural Teaching,* which appeared in 1979, was the first book to offer a comprehensive approach to multicultural education from the perspective of the K–12 curriculum. Since then, many books have presented a broad appproach to multicultural education, ranging from texts focusing on primary students and those representing the self-contained classroom, to this book, still one of the few promoting integrated multicultural thinking across the content areas and throughout the grades. An additional category of multicultural teacher education texts covers the foundations approach.

Social Reconstructionism

Active efforts to bring about a change in thinking and behavior have always been integral to our society. Activism, involvement rather than passive acceptance, is another approach to multicultural education. Refusing to be victimized, we all have a responsibility to speak out against injustice, discrimination, and prejudice and to work to ensure that human rights are upheld for all. Individual involvement in this social reconstructivism will vary, but increasingly, educated Americans are intervening when unthinking individuals tell stories that insult certain ethnic groups or use insensitive language. Others join groups that work actively to achieve and maintain civil rights for specific groups. It is important to take a stance and to make our viewpoints known. Teachers have a special responsibility to manage classroom procedures and to plan the multicultural curriculum appropriately.

Global Education

Multicultural education can also be defined to include the study of other countries, the concept of the world as a global village, and recognition of the need for everyone on this planet to collaborate to ensure clean air and preserve our resources. Focus on international studies brings an awareness of the shared concerns of nations around the world. It leads to a greater understanding of other people and the universal issues human beings face. Ecologically and economically, we will always be interdependent. Such studies engage us in reading the literature and becoming familiar with the cultures of specific groups around the world that may speak the same language or share a religious belief, thus helping to broaden studies across the total curriculum in the United States. We recommend these topics as complementing multicultural education rather than competing with it. Despite the dangers of exotic "tourist" studies that separate us from people in other countries, we believe that students will learn more about themselves when they realize other human beings face similar struggles.

With the increasing diversity of classroom populations and cultural complexity of communities served, it became clear that everyone, not just so-called minorities, needed to be prepared to function well in a multicultural world. Multicultural education was required that provided for both content and skills but also included reformulation of our concept of the teaching and learning process. Approaches that emphasized human relations, countered assimilationist ideology, and demonstrated the connectedness of humanity were all necessary for the development of an effective multicultural program. Creative and critical thinking, the ability to work effectively in diverse settings and groups, and wider social awareness of the complexity of human cultures had to be combined with an active consciousness of structural social inequities found throughout education, such as discrepancies in available school resources, differences in teacher hiring and training practices, academic tracking that privileged some students over others, and standardized achievement assessment programs. Students had to be seen as competent individuals, not deficient because of their diversity, with knowledge and experiences that should be brought into the classroom. Teachers could change from the role of all-knowing experts to that of learners when they began to listen to their students.

If each person in this world will simply take a small piece of this huge thing, this amazing quilt, and work it regardless of the color of the yarn, we will have harmony on this planet.

~ CICELY TYSON

Our Model of Multicultural Education

Multicultural education is fundamental to all learning. It is an integral aspect of the discussion about fair behavior on the playground that might concern primary students. It underlies the conflicts and concerns that intermediate students face as they develop as individuals. And it explains why recognizing the destructive power of racism is a significant part of the high school learning experience. Multicultural education belongs in science, history, mathematics, language arts, social studies, and the arts. Teaching multiculturally requires the efforts of committed professionals and community members working cooperatively at all levels of education. Multicultural education is for and about everyone. It must promote an antivictim consciousness in historically oppressed groups as well as increase understanding in those who belong to the dominant groups to the extent of the privileges they accrue just by being born to that group.

In this book, we propose a model of multicultural education as the best education, the one that every parent would wish for their child. We include students of all backgrounds while we provide a positive learning environment and teach about different groups from many perspectives. All students need access to the skills and knowledge that will be required for living well in a rapidly changing world. An education in diversity is also an education in human unity, as stated in the motto *E Pluribus Unum.*

Many multicultural programs have been criticized for a superficial approach, often called "heroes and holidays" or "food and festivals." To be effective in developing cultural competence, true multicultural education must:

- Illuminate the nature of power and privilege exercised by the dominant group and show how it impacts other groups;
- Provide flexible learning environments that will support all students;
- Integrate multicultural concepts into all subjects, all grades, for all students;
- Uncover and confront biases, prejudices, and stereotypes;

- Encourage student efforts as learners through high expectations;
- Organize curriculum to provide extensive opportunities for students to work with diverse others and engage in learning conversations;
- Defy assumptions of passivity in oppressed groups, for example, by showing enslaved Africans actively revolting against their conditions; and
- Demonstrate the malleability of culture, for example, by bringing the story of Native Americans from the past into the present.

Esteem, Empathy, and Equity are the foundation for our multicultural model as we combine these premises to demonstrate how we can build support for all students' learning. The central elements are introduced here and developed further in the next chapter. **Self-Esteem** is basic to effective learning. Real learning requires that students take risks, persevere despite setbacks, and maintain confidence in their ability to succeed. Members of many historically oppressed groups have internalized feelings of inferiority and self-hatred. These can be expressed as hostility toward authority, fear of change, and dislike of exposing oneself to failure. Building student self-esteem is an essential part of any program that proposes to support students as learners.

    Empathy enables people to make connections with others, accept differences as well as similarities, and collaborate effectively while acknowledging the diversity of perspectives. As we work with students, we aim to give them "roots as well as wings," leading them to multicultural understandings through "windows as well as mirrors." Development of empathy is a necessary part of the program in order for students to understand that there is more than one way to live in the world, and the life that they know is not the only acceptable way to be a person. **Equity** must be considered, not just equality. When we evaluate programs for equality, we are asking whether they provide the same resources and support for all students. Education for equity, however, requires recognition that students do not come from equal playing fields. All students must be given the real possibility of access to the resources that count in order to achieve their potential. Differences in school funding, teacher experience, and community support are examples of how specific groups of students have consistently been denied equitable opportunities for success.

❖ Defining Key Terms

In this last section of this chapter we present a list of important terminology used in multicultural education, with which you should be familiar. Discuss these concepts further in your Cooperative Learning Group. You can add to the list as you encounter new words.

Ways We Categorize Humans

We divide humans into many groups, such as race, social class, culture, and ethnic groups.

Race
For many years attempts were made to justify different groupings of humans into races, using science to claim that some races were more developed than others and were, therefore, biologically intended to dominate. The basic type was European, of course,

as were the scientists, and the races declined in importance as they diverged from that norm. Despite the great variation found in human appearance, we now know that there is no biological basis for racial divisions. Populations vary among themselves more than they vary across physical types. Certainly the physical characteristics you find in the many different groups living in Africa illustrate an enormous range of human variability, not consistent with what is usually thought of as the Black race. Our use of the term *race* today is socially determined, and different cultures use different criteria for categorizing people into "racial groups" that are not necessarily the same ones we are familiar with. For example, in the United States, people who are half-White and half-Black are usually called Black, whereas many countries have a separate category for people of mixed heritage. Cross racial marriages were illegal in many states until recently. White people had to pretend to be Black in order to marry an African American. The 2000 census gave respondents their first opportunity to identify as members of more than one race. Public conversation on the topic of mixed race identity illustrates the complexity of this issue.

Social Class
We like to think of the United States as a "classless" society, compared to other cultures which make more rigid distinctions. But *social class* plays a major role in our society. Social class is most easily defined as one's possession of income/assets (often referred to as Socioeconomic Status, or SES). However, other factors may be considered. The prestige value of some jobs, such as teaching, can overrule a lower income and raise one's social class. Becoming a teacher or a nurse was always considered a means of achieving upward mobility for working class families. Working for a non-profit foundation may reduce one's income but does not affect the social class standing one was born with. Women tend to "marry up" the social class ladder while men sometimes "marry down." As journalist Eugene Robinson comments: "Even more troubling is that our notion of America as the land of opportunity gets little support from the data. Americans move fairly easily up and down the middle rungs of the ladder, but there is 'stickiness at the ends'—four out of 10 children who are born poor will remain poor, and four out of 10 children who are born rich will stay rich." Despite our ideology that "anyone can grow up to be President," the reality is otherwise. In fact, a graph strictly based on income directly predicts one's health, longevity, and general satisfaction with life. Social class, like "tracking" in schools, is difficult to shed and controls access to all important resources in a society.

Culture
This word is easily used without much critical thought. If you ask a group of people to suggest definitions, they are most likely to begin with highly visible, surface aspects such as clothing, food, and holidays. A deeper level would focus on behavioral dimensions such as social roles, learning styles, religion, and communication of values. But culture also covers abstract factors that are more difficult to uncover and identify, such as all the complex assumptions we make about others and messages we send about ourselves without being conscious of them. It is easier to speak of the "culture" of a distant tribe than to examine carefully the many cultures around us or our own cultural group, because they are

DID YOU KNOW?
◄○►

The Surui tribe, living deep in the Brazilian rain forest, who first made contact with the outside world less than forty years ago, are now competently combining their traditional bows and arrows with modern technology such as Google Earth to help protect their 600,000 acre reserve from the miners and loggers who have devastated so much of the irreplaceable Amazon resources. Chief Almir Surui, the first of their tribe to graduate from college, discovered Google Earth while traveling and, adjusting rapidly to new ideas, asked about adapting Google technology to help the Surui monitor their reserve and raise international awareness of the problems in the Amazon.

According to Google's project manager, Rebecca Moore, speaking of the company's intent to train the Surui in using the unfamiliar machines: "We traveled to the Amazon rainforest expecting to be the teachers. But the story of the Surui as they engage with the modern world holds lessons for all of us, and if we pay attention, we may have more to learn from them than they from us." The high-quality imagery will enable the Surui to tell stories about their culture and historical traditions as well as provide updates on the planned reforestation of land lost to illegal activity. For example, between August 2007 and August 2008, 3,145 square miles of rainforest were destroyed, an increase of 69 percent over the previous year. In fact, about 20 percent of the Amazon region has already been deforested.

part of the sea in which we swim. In addition, people tend to make generalizations about cultures as if they were fixed instead of flexible, continually adapting to outside forces. As a result, statements about Vietnamese American or Samoan American culture, for example, rarely provide useful information about individuals because all cultures are dynamic, that is, constantly changing. It is overly simplistic to make judgments about others based on the notion of a "single" culture. Individuals incorporate many factors into their identity which are influenced by the culture they were brought up in, yet they continue to change and adapt as they encounter new experiences.

Ethnic Group
One's ethnic group refers to the region, nation, or distinctive group with which one identifies, either directly or as a heritage. Membership in a particular ethnic group is usually clearly defined by language, religion, or other major factors. The fact that the fragmentation of the Balkan nations led to "ethnic cleansing" is an example of how group identifications can persist over centuries, so that people who had lived peacefully next to each other one day could begin mass killings of their neighbors the next. Serbs, Croats, and Bosnians, once they had the opportunity, carried out longstanding grievances against each other and were unwilling to negotiate political power. In Africa, the national borders created by European colonizers did not reflect tribal (ethnic) territories, with the result that many animosities between cultural groups (people with different traditions and ways of life) persisted and turned into active hostility when one group was perceived as holding too much

official authority over another. For example, the inability of Hutus and Tutsis to share power in Rwanda led to mass executions on each side, where once they lived in the same villages and even intermarried. Similar conditions are present in the Sudan (Muslims and Africans) and occurred recently when Eritrea broke away from Ethiopia. A large country such as China includes more than fifty distinct ethnic groups (with different languages, traditions, lifestyles, and values) although the Han are the majority group (over 90 percent) and the ones who control the social and political structure.

Group Names

It is important to stay aware of how groups call themselves, what they want to be called, and what is considered disrespectful. No one uses the old, insulting terms for Poles, Italians, or Chinese. But shortening Japanese to Jap is also demeaning. If you are using materials written in another time, you may have to explain what some terms meant and why they aren't used anymore. Several books have raised issues of censorship, such as *Huckleberry Finn* for its use of the N-word, now considered too degrading to say aloud in public although used among some groups to establish insiderhood. Often, names that were in common use for many years have been replaced by the groups themselves as part of their attempt to create a more positive identity. For example, the term *Inuit* is now used instead of Eskimo and the Gypsies prefer to be called *Roma.*

   • *African American:* This is the preferred term of respect, along with *Black* (note the capitalization, also for *White*). The African part of the heritage may be indirect, as many people come from the Caribbean (Dominican Republic and West Indies, for example) or Latin America (such as Guyana or Cuba).

   • *Latino American:* This term is preferred over Hispanic American because it evokes Latin America rather than Spain. Unlike Asian or African American, *Latino* does not identify someone by race but by ethnic group identity. Latinos may be of any race or combination of races. However, you should beware of generalizations here, too, as the experiences of Mexicans, Central Americans, and South Americans will be very different. South America also includes Brazil, where Portuguese is spoken, not Spanish. Puerto Ricans should be considered a separate group, not only because of shared culture and traditions, but because they are legal citizens of the United States (though they still can't vote). Recently, Puerto Ricans have adopted the term *nuyorican* to refer to themselves. Indigenous Indian groups have a signficant presence in many of these countries which means that some Latino immigrants may not even speak Spanish, but only their Indian language. In addition, because this term also includes Latinos who have lived in the United States for many generations, you cannot make assumptions about the extent of shared cultural values or language. For example, May 5 (Cinco de Mayo) has become a major celebration for Latinos in the United States, while Mexicans celebrate September 15 (El Día de la Independencia) instead. Also, many Latinos speak English very well while they may or may not speak Spanish. The distinction between Latino (male) or Latina (female) is sometimes used, based on Spanish language gender. *Chicano* is another, older term, used in the time of labor rights activism, to refer to Mexican Americans, particularly in California. *La Raza* (meaning, *The Race*) has also been used to represent the development of Latino culture specific to the United States.

• *Asian American:* This term has replaced Orientals as a group label, but *Asian* (which includes *Pacific Islander* in the U.S. Census data) covers such diverse populations that relying on generalizations is dangerous; the term obscures many significant differences, rather than illuminates. Whenever possible, specify the particular heritage, such as Chinese, Japanese, Khmer, Hmong, Filipino, or Samoan, for example. While many Asian American children have experienced notable success in schools, especially those families from China or Japan, others have adapted less readily to U.S. expectations. All Asian Americans resent being lumped together as "the model minority." People from the Indian subcontinent (the countries of India, Pakistan, and Bangladesh) are called *South Asians.* They often come to the United States via the West Indies or South Africa, where they were known as Asians.

• *Native American:* While this term may be the most respectful, many people continue to use American Indian for convenience. (Note that the U.S. Census data includes Native Hawai'ians and Alaska Natives along with Native Americans.) Because the material culture of Indian tribes varies widely, from the Passamaquoddy and Abenaki in the East, the Navajo, Zuni, and Hopi in the Southwest, to the Haida and Tlingit of the Pacific Northwest, as do as their experiences with White colonization, it is particularly important to specify the tribal group to which you refer. In addition, many Whites, upon first encountering Indian tribes, gave them "English" names that had come from the Indians' enemies, which were often degrading. Therefore, pay attention to the name that the tribe prefers to use for itself, such as *Lakota* rather than *Sioux.*

• *White: European Americans,* or *Whites,* tend to think of others as belonging to a racial or ethnic group, not themselves, because they are the dominant group against which the others are measured. Many "White" students wonder where they fit in. As Anthony Lising Antonio, professor at Stanford, says: "The fact is we still don't understand what 'whiteness' is. It's been such a norm that we haven't defined it, and I think White students might feel like they're in a cultural vacuum, whereas other folks— the Asians and the Latinos, for example—have something tangible to call their culture." For that reason, it is particularly important that White people preparing to be teachers need to reflect carefully and critically on their own values, cultural traditions, and attitudes in order to understand that they do carry a culture along with them, although it has not been made visible before.

• *Minority Group: Minority* is a confusing term today and refers only to relative status, since minorities are no longer a minority in the population. Many people prefer the term *"people of color,"* although that appears to emphasize "race" rather than social position. Another possible choice has been *"historically underrepresented,"* which focuses on a history of discrimination rather than number and is more inclusive, applying to working class Whites, for example. Most people use *minority* as shorthand for the complex interrelationships of these groups.

• *LGBT:* This convenient acronym for *lesbian, gay, bisexual,* or *transgender* is being used more frequently. It avoids the ambiguity of homosexual, which can refer to men or women while lesbian is used only for women. Gay and lesbian have also been reclaimed as labels to be proud of. LGBT also acknowledges the broader range of gender identity and is obviously intended to include people dressing as another gender (for performance art or to take on a different identity) as well as people who feel they were born into the wrong gender. The term reflects total acceptance of gender differences, as does *queer,* as in "queer" culture, which affirms diverse choices of how identity is expressed.

Factors Affecting Human Relations

There are many terms expressing concepts related to tolerance, or getting along with others. Several basic terms, such as *prejudice, stereotype,* and *discrimination,* are presented below.

Prejudice

A *Prejudice* is a judgment or attitude, often accompanied by matching behavior, toward a group, based on generalizations (stereotypes) rather than experience. It is normally used in a pejorative sense, referring to a negative attitude, but by definition can be positive, as in "I am prejudiced in favor of classical music." The main idea is that of judging someone (or something) before you know enough to form an opinion.

Stereotype

The word *Stereotype* refers to categories in which people are placed, along with strong positive or negative associations. These generalizations may be attempts to provide affirmative information about a group, such as, "Latinos value family very highly," but even positive statements are harmful because they conceal individual variability under a guise of uniformity. Using generalizations about groups in this way is called "essentializing."

Discrimination

Discrimination, which means differences in the treatment of groups, is another term that is capable of being used in a positive or negative context. However, as the Supreme Court pointed out in *Brown v. Topeka,* "separate but equal" was only a cover for providing substantially inferior education to Black children. Racial discrimination has been found in all aspects of society, such as hiring, college admissions, housing availability, opportunities to get ahead, and access to loans for businesses. In addition, greater attention to legal remedies for racial discrimination has led to making discrimination against other groups, such as women, the disabled, and gays/lesbians, illegal as well.

The –Isms

The following words are formed on the model of "racism," and illustrate the range and variety of discrimination against specific groups.

Racism

This word refers to derogatory attitudes or ideas, discriminatory action, and belief in the inferior status of another group, determined by "skin color." *Racism,* of course, is a highly loaded term and should not be used casually or without reflection. Most people prefer not to talk about it. Nonetheless, it is always there, lurking in the background, and needs to be brought into open and honest discussion.

Sexism, Classism, Ageism, and Ableism

These terms are used to label similar derogatory attitudes, denial of equal access and legal rights, and application of inferior status to, respectively: women, working class people, the aged (or youngsters, depending on context), and people with disabilities. Calling adult women "girls" is an example of sexism. Classism occurs when people assume that everyone comes from the same middle-class background that they do or that any other background represents a deficit to be corrected. Older people often find themselves dismissed or invisible in a youth-oriented culture, for example, when they are forced to retire at a specific age regardless of their ability to perform the job. Using a wheelchair for mobility has become a common symbol for "handicapped" people. People who have disabilities prefer to be considered as a person first and not have people ignore them, speak to another instead of directly to them, or treat them as mentally incompetent because they require assistance. For example, special needs children can be called "children with autism," or "children with Down syndrome." Such focus on the disability as a primary identity has led to discrimination called "ableism." You may encounter other words using the ending –ism to indicate similar discrimination as different groups claim their rights.

Heterosexism

The term *heterosexism* reminds us of the preeminent norm that sexuality is limited to behavior associated with a couple consisting of a man and a woman. The social pressure is reinforced by fears of crossing the boundaries or norms. This prejudice, called *homophobia,* reflects how strongly people can feel threatened by deviation from the perceived norm. It also occurs in the mindless use of the phrase "That's so gay," which is offensive whether or not it is deliberately intended to be insulting.

Ethnocentrism

This belief that one's own group represents the best or the only correct way to do things is one of the broadest kinds of prejudice against which others should be measured is based on the belief that their group is the center of the universe. Such assumptions stand in the way of being able to affirm differences among people and empathize with others in order to work comfortably in diverse settings. Multicultural education aims to counter this kind of thinking.

CONNECTIONS

The underlying goal of multicultural education is to provide the best education to all students, regardless of their race, gender, language, and so on. We must develop our awareness of the way "White" norms are unconsciously enforced, identify sources of bias, and consider the different kinds of power present in the classroom. Instead of sweeping differences under the table, we bring them to the forefront, acknowledging that all students are different from one another and that a variety of approaches are required to reach every student. In order to achieve our goal of including all students, we must learn how to treat these differences as strengths.

After reading this chapter, you should be able to analyze and discuss the implications of the concept that there is not one "American" culture. You should be able to describe the nature of community in a country made up of many cultures. Because we all identify with many groups, we need to be more aware of how they affect our attitudes and experiences (as a "lens") as well as how others see us. We understand the need to be seen as individuals, not just members of one group. In addition, we recognize how the dominance of particular groups ("the norm") is enforced in ways that may become insidious, creating unconscious prejudices. You should be able to describe how these persistent negative attitudes and the discrimination that people experience lead to such conditions as oppression, marginalization, invisibility, and silence, and how these may have a negative impact on a student's ability to learn. In the next chapter, we will focus on how changing metaphors of teaching and learning can help us develop different approaches to instruction that include all students and examine how these can best fit our goals for multicultural education.

GETTING INVOLVED

❖ The Reflective Teaching Portfolio

As a way of modeling effective teaching and learning, each chapter in this text ends with suggested activities for preservice or practicing teachers. The Reflective Teaching Portfolio is an example of using personal writing to reflect on and learn from new experiences. Research shows that **Writing to Learn** (what you **Think**) is an effective way to help students process what they learn and connect it to what they already know.

Setting up the Portfolio

At times, you may be asked to reread an earlier entry and to make comments next to it regarding any changes in your thinking. (For that reason, you will be writing on only one side of the paper, leaving room for later comments on the opposite side.) In the same way, you may share some of your writings with the instructor as part of a Portfolio Assessment plan, or with other students in a Cooperative Learning Group (described below), to provide starting points for discussion or further action. In addition, you will have noticed that each chapter begins with an opening quote and that there are other quotations scattered throughout the chapters. An instructor might choose to display a quote for you to respond to, writing in your portfolio as students arrive and settle down at the beginning of class.

To create your Reflective Teaching Portfolio, you will need to purchase a notebook with rings so that you can remove items or add them as necessary. Have fun—no one has to see anything that you write unless you wish. Select your favorite colored paper, lined or unlined, and a comfortable pen that you can attach. A really small notebook may conveniently fit in a pocket but is often too small for the longer writing you will be doing. A backpack/briefcase may hold everything you need but can become too heavy to carry everywhere. It's a good idea to select a notebook that's "not too large or too small but just right for you" that you can always have with you in case you want to write down a good thought or question. Include dividers of heavy paper or use stick-on tabs to separate the pages according to your course syllabus. Perhaps you can add some pockets in case you have small items to include. Begin your notebook by writing responses to these opening questions:

- Who am I?
- What does multicultural education mean to me?
- Why is multicultural education important?

Remember to write on one side only, leaving space for additional thoughts. Date this page and save it for later reflection when you finish the course.

Reflective Teaching Portfolio Activities

1. List as many different groups as you can think of that you belong to, for example:

   Student teacher
   Methodist
   Like to Dance
   Brought up on farm
   Female
   Adopted

   Review your list and write notes about what these identities mean to you. Which five are of the greatest importance in your life? Put them in order of importance from the most to the least important.

2. Take out your list of your most significant identities. Cross off the third item on the list. Imagine that from this moment you can't bring that part of yourself into the class, into school, or into your public life. How would you feel? How might this affect your self-confidence as a learner? Your ability to speak up in a group? Write about your reactions to share later with your cooperative group. Did others have similar responses? What part of themselves did they have to eliminate?

❖ Working with a Cooperative Learning Group

In addition to the Portfolio suggestions, each chapter will include possible small group activities. Here again we are modeling effective teaching and learning because we know that students learn **socially**, by talking and listening to each other, and **actively**, by expressing their thoughts to others. If working in cooperative learning groups is new to the students or the instructor, you might begin by working in pairs. When one person is talking and the other listening, use a timer to change partners. Small groups usually range from three to five students. More directions about setting up cooperative learning groups will be found in Chapter 3.

Beginning to Work in Groups

The Cooperative Learning Group activities provided in each chapter are intended to provide students with an additional opportunity to process and reflect on new ideas. The conflicts created by different people presenting and defending their ideas, along with the resolution, may be considered the most elemental form of learning. As you explain what you think, you have to listen to yourself more carefully and consider the response of others. The discomfort of attempting to move beyond these differences of opinion creates the disequilibrium that allows us to accept new ideas and restructure old ones, just as the constructivist theories of Piaget and Vygotsky guide our understanding of child development.

Cooperative Learning Group Activities

1. As a group, brainstorm what you would like to know about the other people in your class with whom you will be working closely. Develop a list of questions to ask each other based on this information. Have the questions posted where everyone can see them. Then work in pairs to interview each other. One person begins the interview, using the questions on the list as a starting point and exploring other topics that arise. Use a timer to tell you when to switch roles so each person in the pair has equal time to talk. Afterwards, each interviewer introduces the other person to the class, mentioning points of common interest and including specific details that make this person special.

2. Reread the quote from Rabbi Hillel that opens this chapter. In 1961, almost 2000 years later, John Lewis, a civil rights activist, echoed these words in urging people to join Freedom Bus Rides and stop discrimination against African Americans:

    If not us, then who? If not now, then when? Will there be a better day for it tomorrow or next year? Will it be less dangerous then? Will someone else's children have to risk their lives instead of us (sic) risking ours?

    What do you think is worth fighting for today, 50 years after Lewis's exhortation? What would you urge people to do? Discuss with your group.

3. Consider the extraordinary popular reaction to the gound-breaking presidential election of 2008, in which we Americans chose an African American to lead our country, for the first time in history. Discuss with you group how you would communicate the historic significance of this event to your students. Begin collecting information to use for teaching. You might start with a book for young students such as Marlene T. Brill's *Barak Obama: Working to Make a Difference* (Millbrook, 2006). Older students will enjoy discussing the ideas presented in Obama's book *The Audacity of Hope: Thoughts on Reclaiming the American Dream* (Crown, 2006). This book is especially practical because it is available in audio format, read by the author, and can be shared with students of varying reading abilities.

EXPLORING FURTHER

At the end of each chapter, we will suggest a few readings we recommend you investigate should you want to follow up on topics mentioned in the chapter. They include books of enduring interest that you might consider buying for your own library as well as books that promote discussion and controversy as you continue your education. The basis for a professional bibliography of multicultural theory and research is provided as part of the book's endmatter, along with two appendices of special interest, "Recommended Authors" and "Recommended Films."

Gloria Anzaldúa. *La Frontera/The Borderlands,* 2nd ed. Aunt Lute Books, 1999. Poet and author muses on her life between cultures, as she creates a unique identity as a Latina American.

Lisa Delpit. *Other People's Children: Cultural Conflict in the Classroom.* The New Press, 1995.

Paulo Freire. *Teachers as Cultural Workers: Letters to Those Who Dare Teach.* Westview Press, 1998. Brazilian educator who worked with illiterate peasants is credited with introducing teachers to interpreting their work as "critical pedagogy." See also his first book, *Pedagogy of the Oppressed.*

Johnathan Kozol. *The Shame of the Nation: The Restoration of Apartheid Schooling in America.* Crown, 2005. Renewed indictment of conditions experienced by low-income students in this country, showing the vast difference in resources between poor and rich schools.

Richard Rodriguez. *Brown: The Last Discovery of America.* Penguin, 2003. Contrasts modern gains and losses from the increasing diversity and changing cultures of this country.

Ronald Takaki. *Debating Diversity: Clashing Perspectives on Race and Ethnicity in America.* Oxford University Press, 2002.

CHAPTER 2

Becoming a Culturally Competent Teacher

Welcome
Bienvenidos
Hawn txais tos
Chào Qúy Vị
ԲԱՐԻ ԳԱԼՈՒՍՏ
歡迎
សូមស្វាគមន៍
Maligayang Pagdating
어서오십시요
ຍິນດີຕ້ອນຮັບ
Bem Vindos
ПРИВЕТСТВИЕ

The first chapter of *Multicultural Teaching* looked at the concept of multicultural education, the principles underlying multicultural thinking, how such thinking changed as the world changed, and the varied assumptions implicit in educational programs implemented under this rubric. In this chapter, we focus more closely on those factors that are crucial to the success of such a program: **teachers** and **students**. Multiculturalism gives us a lens through which to look at what takes place between teachers and students in schools and to define what must be changed in that relationship in order to achieve the goals that we set in Chapter 1. The third chapter, "Multicultural Teaching Strategies," will demonstrate how learning can be organized to foster multicultural understandings. Throughout these chapters, our model of **Esteem, Empathy,** and **Equity (3E)** provides a structure on which to build a multicultural program as well as an evaluation measure for a successful program.

The chapter opens with a brief self-check assessment. You can think of it as a kind of pretest to help you define where you are now, at the beginning of your process of becoming a multicultural teacher, and to understand some of the learning that will be expected of you. When you have finished this course or this book, you will have the opportunity to look at this self-assessment again and to reflect on the changes that you find as well as to plan for your continuing development as a multicultural teacher.

In the first part of this chapter, our 3E model is described in detail in order to explain its implications for education. We claim that a new way of looking at education is required to prepare students to be successful under the changing conditions of tomorrow's society. As a result, we must ask questions such as, "What kinds of teaching will be needed to support students in an increasingly diverse world?" "What kinds of teacher preparation will be needed if we hold teachers responsible for 'teaching multiculturally?'" The 3E model enables us to seek new metaphors for teacher roles and their relationships with students.

The next part explores more closely what we mean by becoming a multicultural teacher, a teacher who is capable of meeting the needs of diverse students and providing pedagogical support as appropriate. Creating a community in which everyone can learn successfully and develop according to their abilities is a fundamental aspect of multicultural teaching. We illustrate this process with sample activities and resources.

This is followed by a section exploring what the classroom might look like when we carry out our ideas for putting the student at the center of learning. Once the students become the experts on whose resources we draw for our curriculum, what becomes of the teacher's role? We show examples of ideas and activities to demonstrate how this might be carried out.

Finally, in the last section of the chapter we explore how to pull these connections among teachers, students, and learning together through thematic teaching. We supply approaches for a thematic unit focused on sex, gender, sexism, and related social issues, called *Transforming Assumptions about Gender Roles,* as an outline that you can adapt to your particular needs.

The underlying goal of multicultural education is to provide the best education to all students, regardless of their race, gender, language, and so on. We must develop our awareness of the way "White" norms are unconsciously enforced, identify sources of bias, and consider the different kinds of power present in the classroom. Instead of sweeping differences under the table, we bring them to the forefront, acknowledging that all students are different from one another and that a variety of approaches are required to reach every student. In order to achieve our goal of including all students, we must learn how to treat these differences as strengths. In this section, we present the concept of *inclusion* as the hallmark of multicultural education, the stamp by which you can recognize its authenticity.

❖ Beginning with Self-Assessment

Let's begin our discussion with a self-assessment profile, so that you can see more clearly where you are in the process of learning to teach multiculturally, just as you would do with your students before introducing a new topic. As you review each item in Table 2.1, check the box that corresponds with **Well Prepared** (I know this material, can share it with others, and use it in teaching), **Adequate** (I feel OK, but I know some areas less well than others), and **Needs Study** (I need to know more before I can really apply it to my teaching).

TABLE 2.1   Multicultural Education: Theory and Practice

Well Prepared	Adequate	Needs Study	
			1. The United States is a Multiculture, a society comprising many diverse cultures. All of living, including schooling, involves contact between different cultures and is, therefore, multicultural. No one culture can be considered more American than any other.
			2. Thinking in the United States is gradually moving away from the goal of assimilation toward recognizing and affirming the diversity in our society (the "tossed salad," or "mosaic" metaphor).
			3. Multicultural education is too complex and pervasive a topic to be encompassed in a single course for teacher educators. All aspects of education must reflect multicultural awareness. Curricula for grades K–12 must be designed to teach all students about our multiculture and to provide individualized support (equity) for all learners in all subjects.
			4. K–12 curriculum planning must be student-centered and designed to promote *Esteem, Empathy,* and *Equity* for all children in all subjects. Multicultural teaching means using the best teaching practices to enable all students to achieve their full potential.
			5. Although every child grows up within a particular culture, he or she is shaped over the years by additional influences, such as education and personal interactions. Education can guide students to become more aware of and take pride in their individual cultures and their heritage. Children do not need to deny their heritage in order to participate fully in a different culture.

(continued)

Well Prepared	Adequate	Needs Study	
			6. Children enter school with a store of prior knowledge, closely aligned with their individual experiences or cultural heritage, on which teachers should build. Their native languages are valued and nurtured as they learn English and other new content.
			7. Teachers need to be aware of their own cultural backgrounds and assumptions. They need to be aware of how these biases might influence their expectations of students and their interactions with others. Open dialogue with students will acknowledge these cultural influences as equally valid. Both teachers and students must learn to-gether about different ideas and ways of thinking.
			8. Multicultural teaching is exciting because it is grounded in lived experience. Through active, varied learning strategies, students become personally engaged in their learning. At the same time, teachers must be willing to let go of some authority so that students can make their own choices.
			9. Multicultural education, global studies, and inter-nationalization of the curriculum are related in their focus on human interdependence. Thus, similarities and differences in human needs suggest cross-curricular approaches so that the three are not just options or add-ons to the curriculum.
			10. Multicultural education deals with behavior and attitudes as well as knowledge. We guide students to be aware of their own thinking and to listen to others. We guide them to make critical choices based on analytic reasoning, problem solving, and group decision making. Because changes in attitudes and the development of empathy take time, assessment must be flexible to reflect diversity in student learning.

Where are you in your development as a multicultural teacher? In which areas do you feel the greatest need for additional support and practice? What have you learned about yourself? Remember you are just starting out on a long process. Multicultural education is a broad study, requiring more than just one course or textbook; it is part of your commit-ment to lifelong learning. Use what you have learned here to construct a personal plan of study: identify areas that you, as an individual, would like to explore; think of experiences, people, and places you have access to (not just course requirements) that might provide important insights; imagine yourself meeting challenges to long-held beliefs or holding confrontational conversations without feeling personally threatened. After you have completed this assessment, file it in your Reflective Teaching Portfolio to review later, perhaps with your Cooperative Learning Group or as part of your final evaluation conference.

Presenting the Model: Esteem/Empathy/Equity (3E)

We present the 3E model, shown in Figure 2.1, as the foundation for multicultural education because we believe that the three elements—*Esteem, Empathy,* and *Equity*—are central to working with students to achieve multicultural goals. When we teach multiculturally, we will use the 3E model to ensure that the following basic objectives are met:

1. Develop students' identities as individuals of worth so that they can contribute to the class and have the motivation to persevere after making mistakes.
2. Value differences of opinion and understand how these differences enhance students' ability to make decisions at different times.
3. Understand different perspectives and what factors influence one's perspective.
4. Learn about one's heritage and that of others without stigmatizing anyone.
5. Promote global ways of thinking and understand the interdependence of humanity.
6. Recognize and accept the responsibilities of a citizen in a multicultural society.

All of these objectives must be incorporated into each instructional area.

Our emphasis on the *Esteem, Empathy,* and *Equity* model for multicultural education begins in early childhood and continues throughout a student's development. Reinforcing these efforts through cooperative planning within a whole school promises to achieve significant results from preschool through middle school and into high school. Multiculturalism is not a

FIGURE 2.1   The 3E Model for Multicultural Education

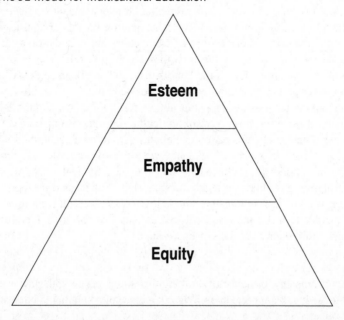

medicine with which we can inoculate children at one point in time. Rather, these understandings and attitudes must grow slowly as the result of small incidents, repeated acts of kindness, and carefully designed instruction over a period of years.

A model should do more than offer a label for a collection of principles. The 3E model graphically represents our thinking about multicultural education. It is, first of all, designed to put the student at the center. The three elements are connected in a triangle. Esteem is the foundation because that aspect of the student must be addressed before we can go on to work with Empathy, just as children who come to school hungry must have that need met before they can learn. In the same way, the development of Empathy is necessary in order to work with in supporting student Equity. This model also incorporates the two sides of multicultural teaching: the **content**—what we teach and the **process**—how we teach.

Esteem

Young children come to school expecting success. After all, they have already learned much about their native language, they have learned to walk, and they possess many other skills as well. But the school experience can be disconcerting for many because it is so different from what they are familiar with. They are expected to follow many strange new rules and they are treated as one among many, instead of one precious individual. The path to success is less certain and praise for their accomplishments is less frequent. Suddenly, learning is something that they are graded on, unlike walking, something they can pass or fail, something that has a correct answer. "Doing school" means understanding that there is only one way to be right (doing what the teacher expects) and so many ways to be wrong. People who mock the concern for supporting student self-esteem have forgotten how painful it may feel for young students to fail publicly, to be slow when everyone else is quick, or to be constantly bewildered by so many different expectations.

Students spend their early years in school negotiating a new identity in this environment. Gradual loss of self-esteem is common and hinders students' potential for achievement. Multicultural education must focus our attention on this crucial aspect of student thinking through the critical early years to provide a strong foundation as the demands on students as learners increase. By the time they reach high school, peer pressure and the power of puberty are only a few of the factors that fall heavily on students, and their sense of self-esteem is essential in coping with issues of body image (from obesity to eating disorders) and making responsible decisions about their bodies (sex and drugs).

Strong self-esteem is promoted in multicultural programs that connect with students at deeply personal levels. Instead of celebrating traditional school holidays, such as Christmas, that exclude groups of students, we affirm diversity by celebrating the great variety of ethnic holidays embraced by our students. Students develop self-awareness skills by exploring their heritage and values, as embodied in favorite foods, the language of the home, and family relationships, and learn to draw strength from their cultural backgrounds in order to make informed choices as they develop their identities. Their self-esteem helps fulfill their need for self-expression.

Empathy

The faculty of empathy, or habits of thinking that we associate with practicing empathy, is based on the feeling of connectedness. Without a sense of belonging, all that students have is boredom or isolation. Even at a young age, children are capable of being sensitive to the needs of others. Preschool children can pretend-play parental roles, offering comfort to a baby doll, for example. A lack of awareness of the feelings of others may be a symptom of autism, a developmental/brain disorder. Young children can demonstrate powerful instincts to reach out to others, to be useful, and to engage in activities requiring cooperation. But this sensibility or "emotional intelligence" shows up less frequently in the teenage years, especially among boys, where it may be stigmatized as a sign of weakness or femininity.

A multicultural program provides opportunities for students to develop their ability for empathy and find positive ways to express their feelings. They need to find heroes who model extraordinary accomplishments, as well as examples of everyday people who have overcome obstacles like their own, that will give them examples of how doing things for others can help them feel better about themselves.

Equity

We recognize that students do not come from an equal playing field, and so we promote opportunities for learning that allow all students to flex their strengths and to make a contribution. All children need places to play, to study, to explore. Members of all groups need to find their own voices in order to be both visible and proud. Education plays a significant role in teaching students skills and information that society considers important, or "cultural capital," but it also limits the access of specific groups of students to these socially privileged areas. Focusing our attention on equity means that we want to reduce the school's role of gatekeeper, that of deciding who will have access to valued items and who will not. In the past, people commonly assumed that certain groups of people were not as capable as others, for example, women, limited English speakers, and children from lower social class families. We need to examine closely any assumptions that we still hold about what students are capable of achieving, once they are given the chance.

In our multicultural curriculum we have to be careful to include examples of all aspects of human life. A study of enslaved Africans must counteract images of passivity by showing how they constantly resisted, rebelled, and actively sought freedom. A unit on Jewish Americans must tell a wider story of Jewish history than just that of being victims of the Holocaust. Native Americans need to be shown in the curriculum as people living in the modern world, not just historical images that support stereotypes of people hunting buffalo or living in tepees.

Helping students learn to get along, to feel better about themselves, and to become sensitive to the needs of others is a starting point for multicultural education but not the complete answer to what we need. We must prepare students to be active participants in their community and their learning, to comprehend that no one stands alone in the struggle for social justice, and that we will all benefit from working together for the welfare of everyone.

A Student-Centered Approach

Effective multicultural education must be student-centered if it is to be equitable. In learning to teach for diversity, we need to perceive students as individuals, being careful to avoid generalizations that lead to stereotyped thinking. Student-centered instruction recognizes student learning as the ultimate aim of education. We want students to be self-motivated

DID YOU KNOW?

◄◇►

In a middle school in the South Bronx, New York, once considered a dangerous and discouraging place, Ramón Gonzalez has given up his dream of being a lawyer and now, as the school principal, is spearheading a successful approach to engage these neglected students. He overhauled the whole learning environment, including implementing a longer school day and classes on Saturday, to give students more opportunities. His students respect him; they can tell that he really cares. They are the poorest of the poor—90 percent are eligible for a free lunch, 15 percent live in shelters, and 20 percent need help learning English. He understands; he grew up in a similar environment in Harlem.

He created a special school here, the Laboratory School of Finance and Technology, in 2003, because he found the students had real abilities and desires to achieve that weren't being supported. For example, many students couldn't get past a job interview with their criminal records, so they ended up directing their skills into the underground, illegal economy. But what they really wanted to do with their lives was learn to work with computers and make money from good jobs. Due to Ramón Gonzalez's high expectations of the students and the school staff, the Laboratory School proved that all students, even the ones from the worst backgrounds, could succeed academically. He concludes, "I love this job because every day we get a chance to change lives. By the time kids get to high school, a lot of decisions are made. Now, they're still searching."

learners, to inquire and to discover, and also to question established practices or assumptions. At the same time, students need to be aware of the responsibilities that are directly related to choice and decision making.

We talk of student self-esteem as the foundation for learning; we recognize that all students need a sense of worth—an "I can" attitude—if they are to strive to achieve. We are concerned about the classroom climate as we try to build an attitude of trust between student and teacher. We try to let students know that making mistakes is an essential part of real learning, so that they will dare to take risks as they brainstorm and solve problems together. We need citizens who have genuine self-esteem, for they are the people who can reach out confidently to others with empathy and caring.

As we plan a multicultural program, we consider how we will provide for the needs of our students.

All children have the right to:

- An education appropriate for his or her needs.
- An education which respects each student's culture, race, gender, socioeconomic background, and home language.
- Schools and educational programs which are effective.
- Educational programs that prepare them for jobs, for lifelong learning, for family life, and for citizenship in a democracy.
- Education in a safe, caring environment.

In addition we stress the need for acknowledging differences while also recognizing the strengths of each individual child. For example, rather than operating with the deficit model that labels a child as "non-English proficient," we need to retrain ourselves to think more positively: "Here is a child who knows how to speak Japanese" or "This boy has lived in Mexico and can read Spanish." There is never a reason for students to feel bad about who they are.

So, we encourage students to tell their stories. We let them share what they have to contribute whether it is through storytelling, writing poetry, or painting a picture. Each child should know that he or she is a valued member of the group.

Note that different cultures may indicate respect for elders, for example, by *not* looking directly at another person. Such differences between "school culture" and "home culture" can be dealt with explicitly, in the same way you talk with students about when it is appropriate to use an "inside" voice and an "outside" one. As you discuss these differences, be careful to point out to students that it is OK to switch between the two codes of behavior.

Encourage students to discuss any related topics that come up. Younger students might talk about being kind to others, for example, making a newcomer welcome. Older students may be interested in how to dress, perhaps, when you go to the local grocery store to apply for a job. We need to listen to what our students are saying to each other, especially when they think we are not paying attention, in order to prevent the acceptance of biased speech and racially hostile attitudes. Begin a discussion with your students by sharing a book such as:

For primary students:

> Michelle Edwards. *Pa Lia's First Day.* Harcourt, 1999. A second-grade Hmong girl's first day in a new school.
> Louise Erdrich. *The Birchbark House.* Hyperion, 1999. A young Ojibwa girl grows up on an island in Lake Superior in the mid-1800s.

For intermediate readers:

> Jon Hassler. *Jemmy.* Fawcett, 2000. Jemmy is half-Chippewa and half-White and has conflicts over her family responsibilities.
> Avi and Rachel Vail. *Never Mind! A Twin Novel.* HarperCollins, 2004. Meg is ashamed of her twin Edward and is terrified her friends will find out about him.

As you discuss the book, have students define the key terms of *prejudice, racism,* and *stereotyping* in their own words.

Have students cite examples of each of these from their own experience. Discuss how to recognize prejudice, possible responses to racist remarks, and the harmful effect these have on everyone involved. Students can complete the following sentences individually or in groups.

> Prejudice means _____.
> I don't like it when someone calls me a _____.
> People assume I am _____.
> Racist attitudes hurt because _____.

The "Hidden Curriculum"

We need to remember that curriculum consists of more than consciously, carefully planned messages presented through lectures and in textbooks. Children also learn concepts and attitudes through the hidden or covert curriculum that may not be recognized and is almost never assessed. Consider what students are learning from the speech and behavior of these teachers:

> *Motherly Mrs. McIntyre loves children and loves to teach first-grade reading. She always brags to the principal about the wonderful readers in her Great Books group and has one of them read aloud when he visits the classroom. (How do the less able students feel? What knowledge and attitudes are they internalizing?)*
>
> *Jim Melville loves to teach fourth-grade language arts. He reads aloud to his students and brings in piles of books from the library. He tells students that he always picks out books about boys because he knows boys hate stories about girls but girls enjoy the adventure stories about boys. (How might this practice affect the self-esteem of girls in this classroom? What are the boys and girls learning?)*
>
> *Eighth-grade history teacher Donna Fosdick has regular celebrations for Martin Luther King's birthday and Cinco de Mayo. She comments that she can't afford more time from the curriculum for extra observances. (Is there more to understanding other cultures than just observing these few holidays? What do students learn from hearing this attitude expressed? What are they failing to learn?)*

Children are very attentive to the hidden messages communicated by teacher behavior. We need to be aware of our own stereotyped thinking that causes us to behave, for example, as if all children have the same support at home or that everyone in a class shares the same values. Beware of generalized evaluative statements such as "That's good" whenever students make a contribution. Students quickly learn to perform for teacher approval instead of their own satisfaction. We need to be aware of our role as the adult who models respect and caring for students in the classroom.

In offering an inclusive educational program that serves the needs of all students, we want to refrain from:

- *Trivializing:* Organizing activities only around holidays or only around food; involving parents only for holiday or cooking activities.
- *Tokenism:* Displaying one black doll amidst many white dolls or having only one multicultural book among many others; any kind of minimal display in the classroom.
- *Disconnecting cultural diversity from daily classroom life:* Reading multicultural books only for special occasions or teaching one unit related to cultural diversity and never addressing the topic again; for example, featuring African Americans only during Black History Month in February or talking about Native Americans only in relationship to November's Thanksgiving celebration.
- *Marginalizing:* Presenting people of color only in a limited context, such as the past or as victims. Instead, provide modern examples of groups coping with contemporary issues.
- *Misrepresenting American ethnic groups:* Using books about Mexico, Japan, or African countries to teach about contemporary cultural groups in the United

States. Don't confuse their heritage with the culture they are creating in this country.

- *Essentializing:* Expecting individuals to reflect generalizations about the group they belong to, treating them the same.
- *Tourism:* Presenting different customs or beliefs as exotic rather than a normal part of one's life.
- *Denying conflict:* Allow discussion of conflicts into the classroom and model active listening and conflict resolution skills.

Creating a Community of Learners

Good teachers make all the difference. In many states, too few students have access to experienced and qualified teachers, and the poorer the school the less likely it will attract the most effective teachers. When school districts post low scores, it is often the teachers who get the blame. But teachers are not the villains. Students still respond to an individual who offers them respect, care, and dignity.

Building a community in which students are free to learn and feel welcome to bring all of themselves into the classroom is the task of multicultural education. In order to accomplish this, we have to explore the role that the teacher plays in this kind of classroom and how that might be different from the traditional roles. We have to change our beliefs and behaviors as teachers. Most often, the teacher is the one from whom knowledge flows, and the students passively accept what they will be required to feed back to the teacher as evidence that they have learned what they should. But this picture of teaching resembles the process of stuffing a sausage and has the equivalent appeal to students. Other images or metaphors that can be used to describe teaching include:

- The Banker—The teacher makes deposits, and the student makes withdrawals.
- The Sage on the Stage versus the Guide on the Side—This picture contrasts the expert lecturer at the front of the room, facing the students, with a teacher who moves around the room, offering assistance as needed.
- The Gardener—This kind of teacher starts with the seed of an idea and fosters its development through student learning.
- The Librarian—This model provides information, shows students where to find what they are looking for, and answers student questions.
- The Coach—In this role, the teacher offers encouragement and advice on how to improve student understanding.

Which of these metaphors or models have you experienced as a student? Which of them, if any, appeals to you? In general, traditional models depend on thinking of the student as an empty vessel and the teacher as the main source of knowledge and authority. It is difficult to find a different perspective to apply to student learning when so much of teaching is focused on getting through the material or teaching to the test.

When we test students on the content we have taught and they don't do well, we have no means of understanding what went wrong. Did the teacher present the material poorly? Was the level appropriate for the student? (Was the student even listening at the time?) Did the student not understand the exam question or become confused by the choices offered?

To put it another way, when the student selects the wrong answer, where does the fault lie? Do we blame the student, the teacher, or something in between?

In the typical classroom, only one person has authority and has the power to make decisions affecting others, and that is the teacher. The teacher determines what behavior or response is allowed; the teacher plans and directs the learning for the group. Few, if any, options are open to the student. Students react in many different ways to express their feelings. They might withdraw by daydreaming or passing notes to each other or they might actively resist the structure by interrupting the lesson, causing trouble, talking back, or doing anything to break the cycle of boredom and to demonstrate their refusal to accept the teacher's authority. If real learning is ever going to take place, the teacher must earn his or her position of authority and decision making must be shared with students in order to construct a community.

A community of learners is a group in which everyone is engaged in learning from each other and everyone shares in the responsibility to enable the learning to take place. In a community everyone participates because they know it is a safe place to bring themselves, their prior knowledge, their experience, their identities, and their concerns. Community members engage in conversation and respectful dialogue in which they listen to each other. Students work out their ideas by talking them through, testing them against others, and freely exploring the possibilities of their ideas.

Teachers and students may come from very different backgrounds. In addition, school may be an unfamiliar environment, with new and strange conventions to follow, for many students. When all are learning together, teachers as well as students, everyone can build bridges and make connections, drawing on what they already know, to make the new setting safe for the risk-taking and mistakes that accompany learning.

Creating an Inclusive Classroom Culture

What does an inclusive multicultural classroom look and feel like when you walk in? The first aspect you would notice is that everyone is engaged in some way. There are no students hanging out passively in the back. The teacher may be working with a small group of students or walking around the room checking in with each student. There is a steady buzz of conversation as students talk with each other and ask each other questions. The seating is organized so that it can be changed depending on the activity. The students seem proud of their accomplishments and examples of student work cover the classroom walls.

Planning for such an inclusive classroom culture must take into account many elements, for example:

- Rules—Each class must draw up and agree upon rules for respectful language and behavior, as well as the consequences for failing to uphold these rules.
- Community—Each class will build shared experiences through reading books together and participating in discussions that create a common background to draw on.
- Organization—The power to make others do something must be shared among all, not just a few, and rotated. Everyone gets a turn to be responsible for a task, not just the student who is always the first one to raise a hand, answer questions, or volunteer.

IDEAS IN ACTION!

An Urban Odyssey

It was called an Urban Odyssey, a trip through four of New York City's boroughs for twenty teachers from all over the country and from every kind of school. The purpose of this expedition was to make them better teachers by motivating them to examine their beliefs and biases. Sleeping on the floor in community centers, they were immersed in the life of the neighborhood, often for fifteen hours a day, participating in activities as diverse as climbing a rope course, learning salsa dancing, visiting a Sikh temple, and handing out sandwiches to homeless people in a park. One participant commented, "I was surprised to find out how much I had to learn, not only from the students I met, but also from working together with the other teachers to answer the challenges of the trip."

Present this challenge to your students: If you could invite twenty teachers from around the country to visit this community, what would you like to show them? What would surprise them about your area? What might be unfamiliar to someone from another part of the country? What knowledge and attitudes would you like them to take away from this visit?

- Values—Each class has the responsibility to discuss the difference between helping each other and stealing someone else's work and passing it off as your own.
- Evaluation—The students will be encouraged to measure success by their own improvement rather than by always competing to be the top student.

A community exists when people share activities and values, when the people feel that everyone is on the same side, reaching for the same goals, and everyone knows that all of them depend on each other. In order for every student to succeed, we need to tap the diversity in each one, because each student is unique. Because everyone will have something to contribute to the class knowledge and welfare at all times, students will feel supported in their efforts by the inclusive classroom culture.

Students Leading Learning

Genuine dialogue is not possible without humility on the part of everyone. Teachers who expect to be obeyed may be surprised to find that students expect them to earn that authority. The common discontinuity, or gap, between White teachers and students of diverse races, ethnicities, and cultures often leads to miscommunication over authority roles and resistance to learning. But for true multicultural education (teaching and learning) to take place, teachers must be willing to give up some of their stance as the authority figure at the front of the class in order for students to claim their own role in learning. For White teachers, this might require making significant changes in their belief system, thought processes, self-concept, interaction patterns, and classroom practices. The subconscious world view that many White teachers carry with them takes the White, middle-class, standard English-speaking way of life as the framework against which all other ways of life are measured. There is no formula for you to follow in adapting to a different culture. However, the best way to begin is always to ask the students what they want from a good teacher. Students say they want:

- High expectations from the teacher for what they can achieve.
- Someone who will show trust in them as human beings.
- A person who cares about them and shows concern.
- Someone who believes in working things out together.
- A teacher who is culturally competent; that is, willing to learn about new customs, new ideas, new identities.

As you consider how you might fulfill these needs when you begin teaching, you are engaging in the process of becoming a multiculturally competent person.

Who Do We Want to Be?

What are our goals for schools? What kinds of students do we want to have? How can we help them get there? So much of school appears to students to be based on an assembly-line process, aimed at creating bored students who come out all the same. What can we offer them instead? Students need to feel that they belong to the class, that they have an important role to play, that they are accepted for who they are, and that they can bring significant aspects of their cultural identity to school. We have to approach our students in a way that will convince them learning is pleasurable and positive learning events are satisfying. We already know what to do. We have to give students choices so that they can pursue their own interests. They can become experts in particular areas and make an important contribution to the class by sharing their information through talking, drawing, acting, performing, making, singing, or otherwise representing what they are excited about discovering. We know that students like to create things. It gives them pride, a feeling of agency, and immediate feedback. Therefore, we need to make it possible for them to put together newspapers, make posters to demonstrate processes, and build their own websites. The way we choose to show off student work communicates what we value. Consider what image you want to project to the community of the learning that takes place in your school. Do you want people to look only at the school's test scores as illustrations of what students are doing in school all day?

The concept that people possess multiple intelligences, that their abilities cannot be represented by a single score on one scale, leads us to look at schooling more broadly. Students are highly engaged in learning when they have opportunities to play with things and encouragement to figure out how to make something work. Students can take their learning outside the classroom and look for different ideas in the wider world that surrounds them. Experiences with physical and artistic expression also allow significant, alternate areas of student minds to be involved in learning. Learning is also taking place when students are having fun. Break down boxed-in, habitual patterns of thinking by sharing books with students that show life as humorous or ridiculous. Intermediate grade students enjoy *Diary of a Wimpy Kid,* by Jeff Kinney (Amulet, 2007), and young adults will be drawn in by the distinctive humor of Sherman Alexie's *The Absolutely True Diary of a Part-Time Indian* (Little Brown, 2007).

DID YOU KNOW?

—◦—

Psychologists can actually see the extra effort that racism causes in brain processing. They use a computerized test called fMRI (functional magnetic resonance imaging) to measure how many seconds faster people associate stereotypically "White" names (such as *Chip*) with positive qualities (such as *heaven*) compared to stereotypically "Black" or "other" names (such as *Jamaal*) with the same positive qualities. The difference in pairings is only fractions of a second for most Whites and some African Americans, but it is evidence that prejudice is a state of mind to which no one can claim to be immune. This brain imaging study does not look at actual signs of racism, but it shows us the effort the brain puts into self-control, to not letting racism bias the brain's reaction. This effort has additional consequences. When the brain is spending time controlling potentially biased reactions, it has less "space" to work on other puzzles. Prejudice is not hard-wired into our brains, but we have to use our capacity to change habitual reactions.

In a student-centered program, literature can be used to open up student thinking, provide insights into the lives of others, and support students' desire for change. Show students how they might respond to a book by introducing them to one of your favorites and reading a special selection aloud. Instead of analyzing the story from an academic standpoint, elicit personal, emotional responses. You can throw out a few open-ended questions and see how students react, or you might read the passage again, more slowly, pausing to savor the language and ideas being presented. Questions to elicit personal responses include:

- What does this story make you think about?
- What comes to mind after reading the story?
- Does this story matter to you? How?

Let the students discover their own way into the story by talking about it with each other instead of focusing on delivering a response they believe you are looking for. In this way, the book comes to belong to the students who have shared it, and students will feel comfortable reading it over and over again. Then, any of the participants, including the teacher, can also refer back to it when making connections to new material.

Culturally Responsive Teaching

If we want all of our students to feel a part of the class, we must provide them with a sense of belonging, the knowledge that they are not the only ones like them. This self-confidence can lead to taking on new ideas, such as standing up for what's right and working out one's problems. We show them how one person can make a difference, no matter what background he or she comes from. Topics such as different family arrangements, feelings that students are afraid to show, such as being shy or fearing that they look stupid, and aspects of life that make it special, such as having friends, helping others, and believing in dreams are all appropriate to bring into the classroom for discussion and sharing, and will remind students that others feel the same way they do, at all grade levels. The following books are helpful in stimulating discussion with different groups of students:

Michael Dorris. *Guests.* Hyperion, 1994. Moss, a Native American boy, resents his father's inviting the "strange white men" to join their harvest feast.

Sharon Arms Doucet. *Fiddle Fever.* Houghton, 2000. A 14-year-old boy in Louisiana wants to learn to play the fiddle like his 'Nonc Adolphe. Set in a small town in 1914.

Brent Hartinger. *Geography Club.* Harper, 2003. A boy keeps his being gay a secret until he finds others like him. They create the "Geography Club" as a cover for their meetings.

Claudia Mills. *Dinah for President.* Macmillan, 1992. A middle school girl runs for president of the sixth grade; humorous.

Mitali Perkins. *Monsoon Summer.* Delacorte, 2004. A girl reluctantly travels with her family to India to work in the orphanage where her mother lived as a child.

The process of creating one's identity is especially difficult for today's students, who face so many different pressures and competing identity groups. All students need to be able to share the problems they face and understand that others may be experiencing some of the same conflicts. A culturally competent teacher can help students ask for help in sorting out conflicts between home and school, or discover a new way to create an identity from blended cultures. The following list of books offers suggestions to support students in their learning about themselves:

Tomie de Paola. *Nana Upstairs & Nana Downstairs.* Putnam, 1998. Rev. ed. A child learns about death.

Mem Fox. *Wilfrid Gordon McDonald Partridge.* Kane/Miller, 1985. A boy looks for his elderly friend's missing memory.

Cynthia Rylant. *The Old Woman Who Named Things.* Harcourt, 1996. This Appalachian woman names only things she will outlive until she falls in love with a shy little dog, whom she names Lucky.

A multicultural teacher will create an environment in which students lead the educational inquiry in the directions that are important to them. Bullying, for example, is a topic of great personal interest to students as it has expanded from verbal and physical attacks at recess or after school to more sophisticated schemes involving the Internet and possibly provoking vulnerable individuals to commit suicide. Bullying is no longer a behavior that can be shrugged off as innocent teasing or a passing stage.

Bullying also affects more than the immediate victim. Children usually are afraid to tell adults about such behavior. Even those who only observe the bullying may be afraid of retaliation. Discuss this problem in general in every class, giving students an opportunity to bring up possible experiences they may have had. Students who are the targets of repeated bullying behavior often show signs of fear and stress, such as:

Fear of going to school
Fear of going to the bathroom

Fear of riding to and from school on the bus
Physical symptoms of illness
Diminished ability to learn

Teach students effective strategies for coping with bullying or potentially threatening situations. The following are some strategies that you can discuss and practice:

Learning to control anger or cool off
Collaborative problem solving
Active listening
Seeking a mediator

Look for the following resources:

Allan L. Beane. *The Bully-Free Classroom: Over 100 Tips and Strategies for Teachers K–8.* Free Spirit Publishing, 1999.

Let's Get Real, documentary film by Debra Chasnoff, Helen S. Cohen, and Kate Stilley. New Day Films. 190 Route 17M, P.O. Box 1084, Harriman NY 10926.

Not in Our Town I and *Not in Our Town II,* PBS video specials. NIOT Campaign/The Working Group. P.O. Box 70232, Oakland CA 94612-0232. (www. pbs. org/niot) Patrice O'Neill and Rhian Miller, producers.

Nan Stein. *Secrets in Public: Sexual Harrassment in Our Schools.* Harcourt, 2001.

❖ Providing for Differentiated Instruction: A Thematic Unit of Study

The thematic approach to organizing learning activities is particularly appropriate for integrating studies across the curriculum. A broad theme study is also conducive to integrating multicultural concepts into the curriculum. Within a self-contained classroom the teacher can readily guide students through an exploration of a general theme (for example, "Survival") while helping them to develop literacy skills as they learn information related to science and social studies, apply mathematical concepts, and include music and the other arts in a rich, meaningful study.

Humanities approaches to the curriculum in the middle years and high school offer many opportunities for this kind of thematic study. Core class arrangements often allow social studies and language arts teachers time to organize such units. Planning together pays off because students can see how learning is connected across many fields as they practice "writing like a scientist" and sharing their findings through artistic displays or dramatic presentations.

High school teachers can use thematic units to provide context for subjects they are covering. Whether in a science or social studies class, students will benefit from reading fiction as well as nonfiction. They will make cross-curricular connections with current issues and reinforce content learning through greater involvement with other subject areas.

Selecting an Appropriate Theme

Focusing units of study on broad themes allows for the greatest involvement of students of differing abilities and interests. Integrated studies include opportunities for students to contribute to the total knowledge gathered by all class members and also to work together on common tasks, thus learning from each other. You can select a topic that is timely and especially useful. The best topics from a multicultural viewpoint will be sufficiently broad so as to include a wide spectrum of ideas representing different cultures, for example:

- Food and Nutrition
- Endangered Animals
- Living in Desert Lands
- Sports around the World
- Transportation
- Reaching Out to Help

Using a Planning Sheet

The planning sheet shown (see Figure 2.2), designed to assist one teacher or a team of teachers in developing a thematic study, can be used in a variety of ways. For instance, a group of teachers might sit around a table brainstorming together the possibilities for developing a thematic study of, perhaps, "Citizenship." Each person could have a copy of

FIGURE 2.2   Thematic Planning Sheet

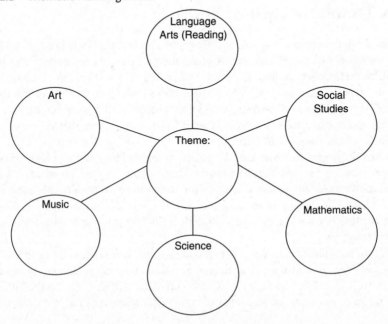

this planning sheet, or you could enlarge the diagram on a large sheet attached to the wall that would enable the group to record many ideas together. Each time the group meets to review their progress, this sheet can be displayed to remind the group of the plan they had generated together.

Students, too, can use this kind of planning sheet as they begin developing a thematic study within their Cooperative Learning Groups. You might change the labels on each circle to reflect skills or specific subject matter instead of courses, for example, reading, writing, history, geography, art, music, biology, and math. If each group selects a theme it wants to explore, this sheet will encourage students to consider how different subject areas contribute to the development of a broad theme. Or, if the whole class is exploring one theme, for example, "Family," an enlarged planning sheet can guide both individual and small group projects as the students integrate their work into the total study. The planning sheet will expand as students uncover new material, and student engagement in learning will increase as they make their own choices about which paths to follow and what questions to ask.

Introducing a Thematic Study

The purpose of the introduction is to engage student interest in the theme the class is going to study. You might choose an introductory approach that begins with:

- Discussing a current news event (an apology for having interned Japanese Americans during World War II)
- Displaying a picture (the plight of the elderly in your community)
- Inviting a guest to speak to the class (a community activist)

To introduce the theme "Persecution," you might read Lois Lowry's Newbery Award-winning book, *Number the Stars,* aloud. This novel for intermediate readers, is set in Copenhagen in 1943 when Nazi soldiers were rounding up Danish Jews. After reading the short novel, challenge students to list all the ideas that were presented by this author. As students suggest ideas found in Lowry's book, write the words and phrases on the chalkboard, linking those that are related (see Figure 2.3). Notice how *clusters* of ideas begin to develop, suggesting further exploration.

Reading this novel may lead to an historical study of Jewish beliefs, the Nazi genocide of Jews in Europe (the Holocaust), or the lives of Jews in the world today.

A novel motivates students to care about the characters and the choices they make. Students will want to know why the Germans threatened the Danes and why the Jews in particular were persecuted. They can depict scenes on a large floor map as they follow events in the story. Small groups can research the history and geography referred to in this novel. As they learn more about the setting, students will begin to ask critical questions, such as:

- What happened to the Jews in other countries?
- Why didn't more people protest actively?
- How did the United States respond?
- Were groups other than the Jews also threatened?

FIGURE 2.3 Clustering Ideas Presented in a Book

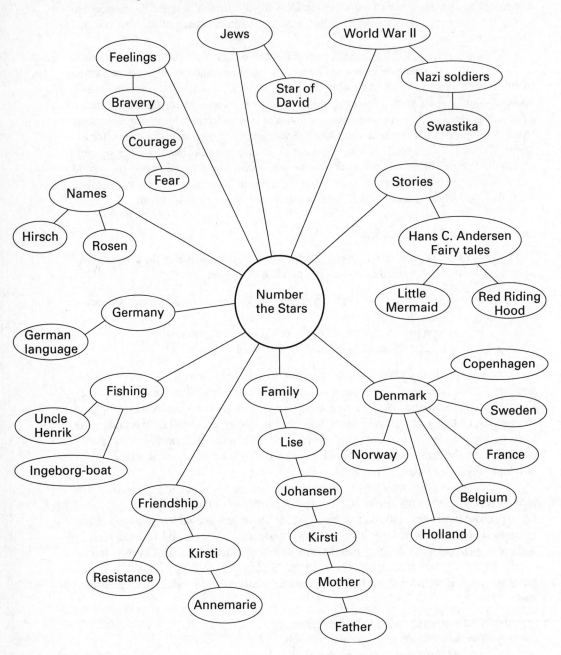

The following books will help students expand their knowledge about this identity group.

Ann Kramer. *Anne Frank: The Young Writer Who Told the World Her Story*. National Geographic, 2007. Provides more context for older students.

Carol Ann Lee. *Anne Frank and the Children of the Holocaust*. Viking, 2006. Stories of other children caught up in the war.

Josephine Poole. *Anne Frank*. Knopf, 2005. A picture book biography with a timeline.

The following are additional books recommended for reading aloud to introduce other similar thematic studies:

The City

Barbara Joosse. *Hot City*. Illustrated by R. Gregory Christie. Philomel, 2004. Mimi and her brother Joe, two African American kids looking for fun, escape the sizzling heat of the city by going to the library and letting their imaginations roam wild. Especially recommended for the outstanding illustrations, saturated with color and dizzy with shifting perspectives.

Walls

Mary Burns Knight. *Talking Walls*. Illustrated by Anne Sibley O'Brien. Tilbury, 1992. This book and its sequel, *Talking Walls; The Stories Continue*, uses a **Wall** as a unifying metaphor to explore ways that people in different cultures are kept apart or held together.

Celebrations

Byrd Baylor. *I'm in Charge of Celebrations*. Illustrated by Peter Parnall. Scribner, 1986. This timeless book encourages us to appreciate every day in a different way. The illustrations suggest the spare openness of the Southwest desert.

Dreams

Arthur Dorros. *Abuela*. Illustrated by Elisa Kleven. Dutton, 1991. Rosalba and her abuela (grandmother) hold hands and fly all over the city, waving to the people below. Lots of details encourage close examination of the illustrations.

Faith Ringgold. *Tar Beach*. Crown, 1991. Children lie on rooftops in the hot New York summer and imagine flying over their neighborhood, looking down from on high. This noted artist fills her pages with fabric art on which she paints her story.

Many of these books raise difficult issues or familiar concerns, using poetic language, so that everyone can make a connection. Selection of an appropriate text can generate sufficient discussion so that you and your students can easily plan a more extensive unit of study.

Developing a Thematic Study Together

Suppose the class plans a thematic study based on "Latino Americans." The purpose of preliminary planning is for students to identify the tasks they need to undertake. They might create notebooks with headings to guide their research, such as:

- What We Know Now
- What We Need to Find Out
- Where We Can Find What We Need?

At this stage students can work in small groups to share the search for information. Working in Cooperative Learning Groups encourages greater participation by all students. It also provides the opportunity for students to get acquainted with each other, thus generating *empathy* as they work. In addition, working as part of a team gives each student more confidence, thus adding to each one's *self-esteem*. After making lists, the class can assemble the results of all groups on a Wall of Information to which any students can add as they come up with more ideas.

The tasks listed under "What We Need to Find Out" can be distributed among the learning groups. Groups can then focus on the next stage—locating resources. Later, the class can brainstorm various ways to share the information gathered.

Students can visit a library as a class or in small groups to find information specific to their portion of the assigned task. If you let the librarian know what topics students will be looking for before they arrive, that person can help them use the computers to locate books, newspapers, and other print material and guide them to additional multimedia resources, such as films and audio tapes.

Students should also be encouraged to identify other means of locating information, for example, the telephone, personal interviews, writing letters, or sending email requests. You may need to plan lessons on using such skills as interviewing and writing business letters as the study progresses. Students should also learn to write follow-up thank you letters to people or organizations that have helped them.

Once the students feel satisfied with the information they have collected, they will be eager to show others the results of their hard work. They can discuss a variety of ways to highlight the significance of their learning, for example:

- Creating an album to put in the school library.
- Producing a poster display with explanations to be mounted in the school entry hall or in a community center.
- Preparing a multimedia presentation for the school.

The assessment of the students' work will be based on two elements: (1) your walking around the groups and noting who is contributing and working well with others, and (2) having the students develop their own assessment scale (rubric, see page 108).

Teaching a Thematic Unit: Male and Female—Transforming Assumptions about Gender Roles

Despite the stereotype that girls are not as good at math, both boys and girls do well on math tests. However, not many girls take the advanced math and science classes necessary for careers in science. Students can create a unit to investigate this and related topics. For example, girls tend to receive less attention from teachers in school partly because they behave well. They may find fewer mentors who might encourage them to consider a range of careers, and they seem less likely to be offered leadership opportunities. Students can participate in a critical analysis of the differences in roles available to women and men. They can learn more about sexism and stereotyping and talk about possible solutions to problems they uncover.

Use the planning graphic shown earlier if you are working with other teachers in middle school or high school, to help you integrate this unit into the year's curriculum. Strategies for getting started include:

- Reading a picture book, for example, *Zora Hurston and the Chinaberry Tree* by William Miller and illustrated by Cornelius Van Wright and Ying-Hwa Hu.
- Sharing a newspaper article about a local event about either sports or politics, in which girls are not represented or are treated unfairly.
- Asking students if they think girls and boys are treated equally in school.
- Brainstorming together or clustering around the word "sexism."

Older students can work in cooperative learning groups to discuss ideas, select a topic they would like to know more about, and develop a plan for working on the project. The following are examples of possible topics for exploration:

- Women Left Out of History
- Contributions of African American Women
- Women as Community Activists

Start by stimulating students to consider their own attitudes. Provide several pictures of groups of important men in which you have inserted a few female faces. How do students react?

Students can also benefit from a quick assessment of their prior knowledge. Ask each one to make a list of ten famous men and ten famous women, excluding popular television, movie, music, or sports stars. Set a limit of five minutes. Then, discuss what they learned from this activity. How did they feel? Was it easy to list as many women as men? What gaps appear in their knowledge of women's accomplishments?

> *In a society where the rights and potential of women are constrained, no man can be truly free. He may have power, but he will not have freedom.*
>
> ~ MARY ROBINSON, Former President of Ireland

Connections across the Curriculum

Begin a Word Wall entitled, perhaps, EXTRAORDINARY WOMEN IN THE UNITED STATES. Add to this list as you continue the study of sex equity, making connections across the curriculum, as suggested below.

Language Arts/Reading Connections.   Read biographies or autobiographies of favorite women writers to find out why they write and what particularly interests them. Share Beverly Cleary's memoir, *The Girl from Yamhill,* or check out Black author Jacqueline Woodson's website, where she answers students' questions.

Social Studies Connections.   Find biographies of women living in the period or region you are studying, such as *Amelia Earhart: The Legend of the Lost Aviator*, by Shelley

Tanaka and illustrated by David Craig (Abrams, 2008) or *A Woman for President: The Story of Victoria Woodhull,* by Kathleen Krull and illustrated by Jan Dyer (Walker, 2007).

Math Connections.   Explore the training of female astronauts such as Sally Ride, Ellen Ochoa, or Mae Jemison, and find out what math skills they need in order to do their job.

Science Connections.   What women have won the Nobel Prize for their achievements in science? Look for biographies such as *Something Out of Nothing: Marie Curie and Radium*, by Carla Killough McClafferty (Farrar, 2006), for older Students, or *Marie Curie,* by Kathleen Krull and illustrated by Boris Kulikov (Viking, 2007) for intermediate grades.

Music, Arts, Sports, Movement, Drama Connections.   There have been many famous women singers and musicians but fewer women who became conductors or composers. A recent series of stamps honoring American choreographers included Martha Graham and Agnes de Mille, but not Katherine Dunham or Isadora Duncan. Look for books that show that the arts are not the sole province of men (mostly European Whites), such as *Frida: ¡Viva la Vida! Long Live Life!,* a group of poems with art by noted Mexican painter Frida Kahlo, by Carmen T. Bernier-Grand (Cavendish, 2007) or the picture book about a renowned Cuban American salsa singer. *My Name Is Celia Cruz: The Life of Celia Cruz/ Me Llamo Celia: La Vida de Celia Cruz,* by Monica Brown (Luna Rising, 2004). These bilingual books will attract student attention.

A Woman's Perspective on History
Women have been left out of the history we usually study but that doesn't mean they were not present. Women disguised themselves as men and fought in the Revolutionary and Civil Wars. Others dressed in men's clothing in order to earn money in jobs closed to women. Find out more about the significant role that women played in the events of their time in the following books.

> Laura Halse Anderson. *Independent Dames: What You Never Knew about the Women and Girls of the American Revolution.* Illustrated by Matt Faulkner. Simon & Schuster, 2008.
>
> Cynthia Chin-Lee. *Amelia to Zora: 26 Women Who Changed the World.* Illustrated by Megan Halsey and Sean Addy. Charlesbridge, 2005.
>
> Bonnie Christensen. *The Daring Nellie Bly: America's Star Reporter.* Knopf, 2003. She kept doing things that ladies didn't do; she championed women's rights and traveled the world.
>
> Pamela D. Edwards. *The Bus Ride That Changed History: The Story of Rosa Parks.* Illustrated by Danny Shanahan. Houghton Mifflin, 2005.
>
> Candace Fleming. *Our Eleanor: A Scrapbook Look at Eleanor Roosevelt's Remarkable Life.* Atheneum, 2005.
>
> Yona Zeldis McDonough. *Sisters in Strength: American Women Who Made a Difference.* Illustrated by Malcah Zeldis. Holt, 2000. Eleven sketches of women who faced varied obstacles, from Pocahantas to Clara Barton.

Andrea Davis Pinkney. *Let It Shine: Stories of Black Women Freedom Fighters.* Illustrated by Stephen Alcorn. Harcourt Brace, 2000. Short pieces about women, both legendary and little known.

Anne Rockwell. *They Called Her Molly Pitcher.* Illustrated by Von Bahler. Knopf, 2002.

As students learn more about these special women, they can discuss the different ways they dealt with the following issues: what obstacles the women faced, how they tried to be taken seriously in a man's world, what people's attitudes were toward their goals, and how they coped with the lack of support for their ambition. Have students imagine being part of the family of one of these women. How might the decisions, possibly dangerous and always outrageous, made by the women in the books affect their lives—as a son or daughter, a parent, a partner?

Featuring Women from Different Cultures

Students need to be able to identify with the people in the books they read, to see their lives and concerns represented, and to learn about people like themselves that they can be proud of. Fill your classroom with literature about people of all nationalities, races, and ethnic groups in order to recognize the contributions made by many different people from diverse backgrounds. For example, African American students will be pleased to see books about well-known personalities such as Maya Angelou or Oprah Winfrey. But all students will benefit from being exposed to many other African Americans who have been honored, in order to counteract the negative images and racism that surrounds us.

Picture book biographies are especially effective with students of all ages because they focus on "stories," lending a personal slant not always found in factual accounts. Look for examples to read aloud, such as the following:

Jeri Ferris. *With Open Hands: A Story about Biddy Mason.* Lerner, 1999. Born a slave, she won her freedom and became one of the richest women in Los Angeles, California.

Eloise Greenfield. *Mary McLeod Bethune.* Illustrated by Jerry Pinkney. Harper Collins, 1994. A story about the life of the pioneering African American educator.

Deborah Hopkinson. A *Band of Angels: A Story Inspired by the Jubilee Singers.* Illustrated by Raúl Colón. Atheneum, 1999. Ella Sheppard, born a slave, toured with the Jubilee Chorus to raise money for African American education and to keep the traditional songs alive.

Barbara Kramer. *Amy Tan: Author of the Joy Luck Club.* Enslow, 1996. One in a series of biographies for older students, this book looks at the Chinese American author's childhood and her struggle to get published.

Reeve Lindbergh. *Nobody Owns the Sky.* Illustrated by Pamela Paparone. Candlewick, 1996. Story of Bessie Coleman, the first African American to earn a pilot's license.

Osceola Mays. *Osceola: Memories of a Sharecropper's Daughter.* Disney Press, 2000. Outstanding oral history.

Maria Tallchief with Rosemary Wells. *Tallchief: America's Prima Ballerina.* Illustrated by Gary Kelley. Viking, 1999. With support from her family, Tallchief overcame objections from her tribe and social barriers to follow her love for dance.

Comparing Accounts

There are often several biographies available about famous women and no two books are alike. Encourage students to explore this opportunity to question the construction of history, the importance of primary sources, and the difference between fact and opinion by comparing several books about the same person. One person who continues to attract interest is Sojourner Truth, born a slave, who grew up to speak for blacks, women, and their rights. Offer students examples of differing accounts of Sojourner Truth such as the following:

Patricia and Frederick McKissack. *Sojourner Truth: Ain't I a Woman?* Scholastic, 1992.

Anne Rockwell. *Only Passing Through: The Story of Sojourner Truth.* Illustrated by R. Gregory Christie. Knopf, 2000.

As students read these books to compare and contrast their coverage, have them consider the following questions:

- Do these books agree on the facts of the person's life?
- What does each book focus on as the motivation for achievement?
- If the books are written for different levels, how is the material adapted?
- Does the author include information on the sources of this material?

Consider what might happen if some of these extraordinary women had a chance to talk with each other and share experiences. Catherine Clinton's picture book, *When Harriet Met Sojourner* (Katherine Tegen, 2007), is based on an occasion when Harriet Tubman's and Sojourner Truth's paths crossed. They grew up in different times, had different educations, and focused their efforts on different aspects of the struggle for social justice. What questions might they ask one another? Would they even get along? What might make their perspectives similar or different? Students can write and perform short skits imagining the encounter.

A Woman's Job Is . . .

Despite discussion of stereotypes and examples from their own experience, many people remain convinced that a woman's primary role is to be a homemaker and caregiver, dependent on another person's earning power to live. As a result, women are often ill-prepared to support themselves and their family when changes in their life make it necessary. Just as much as men, women need to be encouraged to consider their skills and interests in order to achieve the necessary training for a career. Both girls and boys can talk about possible jobs, how they are achieved, and how people can balance a work life with the responsibilities of the family. Surround students with information about women who have chosen satisfying careers and the difficulties they have faced and overcome.

Nic Bishop. *Digging for Bird-Dinosaurs: An Expedition to Madagascar.* Houghton Mifflin, 2000. Photos of paleontologist Cathy Forster at work in the field.

Penny Colman. *Rosie the Riveter: Working Women on the Home Front in WWII.* Crown, 1997. Nonfiction account of women in nontraditional jobs, for middle school students.

Virginia Meachum. *Jane Goodall.* Enslow, 1997. A biography of a scientist famous for her groundbreaking work studying chimpanzees.

Elizabeth Partridge. *Restless Spirit: The Life and Work of Dorothea Lange.* Viking, 1998. Puts a face on this talented photographer who became known for her powerful images of people during the Depression.

Laurence Pringle. *Elephant Woman: Cynthia Moss Explores the World of Elephants.* Photos by Cynthia Moss. Atheneum, 1997. Shows the biologist's work with elephants.

Trailblazers and Freedom Fighters

Stimulate students to investigate the lives of influential women, past and present. Have students select an individual by drawing a name out of a hat. They can prepare a report on that person's life and present it to the class so that all students learn more about these people. Students can write a diary entry for a significant day in the person's life. They can select artifacts or appropriate objects to accompany their presentation, such as eye goggles, a compass, and a map for Bessie Coleman. The following names provide representatives of different ethnic groups with which to start. You can also add names of local community interest.

Marian Anderson	Gertrude Ederle	Georgia O'Keeffe
Joan Baez	Althea Gibson	Faith Ringgold
Elizabeth Blackwell	Ruth Bader Ginsburg	Wilma Rudolph
Gwendolyn Brooks	Zora Neale Hurston	Maria Tallchief
Hillary Clinton	Judith Jamison	Amy Tan
Bessie Coleman	Wilma Mankiller	Ida Wells-Barnett
Katherine Dunham	Toni Morrison	Babe Didrikson Zaharias

These books will help students begin their study:

Sally Hobart Alexander and Robert Alexander. *She Touched the World: Laura Bridgman, Deaf-Blind Pioneer.* Clarion, 2008. Picture book biography of extraordinary woman who was the only person able to reach Helen Keller and teach her language. This striking book could be used at all grade levels combined with other biographies of Helen Keller.

Don Brown. *Uncommon Traveler: Mary Kingsley in Africa.* Houghton Mifflin, 2000. Although born to a conventional English family in 1862, Kingsley became an adventurer and traveled through West Africa, collecting botanical specimens.

Shana Corey. *You Forgot your Skirt, Amelia Bloomer.* Illustrated by Chesley McLaren. Scholastic, 2000. She thought "proper" clothing for ladies was silly and took action.

Malka Drucker. *Portraits of Jewish-American Heroes.* Illustrated by Elizabeth Rosen. Dutton, 2007. Brief accounts of twenty-one courageous men and women, including Supreme Court Justice Ruth Bader Ginsburg.

Barbara Kerley. *What to Do About Alice? How Alice Roosevelt Broke the Rules, Charmed the World and Drove Her Father Teddy Crazy.* Illustrated by Edwin Fotheringham. Scholastic, 2008. Instead of behaving as a respectable daughter of President Theodore Roosevelt when they lived in the White House, she ran wild, rode her bicycle all over the city, and generally entertained the public.

Kathleen Krull. *Lives of Extraordinary Women: Rulers, Rebels, and What the Neighbors Thought.* Illustrated by Kathryn Hewitt. Holt, 2000. Covers a wide range of subjects, reaching from Cleopatra to Rigoberta Menchú.

Dante Liano. *Rigoberta Menchú: The Girl from Chimel*. Illustrated by Demi. House of Anansi Press, 2000. How a poor Guatemalan woman became an activist for social justice and was recognized for her work with a Nobel Prize.

Sienna Siegal. *To Dance: A Ballerina's Graphic Novel*. Illustrated by Mark Siegel. Simon & Schuster, 2006. Sienna's drive to dance takes her from home in Puerto Rico to Boston and eventually New York City.

Susan Wengraf. *Love It Like a Fool: A Film Biography of Malvina Reynolds*. Film, 2008. Malvina Reynolds used music as her channel for social activism, writing catchy satirical tunes such as "Little Boxes."

Women Put Their Stamp on the World

Have the students paid attention to the images on postage stamps? Many stamps are issued to commemorate a person or event. Women who have been honored with a stamp for their achievements include Ruth Benedict (anthropologist), Virginia Apgar (medical researcher), and Maria Mitchell (astronomer).

Recent stamps have been issued featuring the following women:

- Martha Gellhorn, war correspondent and journalist (American Journalists series)
- Gerti Cori, biochemist (American Scientists series)
- Marjorie Kinnan Rawlings, author of *The Yearling* (Literary Arts series)
- Louise Nevelson, sculptor

In addition, the special stamp issued for the 2008 Olympics in China featured a female athlete. The National Women's History Project (www. nwhp. org) has a poster featuring forty-seven women who have appeared on stamps. Are any of these names familiar? Challenge students to find out more about these women and why they were selected.

The Struggle for the Right to Vote

When the United States declared its independence, White men could vote but not White women, Native Americans, African Americans, or any people without property. White women became social activists as a result of their involvement in the abolitionist movement but were frustrated when they couldn't support their beliefs by voting. As a result, Elizabeth Cady Stanton and Lucretia Mott were inspired to organize a gathering in 1848 in Seneca Falls, New York, to declare the official beginning of the women's suffrage movement. Women were eager to participate in order to become able to enact social reforms. In 1872, after enslaved African men had been made citizens and, therefore, had the right to vote, Victoria Woodhull ran as a third-party candidate for U.S. President on the basis that she was a citizen, too. Later, a few states (such as Wyoming) gave their women the right to vote, but women still needed the federal recognition of a constitutional amendment. That wouldn't come until 1920, when the Nineteenth Amendment passed by a "whisker" and made it possible for women to vote.

Creating a Timeline. Why was there such a long period between the beginning of the suffrage movement and the passage of the Nineteenth Amendment? Have students create a timeline on the wall around the room to mark significant events in the ongoing struggle for women to gain equal rights. They might put the year 1848 near the beginning, 1920 in the middle, and the present year at the end in order to visualize how much time passed and the many small steps of progress. The following books will get them started:

> Ann Bausum. *With Courage and Cloth: Winning the Fight for a Woman's Right to Vote.* National Geographic, 2004. Excellent historical background for middle school students.

> Tanya Lee Stone. *Elizabeth Leads the Way: Elizabeth Cady Stanton and the Right to Vote.* Illustrated by Rebecca Gibbon. Holt, 2008. This book for primary students opens with the question: "What would you do if someone told you you can't be what you want to be because you are a girl?" High school students can explore why many people, including some women, opposed women's suffrage.

> Gwenyth Swain. *The Road to Seneca Falls: A Story about Elizabeth Cady Stanton.* Carolrhoda, 1996. Founding of the suffragist movement by Stanton and Lucretia Mott in 1848.

Here are some dates to put on the Timeline:

1848	Declaration of the Rights of Women, Seneca Falls, announced women's determination to gain the vote.
1852	Harriet Beecher Stowe published *Uncle Tom's Cabin,* which revolutionized people's attitudes toward enslaved Africans.
1869	Women could vote in Wyoming.
1879	Belva Ann Lockwood was the first woman lawyer to argue before the U.S. Supreme Court.
1893	New Zealand gave women the right to vote.
1920	19th Amendment passed giving U.S. women the right to vote.
1925	Nellie Ross became the first woman governor (Wyoming).
1932	Hattie Caraway was elected the first woman senator (Arkansas).
1972	Title IX outlawed sex discrimination and required equal support for men's and women's sports.
1983	Sandra Day O'Connor became the first woman U.S. Supreme Court judge.

What other important events do students want to add? Students can fill in more dates as they accummulate information. The website (www.herstoryatimeline.com) is a good source.

National Women's Hall of Fame

Because women have so often been left out of history, we rarely have the chance to see them in a wide variety of roles: as developers of ideas, initiators of events, inventors, scientists, artists, and world leaders. The National women's Hall of Fame was established so that people could nominate women who should be recognized for their work. They began by surveying more than 300 historians and scholars to determine who were considered the most influential women in U.S. history. They now have a list of 227 names. (For more information, see (www.greatwomen.com.) The following are the top ten names they started with. How many of these women can students identify?

1. Eleanor Roosevelt
2. Jane Addams
3. Rosa Parks
4. Margaret Sanger
5. Margaret Mead

6. Charlotte Perkins Gilman
7. Betty Friedan
8. Barbara Jordan
9. Helen Keller
10. Alice Paul

Boxed in by Gender

All children are put into "gender boxes" when they are born. Adults expect to know whether the baby is male or female (who would dare use blue for a girl or pink for a boy?) and adapt their behavior to the baby accordingly. Starting around puberty, social and peer influences require attempts at "pairing up." Girls go with boys; boys go with girls. But that may not feel "right" to some children, who can experience same-sex attraction at an early age. Because "heterosexuality" is assumed to be the norm (as discussed in Chapter 1), students are unmercifully mocked, harassed, and attacked for perceived violations of these boundaries. Make your classroom a safe place for children to be able to explore being different without being subjected to subtle or extreme pressure to conform.

The fear and hatred of difference can develop into greater acts of violence as children get older. In one incident in 2002, a young girl, Gwen Araujo, was brutally murdered by several boys apparently because they discovered she was born male but was identifying as female.

The following book will engage the interest of high school students:

Lauren McLaughlin. *Cycler*, Random, 2007. Four days a month, the girl shown on the cover of the book takes on the role of a boy.

A book for use with primary grades is:

Justin Richardson and Peter Parnell. *And Tango Makes Three.* Simon & Schuster, 2005. A true story of two male penguins raising a chick at the New York City Zoo.

Positive Models for Young Women

All students will benefit from reading literature that provides positive models for boys and girls, but especially girls. Carefully select the reading choices you supply to ensure that the values being transmitted are multicultural—including diverse students, authentic cultural elements, and realistic backgrounds—and explain to students what you are doing. Seek out contemporary fiction that shows girls becoming problem-solvers, confident leaders, risk-takers, and activists for social justice. The following are examples that will stimulate lively discussion:

For Primary Students:

Lynne Barasch. *Hiromi's Hands.* Lee & Low, 2007. Everybody knows that girls can't make good sushi but Hiromi perseveres and proves them wrong.

Judy Blume. *Soupy Saturday with the Pain and the Great One.* Delacorte, 2007. Another humorous tale of family woes from a noted author.

Mem Fox. *The Straight Line Wonder.* Mondo, 1997. Illustrated by Marc Rosenthal. A parable about the pleasure and loneliness of being different.

James Howe. *Horace and Morris but Mostly Dolores.* Atheneum, 1999. Three rats explore whether boys and girls can be friends.

David Mack. *The Shy Creatures.* Feiwel, 2007. A shy girl imagines herself healing scary monsters.

Megan McDonald. *Judy Moody Declares Independence.* Candlewick, 2005. If the founding fathers can declare independence in Boston, then Judy doesn't see why she has to brush her hair or take care of her little brothers.

Camille Yarbrough. *The Shimmershine Queens.* Putnam, 1989. Self-esteem and achievement help African American girls counter sexism and racism.

For Intermediate Readers:

Dawn Fitzgerald. *Getting in the Game.* Roaring Brook Press, 2005. Seventh grader Joanna really wants to play ice hockey but is discouraged by everyone, even her best friend. Derek, the class bully and hockey star, sees this as a great opportunity to beat her up.

Katy Kelly. *Lucy Rose: Busy Like You Can't Believe.* Delacorte, 2006. Although Lucy Rose is only in fourth grade, multiple responsibilities, expectations, and secrets weigh on her mind.

Patricia C. McKissack. *Abby Takes a Stand.* Viking, 2005. Part of Scraps of Time series. Ten-year-old Abby is influenced by the fight for civil rights. Too young to take part in sit-ins, she finds her own way to make a statement.

Susan Patron. *The Higher Power of Lucky.* Illustrated by Matt Phelan. Simon & Schuster, 2006. Ten-year-old Lucky has a lot of worries on her mind, but a test of survival in the desert helps her understand her feelings.

Jane Shaw. *The Silent Stranger: A Kaya Mystery.* Pleasant Company, 2005. An American Girl adventure about a Nez Perce girl whose encounter with a stranger leads her down an unexpected path.

Kashmira Sheth. *Keeping Corner.* Hyperion, 2007. Twelve-year-old Leela discovers the reality of being a female in India. To regain her life, she must learn to take advantage of the new opportunities for women during Gandhi's struggle for Indian independence.

Gloria Whelan. *Homeless Bird.* Harper, 2000. Even in modern India, a girl's life is limited. When 13-year-old Koly is married to a boy who then dies, she becomes a widow, an invisible, worthless person. Somehow she discovers new life for herself.

For Young Adults:

Sharon Draper. *Fire From the Rock.* Dutton, 2007. Sylvia is excited to be one of the first African American students to integrate the high school in Little Rock, Arkansas, until she experiences the racism, hatred, and hostility directed at her.

Nikki Grimes. *The Road to Paris.* Putnam, 2006. Paris has only known foster homes and as a biracial child feels unwelcome everywhere. She has to make difficult decisions in order to find her true self.

Ann Rinaldi. *Come Juneteenth.* Harcourt, 2007. A complex exploration of attitudes in Texas after the Civil War and why the slaves were not told they were free until two years later. The focus on one family and excellent characterization draw you in so that you can empathize with all sides.

DID YOU KNOW?

—◄○►—

Several thousand people, mainly women, were killed in Europe and the United States before the eighteenth century because they were thought to be witches. However, the persecution of witches had largely disappeared by the time the last trial took place in 1782 in Switzerland When Anna Goeldi, a village woman accused of causing a girl to spit pins and convulse, was tortured and beheaded for being a witch. In 2008, after refusing to consider the case at first, the churches of the region decided that they had made a mistake, that the execution was illegal at the time, and so they officially exonerated her. That meant her name was cleared and her reputation rehabilitated, even if it did take more than 200 years.

Gloria Whelan. *Parade of Shadows*. Harper, 2007. In 1907, 16-year-old Julia convinces her father to let her accompany him to the exotic area of the "Levant." She gets more than expected as she becomes involved in the intrigues and upheaval of the Ottoman Empire just before World War I.

Sexism Is . . .

After students have had some experience looking at issues related to gender equity, it's time for them to make connections and to apply critical thinking skills. They can draw conclusions, make generalizations, and suggest approaches to problems that persist. Give students the stimulus, "Sexism is ———," and have them complete the sentence. Then have all students share their reactions by using "Clustering" (a graphic organizer illustrated on p. 56). As their ideas spread across the paper, have them look for relationships and draw lines to connect items. Older students can be asked to name the relationship or the category to which the items belong, adding additional examples under the same category.

Analyzing Sexism in the Media

Draw student attention to any sex stereotypes that they encounter in their reading. Teach them to consider such topics as:

- Count the number of male characters in the stories and compare this figure to the number of female characters.
- Count the number of times the female is the person who is in charge of the action compared to the number of times the male is.
- Are there differences in the types of activities that the male and female characters are shown engaging in?
- Look closely at the illustrations—do they imply differences between the male and female characters?
- Is the message in the book the same for boys and girls? If it is different, why?

Students can conduct a study of the literature recommended for their age level and summarize what they find. Interesting or surprising data can be shared with other classes or be the subject of a letter to the local newspaper.

Students can also apply these analytic skills to other media such as television, advertising, comic books, and videogames. For example, they could record the Saturday morning cartoons, including ads, on television to determine what messages about appropriate sex-linked behavior are being communicated to the young children, boys and girls, who are the intended audience.

Sources of additional information for teaching about sex equity:

Maria Claudia Andre and Eva Paulino Bueno, eds. *Latin American Women Writers: An Encyclopedia.* Routledge, 2008.

Dianne Ashton. *Women and Judaism in Antebellum America.* Wayne State University Press, 1997.

Ian Ayres and Jennifer Garada Brown. *Straightforward.* Princeton University Press, 2005.

The Book of Latina Women: 150 Vidas of Passion, Strength, and Success. National Women's History Project, 2007.

Stephanie Brill and Rachel Pepper. *The Transgender Child: A Handbook for Families and Professionals.* Cleis Press, 2008.

Robert P. J. Cooney Jr. *"Winning the Vote": The Triumph of the American Woman Suffrage Movement.* American Graphic Press, 2005.

Encyclopedia of Sex and Gender. Gale, 2007.

Lillian Faderman. *To Believe in Women: What Lesbians Have Done for America—A History.* Houghton Mifflin, 1999.

Lisa Tendrich Frank, ed. *Women in the American Civil War.* ABC–CLIO, 2007.

Mary McVicker. *Women Adventurers, 1750–1900: A Biographical Dictionary with Excerpts from Selected Travel Writing.* McFarland, 2007.

Notable American Women, Vols. I–III, Wilson, 2001.

Cokie Roberts. *Founding Mothers: The Women Who Raised Our Nation.* Morrow, 2004.

———. *Ladies of Liberty: The Women Who Shaped Our Nation.* Morrow, 2008.

Joan Roughgarden. *Evolution's Rainbow: Diversity, Gender, and Sexuality in Nature and People.* University of California Berkeley Press, 2005.

Myra Sadker and David Sadker. "Gender Bias" in *Multicultural Education,* 5th ed. Banks and Banks, eds. Allyn & Bacon, 2000.

Bonnie Smith, ed. *Oxford Encyclopedia of Women in World History.* Oxford University Press, 2008.

Barrie Thorne. *Genderplay: Girls and Boys in School.* Rutgers University Press, 1993.

A Culminating Activity

Let students decide on different ways they can share their conclusions at the end of this thematic study. Possibilities include:

- A talk to the PTA
- A puppet show for primary grade students
- An op-ed piece for the local newspaper

CONNECTIONS

In this chapter we have shown how the *Esteem, Empathy, Equity model* directs a student-centered approach to teaching multiculturally.

With an emphasis on learning processes, multicultural teaching attempts to facilitate the learning of every child, assisting each one to reach his or her highest potential. We need to plan instruction that accommodates individual differences and use teaching strategies that ensure successful learning for children with diverse abilities. No matter what race or culture a student comes from, he or she requires teaching that is flexible and adapted to his or her individual strengths and weaknesses. Implementing the *Esteem, Empathy, Equity* model should help you assess the needs of the student, plan an appropriate multicultural program, and deliver this curriculum, having selected the best methods and materials.

The teacher does not abdicate his or her position but rather plans quality learning activities that engage students in active, hands-on experiences and builds on success to develop students' self-esteem. The teacher models appreciation for diversity by building on students' prior knowledge and setting clear, realistic expectations for each student's abilities. Learning experiences are designed to promote student interaction and to generate inquiry and thinking through both talking and writing. Such approaches benefit all students, but they are especially recommended for those who come from cultures that are very different from the school culture or are learning English as an additional language.

In the next chapter we provide examples of teaching strategies that can be used following the 3E model.

GETTING INVOLVED

Expanding Your Reflective Teaching Portfolio

1. Explain in your own words what self-esteem, empathy, and equity have to do with multicultural education. What is the difference between equity and equality?
2. What can you do to create a classroom that says "Welcome" to all students?
3. When your students label behavior or beliefs that they encounter at school as "racist," how would you respond?
4. What do you remember as your favorite parts of school?
5. Who was the best teacher you ever encountered (in school or in a nonformal learning environment)? Identify some of the characteristics that made this person an exceptional teacher.
6. Write a short paragraph about just what "differentiated instruction" means to you at this stage of your training. What is the teacher's role in presenting individualized instruction? Then, begin a list of ways that you could provide support for slower students who might need an extra boost. Make another list of strategies for engaging gifted and talented students in more challenging investigations or projects that will extend their thinking. You can continue adding to these lists as you learn more and also by discussing this topic with your classmates.

Working with Your Cooperative Learning Group

1. Based on the demographics of the schools in your area and the grade level you plan to teach, have each group select a particular ethno/cultural/linguistic group to investigate further, for example, Haitians, Ethiopians, or Koreans. Become an "expert" on this group by extensively exploring it and developing a collection of information, resources, materials, list of community representatives, and literature. Your group can present this to the class and then share its material so that everyone will have a chance to learn more about many different cultures.

2. Find out where your parents and grandparents were born and how you happened to come to live in your present community. How did your parents meet? Think about what values are important to your family, how you celebrate rituals or holidays, and what kinds of foods you enjoy together. Discuss your findings with others in your Cooperative Learning Group. You might bring pictures to show each other or plan to share some foods. List the objectives involved in this kind of sharing and how you might help young students engage in this type of sharing, too.

EXPLORING FURTHER

Robert Coles. *The Call of Stories: Teaching and the Moral Imagination.* Houghton Mufflin, 1989.

Louise Derman-Sparks, Patricia Ramsey, Julie Olsen Edwards, and Carol Brunson Day. *What If All the Kids Are White? Anti-Bias Multicultural Education with Young Children and Families.* Teachers College Press, 2006.

Howard Gardner. *Multiple Intelligences: New Horizons.* Basic, 2006.

Geneva Gay. *Culturally Responsive Teaching: Theory, Research, and Practice.* Teachers College Press, 2002.

Herbert Kohl. *I Won't Learn from You and Other Thoughts on Creative Maladjustment.* New Press, 1994.

Gloria Ladson-Billings. *Crossing Over to Canaan: The Journey of New Teachers in Diverse Classrooms.* Jossey-Bass, 2001.

Nel Noddings. *The Challenge to Care in Schools: An Alternative Approach to Education.* Teachers College Press, 1992.

Teaching Strategies for the Multicultural Classroom

The American people have this to learn:

Where justice is denied,

Where poverty is enforced,

Where ignorance prevails, and

Where any one class is made to feel

That society is in organized conspiracy

To oppress, rob, and degrade them,

Neither persons nor property will be safe.

~ FREDERICK DOUGLASS

In this chapter we introduce a selection of instructional methodologies that are especially adaptable for promoting multicultural understandings. The first part of the chapter focuses on two ways of planning instruction: (1) the Thinking + Learning Plan and (2) Learning Centers. The last part of the chapter describes ten specifically recommended instructional strategies. These strategies will enable you to follow the 3E Model for a multicultural curriculum that we presented in Chapter 2. This model is designed to support the *self-esteem* of each student, develop *empathy* among all students in a classroom, and provide *equity* for the students who are striving to learn. In addition, the strategies that we are recommending will help you integrate multicultural concepts into the various subject areas across the curriculum. All of these strategies will be further illustrated in the chapters that comprise Part II of *Multicultural Teaching,* in which we focus on incorporating multicultural education across the curriculum. The ten strategies we have chosen to recommend in Chapter 3 are:

> Reading Aloud
> Teaching with Picture Books across Levels
> Brainstorming
> Cooperative Learning Groups
> Perspective Taking
> Acting Out
> Readers' Theater
> Using Graphic Organizers
> Reporting
> Assessing Progress

We describe each strategy and also suggest specific ways to implement the strategy, including books and other resources that you may find useful.

The quotation on the opposite page from Frederick Douglass, a noted African American leader, can be copied and enlarged to create an attractive poster to display in your classroom. Discuss with your students what Douglass is telling us. How might his words affect what happens in your classroom? How might his ideas affect behaviors in the larger world? Have teams of students search varied sources to learn more about this man and his life as a renowned abolitionist.

❖ Planning Instruction

This first section provides two suggestions for planning instruction in your classroom:

- Following the *Thinking + Lesson Plan*
- Setting up Multicultural Learning Centers

First, we present the *Thinking + Lesson Plan,* which we use as a model for developing lessons that put the students at the center, allow for differentiated instruction and a variety of learning styles and assessment modes.

In the next part we show how to develop learning centers where students can select from among a variety of activities related to one topic. Here we present examples of a learning center focusing on (1) a state (Alaska) and (2) an ethnic group (Chinese Americans).

Following the Thinking + Lesson Plan

In this section of the chapter we introduce a multicultural lesson plan that you can use as you create lessons that put students in the center and incorporate a number of different strategies for planning, organizing, reporting, and assessing student learning activities. On page 74 we

THINKING + LESSON PLAN FORM

◄○►

Grades _____

Subject of Lesson: _____

Expected Outcomes
Learner will:

1. _____

2. _____

3. _____

Teaching/Learning Strategy:

Resources Needed

Directions

Step I:

Step II:

Step III:

Performance Assessment

1.

2.

3.

present a blank lesson form that you can copy to use as you plan lessons other than those presented in this book. We recommend working together with other teachers to construct plans as you share materials and ideas, for example, new books or media resources.

The Thinking + Lesson Plan is designed to help teachers at any level plan a lesson that will engage students in thinking as well as working with content from different subject areas. In applying this lesson plan to multicultural studies, we expect, of course, to include lessons that support the *self-esteem* of each student, develop *empathy* among students and other people, and provide *equity* for all as presented in the 3E model. How this is achieved will depend on the teacher, how he or she interacts with the students, and his or her expectations for what the students might be able to do.

Given that expectation, we also aim to engage students in thinking beyond the rote memorization of facts. We want them to evaluate information they read or hear, to make judgments about the validity of what other people present as factual. We want them to consider both sides of an issue, weighing the pro- and con positions that might be appropriate. Above all, we want them to be creative, to imagine, to dare to be inventive. We want them to think!

In planning any lesson, it is important to think through the entire process beforehand. First of all, what are your objectives for teaching the lesson? What do you want students to be able to do? Next, you think about how you can achieve these results. How will you engage students' interest? What materials—films, books, pictures, software, objects—will help you stimulate student involvement?

Throughout *Multicultural Teaching,* we include fully developed lesson plans that you can adapt for use in your classroom. The title of each lesson gives you some idea about the focus of the lesson, and we indicate the grade levels that you should be able to use the lesson in with little alteration. In this plan, too, we begin by defining two or three clear objectives and what the students will be doing in the lesson. Then, we provide general directions that suggest resources you will need for the lesson and how to carry out the lesson step-by-step.

One of the most important parts of each lesson is the performance assessment, which includes simple criteria for judging the writing product, participation, and so on. Evaluation techniques may range from acting out to telling to writing—some active performance by the student. Notice that we do not advocate a point system and that criteria are usually attainable by most students.

By following the Thinking + Lesson Plan, you will produce a theoretically sound learning experience for K–12 students. We provide an example of a lesson plan that engages students in grades 6–12 in writing a biographical sketch based on student research on page 76.

Any of the strategies that will be described in the next section of this chapter could be incorporated in the Thinking + Lesson Plans. Developed plans appear in each of the five chapters focusing on the various areas of the curriculum that appear in Part II of *Multicultural Teaching.*

Setting Up Multicultural Learning Centers

In this section we show you how to develop multicultural learning centers. The Learning Center approach to teaching offers a range of possibilities for individualized activities. A small center can be presented on a poster or even tucked into a shoebox.

A SAMPLE LESSON FOLLOWING THE MODEL
─◁○▷─

Thinking + Lesson : A Biographical Sketch

Level of Difficulty: Grades 6–8
Expected Outcomes
Learner will:

1. Read a short biographical sketch of an author.
2. Analyze the quality of the writing.
3. Identify the features of a biographical sketch.
4. Compose a biographical sketch following the model.
5. Expand knowledge about diverse authors and their writings.

Teaching/Learning Strategies

Resources Needed
This lesson should be developed over a period of several days. Duplicate copies of the following biographical sketch of Alex Haley:

    Introducing Alex Haley. Alex Palmer Haley is the well-known author of *Roots: The Saga of an American Family,* which was published in 1976 and made into a stirring film that was presented on television to millions of Americans. Born August 11, 1921, in Ithaca, New York, Alex Haley was the son of a professor.

    Alex Haley served as a journalist in the U.S. Coast Guard. He tells of writing love letters for his fellow seamen who weren't particularly good at writing. He won their admiration and gratitude (and earned considerable money, too) by creating romantic letters that ensured that the men's sweethearts were waiting when they returned to port.

    Haley soon decided that he wanted to concentrate on writing full-time. After struggling for a number of years to earn a living as a writer, he finally succeeded by collaborating with Malcolm X, writing *The Autobiography of Malcolm X,* which appeared in 1965.

    But it was *Roots* that brought Haley real acclaim. Recognizing this unique contribution to American literature, the noted author James Baldwin writes:

> *Roots* is a study of continuities, of consequence, of how a people perpetuate themselves, how each generation helps to doom, or helps to liberate, the coming one—the action of love, or the absence of love, in time. It suggests, with great power, how each of us, however unconsciously, can't but be the vehicle of history which has produced us. Well, we can perish in this vehicle, children, or we can move on up the road.

    After twelve years of painstaking genealogical research, Haley collected the life story of seven generations of his family in the United States and several more generations in a village on the Gambia River in West Africa. He presents these facts in a fictionalized story, a form he calls "faction," a delicate combination of fact and fiction that allows him to flesh out these ancestral characters, to include their thoughts and emotions. The resulting novel has touched the lives of millions of readers in a way that a scholarly report would never have achieved. As Haley knows, "When you start talking about family, about lineage and ancestry, you are talking about every person on earth." Alex Haley died in 1992.

Directions

Step 1: Have students read the sketch of Haley's life. Tell the students this form of writing is called a biographical sketch. Ask students to note and then discuss particular words they find interesting. Identify collectively and list on the board the features of a well-written biographical sketch, for example:

> Tells where and when the person was born.
> Makes clear why the person is known.
> Uses a quotation about the person's work.

Tell students that they are going to write a biographical sketch about any multicultural (broadly interpreted) writer whose work they have read or want to read. (You may brainstorm a list of recommended authors on the board, such as Laurence Yep, Virginia Hamilton, Isaac B. Singer, Francisco Jimenez, or Simon Ortiz.) They may begin with an internet search, but they are to use other resources, too. You may wish to specify that they locate at least two sources other than websites.

Step 2: Take students to the library where they can look for biographies, check out books by the author selected, use the computer, and locate other sources of information. Point out *Current Biography* and *Contemporary Authors* as possible references. Students should take notes from resources they cannot check out. For homework, they are to begin the first draft of the biographical sketch to present in class on the following day.

Performance Assessment

Assessment 1. On the next day review the features of a biographical sketch and make any additions recommended. Then have students work in pairs as they read the first drafts of the sketches and check their writing together against the list of features. The partners should work cooperatively to suggest revisions that will strengthen each paper.

Assessment 2. The aim is to communicate to an audience with clear expository prose that is interesting to read. Students can evaluate the finished products as Grabs Me! (5 points), So-So (3 points), and Not So Hot (1 point). Students should be permitted to improve their writing in order to gain more points. Cooperative learning techniques used in groups can assist each student in achieving the top score. Note that this teaching strategy aims to develop self-esteem by facilitating success. All students are learning to collaborate to reach a goal.

The polished biographical sketches are published in a class book entitled "Authors We Have Known." Students may refer to this book when they are selecting books to read. The collection can be further developed by including book reviews. Note that students are learning about the contributions of members of diverse cultures to what we call "American literature." They learn about these authors as people, and they are introduced to literature they may be motivated to read based on a classmate's recommendation.

More commonly, a center might be developed around a bulletin board display or created on a table in a corner of the room. Here students can select from a variety of activities related to one topic.

Learning Centers offer a versatile method for engaging students in varied activities focusing on studies that cross the curriculum. Students enjoy the change from the more common textbook approach to instruction, including the opportunity to move around the classroom. Because students proceed at their own speed, individual differences are more readily accommodated.

Place the Learning Centers around the room on desks or tables, on the bulletin board, the window sill, the chalktray, an easel, or a bookshelf. Number the places at each center to ensure that too many students don't try to work with one center at the same time. You do need to see that there are ample workspaces within the room to provide room for every student. You can always allocate some places at a library table for "free reading."

Let students help to develop centers as a result of ongoing study in the classroom. Let them suggest a name for each center that they can print on a large sign above the space allocated for the center. Encourage students to use their ingenuity in setting up a center. Plan to have more than one center in operation at any time. Centers should include various kinds of materials that students might use as they work there, for example, paper, pens and pencils, and other interesting supplies, as suggested here:

- Magazines to tear apart
- Crayons
- Staplers
- Scissors
- Rulers
- Colored pens

- Various papers: lined and unlined, drawing paper, colored construction paper, cardboard, posterboard, and corrugated cardboard for construction
- CD players with headphones

In addition to pictures and information displayed to make the center attractive and inviting, there should be a variety of individualized activities. Planned activities should range from easy to more difficult as well as involve using varied skills—listening, speaking, reading, and writing. Include, too, activities that draw from different subject areas and those that stimulate student creativity in music and art.

In this section we show examples of two learning centers that focus on: (1) a state (Alaska) and (2) an ethnic group, (China and Chinese Americans).

Developing a Learning Center: Exploring Alaska

Exploring Alaska: Our Forty-Ninth State

One Learning Center focuses on a single state, Alaska. Here you can see how this center was set up and what was featured at the center. This example suggests possibilities for developing centers on other states or centers on similar topics. Just use your imagination!

In addition to the center itself, we include related activities that can be placed elsewhere in the classroom. Directions for these additional activities might be included at the Learning Center itself, thus keeping everything about Alaska organized in one place.

A Cozy Corner

Using the Learning Center

As you and your students create different learning centers, you need to introduce each new center to the class, showing them all how the center works and what the possibilities are for working at each one. Students may need to sign up for a particularly popular center.

A good way to begin work at learning centers is to post a schedule giving each student a specific assignment for the day. You can prepare the schedule for a week, two weeks, or a month, depending on how long the study will take and how many centers are available. Working in the library could be one center activity that would accommodate a number of students. Your schedule for ten days might look like that shown in Table 3.1.

Enlarging specific centers to provide more activities and seating space will permit additional students to participate. Sometimes, activities can be completed at the student's desk.

Keeping track of materials at each center is another important part of planning. Here are several tips that may help you.

1. Color-code everything that belongs at one center. If the center on Alaska is red, then mark games, task cards, materials, and so on with a red felt pen. Students soon learn to replace task cards or games at the appropriate center.
2. Hang activities in envelopes or plastic bags on the wall where they are visible. Pegboard is ideal for this purpose, but you can improvise with cork bulletin boards or strips of wood on which hooks can be placed. If you have a specially marked hook for each item, you can quickly tell when something is missing at the end of the day.

TABLE 3.1   Learning Center Schedule

Name	M	T	W	TH	F	M	T	W	TH	F
Felipe	1	1	2	2	L	3	3	4	4	L
James	1	1	2	2	L	3	3	4	4	L
Kentu	1	1	2	2	L	3	3	4	4	L
Sandra	2	2	L	3	3	4	4	L	1	1
Hope	2	2	L	3	3	4	4	L	1	1
Harold	2	2	L	3	3	4	4	L	1	1
Marisa	3	3	4	4	L	1	1	2	2	L

Whenever there are problems regarding classroom operations, have a class meeting to thrash out the problems and to determine possible solutions. When students decide on the solution, they will enforce the rules.

As teacher, your role in working with learning centers is to help students organize their work toward a goal and specific objectives. You facilitate and guide the learning experiences and serve as a resource, a person to be consulted when help is needed. You guide the students in assessing their own growth and learning as well as in checking their own work. Respond to student needs, plan strategies for stimulating further learning, and explore new resources and materials that come your way.

Making Task Cards for the Center
Task cards are sometimes called job cards or activity cards. They range from small (about 3" × 5") to large (about 8½"× 11"). The size you choose depends on the age of the students who will use the cards (young children can handle large cards more easily) and on your instructional purpose. You can store them in file boxes, shoe boxes, or tote bags.

Small Cards. Small cards work well for "idea files" to which older students refer individually, for example:

- *Acting Out.* On each card a problem situation is described that calls for role-playing. Activities could be for small groups.
- *Books to Read.* Each card lists the title and author of a book as well as a short synopsis of the story. Students use this file as they are searching for a book to read about Egypt, living in New York City, or any other topic you want to include.

Have students themselves develop these sets of cards. Each person can prepare a card, for example, about the book he or she has read. This activity serves a dual purpose—the students have a purpose for reading, and they create a set of cards about books other students will find interesting. They can add notes such as "If you like mysteries, you'll like this." Preparing "acting out" situations gives students a purpose for writing a short paragraph.

Large Cards. Large cards are usually constructed of sturdy poster board, so they are stiff and durable. These cards are used to present an activity that one or more students will undertake at different times. Directions must be clear if students are to work independently.

A task card for upper-grade students that focuses on the money used in various countries is presented in Chapter 7. When material is prepared for you like this, simply enlarge the material presented. You can also use larger type sizes on the computer to facilitate reading. If directions are short, printing with a felt pen is effective. Throughout this book you will find informative material and activities that can be presented as is or transformed into task cards.

Activities
The following are additional activities to use at this Learning Center.

Create a Book About Alaska. On the cover, draw a picture of Alaska's flag, The Big Dipper with the North Star. Include an outline map of Alaska. On the "Legend," indicate the size of the state and the population (571,951 square miles; 670,053 people, 2006 estimate).

1. Compare the size of Alaska to the size of your state. How many times would your state fit into Alaska?
2. Compare the population of Alaska to that of your state. Draw a circle to represent the population of Alaska. How many of these circles would you need to represent your state?
3. Calculate the "population density." How many people live there per square mile?

Resources:

Debby Dahl Edwardson. *Whale Snow.* Illustrated by Annie Paterson. Talewinds, 2003. A young Inupiaq boy learns about whale culture.

Shelley Gill. *Alaska.* Charlesbridge, 2007. Factual information about the state.

Using the same map, fill in some details.

1. Locate important sites: the capital (Juneau), major cities (Anchorage and Fairbanks), the tallest mountain in North America (Mt. Denali, 20,320 ft.).

2. Draw the route of the Iditarod, the famous annual dog race, showing the start and the finish. What historic event does this race commemorate? How many miles long is the trail? How long does it take to cover that distance?

3. Locate Prudhoe Bay, then Valdez. Now draw the 800 mile-long pipeline that connects them.

Resources:

Debbie Miller. *Big Alaska: Journey across America's Most Amazing State.* Walker, 2006. Facts about the state.

Cherie Winner. *Life in the Tundra.* Lerner, 2003. The biology and physical environment of the country.

Using a map of the United States that includes Alaska, answer the following:

1. Calculate the distance between Mt. Denali (or Anchorage) and Washington, D.C. Calculate the distance between Mt. Denali (or Anchorage) and your state capital.

2. Can you drive from Washington State to Alaska without crossing into another country?

Find Out More about Living in Alaska.

1. What animals live in Alaska? List three and write four facts about each, such as its appearance, where it lives, what it eats, and whether it has predators.

2. Are any of these animals endangered? If they are, what is the reason for the decline in population?

3. Read a nonfiction book about Alaska. Write a description of it and tell whether you would recommend it to others.

4. Read a fictional book about Alaska. Write a description of it and tell whether you would recommend it to others.

Suggested Readings:

Marion Dane Bauer. *A Bear Named Trouble.* Clarion, 2005. A lonely boy connects with a lonely bear cub.

Nicola Davies. *Ice Bear: In the Steps of the Polar Bear.* Illustrated by Gary Blythe. Candlewick, 2005. How the polar bear thrives in the Arctic and its relationship to the Inuit.

Will Hobbs. *Leaving Protection.* HarperCollins, 2004. A sixteen year-old on a fishing boat encounters a mystery.

Melissa Lion. *Upstream.* Wendy Lamb, 2005. A story about a high school girl and her family.

Explore Alaska's History.

1. The United States bought Alaska from the Russians who were there for the fur trade. Are there any traces left of the Russian settlements?

2. Identify the three indigenous groups living in Alaska. (Eskimo/Inuit, Aleut, American Indians).

3. Where do members of these groups live?

4. List three items of material culture from one of the groups (clothes, tools, games, for example).

Resources:

Raymond Bial. *The Inuit*. Benchmark, 2002. The folkways, culture, and language of these indigenous people (formerly called Eskimo).

Kirkpatrick Hill. *Dancing at the Odinochka*. McElderry, 2005. Historical fiction set in the time of Russian occupation.

Russ Kendall. *Eskimo Boy: Life in an Inupiaq Eskimo Village*. Scholastic, 1992. Photographs of a seven-year-old boy show all aspects of his life.

Peter Lourie. *Arctic Thaw: The People of the Whale in a Changing Climate*. Boyds Mills, 2007. The Inupiat people live on the North Slope and have to adjust to a changing climate that disrupts their ancient culture.

Storytelling.   Read an Alaskan folktale. Prepare to tell the story to the class or to your Cooperative Learning Group. Look for books like these:

James Houston. *James Houston's Treasury of Inuit Legends*. Harcourt, 2006. Four folktales, well-illustrated.

Gerald McDermott. *Raven: A Trickster Tale from the Pacific Northwest*. Harcourt Brace, 1993. A folktale representative of Northwest Native tribes.

Special Words from Alaska.   Define these words and explain how they are related to Alaska.

1. mushing

2. mukluk

3. tundra

4. permafrost

Resources:

Robert J. Blake. *Swift*. Philomel, 2007. A boy and his husky struggle to survive in the wilderness.

Nancy White Carlstrom. *Northern Lullaby*. Illustrated by Leo and Diane Dillon. Philomel, 1993. Go-to-sleep book with images based on Eskimo life.

Pam Flowers with Ann Dixon. *Big-Enough Anna: The Little Sled Dog Who Braved the Arctic*. Illustrated by Bill Farnsworth. Alaska Northwest, 2003. Pam Flowers, a musher, trains her smallest dog as lead for a journey across the Arctic.

Ted Harrison. *A Northern Alphabet*. Tundra, 1982. Noted Yukon artist includes many features special to the North.

Mary Beth Owens. *A Caribou Alphabet*. Dog Ear Press, 1988. Focuses on plants and wildlife.

Assessment.

1. Students share favorite pages from their books.
2. Students interview each other about what they learned.

Developing a Learning Center: Exploring China

Getting to Know China and Chinese Americans

Asians are among the many immigrants who arrived on the west coast of the United States, particularly during the Gold Rush. You might read Laurence Yep's historical novel, *Dragonwings*, to the class as a way of introducing the possibilities for a Learning Center that you and your students could develop about China and Chinese Americans who are very much present in our population today.

Begin this Learning Center on a large bulletin board. Place this poster on the upper left fourth of the space.

In the other three-fourths of the space display directions for three activities that students can work at independently. You can begin with these activities, but replace them with others once most of the students have had a chance to work with the first ones displayed at the center.

Activity 1.   Learning to write in Chinese. Copy the directions from a book like Huy Voun Lee's *1, 2, 3, Go!* (Holt, 2000) or Peggy Goldstein's *Long Is a Dragon* (Scholastic, 1993).

Provide sheets of white paper of different sizes and a number of black felt pens. Students will trace around characters that appear in these books.

Activity 2.   What's your sign? Display the Chinese lunar calendar, which is based on a twelve-year sequence of animal symbols. Each animal symbolizes specific traits and characteristics of a person born in that year.

man   beautiful   country

Ox (1973, 1985, 1997, 2009) You have a calm, patient nature. Friends turn to you because you are that rarest of creatures—a good listener. Love bewilders you, so many people wrongly consider you cold.

Tiger (1974, 1986, 1998, 2010) You are a person of great extremes, a sympathetic and considerate friend, a powerful and dangerous enemy. In your career you are both a deep thinker and a careful planner.

Hare (1975, 1987, 1999, 2011) You are blessed with extraordinary good fortune and will inevitably provide financial success. This luck of yours not only extends to your business interests, but also to games of chance.

Dragon (1976, 1988, 2000, 2012) Your reputation as a fire-eater is based on your outward show of stubbornness, bluster, and short temper. But underneath you are really gentle, sensitive, and soft-hearted.

Serpent (1977, 1989, 2000, 2013) You snake people have more than your share of the world's gifts, including basic wisdom. You are likely to be handsome, well-formed men and graceful, beautiful women.

Horse (1978, 1990, 2002, 2014) Your cheerful disposition and flattering ways make you a popular favorite. Great mental agility will keep you in the upper income.

Ram (1979, 1991, 2003, 2015) You are a sensitive, refined, aesthetic type with considerable talent in all the arts. Indeed success or failure will depend upon whether you can shepherd your ability and energy into a single field.

Monkey (1980, 1992, 2004, 2016) In today's parlance you are a swinger. And because of your flair for decision making and sure-footed feel for finance, you are certain to climb to the top.

Rooster (1981, 1993, 2017) You either score heavily or lay a large egg. Although outspoken and not shy in groups, you are basically a loner who doesn't trust most people. Yet you are capable of attracting close and loyal friends.

Dog (1982, 1994, 2018) You are loyal and honest with a deep sense of duty and justice. You can always be trusted to guard the secrets of others.

Boar (1983, 1995, 2019) The quiet inner strength of your character is outwardly reflected by courtesy and breeding. Your driving ambition will lead you to success.

Rat (1984, 1996, 2020) You have been blessed with great personal charm, a taste for the better things in life, and considerable self-control that restrains your quick temper.

Each year has an assigned symbol, so 2001, for example, was the Year of the Snake or Serpent; 2002 was the Year of the Horse; and so forth, like this:

2001	Snake (Serpent)	2009	Ox
2002	Horse	2010	Tiger
2003	Sheep (Ram, Goat)	2011	Hare
2004	Monkey	2012	Dragon
2005	Rooster	2013	Snake
2006	Dog	2014	Horse
2007	Boar (Pig)	2015	Sheep
2008	Rat	2016	Monkey

The Year of the Dragon will come again in 2024 and in 2036 because the symbols repeat every twelve years. In what year were you born? Count backwards to find what year on the Chinese calendar you were born in and what is its symbol.

Activity 3. Draw a map of China, locating some of the major cities—Shanghai, Beijing, Chengdu, Hong Kong. Notice the relative size of China compared to the United States. In area, the two countries are close to the same size (if you include Alaska). But if you compare the populations of each country, the story is quite different.

FACTS AND FIGURES FROM THE WORLD ALMANAC (2008)

Geographic Area:

China: 3,705,407 square miles

United States: 3,718,712 square miles

Population (2007):

China: 1,321, 851,888 people
                         (92% Han; 56 ethnic groups)

United States: 301,139,947 people
                         (82% White/Caucasian, 13% Black; 4% Asian)

Density:

China: 367 people per square mile

United States: 85 people per square mile

China has the largest population of any country in the world. The world population was estimated to be 6 billion in 1999. One person out of five in the world lives in China. In 2007, China's population was estimated to be 1, 321, 851, 888. What is the population of the United States? How many times bigger is the population of China compared to that of the United States?

Approximately 8.7 million residents of the United States were born in Asia; 1.8 million of those come from China. Only Mexico has supplied a larger group.

Library Resources

Include a small library of books as resources for this center on a table placed against the wall below the bulletin board. Check out whatever books your school or local public library have to offer, perhaps some of these:

Alison Behnke. *Chinese in America.* Lerner, 2005. Nonfiction about this ethnic group in the United States.

Lenore Look. *Uncle Peter's Amazing Chinese Wedding.* Atheneum, 2006. A look at Chinese traditions.

Maywan Shen Krach. *D Is for Dou Pu: An Alphabet Book of the Chinese Culture.* Illustrated by Hongbin Zhang. Shen's Books, 1997. A lively, beautiful book, full of information about the life, beliefs, art, writing, and culture of China.

Christoph Niemann. *The Pet Dragon.* HarperCollins, 2007. A playful approach to the Chinese language; uses ideographic forms as characters in a story about a girl and her dragon.

Gloria Whelan. *Chu Ju's House.* Harper, 2004. Fourteen-year-old Chu lives in modern China where people, who can have only one child (or at most two), prefer to have a boy. When her parents have a second daughter, Chu runs away to give her little sister a chance. She suffers, but she does survive and is able to help her sister.

Lawrence Yep, trans. *The Rainbow People.* Illustrated by David Wiesner. Harper, 1989. Stories Chinese Americans told to keep connections with their homeland alive.

Ed Young. *Beyond the Great Mountains: A Visual Poem about China.* Chronicle, 2005.

Creating a Timeline for Chinese Americans

Develop a timeline on a long strip of paper, something like this:

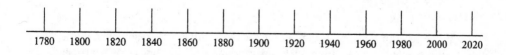

Add illustrations and other information related to the history of Chinese immigration into the United States. Mount the timeline on the wall of your classroom.

Here are a number of events that could be recorded on the timeline:

1785   First record of Chinese in the United States. Three Chinese seamen from the ship Pallas were left stranded in Baltimore.

1854   First Chinese newspaper in America, *Gold Hill News*.

1869   Completion of Transcontinental Railway with aid of Chinese labor.

1882   Chinese Exclusion Act; ten-year ban on Chinese immigration.

1943   Repeal of Chinese Exclusion Act; yearly quota set at 105 permitted to enter United States.

1965   Quota system repealed; permits 20,000 per year.

Research other interesting events related to Chinese Americans that you can add to this timeline, for example, the state of Washington elected a Chinese American as governor within the twenty-first century. Add illustrations and original art to the timeline.

Getting to Know a Chinese American Author: Laurence Yep

Laurence Yep has written a number of books, as noted in the following list.

Sweetwater
Dragonwings (Newbery Honor Book, 1976)
Child of the Owl
The Serpent's Children
Mountain Light
The Rainbow People
Tongues of Jade
Dragon's Gate (Newbery Honor, 1994)
Thief of Hearts
The Dragon Prince
The Imp that Ate My Homework
American Dragons: Twenty-Five Asian American Voices (Editor)

Chinatown Mysteries:

The Case of the Goblin Pearls
The Case of the Lion Dance
The Case of the Firecrackers

Dragon of the Lost Sea Fantasies:

Dragon of the Lost Sea
Dragon Steel
Dragon Cauldron
Dragon Wat

If you have read *Dragonwings* aloud, the class will have already been introduced to this well-respected writer. Bring in as many copies of his books as you can locate. Challenge students to see how many they can read.

A newer book that Laurence Yep wrote with his niece, Kathleen S. Yep, is *The Dragon's Child: A Story of Angel Island* (HarperCollins, 2008). This novel is based on the Yep family history, which was revealed through conversations with his father and the historical record that Kathleen unearthed in immigration archives. Each chapter opens with a question posed by Laurence Yep to his father, who had come to the United States as a young boy: "What was China like?" "Did you want to come to America?" The personal and the historical are blended skillfully in this tale of a scared young immigrant who managed to succeed.

This book ties in with the lesson about immigrants on page 164. Additional resources about experiences at Angel Island include:

www.aiisf.org. (Angel Island's website).

Katrina S. Currier. *Kai's Journey to Gold Mountain*: *An Angel Island Story*. Angel Island, 2005.

Alice K. Flanagan. *Angel Island.* Compass Point Books, 2006.

Another immigrant story, appropriate for older students, is *Snow Falling in Spring: Coming of Age during the Cultural Revolution,* by Moying Li (Farrar, 2008).

Other books that clarify this period of unrest in China, referred to as "The Cultural Revolution" include *Red Scarf Girl,* by Ji-Li Jang (Collins, 2004), and *Revolution Is Not a Dinner Party,* by Ying Chang Compestine Harper, 2006. These books would add to students' understanding of China and its history.

Benefits of Planning Lessons and Learning Centers

Planning lessons offers an opportunity to introduce new multicultural topics as well as to decide how you can integrate these topics into other subject areas covered by the curriculum. Planning a lesson also leads naturally into the consideration of how you will deliver that lesson. The teacher-directed lecture method is only one way of teaching a lesson.

The Learning Centers we have described are excellent ways of organizing a study that may include several sequential lessons and the activities involved. Creating one or a series of centers does require some effort, but once in place using learning centers should provide for differentiated instruction, allowing students to progress at their own rate of speed. Furthermore, such centers can be extended gradually over a period of time, and students will benefit from helping to create new activities, a particular challenge for gifted and talented young people.

❖ Ten Recommended Instructional Strategies

The strategies we describe in this section may not be new to you if you have already taken various methods courses. However, we hope to suggest additional possibilities for implementing these strategies by giving them a clear multicultural emphasis, helping you to become a more successful multicultural teacher, thus enriching the curriculum at any level. The selected strategies include:

- Reading Aloud
- Teaching with Picture Books across Grade Levels
- Brainstorming
- Collaborative Learning Groups
- Perspective Taking
- Acting Out

- Readers' Theater
- Using Graphic Organizers
- Reporting
- Assessing Progress

Each of these strategies will also appear in lessons in the curriculum chapters that make up Part II of *Multicultural Teaching* as we focus on different subject areas of the curriculum. As explained in the description for each strategy, all can be used across the curriculum as well as with students of different ages.

Reading Aloud

Reading aloud to students is an activity that should be practiced in all classes, no matter what grade level or content area. Anyone can read well: you need to read clearly, project to the whole room (instead of into the book), and use expression and pauses to maintain student contact. When you read aloud, students learn by listening.

- They are hearing what fluent language sounds like.
- They experience how language conveys meaning.
- They are learning new information, hearing about themselves, and developing a better understanding of others.
- They make connections with their own experience.
- They learn the meaning of new words in the context of the sentence and the meaning of the passage.
- They are discovering predictable patterns.
- They are building a sense of grammar, of how words are put together to make sentences.

Above all, they are learning that reading (whether fiction, informational, humor, or poetry) is pleasurable. Nothing cements a sense of community as much as sharing the reading experience together. Students are also more likely to read the book themselves after hearing it read aloud. Sharing a good book increases rapport between teacher and students. It includes students of all reading levels. Even preschool children are learning literacy skills when they enjoy "reading" a familiar story over and over again. Students laugh together when something funny happens; they share sadness when a character is in trouble. They develop a common fund of knowledge: "Remember the time when . . . ?"

You can prepare students for new vocabulary by writing a few words on the board to discuss before you begin the reading. You can also enhance learning of comprehension strategies if you stop periodically and ask questions: "What do you think will happen next?" "Why did the character do that?" Model strategies used by fluent readers when you respond to the author's work, question word choices, and think out loud to interpret events and descriptions.

Reading aloud is an excellent way to set the scene for a new topic of study. Nothing gives students the flavor of another time or unfamiliar place than reading a novel set there. It provides a realistic base for discussion of related social issues and differences of opinion. Promote a positive attitude toward reading among all students, by:

- Talking to the class about what you are reading.
- Suggesting that parents give a book to the class for a child's birthday.

- Helping to set up a book club.
- Scattering a variety of types of books around the class for students to pick up and explore.
- Inviting an author or illustrator to come to speak to the class.
- Providing lists of suggested reading to cover all interests.
- Having students ask family and friends about their favorite books.
- Suggesting they read to a younger sibling or friendly neighbor.
- Posting provocative quotations from varied books; for example:

It won't do you a bit of good to know everything if you don't do anything about it.

~ LOUISE FITZHUGH, *Harriet the Spy*

For the life of him, he couldn't figure out why these East Enders called themselves black.... The colors he found were gingersnap and light fudge and dark fudge and acorn and butter rum and cinnamon and burnt orange. But never licorice, which, to him, was real black.

~ JERRY SPINELLI, *Maniac Magee*

The following are suggestions to get you started with reading aloud:

Nancy Anderson. *What Should I Read Aloud? A Guide to 200 Best-Selling Picture Books.*

Jim Trelease, ed. *Hey! Listen to This.* Forty-eight stories for PreK–4.

Jim Trelease. *The New Read-Aloud Handbook.* A guide for parents and teachers.

Jim Trelease, ed. *Read All about It!* Fifty stories for preteens and teens.

Look for some of these fine authors:

Picture Books

Paul Goble, *Iktomi Loses His Eyes*

Trina Schart Hyman, *Little Red Riding Hood*

Allen Say, *Grandfather's Jouney*

Dr. Seuss, *The Butter Battle Book*

Jacqueline Woodson, *The Other Side*

Patricia McKissack, *Days of Jubilee*

Chapter Books

Christopher Curtis, *Bud, Not Buddy*

Roald Dahl, *James and the Giant Peach*

Sharon Draper, *The Battle of Jericho*

Virginia Hamilton, *Cousins*

Paula Fox, *Slave Dancer*

Wilson Rawls, *Where the Red Fern Grows*

Mildred Taylor, *Roll of Thunder, Hear My Cry*

Laurence Yep, *Dragonwings*

Young Adult

Avi, *The True Confessions of Charlottle Doyle*

Walter Dean Myers, *Amistad; A Long Road to Freedom; Fallen Angels*

Gary Paulsen, *Hatchet; Nightjohn*

Louis Sachar, *Holes*

Alice Walker, *The Color Purple*

Teaching with Picture Books across Grade Levels

Picture books are not just for children, as shown by the popularity of Dr. Seuss's *Oh! The Places You'll Go*. There are picture books available for almost any topic that you might teach. A picture book is typically short (about 30–40 pages), but in the best ones the poetic text and extraordinary illustrations each contribute to the overall impact of the book. Picture books are especially effective because they can be shared with a class of older students within the usual class period and you will still have time for discussion about issues or ideas brought up by the book. In addition to the advantages of reading aloud, as presented earlier in this section, teachers have used picture books with older students in middle and high school to:

- Serve as a springboard for student thinking.
- Introduce writing and oral language activities.
- Present provocative topics that motivate critical thinking.
- Allow students to inhabit different cultures and absorb information about people living in other countries.
- Introduce students to varied genres: biography, fairytale, historical fiction.
- Personalize examples of social injustice.
- Build awareness of our literary heritage.
- Highlight language in different ways.
- Suggest examples of a variety of art techniques.
- Introduce a broad thematic study the class will undertake.

Brainstorming

Brainstorming is a strategy that invites all students to contribute and is appropriate for all K–12 students. You might introduce this strategy with primary students by having them name words beginning with B or name as many animals as they can in ten minutes. They can suggest possible titles for a story about two bears in Alaska, for instance, before they begin writing. Leave this list on the board to continue to inspire new ideas.

This technique is worth practicing in many settings because it encourages divergent thinking and makes it possible for people to come up with ideas they didn't know they had, for example, a group of scientists who are studying a disease or community activists looking for new ways to solve a problem. You can use brainstorming in the classroom effectively with students in upper elementary, middle school, and high school as a way of discovering what issues are bothering them or concerns they may have on their minds.

The ground rules for brainstorming are simple. Introduce the topic or question and then invite students to respond as quickly as possible with whatever comes to mind. Offer students a choice of materials to use to record their ideas, such as thick felt pens, large sheets of paper on the wall, or directly on an overhead transparency. You might even have two students writing on a board to keep up with the flow of ideas.

1. Begin with a problem or question that is as explicit as possible.
2. The emphasis is on generating as many ideas as possible; all ideas are accepted, no matter how wild.
3. No criticism of any idea is allowed, nor is self-censorship.
4. Individuals are encouraged to hitchhike on someone else's idea.

Since evaluation is not relevant, the creative part of the brain has the opportunity to spread its wings. Students do not need to be afraid of taking risks, for there are no "correct" answers. Because of this freedom, students will be surprised at the number of ideas they can generate in a short time. These ideas can be put aside to look at later with a critical eye and put into categories or given priorities.

Once students are familiar with brainstorming, the class can use the strategy for various purposes, for instance:

- Generating ideas for solving a schoolwide problem, for example, how to resolve conflicts on the playground without violence.
- Making a list of what students know about a theme that you plan to introduce, for example, Ancient Greece, the discovery of DNA, or English literature by gay or lesbian writers.
- Show the group a common object that is often overlooked or easily discarded, for example, a penny, a coffee cup, a soda bottle, or a paper clip. Ask the students to generate possible alternative uses for this object.
- If they could invent a machine to do anything they wanted, what would they have it do?
- Asking open-ended questions such as "Why should we be concerned about possible changes in the Earth's climate?"
- Suggesting what to do when people use racist, sexist, or otherwise hurtful language.

A related activity, the Word Wall, is an extension of brainstorming. Create a Word Wall using a long sheet of butcher paper. Use this to help students observe words in print and create word lists for current projects. If you plan a theme study on the circus, for example, you might ask students to name the animals, people, colors, and activities that they already associate with the circus. Sharing their prior experience and knowledge engages students in the topic and leads to better understanding. Through reading books and viewing filmed materials, students will add to their knowledge and provide more words for the class collection of circus words. Encourage students to refer to this Word Wall when they need to check their spelling and vocabulary in later writing activities. The Word Wall will grow as you include words from stories and group similar words together to illustrate spelling patterns.

Collaborative Learning Groups

Working in small groups enables students to talk to and to learn from each other, rather than always passively listening to a teacher lecture. In addition, as they express their ideas, they learn more about each other and share different perspectives as they work to a common goal. If working with collaborative learning groups is new to you or your students, you may want to begin with pairs of students. Assign students to work together so that they do not automatically select their friends. Set time limits so that each partner gets an equal opportunity to talk. Small groups can include 3–5 students, depending on the size of the room. Each group needs a space to gather, and you need to be able to circulate easily to check on their progress for informal assessment of student achievement and learning.

Before forming groups, have students discuss appropriate assessment. How can their individual contributions be recognized as well as the work produced by the whole group? Students need to be able to put the expectations for achievement into their own words. Groups may stay together for the term or you may choose to vary their composition depending on the task. It helps to assign specific roles in the beginning and to discuss what is expected of each person. Switch roles often so that students have the chance to practice different skills. Students can draw role cards to start and later pass the card to the left or right to change positions.

Possible role assignments include:

- Recorder: takes notes for the group; rereads notes aloud to help others remember.
- Leader: makes sure everyone gets a chance to talk; paraphrases what others say to make sure they are understood.
- Encourager: checks that everyone is contributing; makes sure that everyone is given enough time to express their thoughts fully.
- Questioner: asks others "what would happen if . . ."; turns ideas around and tests them.
- Reporter: responsible for reporting group discussion to the class; shares results with other groups.

After completion of collaborative group activities, ask students to consider what went well and to analyze how to make their group work more effective. A variation of working in collaborative learning groups is called group decision making. High school students might enjoy this exercise, prepared by NASA, to practice individual decisions, group discussion, and group consensus. The requirement of reaching a consensus is based on real life decision making.

Decision by Consensus (Prepared by NASA)

Individual Decision.   *Instructions:* You are a member of a space crew originally scheduled to rendezvous with a mother ship on the lighted surface of the moon. Because of mechanical difficulties, however, your ship was forced to land at a spot some 200 miles from the rendezvous point. During the landing, much of the ship and the equipment aboard were damaged, and since survival depends on reaching the mother ship, the most critical items still available must be chosen for the 200-mile trip. Below are listed the fifteen items left intact and undamaged after landing. Your task is to rank them in order of their importance in allowing your crew to reach the rendezvous point. Place the number 1 by the most important item, the number 2 by the second most important, and so on through number 15, the least important.

_____Box of matches
_____Food concentrate
_____Fifty feet of nylon rope
_____Parachute silk
_____Portable heating unit
_____Two .45-caliber pistols
_____One case of dehydrated milk
_____Two 100-pound tanks of oxygen
_____Map of the stars as seen from the moon
_____Life raft
_____Magnetic compass
_____Five gallons of water
_____Signal flares
_____First-aid kit containing injection needles
_____Solar-powered FM receiver-transmitter

Group Consensus. This is an exercise in group decision making. Your group is to employ the method of group consensus in reaching its decision. This means that the prediction for each of the fifteen survival items *must* be agreed upon by each group member before it becomes a part of the group decision. Consensus is difficult to reach. Therefore, not every ranking will meet with everyone's complete approval. Try as a group to make each ranking one with which *all* group members can at least partially agree.

Here are some guides to use in reaching consensus:

• Avoid arguing for your own individual judgments. Approach the task on the basis of logic.
• Avoid changing your mind only in order to reach agreement and eliminate conflict.
• Support only solutions with which you are able to agree to some extent, at least.
• Avoid conflict-reducing techniques such as majority vote, averaging, or trading in reaching decisions.
• View differences of opinion as helpful rather than as a hindrance in the decision-making process.

On the Group Summary Sheet place the individual rankings made earlier by each group member. Take as much time as you need in reaching your group decision.

TABLE 3.2 Group Summary Sheet

	Individual Predictions												Group Predictions
	1	2	3	4	5	6	7	8	9	10	11	12	
Box of matches													
Food concentrate													
Fifty feet of nylon rope													
Parachute silk													
Portable heating unit													
Two .45-caliber pistols													
One case of dehydrated milk													
Two 100-pound tanks of oxygen													
Map of the stars as seen from the moon													
Life raft													
Magnetic compass													
Five gallons of water													
Signal flares													
First-aid kit containing injection needles													
Solar-powered FM receiver-transmitter													

Group_____

Key: Take the difference between your ranking and the ranking on the key. Add the differences. The lower the score the better. These answers are based on the best judgments that are now available. They are not absolute answers.

15 Box of matches — Little or no use on moon.

4 Food concentrate — Supply of daily food required.

6 Fifty feet of nylon rope — Useful in tying injured together; helpful in climbing.

8 Parachute silk — Shelter against sun's rays.

13 Portable heating unit — Useful only if party landed on dark side of moon.

11 Two .45-caliber pistols — Self-propulsion devices could be made from them.

12 One case of dehydrated milk — Food; mixed with water for drinking.

1 Two 100-pound tanks of oxygen — Fills respiration requirement.

__3__ Map of the stars as seen from the moon	One of the principal means of finding directions.
__9__ Life raft	CO_2 bottles for self-propulsion across chasms, etc.
__14__ Magnetic compass	Probably no magnetized poles; thus useless.
__2__ Five gallons of water	Replenishes loss by sweating, etc.
__10__ Signal flares	Distress call when line of sight possible.
__7__ First-aid kit containing injection needles	Oral pills or injection medicine valuable.
__5__ Solar-powered FM receiver-transmitter	Distress-signal transmitter—possible communication with mother ship.

Critique.   Following the exercise, discuss the sources of the problem-solving techniques. How often did individuals use their feelings in working out the problem? How often did critical analysis dominate? What kind of balance existed? How did their knowledge of the familiar world allow them to work with the unknowns? What did they learn about their own learning styles? Did they work better in groups or alone? Did they score higher as a group, or was the individual score better? How did the scores compare with the group average? Did they enjoy the individual work more than the group work?

Perspective Taking

Looking at a subject from someone else's perspective requires considerable skill. It involves looking through a different lens and/or standing in someone else's shoes. Students need to practice seeing something from another person's point of view.

As you read books together, you can discuss whose point of view is being presented by the author. Who is speaking? Have students try to rewrite a passage from a story, describing an event from a different point of view. In the well-known nursery tale *Red Riding Hood*, for example, the story could be told from the point of view of Red Riding Hood's mother, her grandmother, Red Riding Hood herself, the woodsman, and even *the wolf!*

Several authors have done just that—rewritten a story, for example, *The Three Little Pigs* from the perspective of the big bad wolf. To show students clearly the effect of the point of view an author chooses for a story, read the original story of the three pigs and their adventures as they build new houses, the first of straw, the second of twigs, and the third of bricks.

Remind your older students of this nursery tale as you relate how the wolf comes along and says, "Little Pig, Little Pig, Let me come in or I'll huff, and I'll puff, and I'll blow your house in!" (Encourage your students to join in this chorus as it is repeated in the story.) And, of course, the wolf does blow down the house of straw, followed by the house of twigs, so all three pigs end up in the house of bricks.

Not to be outdone, the wolf follows along and threatens to blow the brick house down. Of course, he can't. So he climbs onto the roof and tries to enter the house via the chimney. If you remember, he lands in a huge pot of boiling water and runs away wailing, never to be seen again. (Reminder: students from cultures other than European American may not know this story, so here is a good opportunity to introduce it to them.)

IDEAS IN ACTION!

Developing Community Competence

In 1966, a schoolteacher named Eliot Wigginton began his career in an isolated area of north-eastern Georgia, among the poorest of the poor. Students from this region, Appalachia, had always been written off as having no academic potential, nothing to contribute to the world outside.

This young man discovered that the curriculum he was supposed to impart made no sense to his students because it had no connection to the way they lived. As a novice teacher, with no one to tell him that it couldn't be done, he was inspired to base his teaching on areas with which the students were familiar. Accordingly, he sent them out into their own community to interview people, to explore the accumulated wealth of knowledge that their own people had developed in order to live there, and to learn to pay attention to the community competencies that they had never noticed all around them.

This project was wildly successful and brought national recognition to the community as students wrote up their findings and published book after book. The stereotype of Appalachians as ignorant and incapable of learning was proven false, as the students continue to make discoveries. Their first results appeared as magazine articles in the 1970s, which they then collected and published themselves as *Foxfire*, from Rabun Gap, Georgia. This quickly led to a series of publications, the most recent of which is *The Foxfire 40th Anniversary Book: Faith, Family, and Land,* eds. Angie Cheek, Lacy Hunter Nix, and Foxfire students (Anchor, 2006).

To see this region through loving eyes, look for the following books by Cynthia Rylant, in which she celebrates her homeland of Appalachia:

Ludie's Life. A story in verse about poor women in West Virginia
Missing May. The extraordinary courage of twelve-year-old Summer, who must make a life for herself and her uncle in West Virginia after her beloved aunt dies.
Silver Packages. In December, a strange man would throw Christmas packages from a train as it went from town to town, for the children in Appalachia, because they were poor.
When I Was Young in the Mountains. An autobiographical portrayal of life with her grandparents.

Another classic book to share with students is *Where The Lilies Bloom* by Vera and Bill Cleaver, which describes how a fourteen-year-old girl manages to keep her siblings from starving by earning money through an Appalachian practice called "wildcrafting," using her knowledge of valuable wild plants to gather them for sale.

What competencies, knowledge, and skills might be hidden in your community? Encourage students to pay attention to possible sources for stories, history, and information worth preserving and sharing with others.

Once they know the original plot of this funny story, read the class a rewritten version that takes the wolf's perspective. Several authors have experimented with changing the point of view of this tale. *The True Story of the Three Little Pigs* by Jon Scieszka (Putnam, 1997), is an excellent model for this writing activity. In this version, the wolf gets to tell his side of the story. Not surprisingly, his version is different from that of the three pigs!

Role-Playing

Prepare a set of cards bearing this kind of information:

Setting: Central Park in New York City

Characters:
 Joe: A ten-year old boy
 Marie: His twelve-year-old sister
 Eduardo: The ice cream man

Situation:
 Joe and Marie want to buy some ice cream, but they have only enough money to buy one kind of ice cream.

Pull one card out of the pack of cards available. Call on students to play roles described on that card. Give them one minute to think about the situation before they act it out for the class. These performances are not expected to be polished.

Give students the chance to act out different roles in hypothetical situations and encourage them to respond immediately with words and action. This type of oral expression is important in a number of ways:

1. It allows students the chance to try out different roles while still being themselves.
2. It gives them a way to take risks as they create in a spontaneous manner.
3. It provides them with the opportunity to express themselves through both language and movement.
4. It demonstrates how different language forms are appropriate in different contexts.

The following are examples of situations that might be used:

- Parent explaining how to use the telephone to small child
- One person teaching another how to fly a kite
- Officer asking child to use a bicycle helmet
- Student applying for job as pet sitter for six cats
- Child apologizing to neighbor for breaking the window

Role play activities that encourage problem-solving skills can be done with the whole class or a small group. You will need to allow time for discussion afterwards. Each student can be assigned a role to play. Possible problem situations include the following:

- Guha is riding his bike and runs a red light—a police officer sees him.
- Xiana comes home too late for supper and her family has already eaten.

- Nguyen is assigned to do the family shopping and when he gets to the checkout counter he finds he forgot his money.
- Lanwei brings home a report card with Cs and Ds.

Role-playing can also be based on a book that you have read aloud to the class. Have groups of students take turns role-playing the same book in turn to see how the interpretations differ. Here is a chance for students to develop empathy as they try to imagine what a girl or boy from a different culture might be thinking or saying, how they might be engaged in the family activities, for example, plowing a field or gathering grain.

All students can participate in such activities so that their self-esteem is supported as they also develop empathy for the feelings of other people. Role-playing offers something for all students and can be used successfully in every classroom.

Acting Out

Students enjoy acting out. There are multiple ways of engaging them in simple dramatizing activities that serve to further their comprehension of literature and/or social studies content. Try conversations, short skits, puppetry, and role playing to engage students in interpreting an event or discussing a topic in a different way.

Story Dramatizations

Read a story aloud to the class, for example, a folktale from Russia like "Baba Yaga." Then call on a set of students to act out the story. Encourage them to improvise dialogue, as appropriate.

After this set of students acts out the story, have students tell the actors what they especially liked about the performance. Then, have the first students choose other students to play their roles.

After working with a simple folktale, introduce the class to tales from other lands, perhaps a country they are studying in social studies, for example, Japan or Ghana. Many picture books present folktales with attractive illustrations that facilitate the dramatization, Blair Lent, for example, retold and illustrated an excellent version of *Baba Yaga*. Look for others in the children's section of the library under the nonfiction number 398.

Additional Useful Strategies

- Charades—titles, expressions, events
- Who Am I?—noted actors, national leaders
- Readers' Theater—combined with some actions
- Folkdancing
- Exercises
- Games with Motions—Simon Says, Squirrel-in-the-Cage

Puppets

Many students who are shy about talking in class will open up when they can talk through hand puppets that look like different kinds of people or animals. Divide the students into small groups to work with the puppets and give some short assignments to get them started.

The first step is for each student to introduce his or her puppet to the others. The puppets can ask each other's names and ask questions about the other puppets. All the puppets in the group can have a conversation together.

Students can also use puppets to act out events, such as the most important thing that ever happened to them, or portray favorite activities.

The group members can work together to create a play for their puppets. (Suggest topics if necessary.) After they have decided what they want to do, the students can present the puppet play to the class. If the children in a group are interested, ask them to write their play so that they can present it again and others can read it.

Students can also create a puppet theater to use with more elaborate productions. Using a large box, cut out an opening in one side, high enough to allow students to crouch below the "stage." Students will enjoy embellishing their very own theater.

Stick Puppets. The stick puppet is versatile and can be created easily by primary grade children. Popsicle sticks or tongue depressors form the base of the puppet. Children can cut out heads of people or animals or they may wish to create their own fully drawn figures to glue on the sticks.

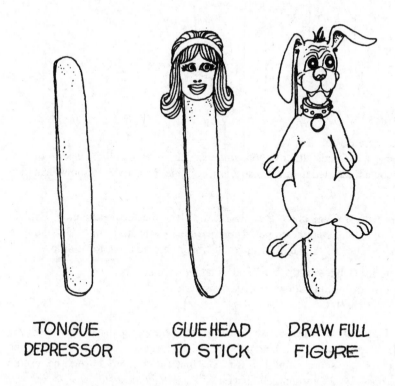

TONGUE
DEPRESSOR

GLUE HEAD
TO STICK

DRAW FULL
FIGURE

Paper Bag Puppets. Puppets can be constructed quickly and easily by using readily available paper bags (see page 102).

Readers' Theater

Organizing the Presentation

Readers' Theater is a dramatic structure that students can use to highlight aspects of topics they have become interested in or to present as a culminating activity to show what they have learned.

Planning.   Talk with students about the idea of a readers' theater presentation. Explain that the presentation is read, not acted out. The presenters sit on stools or chairs and read their assigned parts. Discuss the kinds of materials that might be used, for example:

- Short stories (fables, myths, etc.) and excerpts from novels
- Sayings, proverbs, quotations, poetry, song lyrics
- Factual statements

Searching for Material.   Plan a visit to the library as the groups search for material related to the selected theme. If you notify the librarian ahead of time, she or he will be able to locate appropriate sources for class use. The material does not have to be written in play form for this kind of presentation, as you will see in the next step.

Preparing the Script.   Duplicate copies of folktales or poems that students plan to use. These copies can then be marked and revised as the group deems appropriate. There may be three or four roles to read plus one or more narrators who read the descriptive passages. Students can invent dialogue to add interest and to develop a character.

Rehearsing.   One student should be the director to signal the group when to stand and to sit. This person listens during rehearsals, ensures that students read clearly and effectively, makes suggestions for timing, and so on. Poetry and nonfiction can be divided in various sections or verses, A number of students can read to provide variety.

A Civil Rights Readers' Theater

Students might want, for example, to focus on the African American struggle for civil rights. They can seek out materials about such topics as Freedom Riders, sit-ins, school integration, or the words of such well-known figures as Dr. Martin Luther King, Jr. Ruby Bridges, or Marian Anderson. Made-up reactions from ordinary people, onlookers to these historic events, can be added as well.

Tell the students that they are going to prepare a Readers' Theater presentation about the Fight for Freedom. Each person will read a selection, sitting down and facing the audience. Everyone will need time to rehearse so they know the words very well and don't stumble. If they are comfortable with the material, they will probably be able to look up occasionally at the audience. Two students might take turns reading the same selection, or a group of three to five people could read a poem together as a chorus.

Students can work in small groups to choose their readings and to think about how to present them. They can add music, art, movement, or singing to their presentation where it is appropriate. As groups practice, have several other students serve as an audience to make suggestions for improvement of the presentation.

Make a list of all presentations and presenters on the chalkboard so the class can plan the organization, considering:

- Introductory information
- Order of selections
- Art or music to enhance the presentation

Students can hold their copy of the part they will read in a black folder made from 12" × 24" construction paper, so they will look professional.

This presentation may be given before another class or two, which would give the speakers additional opportunities to polish their reading. Then the group might offer to present *Fight for Freedom* to the PTA or a community organization. Although planning a Readers' Theater presentation may appear to be a lot of work, this activity boosts everyone's self-esteem, as they have many opportunities to work together and each one can contribute to the group effort in different ways.

Group Reading

A variation on this technique is called group reading. In this activity, every student in the class begins with the same collection of reading material—for example, a book, a story, an article, or a newspaper. Each student chooses a phrase or line to underline. Then a leader selects students to read their individual lines, one at a time. The order in which students read is random, and more than one student may have chosen the same line. Some students may speak more than once. As they read aloud, students are creating a new story. Record the session so students can hear the results of their composition.

Students may begin by selecting a passage from one of the books they are reading. As they copy the passage, they decide where to break the lines to create a poem. Then they share their "poem" with the class. In this way, students learn to look at language in new ways.

For example, instead of reading his well-known speech, "I Have a Dream," students might honor Dr. Martin Luther king, Jr. by underlining various passages from different speeches he made. Then they can read the selections in any order they choose. This will create an innovative portrait of the familiar hero.

Using Graphic Organizers

Various kinds of graphic organizers can help students organize their thinking as they prepare to write a report. Developing a kind of visual representation of ideas also serves to help students expand their ideas as they explore a topic. Such organizational thinking is a stimulus to creativity. Throughout this book we demonstrate the use of various graphic organizers to which you can refer, for example: Clustering (page 56) and Venn Diagram (page 136).

Another useful type of organizer is mapping, which is a versatile way of picturing the plot of a story, the sequence of an event, or the intricacies of a complex topic. Figure 3.2 is a simple example of mapping that records the components of the familiar story "Goldilocks and the Three Bears."

Figure 3.2   Mapping

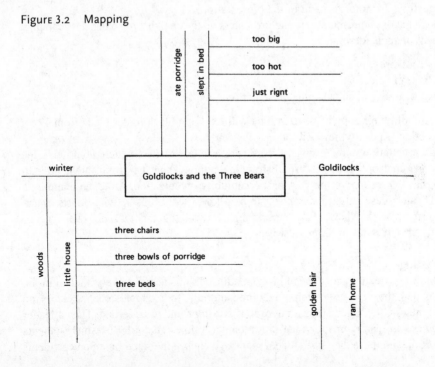

FIGURE 3.3   Describing a character

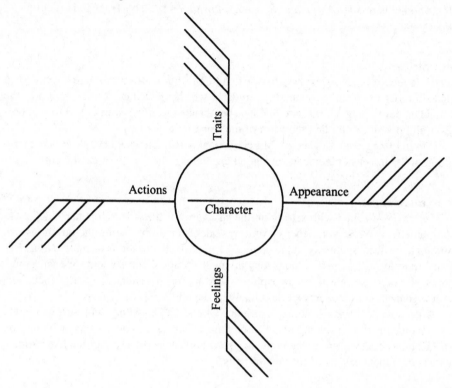

Encourage students to invent different ways of organizing their thinking using original graphic organizers such as the one shown in Figure 3.3.

Reporting

Reporting data that one has collected can be done in a variety of ways. Most students envision a report as a form of expository writing, a series of paragraphs that usually is an essential part of a formal research paper that contains these four parts:

- Statement of the Problem
- Description of the Research Procedures
- Summary of the Findings
- Conclusion

Reporting, as you can see, is only one part of the full research paper. It is likely, however, to be the most interesting.

As teachers, we can invite students to present the findings of whatever research they undertake in a more creative way. Perhaps, if we suggest a few interesting ways they might try, they will be motivated to create additional methods. For example, show the students alphabet books that report an amazing amount of information. One outstanding publication is *D Is for Democracy: A Citizen's Alphabet,* by Elissa Grodin (Sleeping Bear Press, 2004). Another is *A Is for Astronaut: Space Exploration A to Z,* by Traci Todd (Chronicle, 2006).

Comic Strips

One way to rewrite a news story or a familiar children's book is to turn it into a comic strip format. In order to create a comic strip, students will have to focus on the action of the story and on developing appropriate dialogue for the characters. A comic strip format provides useful practice in finding the heart of the story.

The Iliad and the Odyssey, by Marcia Williams (Candlewick, 1996), a comic strip retelling of the famous epic poems, is a good example to share with older students.

The I-Search Paper

Ken Macrorie is credited with setting up the structure for the I-Search paper. The key to writing an effective research paper is to have students begin by listing the questions that they want to answer. Students can generate a list of possible questions on a topic as a class and then develop more specific questions in small groups. Each student, or each group, chooses one of these questions to explore. This approach results in greater focus and clearer organization as students are less likely to accumulate a list of facts.

After students have had some experience with short expository writings, you might like to involve them with writing an I-Search Paper. The paper should focus on a question of special interest or concern to the individual students. The paper is organized like a formal research study that consists of four major parts:

Part I: Statement of the Problem.   In just a few sentences, the student states the question or problem that he or she is going to study.

Part II: Research Procedures.   The second part of the research is the actual study. The student should outline the process which he or she proposes to undertake, Depending on the topic, the student will obtain books and magazines or journals that provide information about the subject. He or she will also check specific websites or search topics through a browser to collect information. The student will record the process followed during the research.

Part III: Summary of the Findings.   In this part the researcher summarizes all of the findings gathered through the research process. The findings can be grouped in various ways according to the topic being studied. Some of the findings may be presented as graphs or charts.

Part IV: Conclusion.   This statement relates directly to the statement of the problem. Is there an answer to the question posed? Are there conclusions reached after studying the subject? Perhaps there is a need for further research.

Assessing Progress

What is assessment? It is more than giving each student a grade on a report card. It is more than testing students to see how much they know. Assessment is an essential aspect of teaching; it is part of the ongoing teaching/learning process. Effective teachers use assessment to:

- Clarify what they expect to teach and, therefore, what they will assess.
- Determine just how far along students have progressed in learning at any given point.
- Show the teacher what remains to be taught or if something needs to be retaught.
- Discover how much a student has learned about a given topic or process.

Teaching begins where the student is, but if you don't know where that is, how can you plan effective instruction? Before beginning a thematic study, therefore, the first thing you should plan is a pretest to assess what students already know.

Many teachers use a graphic organizer called KWL to guide students to assess their own progress. Students, often working within a cooperative learning group, make an assessment at each of three stages, thus:

K—What we already *know* about this topic—pre-assessment.
W—*What* we hope to find out about this topic—planning research.
L—What we have *learned* about this topic—post-assessment.

Although it is often overlooked, assessment is an important part of teaching. It is an essential component of any lesson plan. Assessment supports instruction and informs the teacher at all stages, for example:

Diagnostic—The diagnostic assessment is not graded. It simply informs the teacher about what each student knows and what he or she is able to do. This assessment tells the teacher where to begin teaching and perhaps what methods may work best.

Formative—This ongoing assessment measures a student's progress and shows both teacher and student where he or she is on the learning ladder and how many more rungs are yet to be climbed. It indicates clearly just how the teacher can best help the student move ahead.

Summative—This final assessment should reveal exactly how much a student has learned. This assessment may be in form of a test, a project, or a performance, something that was clearly indicated from the beginning of the study as the expected criterion of success.

As many educators realize, students are more likely to become engaged in a task when there is:

- *Task clarity*—when they clearly understand the learning and know how teachers will evaluate their learning.

- *Relevance*—when they think the learning goals and assessments are meaningful and worth learning.
- *Potential for success*—when they believe they can successfully learn and meet the evaluative expectations.

Define the objectives for the students and for yourself before you begin any unit of study. Let the students know what kind of performance you expect. You want to be sure you have a clear goal in mind that you can convey to the class. Begin the study with this end in mind. Each decision you make must then move you toward that goal—your state standards, resources, learning activities, assessments, etc.

Have students keep a portfolio of their work. In an English class, for example, students will complete a number of writing tasks. It will be helpful for them to review periodically the writing they have done and to note how much their writing has improved over the past few months. Such self-assessment is motivating as they begin the next assignment.

Involve students in defining standards for success. Have them devise a nine-point rubric, for example, that might be used in assessing persuasive essays written in response to a prompt that all students in a school district are expected to write as an annual testing of writing. By constructing a rubric themselves before any writing test is administered, students decide what components are most important as they write—clarity, spelling, vocabulary, neatness, and so on. You might develop a rubric such as the one below to be used when organizing and assessing the Reflective Teaching Portfolio activities suggested at the end of each chapter.

Rubric for Reflective Teaching Portfolio

9 All entries included
   Exceptional quality of writing, thoughtfulness
   Well organized; Table of Contents
   Interesting additional materials integrated into journal

7 All entries included
   Entries of uneven quality; some very well written
   A number of additional materials included

5 All entries included
   Very short journal entries
   Little additional material

3 Minimal effort made

1 Very little effort made

Grades 9 = Outstanding—A
       7 = Very Good—B
       5 = Adequate—C
       3 = Insufficient—D
       1 = No Credit—F

After the rubric is completed, each student should have a copy to keep in his or her writing portfolio. This is especially helpful for students in middle school and high school as they are engaged in more writing activities. The creation of one rubric is not an end in itself. Criteria for effective writing should be an ongoing conversation, particularly as student abilities and experience grow.

Our chief focus should be on developing habits of mind as students engage in reading, writing, and discussing issues related to the big questions we face in life. We want to engage them in higher order thinking skills as they learn to compare, to judge, to argue, to state a sound opinion, to evaluate, to make intuitive leaps, to initiate new ideas, to self-assess throughout the learning process. We want them to continue responding to the thrill of learning. (Adapted from "Spotlight on Assessment" in *California English,* September, 2007.)

CONNECTIONS

In this chapter we have focused on planning instruction, using techniques that promote hands-on activities requiring students to engage actively in listening, speaking, reading, and writing about ideas. We included a student-centered Thinking + Lesson Plan that aids teachers in creating multicultural lessons across the curriculum. We also described the use of Learning Centers that are conducive to individualized learning. These two methods of planning instruction offer structure for daily learning activities, yet they provide for infinite variety.

In addition, we shared ten teaching strategies that teachers have found successful in teaching in K–12 classrooms. Moving beyond the usual pencil and paper activity, many of these strategies allow students to move around the classroom. They stimulate interaction among students, and serve to encourage all students to enjoy learning, to be glad to be in school, and to be excited about what comes next. The strategies were selected to engage students in exploring literature, in thinking about important issues, and in expressing their own ideas.

These strategies will be further demonstrated in the curriculum chapters that make up Part II of *Multicultural Teaching.*

GETTING INVOLVED

Expanding Your Reflective Teaching Portfolio

1. Of the ten teaching strategies presented in this chapter, which one appealed most to you? Why did you particularly like that strategy? How would you imagine that you could use the strategy effectively?
2. What books have you read so far in this course? Discuss one that you would recommend to all of your classmates. Why?
3. What do you hope to achieve in your classroom?

Working with Your Cooperative Learning Group

1. Choose a topic that interests your group, one that you think would be exciting to explore with a classroom of students. Designate one person to take notes as you begin listing what you know, as a group, about this topic.

   Next, list questions that would be interesting to investigate related to this topic.

   Last, brainstorm ideas for locating information about the topic, especially information relevant to the questions your group has listed for investigation.

2. Talk about the ten strategies that are described in this chapter. Is there one or more that is entirely new to you, for example, Readers' Theater? Plan to prepare a lesson following the strategy you have identified. Present this lesson to the rest of your class just for practice. Discuss problems that you may have encountered. Invite classmates to suggest ways of improving the lesson.

3. Tell the other members of your group about a book that you have read that you think would be especially appealing to middle school and/or high school students.

4. Develop a learning center for your state. Each group can focus on designing one activity or station for students. Collect the supplies and other resources you would need, and plan how you would assess student learning.

EXPLORING FURTHER

Mary Cowhey. *Black Ants and Buddhists: Thinking Critically and Teaching Differently in the Primary Grades*. Stenhouse, 2006.

John Dewey. *Democracy and Education*. Free Press, 1966 (1916).

Mike Rose. *Possible Lives: The Promise of Public Education in America*. Houghton Mifflin, 1995.

Nancy Schniewind and Ellen Davidson. *Open Minds to Equality: A Sourcebook of Learning Activities to Affirm Diversity and Promote Equality*. Rethinking Schools, 2006.

Beverly Daniel Tatum. *Why Are All the Black Kids Sitting Together in the Cafeteria and Other Conversations*. Basic, 1997.

Richard Wright. *Black Boy (American Hunger): A Record of Childhood and Youth*. HarperCollins, 2005.

Malcolm X with the assistance of Alex Haley. *The Autobiography of Malcolm X*. Ballantine, 1999.

PART II

Integrating Multiculturalism Across the Curriculum

Multicultural studies belong in every part of the K–12 curriculum. Above all, we plan learning activities that (1) support the self-esteem of each student, (2) develop empathy among members of the classroom community, and (3) provide equity for all students as they strive to achieve to their fullest potential. In addition, teachers of all subjects owe it to their students to consciously recognize the contributions of diverse peoples to the knowledge base in each field. At all levels, we need to introduce students to authors, scientists, and scholars from all parts of the world, and to global leaders who may speak languages other than English. We will expose students to literature about children and men and women from different countries who have hopes and dreams much as they do, thus expanding their worlds.

We will introduce students to persons who serve as role models, who lead the way in living successfully in a nation and a world inhabited by people who share this planet, for example, the stalwart Nelson Mandela, who commented upon being released from prison after many years:

> I have fought against white domination, and I have fought against black domination. I have cherished the ideal of a democratic and free society in which all persons live together in harmony and with equal opportunities. It is an ideal which I hope to live for and to achieve. But if needs be, it is an ideal for which I am prepared to die.

In Chapters 4, 5, 6, 7, and 8 we focus on specific areas of study: language arts/reading, social studies, science, mathematics, and the arts, suggesting learning activities recommended for teaching multiculturally. Chapter 9 is unique, featuring a calendar that presents a wealth of multicultural information selected to enhance teaching in any classroom. Our aim throughout the curriculm is to teach students to respect the diverse people in their school, in our country, and in the world, and to learn how to get along together with those who appear to be different.

CHAPTER 4

Multicultural Language Arts/Reading

> *Nobody can make*
> *You feel inferior*
> *Without your consent.*
> ∼ ELEANOR ROOSEVELT

The language arts—thinking, listening, speaking, reading, and writing—are foundational skills for study across the curriculum. These skills are interrelated in that they all entail the use of language. As California State Superintendent of Schools Jack O'Connell and President of the California State School Board Ken Noonan state in the foreword to the 2007 *Reading/Language Arts Framework for California Public Schools:*

> Literacy is the key to participating and succeeding in a democratic society and global economy. Without the ability to read, write, and communicate with competence and confidence, our children will have limited opportunities for academic and career success. Reading, writing, listening, and speaking are the foundation for learning.

As babies, children listen to the language used by others around them, and through listening, they learn to speak the language they hear, to communicate orally. Then, they begin to observe written language that communicates messages in a different way. As researchers tell us, children should learn to read much as they learn to speak, by deriving meaning from print in their environment and from real children's literature. They learn to read the written language and then to communicate their own messages by writing something others can read.

Writing is the most difficult language skill to learn because it requires the student first to produce thoughts that are then expressed grammatically, using conventional spelling, punctuation, and legible writing. These processes of learning to use language are much the same no matter what language we speak or write.

Although reading is often treated as a separate skill that tends to dominate the elementary school curriculum, we see it as closely aligned with writing, because both are integral parts of the process of using our written language to exchange meaning. Both reading and writing, as well as thinking, listening, and speaking, are used in studying all subject areas in the K–12 schools, as noted in this chapter and those that follow.

In addition to such performance skills, language arts also includes the study of language and literature. We consider the study of language to be so critical to multicultural education that we have devoted an entire chapter to that subject (see Chapter 10). Our multicultural explorations will lead us to observe, for example, that some languages are easier to write (spell) than is English with its Germanic roots, which show up in such words as *night* and *right*. As for literature, you will find that it permeates the whole K–12 curriculum as a rich resource for learning multiculturally about every subject area we study.

The quotation on the previous page sets the stage for our investigation of multicultural language arts and reading. Eleanor Roosevelt was a brilliant woman who still gives us something to think about.

❖ Multicultural Language Arts Activities that Support Esteem, Empathy, and Equity

The use of language is an integral part of human existence. It is essential that children learn to use at least one language effectively as they interact within a classroom and later in society at large. In the United States, it is essential that everyone learn to use the dominant language of commerce, English. The classroom provides a safe environment for practicing language skills as children talk together, learning how to exchange ideas with others, to communicate. Here we suggest learning activities that support the 3E model we introduced in Chapter 2 as the foundation for effective multicultural education. We focus first on supporting self-esteem, then developing empathy for others, and last, providing equity for all students.

Supporting Esteem

Students' self-esteem is best supported when they engage in activities at which they can succeed. It is important to plan for success!

Listen!

Talk about the listening process with students. Make a list of what they learn by listening as opposed to reading. Notice that listening to learn something requires intent. Students have to want to hear, and they must concentrate to listen effectively. They may also need to take notes.

Have students work in pairs as they listen actively to each other. First, for example, Joe tells Deanna about the place where he was born, what he remembers hearing about the town, the house the family lived in, and how he got his name. Deanna tries to repeat everything she learned from Joe; he can make corrections as she talks. Then, it is Deanna's turn to talk while Joe listens actively and summarizes everything he learned about Deanna. This is a particularly good activity early in the year when students are less likely to be well acquainted.

Developing a Positive Classroom

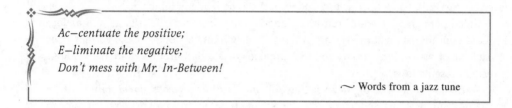

Ac–centuate the positive;
E–liminate the negative;
Don't mess with Mr. In-Between!

~ Words from a jazz tune

Talk with the students about the importance of being positive in their relationships with others. Discuss how negative comments can be hurtful to others. An old saying they might remember is, "If you can't say something nice, don't say anything!" Copy the motto above for display in your classroom. Invite students to decorate copies of the motto for display in school hallways, lunchrooms, and so on.

Talking about Multicultural Picture Books

Have upper elementary school students work in Cooperative Learning Groups as they read multicultural picture books together. Give each group a number of multicultural picture books to share. Each student takes a turn reading a book aloud to the others, sharing the illustrations as they go. As each book is completed, the group discusses what they liked about that presentation in story and pictures. After each person has read a book aloud, the group can vote on which book they liked best of those they read.

Some books on multicultural themes that you might include are:

Jennifer R. Elvgren. *Josias, Hold the Book*. Illustrated by Nicole Tadgell. Boyds Mills Press, 2006. Josias learns how to raise better beans for his family by reading a book in school.

Tony Johnston. *Angel City*. Illustrated by Carole Byard. Philomel, 2006. An elderly African American man hears the cry of a baby in the Dumpster. He rescues the tiny Mexican child and raises it with the help of his Los Angeles neighbors; based on a true story.

Barbara Kerley. *A Little Peace*. Illustrated with author's full-color photographs. National Geographic, 2007. Pictures of children playing around the world; thoughts on how we can promote peace.

On another day, each group can present the multicultural picture book they thought was best of all to the entire class. After all books have been presented, the class can list what qualities they feel are needed for such a book to be considered really good.

IDEAS IN ACTION!

Promoting Multicultural Reading

For some time, Sonoma County, California, libraries have been sponsoring **The Big Read**, a month-long effort to encourage reading by people of all ages in the community. Each year a book is chosen, for example, in 2008 it was *To Kill a Mockingbird* by Harper Lee. An earlier choice was *The Grapes of Wrath*. Clearly the criteria for making a selection did not include "newness," but rather quality of writing and impact on the reader's thinking.

Funded partially by a grant from the National Endowment of the Arts as well as local media and educational institutions, this program makes multiple copies of the current selection available at the thirteen county libraries, provides discussion groups, dramatic readings, and media presentations.

Information about **The Big Read** can be obtained at *(www.bigreadsonoma.com)*.

Write a proposal for conducting a similar reading program in your area. Present this proposal to such groups as a city chamber of commerce, a city council, a library board, the Lions Club, the Rotary Club, the American Association of University Women or your school board. Any group could initiate this worthwhile community-wide program, which is sure to have broad appeal.

Developing Empathy

Empathy develops as students get to know each other. Working in pairs or small groups encourages sharing and discussing personal feelings. Following are selected learning activities that will help students learn to empathize with others in the classroom. Talk about what empathy is and why it is important in a democratic society.

Keeping Diaries

Have students make booklets (see Chapter 8) in which they can keep diaries, noting what is happening in their lives and how they feel about it. In pairs or small groups they can take turns sharing an entry of their choice from their diaries. The other students can respond to what each student shares. Composing diary entries not only has students observing writing skills but also helps them to develop empathy as they express personal feelings about things they may be experiencing.

Students aged 10–14 might enjoy reading such books as the following, which are presented as diaries:

Claudia Mills. *Totally Made-up Civil War Diary of Amanda MacLeish*. Farrar, 2008.

Rebecca Ruff. *Sarah Simpson's Rules for Living*. Candlewick Press, 2008.

Role-Playing

Role-playing is a versatile oral activity that allows students to express their opinions in a realistic situation. They can literally stand in someone else's shoes as they speak in the role they have assumed. Ideas for role-playing come from all areas of the curriculum, for instance:

- A group of parents discussing a city problem.
- Children greeting a new student from Vietnam.
- A Japanese American family talking after they arrive at an internment camp.
- The Abenaki tribe holding a feast in 1700.

Role-playing may be performed by a group of three to five students as the others observe and take notes. After the performance, class discussion focuses on the strengths and weaknesses of the performance, for example, the language used and the appropriateness of the topics discussed. After this analysis, another group can perform with the same roles and situation.

At other times, the whole class can role-play a situation, such as plantation life in 1800. Before beginning this activity, of course, students need to study to determine what the various roles would be. Group activities in specific areas of the room might focus on the slave quarters, the barn where horses are shod, or a group of runaways in the woods. Simple costuming lends interest to this dramatic play.

Role-playing can lead to formal debate as students discuss the pros and cons of an issue. After arguing informally in role-play, students may be stimulated to search out more information to be presented in a panel discussion or debate. These oral activities lend interest to learning, and they provide a firm foundation for writing to express opinions. They also teach advanced thinking skills. Role-playing is discussed further in Chapter 3.

Creating Classroom Libraries
The president of the International Reading Association in 2003, Jerry Johns, presented a powerful message on the importance of libraries in promoting students' reading abilities. He notes that "reading for pleasure begins with access to books and time to read them." To support access to books, the International Reading Association advocates the importance of having classroom libraries with at least seven books per student and staffed school libraries with at least twenty books per student in the school. Although most educators support the presence of school libraries in all schools, with funding problems such libraries, particularly in elementary schools, are often eliminated. Students can conduct a campaign to collect books in their neighborhood, making posters, canvassing door-to-door, and writing letters to the newspaper. They can create a classroom library that they can share.

Talking about Names
Naming practices around the world are interesting to all of us. How are names chosen? What do different names mean? Here is an engaging topic that will involve all students as they begin a new school year. Students' names are key elements of their identity, especially their first names. Provide opportunities for students to explore their names and how they feel about them as well as to investigate names in other cultures.

Choosing Names.   Ask children about their first names. How do they feel about their names? Are they named after someone, perhaps an aunt or grandfather? Perhaps they have a family name, like Jamison, or an invented name composed of both parents' names, such as Rayella. Have them write on one of these topics:

- My parents named me _____ because _____.
- I like my first name because _____.
- I wish I could change my first name because _____.
- If I could choose a name for myself, it would be _____ because _____.
- If I had a child, I would name the baby _____ because _____.

Read aloud *Chrysanthemum* by Kevin Henkes, the story of a young mouse who loves her unusual name until she starts school. Then the others make fun of her, saying her name is too long and not appropriate for a mouse. But one of her teachers helps her learn that her name is as special as she is.

Explore naming customs in different cultures. Catholic children choose a saint's name when they are confirmed. What does this mean? Jewish children are named after relatives but never living ones. Alex Haley begins his classic work *Roots* with a moving description of an African naming ceremony. Chinese children are given a "milk" name as babies to confuse evil spirits. Do students know of other naming customs?

What's Your Name? From Ariel to Zoe by Eve Sanders presents history and stories about names from many cultures. Many websites provide information about child names, such as (www.parentsoup.com/babynames/finder).

My Name Design.   Help students see their names from a different perspective by having them make designs based on their first names (see Figure 4.1). Follow these instructions: Fold a piece of paper in half lengthwise. With the fold on the bottom, write the name, making sure that each letter touches the fold. Letters that extend below the line can be raised so they fit on the same level. Now hold the folded paper up to the light and trace the name in reverse on the other side. Open up the paper to find an abstract design. This can be colored in or decorated to make an imaginary figure. Display these on the bulletin board or use them to make covers for collections of student writing.

Name Acrostic.   Use your students' names often in puzzles or wordplay. A creative activity is to develop an acrostic based on a name. Students write their name vertically down the left side of a page. Then they fill in the acrostic with adjectives (or phrases) describing themselves, beginning with each letter of their name, as shown on the next page.

FIGURE 4.1   First Name Designs

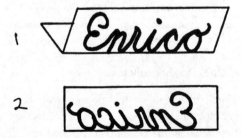

K ind
H elpful
A miable
L ight-hearted
I ntelligent
D aring

You can make the task easier by allowing students to start to the left of their letter. This increases the number of words they can use.

     b **L** ack
      A mbitious
     a **M** azing
    pr **E** tty
      L ively
 friend **L** y
  hon **E** st

Students with short names can include their middle or last name to make the acrostic more interesting. Students with long names can choose a short version. You may want to award points for the number of letters to the right of the name or for the most unusual words chosen.

Encourage students to check the dictionary to find creative word choices and to expand their vocabulary. They can explain their selections to the class.

Studying the Work of an Author Who Writes on Multicultural Themes: Jacqueline Woodson

The class could study the work of a number of authors, but we have chosen one who has written books across levels, from picture books through books for older readers. Jacqueline Woodson is an African American author and a lesbian whose work is highly respected. Her books include the following:

Picture Books

Coming on Home Soon. Illustrated by E. B. Lewis. Putnam, 2004.

The Other Side. Illustrated by E. B. Lewis. Putnam, 2001.

Visiting Day. Illustrated by James E. Ransome. Scholastic, 2002.

Grades 4–7

Feathers. Putnam, 2007.

Locomotion. Putnam, 2003.

Show Way. Illustrated by Hudson Talbott. Putnam, 2005.

Grades 6–10

After Tupac and D Foster. Putnam, 2008.

From the Notebooks of Melanin Sun. Scholastic, 1995.

Hush. Putnam, 2002.

I Hadn't Meant to Tell You. Putnam, 1994.

If You Come Softly. Putnam, 1998.

Miracle's Boys. Putnam, 2000.

As you introduce this author to your students, begin reading one of books that you especially like to the whole class. Assign two gifted students the task of checking Ms. Woodson's biography on the Internet. They can report their findings to the class, putting multiple copies of the printout where students can obtain a copy to read, if they like.

Depending on the grade level you teach, give each Cooperative Learning Group one book to begin reading together. Students should keep a journal in which to record their reactions to this author's work as they hear more. A special section can be allocated to the book

DID YOU KNOW?

According to the Global Reading Test given to fourth-grade students in 2001 and again in 2008, little or no improvement was seen at that grade level in the United States during that eight-year period. In fact their ranking was considerably lower in 2008 than it had been in 2001.

In 2001, the average score for U.S. fourth graders ranked third in the world. In 2008, the average score for U.S. fourth-grade readers tied with two other countries for eleventh place. Countries that scored higher than the United States and those that tied with the United States were:

Russia
Hong Kong
Singapore
Luxembourg
Hungary
Italy
Sweden
Three Canadian provinces: Alberta, British Columbia, Ontario
United States, England, Netherlands (tied)

What does this say for our efforts to meet testing standards demanded by the Reading First program, which has been the foundation for No Child Left Behind legislation in the United States for the past eight years?

Plainly, reading teachers and librarians need to re-examine the strategies we use for teaching children how to read. We need to engage elementary students in gaining meaning from the real language that appears in their environment and from real literature, both fiction and nonfiction, written by talented authors.

you are reading aloud together while another section can bear the title of the book their Cooperative Learning Group is reading together. On one day, give each group a copy of one of Woodson's picture books to read and examine. They can write their comments in their log.

As a culmination for this study of Jacqueline Woodson's writing, students can plan a display in the school library or in the hall outside the principal's office. They might create a large mural depicting the various characters Woodson has described or a map showing the settings for the different books. Suggest that a city- or county-wide group fund the appearance of this author for the general public in your area.

Other multicultural authors whose work crosses levels that you might like to study include:

- Pat Mora—Latino culture
- Cynthia Rylant—low-income Whites in Appalachia
- Walter Dean Myers—African Americans

A Thinking + Lesson Plan: Getting to Know Your Neighbors

Carry out the Lesson Plan on p. 123. Talk about the riots in Los Angeles that are described in *Smoky Night*. Ask if students have experienced similar events. Were they frightened like the people in this book? Have any of them stayed in a shelter? Let students write about experiences they may have had in which they were frightened. Students can read what they wrote aloud in their Cooperative Learning Groups.

Understanding Others

Show middle or high school students a number of large pictures of people. Ask them to look at each picture in turn and to write several sentences about the person they are viewing, for example:

This man is very happy.
He is tall and handsome.
He has a good job and earns a lot of money.

Compare what different students have written about several of the people. Discuss the fact that we often make assumptions about people that we see in the street or even about other students in the classroom. Someone could be feeling terrible, and we don't necessarily know.

Pass out copies of the following poem, saying, "Here is a poem about a man who everyone thought was happy. Read it, and see what you think."

RICHARD CORY

Whenever Richard Cory went downtown,
We people on the pavement looked at him:
He was a gentleman from sole to crown,
Clean favored, and imperially slim.

And he was always quietly arrayed,
And he was always human when he talked;

But still he fluttered pulses when he said,
"Good morning," and he glittered when he walked.

And he was rich—yes, richer than a king—
And admirably schooled in every grace:
In fine, we thought he was everything
To make us wish that we were in his place.

So on we worked, and waited for the light,
And went without the meat, and cursed the bread;
And Richard Cory, one calm summer night,
Went home and put a bullet through his head.
                    —Edwin Arlington Robinson

Ask several students to locate the Simon and Garfunkel song that they wrote about this poem, called "Richard Cory." They can compare the two versions of this brief story of a man's life. Have students write in their journals about what they have learned through this learning activity.

International Pen Pals

Your students might like to write a letter to the editor of a major newspaper in a city such as Buenos Aires, Prague, or London. Research on the Internet will produce addresses for newspapers around the world. Here is a real letter that appeared in the San Jose (California) *Mercury News*.

Dear Editor:

We are children who live in Israel and we like to collect stamps and trade stamps with people around the world. We really like stamps with animal pictures. When we get stamps from different places, we learn about your country, and we learn about you.

We are a girl and a boy, ages 13 and 10. If you print this letter, maybe people will send us stamps and we will send them our stamps. Our address is 9 Lotham Street, Efrat, Israel.

Thank you,

Rivka Bedein
Elchanan Bedein

Your class might begin by writing letters to the editor of some of the newspapers your research has produced. The Internet is also a great source of pen pal contacts with whom you can often correspond via email.

Reading Aloud

Reading books aloud to a class has many benefits. This strategy is discussed in detail in Chapter 3. Select multicultural titles by talented authors, for example, Virginia Hamilton, a prolific African American writer. Her book *Cousins* is a complex realistic novel that provides many interesting multicultural topics to discuss and to write about, such as the elderly, relations with family, and personal responsibility. Other books that present multicultural themes include:

A THINKING + LESSON PLAN

―◄○►―

Getting to Know Your Neighbors

Grades 4–12

Expected Outcomes

Learners will:

1. Listen to the picture book *Smoky Night* by Eve Bunting.
2. Discuss the riots and how people felt about them.
3. Write a summary of what people learned through this shared experience.

Teaching / Learning Strategies

Directions

Resources Needed

Obtain one or more copies of *Smoky Night* by Eve Bunting and illustrated by David Diaz (Harcourt Brace, 1994).

Step 1: Read this short picture book aloud to the class.

Step 2: Talk about what happened in the story and how Daniel and his mother felt as they watched from their window.

Step 3: What incident did the author describe that changes the direction of the story? What wise words did she have Daniel say?

Step 4: Write a short paragraph about what you learned through reading this picture book. Why did the author choose to write about this topic? Have students bring their paragraphs to a Writing Conference for evaluation.

Step 5: Tell the class that the artist, David Diaz, won an award (the Caldecott) for the best illustrated book of the year. Have students examine this man's work to observe the kind of art he used in the book.

Performance Assessment

Students write paragraphs about the lesson learned:

3   More than five sentences; clear; few spelling errors.
2   Three to five sentences; coherent.
0   Fewer than three sentences.

Primary

Ashley Bryan. *Beautiful Blackbird*. Atheneum, 2004.

Nikki Grimes. Illustrated by Bryan Collier. *Barack Obama: Son of Promise, Child of Hope*. Simon & Schuster, 2008.

Janet S. Wong. *Buzz*. Illustrated by Margaret Chodos-Irvine. Harcourt, 2000.

Elementary

Christopher Paul Curtis. *Bud, Not Buddy*. Random, 2002.

Patricia C. and Frederick L. McKissack. *Days of Jubilee: The End of Slavery in the United States*. Scholastic, 2004.

Middle School

Sharon M. Draper. *The Battle of Jericho*. Atheneum, 2004.

Sharon G. Flake. *Money Hungry*. Hyperion, 2003.

A THINKING + LESSON PLAN

Writing a Book Review

Grades 5–8
Expected Outcomes
Learners will:

1. Read a book review.
2. Identify characteristic features of this form.
3. Write a book review that includes these features.

Teaching/Learning Strategies

Resources Needed
Locate the review of a book that you would like students to know or perhaps an author you would like to introduce. Duplicate a class set of copies of the review. (You can write one yourself following the model presented here.) This lesson requires at least two class periods.

Directions
Step 1: *Read the Book Review:* Where the Red Fern Grows

Wilson Rawls was a country boy from the Ozarks. He spent much of his time roaming the hills with a blue tick hound, hunting and fishing, enjoying the out of doors.

It was natural, then, for him to write a book about a boy who wanted hunting hounds, a boy who also roamed the hills and river bottoms of the Cherokee country so familiar to Rawls. In the introduction to the book he describes the setting, thus:

> Our home was in a beautiful valley far back in the rugged Ozarks. The country was new and sparsely settled. The land we lived on was Cherokee land, allotted to my mother because of the Cherokee blood that flowed in her veins. It lay in a strip from the foothills of the mountains to the banks of the Illinois River in northwestern Oklahoma.

Where the Red Fern Grows is a story of love for family, for animals, and for this country. It is also a story of adventure as Billy achieves his greatest dreams.

Ten-year-old Billy wanted a pair of coon dogs, but hounds cost more money than the family could possibly afford. Determined, Billy began saving his money, storing it in an old K. C. Baking Powder can. After almost two years, he had fifty dollars, enough to buy the two redbone coon hound pups that would change his entire existence.

Billy, Dan, and Little Ann spent their lives together from the time he brought them home. As he said:

> It was wonderful indeed how I could have heart-to-heart talks with my dogs and they always seemed to understand. Each question I asked was answered in their own doggish way.
>
> Although they couldn't talk in my terms, they had a language of their own that was easy to understand. Sometimes I would see the answer in their eyes, and again it would be in the friendly wagging of their tails. Other times I could hear the answer in a low whine or feel it in the soft caress of a warm flicking tongue. In some way, they would always answer. (p. 68)

The high point of the book is Billy's winning the gold championship cup in the annual coon-hunting contest. With the cup came a large cash prize that answered his mother's prayers for a new house.

Billy continued to hunt with his dogs until one night they met the "devil cat of the Ozarks, the mountain lion." His brave little dogs tried to save Billy from the lion, whose "yellow slitted eyes burned with hate." Although Billy finally killed the huge animal with an ax, the dogs were badly wounded. Old Dan died from his injuries, and Little Ann soon died, too, of heartbreak at losing her hunting companion. Billy sadly buried the two dogs in a beautiful spot on the hillside.

As the family was leaving the Ozarks the following spring, Billy ran to this grave for one last farewell. It was then that he saw the beautiful red fern that had sprung up above the graves of the little dogs. He remembered the old Indian legend that "only an angel could plant the seeds of a red fern, and that they never died; where one grew, that spot was sacred." As they drove away, the family could see the red fern "in all its wild beauty, a waving red banner in a carpet of green."

Fast action, human interest, and believable characters make this a book for readers of all ages. A master storyteller, Wilson Rawls has shared a piece of himself.

Step 2: *Stimulus (Prewriting)*
Give students copies of the book review you have selected. Read the book review aloud slowly as students read their copies. (This is especially helpful for less able readers and ELL students, and it helps keep the class together for the purposes of the lesson.) Then have students return to the beginning of the review and direct them to identify the kinds of information the author included in the review.

Features of a Book Review
1. Includes quotations from the book.
2. Comments about the content presented by the author.
3. Tells something about the author, biography.
4. Expresses personal reaction to the book.
5. Includes the title and author of the book.

Direct the students to bring a book that they have already read to class the next day.

(continued)

Step 3: *Activity (Writing)*
See that each student has a book to review. Display the Features of a Book Review list that the class compiled. Go through the features one by one with the class as students take notes based on the books they are reviewing. Tell students to complete the first draft of the book review they have begun as homework.

Step 4: *Followup (Postwriting)*
On the next day students should have the first drafts of their book reviews and copies of the book to be reviewed. Have students work in Cooperative Learning Groups of three to five students. Each student is to read his or her book review aloud as the others listen to see if all features on the list have been included. After listening to a review, each member of the group should answer the following two questions for that writer:

1. What one aspect of this review was especially well written?
2. What one recommendation would help improve the writing?

The next day, revised versions of the book reviews can again be shared in the same editing groups. Each writer should point out exactly what changes were made from the first draft. Any further changes should be made, as needed.

Performance Assessment
Before completing the final draft of the book reviews, students should work as a class to determine just how these reviews will be evaluated, for example:

A Simple Rubric or Standard (some recognition for excellence)

10 Uses excellent detailed description.
     Shows clear personal involvement.
     Includes important biographical information.
     Speaks clearly to the audience.
     Includes all features listed, very well presented.

 5 Presents all features adequately.
     Needs further revision.

 2 Presents most features, very weak writing.
     Needs extensive revision.

Students who are involved in determining evaluation measures for their own work are assuming responsibility for their work, and they can help each other so that potentially everyone in each group can get the top score. Students learn much about writing by reading and evaluating each other's writing.

When book reviews are fully revised, they can be published instantly in a three-ringed notebook that bears the title *Books We Recommend*. Have someone decorate the cover. This collection, containing something by everyone in the class, should be available for reading in the classroom and, later, in the library.

Providing Equity

We provide equity when all students have an equal opportunity to participate in an activity. Shared activities in a classroom over time develop a healthy sense of belonging and feeling positive about coming to school.

Reading Novels Aloud

We learn language by listening to native speakers of a language. Students also enjoy hearing the teacher read a story aloud to them. As they laugh together or share tragic events described in a book, students develop a pleasant rapport with each other and their teacher.

Sharing novels chapter by chapter is something students long remember. Here are two good choices:

> Margaret P. Haddix. *The House on the Gulf*. Simon & Schuster, 2004. A short mystery story that provides insight into family relationships and how this family survives. Grades 4–7.
>
> Kirby Larson. *Hattie Big Sky*. Delacorte, 2006. All students will enjoy following the adventures of Hattie, a girl who attempts to homestead in Montana. Grades 6–10.

Reading Picture Books Aloud

Reading a picture book aloud to older students takes only a short time, but the whole class can immediately discuss the story that has been presented or respond to it in writing. Show students the wonderful illustrations as you read so that they learn to "read" the art as well as the text. Look for some of these books:

> Christine Farris. *My Brother, Martin: A Sister Remembers Growing Up with the Rev. Martin Luther King*. Illustrated by Chris Soentpiet. Philomel, 2003. Insight into the life of Martin Luther King Jr.; might be linked to social studies investigations of the civil rights movement. This fine illustrator immigrated from Korea at a young age. (See the interview in *Language Arts*, September, 2005.)
>
> Brian Floca. *Lightship*. Atheneum, 2007. A simple, but interesting, nonfiction book that may "hook" reluctant readers. Be sure students notice the ship's cat that appears in the illustrations. Read the historical note at the end of the book which explains the practice of using a lightship where a lighthouse could not be built. Other picture books by Floca include *The Racecar Alphabet* and *Five Trucks*.
>
> Jeannette Winters. *The Librarian of Basra: A True Story from Iraq*. Harcourt, 2005. Alia saves the books from a library that later is burned to the ground.

Planning a Thematic Study: Religions of the World

A study of a broad topic offers opportunities for all students to participate in planning and in gathering information. Be sure to bring in books that are appropriate for readers of different levels; begin your search for materials in the children's section of the library, asking the librarian to help you locate things you might find helpful. *Religion* is a subject that we Americans don't know as much about as we might. Since we tend to fear that which we don't understand, a study of world religions would be a worthwhile endeavor in the middle school and/or high school. Guide students to generate questions about religion that they might have:

- What are the different religious beliefs that people have around the world?
- How did each religion get started?
- How are religions alike?

Begin this study by having students brainstorm what they know collectively about religions of the world. Write this information on a chalkboard or make a Word Wall (see Chapter 3) that can remain on display so that students can size up what they may need to learn. They can also add information as it is discovered.

DID YOU KNOW?

—◁◦▷—

Where in the world is Bhutan? What religion(s) do the Bhutanese follow?

In the March, 2008, issue of *Smithsonian*, the editors feature a fascinating article about Bhutan, located just south of Tibet. Not surprisingly, the Bhutanese follow a form of Buddhism, Tantric or Vajrayana.

Take the class to the local library, so they can find appropriate reading material. Or, bring in a variety of books about different religions, being sure to include materials for various reading abilities, for example:

General Interest

Islam. One of the many titles in the *Eyewitness Series* which includes such topics as *The Civil War, Africa, Everest, Technology,* and *Presidents* published by DK Publishing, Inc. (375 Hudson St., New York, NY 10014). Many of these titles can be found in bookstores.

Doreen Rappaport. *In the Promised Land: Lives of Jewish Americans.* Illustrated by Cornelius Van Wright and Ying-Hwa Hu, HarperCollins, 2007. Thirteen influential men and women are featured in this attractive oversized picture book, which describes a significant moment in each life. Although most of those included are historical figures, two—Ruth Bader Ginsburg and Steven Spielberg—are still active in the American scene. For more information about Jewish Americans, see www.amuseum.org/jahf, published by the Jewish American Hall of Fame.

Reading Nonfiction Books about Lives in Which Religion Was Important

Binka LeBreton. *The Greatest Gift: The Courageous Life and Death of Sister Dorothy Stang.* Doubleday, 2007. The story of a female missionary in a small town along the Amazon.

Andrew C. Revkin. *The North Pole: Puzzles and Perils at the Top of the World.* Kingfisher, 2006. Articles from the archives of the *New York Times.*

Jonny Steinberg. *Sizwe's Test.* Simon & Schuster, 2008. Informative literary journalism about AIDS written by an author from South Africa.

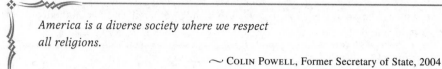

> *America is a diverse society where we respect all religions.*
>
> ~ COLIN POWELL, Former Secretary of State, 2004

Thinking + Lesson Plan: Reading Biography and Other Nonfiction
This lesson focuses on religion. Be sure to include books that talk about religion as seen through the eyes of different people. Look for biographies of Cassius Clay, world-renowned boxer, who changed his name to Muhammed Ali, for example, and turned to Islam in the later years of his life. Stories of missionaries might also be interesting.

Check the library computer for other biographies and nonfiction that you might include. This lesson ties in with the thematic study of religions developed above.

A THINKING + LESSON PLAN

-◄o►-

Reading Biography and Other Nonfiction

Grades 6–12

Expected Outcomes

Learners will:

1. Read a biography or other nonfiction related to religion.
2. Keep a journal as they read.
3. Write a short essay about the religion described.

Teaching/Learning Strategies

Resources Needed

Bring a collection of biographies about people in whose lives religion played an important role (ask your librarian for help). Include nonfiction books about religions, too. You need more than one book per student in the class.

Directions

Step 1: Invite students to browse through the books displayed on a large table or along the window sill. They are to select a book that they will read and report on. As they make their selections, they return to their seats and begin to read.

Step 2: Provide a sheet of directions entitled "Presenting an Oral Report" (see p. 132). Set a date when the reports will be presented in class orally.

Step 3: Students will take notes as they read, following the directions you give them. You may be able to use one or more class periods for reading these books; however, if more time is needed, the reading will be completed at home.

(continued)

Step 4: Oral reports will be presented. You may wish to invite another class as an audience for these presentations.

Performance Assessment

1. Students will give an oral report using notes, but not reading the report.
2. Several students will complete evaluations for each report (rotate positions for this role).

Evaluation will follow this rubric:

5 Well-organized; presented confidently.
3 Rather short; some stumbling over sentences.
1 Too short; inappropriate behavior (giggling, joking, etc.).

❖ Integrating Language Arts Instruction into Other Curriculum Areas

Using the language skills—thinking, listening, speaking, reading, and writing—is obviously necessary as we engage in the study of any subject. As students listen and read, they are learning and absorbing information that someone else has provided. Then, they think about this information, pondering, analyzing, questioning, and evaluating what they have learned. And, finally, they communicate their thoughts about this information. They speak to others, discussing, arguing, and persuading, and they may further communicate this thinking in written form so that their thinking can be saved and read by others. In this section, we explore strategies that encourage students to use language skills effectively as a way of studying the social studies, science, mathematics, and the arts.

The Language Arts and Social Studies

Reading and writing about social studies topics is a natural. The media report daily on events related to social justice, ethnic celebrations, and facts about the increasing diversity in the U.S. population. Encourage students to peruse the newspaper and to bring in clippings about such multicultural information to share with the class.

Create a Bulletin Board Display
Each month assign one Cooperative Learning Group the responsibility for preparing a display to which other students can add information. Provide colored paper and other supplies they can use to make the display attractive. Students will have fun inventing provocative captions, for example:

N ORTH
E AST
W EST
S OUTH

Designate a specific time each Monday, perhaps, for students to present information they have discovered that will interest the class. Clippings or notes and short reports can then be displayed on the board where they can be read later.

Reading Multicultural Historical Fiction

Here are recommended examples of multicultural historical fiction for young people of all ages published in recent years:

Primary

Sharon Addy. *Lucky Jake*. Illustrated by Wade Zahares. Houghton Mifflin, 2007. Jake helps his miner father earn money by planting corn and making fritters.

Margot Theis Raven. *Night Boat to Freedom*. Illustrated by E. B. Lewis. Farrar, 2006. Christmas John, age twelve, helps his grandmother free other slaves; wonderful art.

Elementary/Middle School

Joan W. Blos. *Letters from the Corrugated Castle*. Simon & Schuster/Atheneum, 2007.

Susan Cooper. *Victory*. Simon & Schuster, 2006. Molly, thirteen, saves Sam, eleven, who is pressed into service aboard a ship, the *Victory,* during the eighteenth century.

Katherine Paterson. *Bread and Roses*. Clarion, 2006. Jake, thirteen, is desperate for work, but the mill workers' strike makes it hard on everyone in early 1900s in Massachusetts.

Tracey Porter. *Billy Creekmore*. HarperCollins, 2007. Orphaned Billy works in a glass factory and later in a West Virginia coal mine; conditions are terrible for child laborers.

High School

M. T. Anderson. *The Astonishing Life of Octavian Nothing: Traitor to the Nation*. Candlewick, 2006. A young slave witnesses unspeakable evil in New England and asks what patriotism means.

Marian Hale. *Dark Water Rising*. Holt, 2006. Seth, sixteen, survives a terrible flood in Galveston, Texas.

Stephen E. Ambrose. *Undaunted Courage*. Simon & Schuster, 1996. The story of Lewis and Clark's great expedition and how researching it directly impacted this author. Check other books by this highly respected author.

A slave is still a slave if she refuses to think for herself.

⌒ Lgbo (Nigerian) proverb

Presenting an Oral Report

Developing the skills required for speaking to a group is important throughout life. Giving a report orally to the class offers students a chance to develop these skills. The social studies offer many opportunities for giving oral (or written) multicultural reports about:

- Famous people in history.
- The development of transportation in the United States.
- Different ethnic groups in our country.
- The contributions of African Americans to the growth of our country.
- Native Americans in the United States today.
- Historical fiction such as the preceding titles.

Prepare a set of guidelines like those shown below to aid middle school and high school students in preparing an oral report.

PRESENTING AN ORAL REPORT

◄○►

Gather information for your report, for example:

- Read a book.
- Search the Internet.
- Observe an event.
- Listen to a speech.

Make a list of things you would like to share with the audience:

Choose a title for your report. You may try something catchy or it may be straightforward, for example, "The Life and Contributions of Tom Jones."

On a half-sheet of paper, list the topics you will talk about in order. Just a word or two will remind you about what you want to talk about first, second, and so forth. Plan to say several sentences about each topic before you go on to the next topic.

Write a final sentence that will end your report, for example:

We owe a vote of thanks to Tom Jones for his invention. Or—
As you can see, Buddhism is an interesting religion.

Practice giving your report out loud at home using your list of topics. You might try standing in front of a mirror as you pretend to talk to an audience.

A THINKING + LESSON PLAN

-◄o►-

A Nation of Immigrants: The Angel Island Experience

Grades 4–10

Expected Outcomes

Learners will:

1. Learn about the immigration process.
2. Listen to personal stories of classmates who have immigrated.
3. Recognize the contributions of those who have immigrated.

Teaching / Learning Strategies

Resources Needed

Obtain a copy of *Landed* by Milly Lee. (Farrar, Straus, 2006.)

Directions

Step 1: Read this picture book aloud. Show the pictures to the class as you read each page.

Step 2: Have the class describe the process that Sun had to go through before being admitted into the United States. List these steps on the chalkboard.

Step 3: Have students research Ellis Island and the entry process that immigrants experienced on the East Coast.

Step 4: Each student should read a novel about an immigrant and write a report about his or her experiences.

Performance Assessment

1. Each student receives + or – depending on class participation and the completion of a novel.
2. Students will prepare written reports about the book they read. These reports will be filed in a class book called "Immigrants We Have Known." Students can refer to these reports in locating another book to read. Reports will receive scores according to this rubric:

    5 Clear report of the person's life; few errors in spelling.
    2 A report that is not as clearly presented.
    0 No report completed.

The Language Arts and Science/Mathematics

Talk with students about how scientists and mathematicians use language as they engage in their work. Students can make a list of various ways men and women engaged in these careers use language, for example, by taking notes, discussing a problem with colleagues, writing a report of their findings, and reading research.

Writing Science

As students conduct research, they should keep a journal in which to record the procedures they followed, for example:

- I collected books about frogs.
- I made a list of questions I had about frogs.
- I read about frogs and took notes to answer my questions.
- I wrote a report using my notes.
- I drew pictures of some of the frogs that live near us.

Each of these steps can be presented on a new page in the journal. Some of the steps will require only a page or two, but taking notes will, of course, require a number of pages. The first draft of the report can be in the journal, too, although the final report may be prepared on a computer.

Publishing a Report

To encourage students to make their reports interesting, show them examples of how some authors have presented information. An attractive book about frogs, for instance, is *Frogs Sing Songs* by Yvonne Winer, illustrated by Tony Oliver. (Charlesbridge, 2003). This author/illustrator team is from Australia.

Another example takes the format of an alphabet book, as in *Gone Wild: An Endangered Animal Alphabet* by David McLimans. (Walker, 2006). Factual information is presented for each animal as well as an artful presentation of the letter in which the animal appears.

Analyzing and Comparing: Using the Venn Diagram

The Venn diagram is used in mathematics to compare two sets. This method can be used to compare two concepts or books. After each student has read a novel about young people living in another land, ask each one to complete a Venn diagram that compares his or her life with that of the book character, for example:

Barbara Cohen. *Seven Daughters and Seven Sons.* Harper, 1994. This book is based on an Iraqi folktale that demonstrates the worth of daughters. Buran disguises herself as a man to help her family, and all kinds of adventures follow. It's really an exciting story.

In sections 1 and 2 of the Venn diagram, unique characteristics are listed for each person. In section 3, the student lists adjectives that describe both, showing how they are alike (see Figure 4.2). After completing the Venn diagram, each student writes a five-paragraph essay following this pattern:

Paragraph 1: Introduction
Paragraph 2: Description of herself or himself
Paragraph 3: Description of the book character
Paragraph 4: Summary of how the two are alike
Paragraph 5: Concluding paragraph

This exercise may lead students to observe that people are more alike than different, particularly when they consider their personal characteristics and problems. Once students know how to use this diagram, they can use it to guide comparisons of more complex topics, for example, two ethnic groups, two religions, or two forms of government.

FIGURE 4.2   Venn Diagram

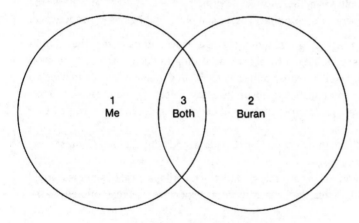

1. Adjectives That Describe Me   2. Adjectives That Describe Buran

1
Me

3
Both

2
Buran

3. Adjectives That Describe Both of Us

Describing a Mathematical Process

Often a mathematician will describe a mathematical process as he or she works with figures on the chalkboard. Thus, those who are watching (students or colleagues) can observe the process and learn how to follow that process later themselves.

Challenge students to describe a mathematical process first orally and then in writing. The object is to make the description so clear that the listener or reader can follow the process independently. Students might, for instance, think about the process of multiplying 368×472. What do you do first? And then? Have two students work together as they check on each other to be sure that no step of the process is omitted. They can take turns going through the process orally before describing it in writing together.

IDEAS IN ACTION!

An Essay Contest

In 2008, the National Geographic Society conducted a "Hands-on Explorer Challenge" contest co-sponsored by Johnson & Johnson for students ages 9–14. Each entrant was to submit a 300-word essay and an original photograph following these directions:

- Write an original personal essay in English that is no more than 300 words telling us how you actively explore your world and the most interesting things you have found in it ("Essay"). Then take a photograph of what, where, or how you explore the subject of your essay ("the Photograph"). You must be the photographer. The Essay and the Photograph must each be a single work of original material created by the contestant entrant. By entering the Contest, entrant represents, acknowledges and warrants that the submitted Essay or the Photograph are original works created solely by the entrant and that no other party has any right, title, claim or interest in the Essay or the Photograph.
- Photograph must be submitted in the form of a print between 3" × 5" and 8" × 10" (taken with film or digital camera). No electronic, slide, or non-print submissions will be accepted.

Further specifications followed regarding the photograph and how entries were to be submitted. Essay/photograph entries were judged by experts according to such criteria as the clear relationship between the essay and the photograph, expression of genuine interest and passion for active exploration as well as journalistic quality of the essay. Selected candidates were interviewed by telephone. Prizes were exploratory trips for fifteen winners, each accompanied by a legal guardian.

For information about this contest, contact: NG Kids, Hands-On Explorer Contest, 1145 17th St., NW, Washington DC 20036.

Follow this model for a contest in your school or district. Perhaps local businesses would sponsor a similar contest. The prizes don't have to be as expensive as those offered by the National Geographic Society.

The Language Arts and the Performing Arts

How are the language arts and performing arts related? Of course, both are a means of expressing ideas, ways of communicating wit h others, for example, recording historical events. We admire and talk about the paintings of Rubens and Warhol. We read music recorded in a special kind of writing by talented musicians. We listen to singers as they perform, perhaps acting out a dramatic opera by Verdi or Puccini. We clap enthusiastically and tap our feet in response to the jazz of Preservation Hall's musicians playing "As The Saints Go Marching In!" Students can explore this relationship further.

Creating a Word Wall for Music

Mount a large sheet of butcher paper on the wall where the class can record words related to music. Begin by brainstorming words in categories they know (see Table 4.1).

TABLE 4.1 Words About Music

Instruments	*Terms*	*Musicians*	*Forms*
Guitar	Quartet	Duke Ellington	Song
Clarinet	Pianissimo	Aretha Franklin	Tune
Piano	Trill	Bruce Springsteen	Concert

As students participate in creating this Word Wall and pore over it later, they expand their interest and knowledge about language as well as music.

Examining the Arts in Picture Books

Picture books today are illustrated by talented artists. In many picture books the art is as important as the author's text. Children need to learn to read the pictures as well as the words to gain the full meaning of the book.

In many cases the same person writes the story and produces the art. This is true of books by Lois Ehlert, who conveys information in both pictures and words. A good example is *Leaf Man* (Harcourt, 2007), in which Ehlert presents large pages full of colorful fall leaves. She talks about the figures of a man formed by the leaves and other parts of a tree. Older children will be able to identify leaves of trees that they recognize—oak, maple, elm, even a gingko. Looking at this book will stimulate creative thinking as children press leaves, then fasten them to colored paper to form animal shapes.

Learning Folk Dances

Take students to see people performing different folk dances. Or, invite dancers to come to your school to perform for the entire student body. Showing videos of such performers will also help to engage students with the idea of performing dances and what each one looks like.

Invite parents or older siblings to come to school to teach children how to perform different dances. Begin with easier circle dances in which all of the students can readily participate.

Engaging Students in All Language Processes across the Curriculum

How can you teach students to listen while learning history content? Or, how about developing critical thinking skills while learning something about biology? Keep the objectives for the multicultural curriculum listed in Chapter 2 in mind as you plan these activities. Following are suggestions that should trigger ideas:

Listening:

- Retell a folktale the teacher has read aloud, for example, "Clever Gretel."
- Act out an Indian trickster tale after hearing it at the Listening Center, for example, "Raven the Trickster."
- Summarize the life of a writer after listening to *The Lives of Writers* (Audio Bookshelf, 1995).

Speaking:

- Discuss the problems that Karana faced in *Island of the Blue Dolphins* by Scott O'Dell.
- Tell a "flannel board story" to younger children, for example, *John Henry.*

Reading:

- Read a poem by Langston Hughes aloud as a selection from a class presentation on poetry.
- Review a book about someone who lives in another country, for example, *Winding Valley Farm: Annie's Story* (Poland).

Writing:

- Keep a process journal while reading a book about the Japanese American internment, for example, *Journey to Topaz* by Yoshiko Uchida.
- Use mapping to outline the life of a famous woman leader, such as Indira Gandhi or Mother Teresa.
- Write "memory stories" after reading *I Was So Silly* by Marci Curtis.

Thinking:

- Compare your life with that of Lisa in *Lisa and Her Soundless World* by Edna Levine (deafness).
- Write questions to ask Katherine Paterson after reading *Come, Sing, Jimmy Jo* (Appalachia).

CONNECTIONS

The language skills—thinking, listening, speaking, reading, and writing—plus the content areas of language and literature are essential for learning across the curriculum. Helping all students to gain facility with communication skills is an important responsibility for each teacher. At the same time, he or she is also concerned with supporting each child's self-esteem, developing empathy among students, and providing equity for each one.

The teacher's knowledge about how children learn to speak language and how they should learn to read language in much the same way affects how well he or she will be able to guide diverse students in their language development. The teacher's knowledge about appropriate literature that is available helps her or him to tap a rich resource that supports multicultural teaching.

GETTING INVOLVED

Reading about ideas for teaching is certainly helpful, but it is even more important for future teachers to become actively involved in preparing lessons and in exploring resources that will support instruction.

Expanding Your Reflective Teaching Portfolio

1. What does this quotation suggest to you?

   He has the right to criticize, who has the heart to help.

   —Abraham Lincoln

   Write your response in your portfolio. How can you use this activity with students? Begin to collect useful quotations on 3" x 5" file cards for use in the classroom.

2. Select a book mentioned in this chapter to read. Plan a lesson around the book using the lesson plan presented in Chapter 3.

Working with Your Cooperative Learning Group

1. Share the lesson you have prepared with members of your group. Encourage your classmates to suggest ways of improving the lesson. You, in turn, can help each of them to improve their lessons too.

2. Choose a topic that members of your group would like to develop together to produce a thematic unit which all of you can use. For example, if your group chooses to develop a study entitled "Native Americans in the United States in the Twenty-first Century," you might begin by brainstorming along these lines:

   • What do we know together now?
   • What do we need to learn?
   • How can we go about the task?

3. Obtain a copy of Frank Smith's "Twelve Easy Ways to Make Learning to Read Difficult (*And One Difficult Way to Make It Easy"), *Psycholinguistics and Reading* (Holt, 1973), pp. 183–196.

   Also obtain a copy of *Language Arts*, September, 2008, which presents a discussion of "how we teach reading." Discuss how you can implement the recommendations of researchers such as Kenneth Goodman, Yetta Goodman, and Frank Smith as you engage students in reading.

EXPLORING FURTHER _____

Jenny M. Bender. *The Resourceful Writing Teacher: A Handbook of Essential Skills and Strategies*. Heinemann, 2007. Detailed instructional strategies that help students in grades 3–8 write successfully.

Thomas Bever. *All Language Understanding Is a Psycholinguistic Guessing Game— Explaining the Still Small Voice*. In Patricia Anders, ed., *Defying Convention, Inventing the Future in Literacy Research and Practice: A Tribute to Ken and Yetta Goodman*. Erlbaum, 2009.

California Department of Education. *Writing, Speaking, Reading, Listening: Reading/ Language Arts Framework for California Public Schools Kindergarten through Grade Twelve*. California Department of Education, 2007. An excellent outline of what students need to learn at each level.

Kenneth Goodman. *The Truth about DIBELS: What It Is and What It Does*. Heinemann, 2006. Discussion of the method of testing students' reading ability following the Reading First program included under NCLB legislation.

Sam M. Intrator and Megan Scribner, eds. *Teaching with Fire: Poetry That Sustains the Courage to Teach*. Jossey-Bass, 2003. A collection of eighty-eight poems by noted American poets that will be useful in grades 5–12.

CHAPTER 5

Multicultural Social Studies

> ### *The New Colossus*
>
> *Not like the brazen giant of Greek fame,*
> *With conquering limbs astride from land to land,*
> *Here at our Sea-Washed, sunset gates shall stand*
> *A mighty woman with a torch, whose flame*
> *Is the imprisoned lightning, and her name*
> *Mother of Exiles. From her beacon-hand*
> *Glows world-wide welcome; her mild eyes command*
> *The air-bridged harbor that twin cities frame.*
> *"Keep, ancient lands, your storied pomp!" cries she*
> *With silent lips: "Give me your tired, your poor,*
> *Your huddled masses yearning to be free,*
> *The wretched refuse of your teeming shore.*
> *Send these, the homeless, tempest-tost to me.*
> *I lift my lamp beside the golden door."*
>
> ~ EMMA LAZARUS

The term "social studies" refers to a broad category of subjects taught in the elementary school as well as the middle school. These studies tend to focus on geography and history. In the high school, such studies are likely to focus on single subjects, for example, American History or World History, and Civics. In this chapter, we will emphasize how multicultural themes derived from the social sciences, such as family, freedom, and citizenship, strengthen the teaching and learning of a diverse student body in the elementary, middle, and high schools.

Immigration is a theme that has always been an integral part of American history, for we are a nation of immigrants. Newcomers are welcomed by the great Statue of Liberty, the symbol of freedom that stands in New York Harbor. This statue bears a poem by Emma Lazarus, "The New Colossus," part of which we have printed for you on the previous page. Today, immigration issues spark heated debate that engages us all.

In Chapter 5, we provide examples of teaching strategies and resources that are available to teachers at all levels and direct you to begin creating multicultural social science lessons that you can adapt to your own classroom. First, we introduce you to possibilities for developing an exciting curriculum by following the 3E Model, on which we base all efforts to teach multiculturally. Then, because the social studies tend to lose space in a crowded curriculum that places greater emphasis on reading and mathematics, we encourage you to follow best teaching practices by integrating social science concepts into such other studies as language arts, science, mathematics, and the arts.

❖ Social Studies Activities that Support Esteem, Empathy, and Equity

As we did in the preceding chapter, which focused on language arts/reading, we are including a section in this chapter that features social studies learning activities that carry out the 3E model. We begin with activities that support self-esteem, move on to activities that tend to develop empathy among students, and then present activities designed to provide equity for all of the students in a classroom.

Supporting Self-Esteem

Students need positive feelings of self-esteem in order to succeed in school. They need a sense of belonging and the knowledge that the teacher cares about them. So, from the very first day, we reach out to touch each one in some personal way. Try some of the following ideas.

Who Is It?

Play a game with students as they become acquainted at the beginning of the year. Provide a few clues that identify one student, for example:

> His initials are C. B.
> He lives on Meadowlark Avenue.
> His family used to live in Galveston, Texas.
>
> Who is it?

If no one can guess, ask the student to identify himself, thus: I am Carl Benton. I live on Meadowlark Avenue, and my family used to live in Galveston, Texas.

Notice that you have told the students something about Carl that they may remember. Each day continue introducing students in this way, which makes each one feel special.

Meet Juanita Espinosa

Prepare a small display area where the Student of the Week is featured. The student can bring in photographs or draw pictures of family members. He or she may complete and post a survey prepared by students in the class, for example:

My favorite color is _____.

On Saturday I like to _____.

The song I like best is _____.

My best friend is _____.

I especially like to eat _____.

When I am twenty, I hope to _____.

Recognizing Students in the Classroom

Make copies of your class list. Place a copy on a clipboard. Especially during the first month of school, make a point of walking around the room as students are working. Ask a question or comment about what a student is doing, addressing each one by name.

Discreetly, place a check by that student's name. The next day repeat this procedure, making sure you address different students. At the end of a week be sure that you address those students you may have missed. Addressing students directly lets them know that you recognize the fact that they are there in your class and that you care enough to say, "Hello."

Recognizing What Each Student Knows

Make sure that you discover the interests and abilities of each of your students. Students who speak a language other than English obviously have the knowledge of a language and culture to share with the class when appropriate. But you may not know that Clarita takes dancing lessons or that Dmitri has grandparents to whom he writes in St. Petersburg. Some students may be engaged in raising vegetables with their parents, cooking, or caring for a new baby. They may have learned to make *ojos de dios* or *luminarias* as part of family activities.

Introduce a discussion of this topic by reading the classic *Crow Boy* by Taro Yashima. This story tells how uncomfortable a country boy feels in a classroom until the class finds out that he can imitate the different calls of crows.

Reading Books Aloud

Sharing a book by reading it aloud to a class is highly recommended. After enjoying a book together, students have a common set of references that promote rapport as they study together. Often you will choose books that support the topics being studied within the social studies curriculum, for example:

Primary Grades

David A. Adler. *A Picture Book of George Washington Carver.* Holiday, 1999. Born a slave, George became a great scientist. He earned a master of science degree and helped farmers improve their crops.

Elizabeth Lightfoot. *Michelle Obama: First Lady of Hope*. Lyons, 2009: A biography of Michelle Obama.

Wendell Minor. *Buzz Aldrin: Reaching for the Moon*. HarperCollins, 2005. Story of an astronaut who was one of the first to step on the moon.

Upper Elementary/Middle School

Cynthia Kadohata. *Kira-Kira*. Atheneum, 2004. The story of a Japanese family who moves from an internment camp to southern Georgia; a Newbery Award-winning book.

Kathy Madden. *Louisiana's Song*. Viking, 2007. Set in the mountains of Carolina, this is a tale of an Appalachian family of ten kids and their parents.

Barack Obama. *Dreams from Our Fathers: A Story of Race and Inheritance*. New York Times, 1995.

Developing Empathy

We want to help students learn to get along. We want to show them how to accept diversity and to demonstrate respect for each other. Make a point of including literature about different ethnic groups in reading and social studies activities. Acknowledge events to be sponsored by specific groups in the community, or let students tell about those they may have attended.

Including Books in Other Languages

As you plan social studies activities, be sure to bring in books in other languages so that those who speak a language other than English can share their abilities with classmates. You might, for example, include a short biography of César Chávez that is written in Spanish along with those written in English. For example, see the attractive picture book *Cosechando esperanza: La Historia de César Chávez* by Kathleen Krull and illustrated by Yuyi Morales (Libros Viajeros/Harcourt, 2003). Those who speak Spanish can tell the rest of the class the story of César Chávez, an American hero. They may also teach their classmates a few Spanish words and expressions, pointing out that many Spanish words look much like the same words in English, for instance: familia, grupo, fiesta, preparaban, rancho, and limonada, (All of these words appear on the first page of this biography.)

Pat Mora has written a folktale in Spanish titled *Doña Flor: Un Cuento de Una Mujer Gigante con un Gran Corazón*, illustrated by Raúl Colón (Knopf, 2005). Ask Spanish-speaking students to translate this tale as they show their classmates the wonderful illustrations.

Some books include both English and another language. An attractive example is *My Name Is Gabito/Me llamo Gabito: The Life of Gabriel García Márquez* by Monica Brown (Luna Rising, 2007). Gabriel is a real person, a respected writer who wrote a memoir called *Living to Tell the Tale* (Knopf, 2003). High school students can compare the memoir by García Márquez to the interpretation by Brown written for younger readers. Note that this picture book was illustrated by Raúl Colón, the same talented artist who illustrated Mora's book described above.

A charming story presented in both Spanish and English is *The Storyteller's Candle*, by Lucía González and illustrated by Lulu Delacre (Children's Book Press, 2008).

Children who arrive from tropical Puerto Rico find New York City a cold, uninviting place. Then, they meet storyteller/librarian Pura Belpré, New York's first Latina librarian, who introduces them to the city's huge library, where all are welcome.

Ask your librarian to help you find other books written in English and another language, for example, Vietnamese, Russian, or Chinese. Bringing in such books shows students that you accept and respect their native language. Although they need to learn English, it is important that they know that their native language is okay, too.

African Americans: Flight to Freedom and the Civil Rights Movement

There are many fine books about the efforts of slaves to flee from oppressive conditions in the South, slaves who crossed the Ohio River to gain freedom. Stories of the Underground Railroad, which aided many, feature heroes and heroines such as Harriet Tubman, who repeatedly guided men, women, and children to safety in Ohio and even into Canada. Bring in some of the picture books about this period. Here are two books for older students:

> Karolyn S. Frost. *I've Got a Home in Glory Land: A Lost Tale of the Underground.* Farrar, 2008. A couple who escaped to the North is captured and threatened with being returned to Kentucky. They are helped to get into Canada. A landmark case determines that they have done no harm and cannot, therefore, be extradited. Thus, Canada becomes a safe refuge for escaped slaves. (See the Thinking + Lesson Plan on *Elijah of Buxton* on page 146).

> Beverly Lowry. *Harriet Tubman: Imagining a Life.* Anchor, 2008. Based on careful research plus imagination, Lowry presents the story of Harriet Tubman's life.

A Thinking + Lesson Plan: Former Slaves Living Free in Canada

Follow the directions for reading *Elijah of Buxton* aloud to your class. This prize-winning book is about a young boy who was the first Black person born free in Buxton, Canada.

Fighting for Civil Rights into the Twentieth Century

African Americans and many empathetic White Americans fought together to achieve equal rights for those with dark skins. Children in the twenty-first century need to hear the stories from the nineteen-fifties and sixties—the work of the KKK, the resistance of many White Americans, often the students themselves, to integrating public schools, the insistence on separate drinking fountains, the seating of Blacks in the back of the bus, the refusal to serve African Americans in restaurants, and so on. Today, we may find these stories of bigotry and racial prejudice incredible. But are these issues entirely gone today?

Have students read both fiction and nonfiction about activities that occurred, especially in southern states. Following is a sampling of books to look for:

> Ann Bausum. *Freedom Riders: John Lewis and Jim Zwerg on the Front Lines of the Civil Rights Movement.* National Geographic, 2006. Forewords by both Lewis and Zwerg, two young men, one White, the other Black, who rode to Montgomery, Alabama, to help obtain equal rights for Black Americans.

> Tonya Bolden. *Tell All the Children Our Story: Memories and Mementos of Being Young and Black in America.* Abrams, 2001. Information about what it has been like

A THINKING + LESSON PLAN

—◄o►—

Former Slaves Living Free in Canada

Grades 6–10

Expected outcomes

Learners will:

1. Listen to the teacher read *Elijah of Buxton* by Christopher Paul Curtis aloud.
2. Respond in a log after hearing each chapter and write a poem based on entries.
3. Participate in a poetry reading.

Teaching/Learning Strategies

Resources Needed

Obtain a copy of the historical novel *Elijah of Buxton* by Christoper Curtis (Scholastic, 2007). If extra copies can be found, bring them to the classroom also.

Directions

Step 1: Tell students something about the history of Buxton, a small town founded in Canada for American slaves who made their way to freedom in Canada (a history is included at the end of the book). Read the first chapter.

Step 2: Have students make logs (see Chapter 8) in which to record their responses following the reading of each chapter.

Step 3: About once each week, have students share their logs with others in their Cooperative Learning Groups.

Step 4: After hearing the whole book, students can write poems about things they noted in their logs.

Step 5: Plan a poetry reading as each student shares one of his or her best poems.

Performance Assessment

1. Completion of daily entries in response to each chapter—Credit/No Credit
2. Participation in a poetry reading—Credit/No Credit
3. Students will nominate specific poems as Best in the Class; they will vote to determine the top three, which will receive an A+ grade.

for African American children living in America, where everyone is supposed to be equal according to the Preamble of our Declaration of Independence. This book is divided into three sections: "Out of Africa," "Longing for the Jubilee," and "Lift Every Voice and Sing"—a fascinating collection of pictures and historical facts.

Tonya Bolden. *M.L.K.: Journey of a King.* Photography by Bob Adelman. Abrams, 2007. A handsome biography of Martin Luther King, Jr. with numerous photos that portray his life, including a nicely presented chronology beginning with his birth in Atlanta in 1929 and ending with the passage of the bill designating the third Monday in January as "Martin Luther King Jr. National Holiday," beginning in 1986.

John Fleischman. *Black and White Airmen: Their True History.* Houghton Mifflin, 2007. A fascinating story of two airmen, one White, one Black, who fought in World War II. John Leahr, a Black man, and Herb Heilbrun, a White man, were classmates in the third grade in Cincinnati, Ohio. As adults, both flew for the Air Force, but Black and White crews were segregated, so the two flyers did not meet until the war was over and they returned to Cincinnati. The Tuskegee Airmen, a group which John Learh helped to found, were being honored. The so-called *Red Tails* had escorted the big bombers into Germany. Herb realized that John might actually have escorted him as he flew through Europe. He and John met and compared notes about their lives. They became friends, visiting each other's families and exchanging war stories, some of which are recorded by this author.

Russell Freedman. *Freedom Walkers: The Story of the Montgomery Bus Boycott.* Holiday, 2006. En masse, the Black population in Montgomery agreed not to ride the city buses, protesting the rule that they could ride only in the back of the bus. As the protest wore on, one elderly man said, "My feet is tired, but my soul is rested." Martin Luther King, Jr. stepped forward as a leader at this time, addressing a packed church:

> There comes a time when people get tired. We are here this evening to say to those who have mistreated us so long that we are tired—tired of being segregated and humiliated; tired of being kicked about by the brutal feet of oppression.

Toni Morrison. *Remember: The Journey to School Integration.* Houghton Mifflin, 2004. A wonderful collection of archival photographs. Morrison imagines what the persons pictured might be saying or thinking; includes "Chronology of the Civil Rights Movement."

Walter Dean Myers and Bill Miles. *The Harlem Hellfighters: When Pride Met Courage.* HarperCollins, 2006. The story of African American men who fought in World War I at a time when bigotry and racism were at their height.

Faith Ringgold. *If a Bus Could Talk: The Story of Rosa Parks.* Simon & Schuster, 1999. An attractive picture book by the talented artist who also wrote and illustrated *Tar Beach.*

Providing Equity

An important responsibility of each teacher is to provide equity for every student in a classroom. We want to ensure that each student has a sense of belonging and the opportunity to achieve to the best of his or her ability. The following learning activities give everyone a chance to become involved.

Bringing Picture Books into the Classroom

Picture books are not just for the primary grades alone. They offer a wealth of information plus wonderful illustrations that provide an engaging resource for students in the middle school and high school, too. Explore both fiction and nonfiction in the picture book section as you plan social science studies. A lovely introduction to the culture of India is presented, for example, in *Mama's Saris* by Pooja Makhijani (Little, Brown, 2007). Illustrator Elena Gomez shows the reader the beautiful cloth which adult women in India wear, so students can readily see why the daughter envies her mother and can't wait until she is big enough to wear a sari, too. Invite a parent to show students how the sari is wrapped to fit a woman's body.

Peter Sis is an author/illustrator of picture books who presents a variety of topics that will be of interest to older students. He tells the story of his own childhood in *The Wall: Growing Up Behind the Iron Curtain* (Farrar, 2007). As he tells us, "I was born at the beginning of it all, on the red side—the communist side—of the iron curtain." He grew up in Russian-occupied Czechoslovakia where he was told what he could draw and what he could think. Eventually, however, the Iron Curtain fell, and he was free! Other titles by this outstanding author/illustrator include:

> *Starry Messenger: Galileo Galilei*
> *Tibet through the Red Box*
> *Madlenka*
> *The Tree of Life: Charles Darwin*

Henry's Freedom Box: A True Story from the Underground Railroad by Ellen Levine and illustrated by Kadir Nelson (Scholastic, 2007) is an amazing story of a slave who mailed himself to Philadelphia and to freedom. Beautifully illustrated, this book presents a true story of how slaves were treated and how some humane Americans helped them escape. Both author and illustrator have produced other award-winning books on topics related to social justice.

The following two books may also be of interest:

Lori Haskins. *Sled Dogs*. Illustrated with photographs. Bearport Publishing, 2006. The Alaskan huskies are both workers and racers. The author tells of a team's trek to Nome, Alaska, carrying medicine in time of need. She also relates tales about winners of the famous Iditarod as well as other dog races. Her photographs present real events that take place, mostly, in our forty-ninth state. Such books may intrigue reluctant readers, particularly boys.

Susanna Pitzer. *Not Afraid of Dogs*. Illustrated by Larry Day. Walker Books, 2006. Many students can identify with Daniel's fear of dogs. In this engaging story, a puppy, Bandit, helps the boy overcome his fears. Students can talk and write about their fears and, perhaps, how they overcame a particular fear.

Developing a Thematic Study: Native Americans, Yesterday and Today

Thematic studies in which an entire class participates offer opportunities for students of varied abilities to become involved. A study titled "Native Americans Yesterday and Today" is particularly appropriate for a social studies/language arts focus. Search the Internet and your local libraries for information and books, both nonfiction and fiction, for example:

Alvin M. Josephy Jr. *Lewis and Clark through Indian Eyes*. Knopf, 2006. In this book we hear the voices of Native Americans and their impressions of the Lewis and Clark expedition. Some of the essays included are based on family stories while some come from the history of the tribes or through the lens of an individual interpretation.

Thelma H. Wyss. *Bear Dancer: The Story of a Ute Girl.* Simon & Schuster, 2006. Based on a true story, the author describes the life of Elk Girl, who loved to ride her sure-footed pony in the Rocky Mountains. One day, however, she is captured by Cheyenne warriors who take her to the Great Plains, which introduces her to a second tribal culture. Then she meets the White men, who aim to kill all the Indians they can. With the help of friends she makes, Elk Girl returns home only to find her tribe decimated, dependent on the White man's largesse.

A Thinking + Lesson Plan: The Trail of Tears

Reading the journal as suggested in the Lesson Plan on p. 150 will introduce your students to the plight of the Cheyennes, a large Native American tribe that had settled, more or less peacefully, in Georgia and South Carolina. The U.S. government arbitrarily decided to remove them from their lands and to force them onto less desirable sites far away in Oklahoma. This journal records the removal journey, a sad event, now referred to rightfully as "The Trail of Tears."

Planning Your Study.   Too often Native Americans have been seen only through the distorting stereotyped images of the romantic nature-lover, the exotic savage, or the source of spiritual wisdom. And now, after many years of hiding it in shame, having some Indian heritage is suddenly something about which to boast. But neither extreme, from the highly romanticized historical picture of chiefs and princesses to the modern Indian of declining culture and casinos, is an accurate depiction of the complexity of the position of Native Americans in the history of this country. Native Americans, although nearly exterminated by the European invaders, are still practicing a living culture as they adapt to a changing world.

Before beginning a study of Native Americans in the United States, use some means of assessing student information and attitudes. This will provide an interesting and instructive comparison at the end of the study. Try some of these ideas:

- Have each student draw a picture of a Native American engaged in some activity.
- Ask students to complete this sentence at least three times: A Native American . . .
- Ask students to list as many Native American tribes as they can.

Put these sheets away until the study is completed. After the study, you might have the students repeat the same activities. Then compare the results.

Native American Tribes.   Many people are confused about the best way to refer to *American Indians* or *Native Americans*. The best solution is to specify the tribe you are referring to, instead of using the aggregate label for an extremely diverse group of people.

Draw a large outline map of the United States on which to locate the various groups of Indian tribes. They can be grouped as follows according to similar modes of living:

- *Eastern Woodland Area:* Algonquin, Delaware, Iroquois, Massachuset, Mohawk, Mohegan, Narraganset, Onandaga, Penobscot, Powhatan, Tuscarora, Passamaquoddy, Pawtuket, Tippecanoe, Wampanoag, Wyandot.

A THINKING + LESSON PLAN

The Trail of Tears

Grades 5–10

Expected outcomes

Learners will:

1. Read a fictionalized journal written by a Cheyenne boy during the Trail of Tears.
2. Respond in writing in a log following each entry read aloud.
3. Participate in a class presentation about what they learned.

Teaching/Learning Strategies

Resources Needed

Obtain a copy of *The Journal of Jessie Smoke: A Cherokee Boy* by Joseph Bruchac (Scholastic, 2001). See if other libraries have the book, too, so the class can have access to several copies of the journal.

Directions:

Step 1:   Introduce students to this book by reading the first chapter aloud to the class. Explain that the book is historical fiction, based on real events, namely, the removal of the Cheyenne Indians from their homeland in Georgia and the Carolinas to Oklahoma, a journey referred to as "The Trail of Tears." Note that the author of this book is Native American; students might look for other books by this respected writer.

Step 2:   Have students make a log (see Chapter 8) in which they will write entries each day. The first entry can include the title and author of the book and a short description based on what you have told them.

Step 3:   Assign able readers specific journal entries to read, one each day. (Be sure less able readers have other ways to participate—art, displays, etc.) Readers can rehearse their readings ahead of time so as to read fluently.

Step 4:   Mount a long piece of brown wrapping paper at the back of the room. Have a team of students develop a map of the journey described (a map is included in Bruchac's book).

Performance Assessment

1. Prepare a presentation for another class to share what students have learned about the Cheyennes and how the White men treated them. Grade as + or – based on participation.
2. Examine each student's log after the study is completed. Enter grades of + or – according to the student's inclusion of appropriate entries each day.

- *Great Lakes Woodland Area:* Chippewa/Ojibwa, Huron, Illinois, Kickapoo, Miami, Oneida, Ottawa, Potawatomi, Sac and Fox, Seneca, Shawnee, Winnebago.
- *Southeastern Area:* Catawba, Cherokee, Creek, Lumbi, Natchez, Seminole, Yuchi.
- *North Central Plains Area:* Arapaho, Arikara, Assiniboine, Blackfoot, Cheyenne, Cree, Crow, Gros Ventre, Mandan, Pawnee, Shoshone, Sioux/Dakota.
- *South Central Plains Area:* Caddo, Chickasaw, Choctaw, Comanche, Iowa, Kaw/Kansa, Kiowa, Omaha, Osage, Ponca, Quapaw.
- *Southwest Area:* Apache, Hopi, Maricopa, Navaho, Papago, Pima, Pueblo, Zuñi.
- *California Area:* Chumash, Hoopa, Maidu, Mission, Modoc, Mohave, Mono, Pit River, Pomo, Tule River, Wailaki, Yahi, Yokuts, Yuma, Yurok.
- *Northwestern Plateau Area:* Bannock, Cayuse, Coeur D'Alene, Colville, Flathead, Kalispel, Klamath, Kootenai, Nez Percé, Nisqually, Paiute, Puyallup, Spokane, Ute, Walla-Walla, Wasco, Washoe, Yakima.
- *Northwest Pacific Coast Area:* Aleut, Eskimo (Inuit), Haida, Lummi, Makah, Muckleshoot, Nootka, Quinault, Salish, Shoalwater, Snohomish, Suquamish, Tlingit.

An excellent resource for information about Indian tribes with maps is Carl Waldman's *Atlas of the North American Indian,* rev. ed. (Facts On File, 2000).

Native Americans in the United States.   There are more than 500 Indian tribes recognized in the United States, with most of them living on reservations in western states (see Table 5.1). Although a small percentage of the total U.S. population (0.6 percent), Indians continue efforts to maintain a living culture.

Native groups in Canada include Indians, Inuit, and Métis (people of mixed heritage). Tribes in Mexico include the Maya, Nahuatl, Huichol, Purepecha, Tarahumara, Mazateco, Zapoteco, Nahua, Cora, Tzeltal, Otomi, and Mixteco. Students can investigate historical and contemporary Native groups in Latin America.

English Words from Native American Languages.   Words borrowed into English show how much the first settlers owed the Native Americans they encountered. Although the inhabitants spoke hundreds of distinct and fully developed languages, most of these words come from the Algonquin family of languages, spoken along the East Coast. Can students guess the English equivalent? Older students can develop a chart to show the relationship.

chitmunk	(chipmunk)	pawcohiccora	(hickory)
aroughcoun	(raccoon)	paccan	(pecan)
squnk	(skunk)	pasimenan	(persimmon)
ochek	(woodchuck)	msickquatash	(succotash)
musquash	(muskrat)	askootasquash	(squash)
moos	(moose)	tamahak	(tomahawk)
aposoun	(opossum)	mohkussin	(moccasin)

National Museum of the American Indian.   In September 2004, the *Smithsonian's* cover displayed a handsome picture of the "new center for the hemisphere's first people," a curving limestone building with the Capitol visible in the background. The National

TABLE 5.1 Native American Population (1990)

Tribe	Population	Percent
Cherokee	369,035	19.0
Navaho	225,298	11.6
Sioux	107,321	5.5
Chippewa	105,988	5.5
Choctaw	86,231	4.5
Pueblo	55,330	2.9
Apache	53,330	2.8
Iroquois	52,557	2.7
Lumbee	50,888	2.6
Creek	45,872	2.4
Blackfoot	37,992	2.0
Canadian/Latin American	27,179	1.4
Chickasaw	21,522	1.1
Tohono O'odham	16,876	.9
Potowatomi	16,719	.9
Seminole	15,564	.8
Pima	15,074	.8
Tlingit	14,417	.7
Alaskan Athabascans	14,198	.7
Cheyenne	11,809	.6
Comanche	11,436	.6
Paiute	11,369	.6
Osage	10,430	.5
Puget Sound Salish	10,384	.5
Yaqui	9,838	.5
All	1,937,391	100.00

For more information about the federal/Indian reservations and trust areas, look at (www.doc.gov/edu/html/indianres. htm).

Museum of the American Indian (NMAI) houses some 800,000 artifacts and 125,000 historical photographs selected to bear the message "We are still here." The art featured ranges from traditional beadwork to paintings by such modern artists as Rick Bartow, a Vietnam veteran and Yurok Indian from Oregon.

This beautiful museum in a prominent position on the Mall in Washington, DC, should help us all recognize the contributions of the many tribes who have lived in the Americas over the centuries, as well as help us see them more clearly as they exist today.

As Ron His Horse In Thunder, president of Sitting Bull College on the Standing Rock Reservation in North Dakota, states:

> Americans tend to clump us all together, not realizing there are vast differences between Indians of various geographic regions, as well as between Indian Tribes with those regions. Too often history books portray us as either savages that stood in the way of progress or as naturalists in tune with nature. But what they don't show is that we made contributions to the United States. They don't tell about how over 50 percent of the world's current food supply comes from plants that Native Americans cultivated. Rarely do they ever show that Native Americans practiced horticulture and we used science to do that. Another contribution is medicine. A good many current medicines in this world came from plants that Native Americans knew about and knew how to use to take care of certain ailments. And they shared that knowledge with the non-Indian world.

Gifts from the Native Americans.   Students will be interested in learning of the many things we gained from the Native Americans. They knew the best trails and ways of traveling across the country by canoe and by snowshoe. They invented hammocks. The Native Americans were the first, too, to grow and use tobacco and rubber. They introduced White settlers to the following foods that we use today:

corn	tomatoes	cranberries	maple sugar
potatoes	vanilla	chicle (for chewing gum)	artichokes
chilies	avocados	beans	hominy
pineapples	peanuts	chocolate	popcorn

Have several students prepare an illustrated chart of these foods. You may experiment with hominy or dishes that are easy to make in the classroom.

Of course, Native American contributions were not limited to food supplies. The following books suggest areas that advanced students can explore:

Jack Weatherford. *Indian Givers: How the Indians of the Americas Transformed the World.* Fawcett, 1989.

Jack Weatherford. *Native Roots: How the Indians Enriched America.* Fawcett, 1991.

Native American Place Names.   Many state names, such as Massachusetts, originated in Native American languages. Names of many rivers, such as the Ohio and Mississippi, and cities, such as Pontiac, Michigan, and Chicago, Illinois, also originated from Native American languages.

Look for evidence of specific tribes. For example, there are many Abenaki place names in Maine, Vermont, and New Hampshire.

Androscoggin	place where fish are cured
Connecticut	the long river
Katahdin	the principal mountain
Kennebec	long water without rapids
Merrimack	at the deep place
Nashua	between streams

For more information on where names come from, see *Indian Place Names of New England* by John C. Huden.

Prepare a map on which to locate Native American names. Include a chart to explain what the names mean and where they come from.

The "New World" in 1492.   What did the world of the Native Americans look like when the European explorers arrived, beginning with Columbus in 1492? Students may be surprised to learn that there were no horses (dogs and turkeys were the only domestic animals). But there were a number of complex cultures, based in different regions, and trading with others. We tend to think only of the great Aztec and Inca civilizations, but there may have been about 20 million Indians in North America around 1492. In the century following, the Indian population dropped by as much as 95 percent.

Dennis Fradin's historical biography *Hiawatha: Messenger of Peace* provides much background information about the Iroquois. Although Hiawatha lived 500 years ago, he made significant contributions to American history. As a leader in his tribe, he helped set up the Iroquois Confederacy, the most politically complex group in 1492. Iroquois customs and beliefs eventually influenced the development of the U.S. Constitution. Also see volumes on the Iroquois and the Mohawk in the Chelsea House series *Indians of North America* for historical data.

For more information on life in 1492, see the following:

Jean Fritz, Jamake Highwater, Margaret Mahy, Patricia and Fredrick McKissack, and Katherine Paterson. *The World in 1492*. Holt, 1992. Provides a detailed description of each part of the world—Africa, Asia, Europe, Australia, the Americas—and how the people there lived at that time.

What Happened to the Native Americans after 1492?   After setting the stage with a picture of the Native Americans before the European conquest, continue the story and explore how the Native Americans were affected by it. Several books deal with specific tribes in specific regions.

Eva Costabel. *The Early People of Florida*. Atheneum, 1993. Presents the history of tribal groups such as Calusa and Tequesta present in 1492. First the Spanish and the French fought over their lands, then the British came.

Louise Erdrich. *The Birchbark House*. Hyperion, 1999. Life of an Ojibwa girl on an island in Lake Superior in 1847.

Paul Goble. *Death of the Iron Horse*. Aladdin, 1993. This picture book tells the true story of the Cheyenne's struggle to preserve their way of life after soldiers and settlers invade their territory with the steam locomotive.

Beatrice O. Harrell. *Longwalker's Journey: A Novel of the Choctaw Trail of Tears*. Dial, 1999. Story based on author's family, how a boy survived a tragic journey.

Kathleen Kudlenski. *Night Bird: A Story of the Seminole Indians*. Illustrated by James Watling. Viking, 1993. An eleven-year-old Seminole girl must leave Florida Everglades in 1840 to move to Oklahoma.

S. D. Lang. *Gift Horse: A Lakota Story*. Abrams, 1999. A boy's rite of passage into manhood.

How Native Americans Live Today. Balance historical information with contemporary accounts that show real people living in today's world. Bring your historical account of Native American life up to the present. Students may be surprised to realize there are modern Native American children like themselves, not just characters out of history. Young Native Americans face many of the same issues concerning growing up that all children face. In addition, they may struggle to learn more about their heritage and the history of their people. They may wonder why people are prejudiced against them or their people. And they face the question of how to maintain their culture in a hostile world. Look for a variety of children's books to show students what it feels like to be a Native American today.

George Ancona. *Powwow.* Photographs by the author. Harcourt Brace, 1993. The Montana Crow Fair is the largest powwow in the country.

Joseph Bruchac. *Eagle Song.* Dial, 1997. Fourth-grade Mohawk boy is teased for being Indian; his father tells class the real story of Hiawatha, the Iroquois leader who sought peace.

Normee Ekoomiak. *Arctic Memories.* Holt, 1990. A picture book of an Inuit childhood in Quebec illustrates a way of life that is almost extinct. Text in Inuktitut and English.

Susan Hazen-Hammond. *Thunder Bear and Ko: The Buffalo Nation and Nambe Pueblo.* Dutton, 1999. Trying to preserve traditions in New Mexico.

Diane Hoyt-Goldsmith. *Lacrosse: The National Game of the Iroquois.* Photographs by L. Migdale. Holiday, 1998. A fine photo-essay.

Sandra King. *Shannon: An Ojibway Dancer.* Photographs by Catherine Whipple. Lerner, 1993. A thirteen-year-old girl's life combines tradition and modern customs as she prepares to dance in a powwow in Minnesota. From *We Are Still Here* series.

David Morrison and George-Hebert Germain. *The Inuit: Glimpses of an Arctic Past.* University of Washington Press, 1996. A young girl tells the history of the Copper Inuit culture.

Laurie O'Neill. *The Shawnees: People of the Eastern Woodlands.* Millbrook Press, 1995. From *Native Americans* series: see also *The Inuit: People of the Arctic.*

Gordon Regguinti. *The Sacred Harvest: Ojibway Wild Rice Gathering.* Lerner, 1992. Color photographs; informative text about processing the rice.

Cynthia L. Smith. *Jingle Dancer.* Illustrated by Cornelius Van Wright and Ying Hwa-Hu. Morrow, 2000. Describes the traditional dance of the Muscogee (Creek) Nation.

Virginia Driving Hawk Sneve. *The Hopis: A First Americans Book.* Holiday, 1995. Abundant pictures of traditional Hopi life.

Frank J. Staub. *Children of the Tlingit.* Carolrhoda, 1999. Many photos of different children from this Pacific Northwest Indian culture.

Rina Swentzell. *Children of Clay: A Family of Pueblo Potters.* Lerner, 1992. Story of a Tewa family in New Mexico.

Linda Yamane. *Weaving a California Tradition.* Illustrated by Dugan Aguilar. Lerner, 1997. Follows eleven-year-old Western Mono girl's life; shows full process of weaving a basket.

Native American Leaders.   Not all Native Americans are chiefs or princesses. Combat such stereotyped ideas of Indians with examples of real individuals as they struggle with questions of identity.

> Joseph Bruchac. *Sacajawea: The Story of Bird Woman and the Lewis and Clark Expedition.* Harcourt, 2000. Skillful writing techniques; alternating first-person narrative by Sacajawea and William Clark.
>
> Nancy Lobb. *Extraordinary Native Americans.* J. Weston Walch, 1997. Sixteen brief biographies.
>
> Morgan Monceaux and Ruth Katcher. *My Heroes, My People.* Farrar, 1999. Brief biographies and thirty-seven striking portraits of Native Americans and African Americans important in settlement of the West; includes the well-known figures as well as lesser known.

Native American Stories and Folktales.   Folklore from the various Native American tribes is an excellent source for learning more about culture and for storytelling activities. Older students can learn one of these tales to present to students in the primary grades. All of these stories adapt well to other modes of oral presentation, such as Readers' Theater. In addition, when you read one of the teaching stories to the class, students can respond to the moral by drawing a picture and discussing what it means to them.

When selecting folktales for use with students, consider carefully the image presented of the people in the group. Many authors have written versions of Native American tales without respect for their authentic cultural background. Contrast these with books by writers such as Paul Goble and Gerald McDermott, who are scrupulous in citing the sources of their stories and in presenting appropriate cultural context in their illustrations. Also look for books by Native American authors, which have become more available as individuals and tribal organizations promote culturally sensitive materials. For example, a booklist of recommended works is available from Oyate, 2702 Mathews Street, Berkeley, CA 94702.

> Shonto Begay. *Ma'ii and Cousin Horned Toad.* Scholastic, 1992. This Navaho teaching tale includes text in Navaho. Coyote is hungry but is too lazy to get his own food.
>
> John Bierhorst. *The People with 5 Fingers: A Native California Creation Tale.* Illustrated by Robert Parker. Marshall Cavendish, 2000. Told in the days when each valley was home to a different Indian nation.
>
> Joseph Bruchac. *Between Earth and Sky: Legends of Native American Sacred Places.* Illustrated by Thomas Locker. Harcourt, 1996. Describes the seven sacred directions that represent the unity of life and our oneness with the natural world, seen and unseen.
>
> Edward Field. *Magic Words.* Illustrated by Stefano Vitale. Harcourt, 1998. Inuit tale from Greenland.
>
> Mary-Joan Gerson. *People of Corn: A Mayan Story.* Illustrated by Carla Golembe. Little, 1995. A creation story.
>
> Paul Goble. *Iktomi Loses His Eyes: A Plains Indian Story.* Orchard, 1999. One of many trickster tales about Iktomi.

C. Shana Greger, retold. *The Fifth and Final Sun.* Houghton, 1994. An Aztec story tells of the origin of the sun.

Leanne Hinton, trans. *Ishi's Tale of Lizard.* Farrar Straus Giroux, 1992. Recent translation of a Yahi tale. Ishi, the sole survivor of the Yahi people, emerged from hiding in 1911.

Gerald McDermott. *Raven: A Trickster Tale from the Pacific Northwest.* Harcourt Brace Jovanovich, 1993. How the raven steals the sun from the Sky Chief so that the people can have light.

Howard Norman. *The Girl Who Dreamed Only Geese and Other Tales of the Far North. . . .* Illustrated by Leo and Diane Dillon. Harcourt, 1997. The best of the oral tradition, taken directly from Inuit storytellers.

Clifford Trafzer, ed. *Blue Down, Red Earth.* Archer, 1996. New Native American storytellers.

Nancy Wood. *Sacred Fire.* Illustrated by Frank Howell. Doubleday, 1998. Pueblo chronicle.

When studying Native American folklore with students, encourage them to look for patterns. Can they find several examples of a "trickster" tale? Compare some Coyote tales with tales in other cultures, such as Anansi stories in African traditions. Are there several versions of one tale? How do the versions differ? In folklore, stories are transmitted orally, so several different written versions may all be authentic. What values do these stories teach?

Making Navajo Fry Bread.   Create a learning center at which children can take turns making a semi-authentic version of fry bread (see Figure 5.1). (The recipe follows on page 158. Teacher supervision is necessary for this activity.)

FIGURE 5.1   Fry Bread Learning Center

Directions

Fill the electric skillet half full of oil. Turn on high to heat.

Measure into bowl:

4 c. flour	1 tsp. salt
3 tsp. baking powder	1½ c. water

Gradually add the water as you stir.

Knead the dough until it does not stick to your hands. Add a little more flour as needed. Divide the dough into small balls. Then flatten them until thin and make a hole in the center like a doughnut. Slide into hot oil. Fry on each side until light brown. Remove and drain on layer of paper towels. Eat while warm.

Games and Sports Originating with the Native Americans. A number of books contain information about Indian children's games, for example:

Gail Farber and Michelle Lasagna. *Whispers from the First Californians: A Story of California's First People.* Magpie Publications, 1994.

Joy Miller. *American Indian Games.* Children's Press, 1996.

Luther Standing Bear. *My Indian Boyhood.* University of Nebraska Press, 1959.

Many of the sports we know today originated in games the Native Americans first played. They played shinny, a game with a puck, similar to ice hockey. Native American children played such games as hide and seek, follow-the-leader, crack-the-whip, prisoner's base, and blindman's bluff. They also had games not unlike hopscotch, marbles, and jack straws.

For more information about Native American sports and how to play them, look for *Sports & Games the Indians Gave Us* by Alex Whitney. This author shows children how to make equipment for use in the games described. Stick dice are easy to make, for example. Use a stick about one-half inch wide and four inches long. With a knife, round off the ends of the stick. Paint one side red and paint a multicolor design on the other side. With the red side counting as one point and the design as two, see who can get twenty points first (see Figure 5.2).

FIGURE 5.2   Stick Dice

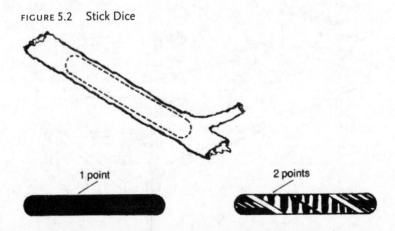

1 point

2 points

Native American Poetry. Share Native American poems with the children in your room. Display the following poem so that students can read and discuss it together.

MAY I WALK

On the trail marked with pollen may I walk,
With grasshoppers about my feet may I walk,
With dew about my feet may I walk,
With beauty may I walk,
With beauty before me, may I walk,
With beauty behind me, may I walk,
With beauty above me, may I walk,
With beauty under me, may I walk,
With beauty all around me, may I walk,
In old age wandering on a trail of beauty, lively, may I walk,
In old age wandering on a trail of beauty, living again, may I walk,
It is finished in beauty.

—Navajo

Reading poetry written by people from another culture is an excellent way of learning about shared values and cultural differences. Feature examples from the following excellent collections.

Shonto Begay. *Navajo: Visions and Voices across the Mesa.* Scholastic, 1995. Art and poetry illustrate the struggle for balance and harmony in contemporary Native life.

Lee Francis. *When the Rain Sings: Poems by Young Native Americans.* Photographs from the Smithsonian's National Museum of the American Indian. Simon & Schuster, 1999.

Hettie Jones. *The Trees Stand Shining: Poetry of the North American Indians.* Illustrated by Robert Andrew Parker. Dial, 1993. These oral tradition poems are really folk chants and songs, preserved for generations and only written down and translated in the nineteenth century. Each is short, identified by tribe, and grouped by similar topic.

Neil Philip, ed. *Songs Are Thoughts: Poems of the Inuit.* Illustrated by Maryclare Foa. Orchard, 1995. Originally collected by Danish ethnologists in the 1920s, these poems are meant to be sung. Includes information on cultural context.

After reading some of these examples, students can choose to write poems based on similar themes of nature or identity. Students can also write poems as a response to the unit on Native Americans to show their reactions to what they have learned.

A Mural of Native American Life. After students have gained information through reading and discussing topics related to Native American life, have them plan a large mural to which each one can contribute. The space of the mural might be considered similar to the map of the United States. Roughly, then, space could be allocated to activities associated with the Plains Indians, those of the Southwest, the Pacific Northwest, and so on. Sketch this plan on the board.

Bring in books with pictures that suggest scenes to be included. Crayons can be used for the figures, and the background can be painted in with pale brown or light green, as appropriate. When the mural is completed, display it in the school hall or a room where all can see it.

A Culminating All-School Assembly. Plan a school assembly to share the results of your study. Let students discuss various ways they can present an informative and entertaining program. Consider some of the following activities:

- An introduction (the purpose of your study and some of the things you learned).
- Presentation of the mural with an explanation of the many Native American tribes in what is now the United States.
- Readers' Theater presentation of folklore from the tribe native to your area, which might include music.
- Demonstration of Native American sports, dances, and so on.
- Creative dramatization of a Native American story.
- An invitation to visit your room to see the things you have made.

❖ Integrating Social Studies into Other Curriculum Areas

Remembering that the most effective teaching allows for the individual differences that appear in every classroom, we include teaching/learning activities here that are inclusive and that provide for the differentiated instruction necessary in teaching a diverse group of students. You might want to review the strategies described in some detail in Chapter 3 as you plan for teaching the social studies.

Social Studies and the Language Arts

Social studies and the language arts are easily connected through listening, speaking, reading, and writing. Literature, both fiction and nonfiction, provides a greater depth of understanding that goes beyond a social studies textbook's presentation of events that occurred in the past. Biography, for example, gives students insight into the efforts of men and women who have played leading roles in developing important domestic legislation and foreign policy. Writing and speaking provide opportunities for students to express their thinking about the pros and cons involved, for instance, with current affairs, with history in the making. For these reasons, particularly in the middle school, social studies and language arts are often taught as a core course that is allocated a double slot of time. Following are suggestions for integrating social studies and the language arts at all levels.

Posting Provocative Quotations

Begin now to collect appropriate quotations related to the social studies that you can use in your classroom. Here are a few to begin your collection:

> *History,* despite its wrenching pain, cannot be unlived, but if faced with courage, need not be lived again.
>
> —Maya Angelou

All history becomes subjective; in other words, there is properly no history, only biography.

—Ralph Waldo Emerson

One faces the future with one's past.

—Pearl S. Buck

History is a guide to navigation in perilous times. History is who we are and why we are the way we are.

—David C. McCullough

What can you do with such quotations? Invite students to create posters by reprinting a quotation in attractive calligraphy. Post a quotation each Monday morning to which students respond in their history logs for the first five to ten minutes of class. Follow up with a short discussion as they share their reactions to the Quote of the Week. Encourage students to contribute interesting quotations that they may discover.

Learning to Participate in Discussions

Students need to learn how to participate in a group discussion, a conversation. Talk about active listening, taking turns, respecting the views of others, and being informed about the topic under discussion. Knowing how to participate in a discussion is not as easy as it sounds. Talk about what it takes to be successful. Then, for example, tell students on Monday that they will be discussing a specific topic on Thursday, such as:

- Problems faced in African countries today.
- A book the class has just finished reading, for instance, *Elijah of Buxton* by Christopher Paul Curtis (Scholastic, 2007).
- The solution to a school problem, perhaps fighting on the campus.

Students have time, thus, to prepare for the discussion. They can develop an entry in their class logs listing questions they have or would like to discuss about the assigned topic or listing things they might share with others during the discussion—facts, a personal experience, and so forth.

Linking Literature and Social Studies

Plan to read a book aloud to the class that relates to a themed study you expect to develop. For example, read *Roll of Thunder, Hear My Cry* to a class of fourth graders or *To Kill a Mockingbird* in ninth-grade English to set the stage for a study of segregation and its effect on the schooling of children in the United States. Or, provide a short reading list from which high school students can choose a book to read that amplifies the understanding of a literature selection that all will read. For example, if the class reads *The Known World* by Edward P. Jones, list such related books as *Beloved, The Narrative of Frederick Douglass, The Souls of Black Folks,* and *Kindred.*

Reading Biographies

Bring in an assortment of biographies of interesting people to stimulate students to read about people who interest them, for example, sports figures. To provide differentiated instruction, include several outstanding illustrated books that may lure reluctant readers into reading. Look for some of the following:

Ellie Crowe. *Surfer of the Century: The Life of Duke Kahanamoku.* Illustrated by Richard Waldrep. Lee & Low, 2007. Beginning with the traditional cry, "Surf's up!" this picture book narrates the life of a great Hawaiʻian surfer who broke swimming records in the Olympics of 1912. Duke's creed begins: "In Hawaiʻi we greet friends, loved ones or strangers with Aloha, which means with love."

Roxane Orgill. *Mahalia: A Life in Gospel Music.* Candlewick, 2002. The life of a woman who was born poor, yet rose to fame through her powerful voice; illustrated with archival photos.

Charles R. Smith, Jr. *Twelve Rounds to Glory: The Story of Muhammad Ali.* Illustrated by Bryan Collier. Atheneum, 2007. Written in simple yet poetic language, this book includes interesting quotations, for example:

> "Daddy, I go to the grocery and the grocery man is white. I go to the drugstore and the drugstore man's white. The bus driver's white. What do the colored people do?"

Large illustrations depict the complex life of this American hero, Cassius Clay, who surprised the world by turning to Islam and shedding what he called his "slave name."

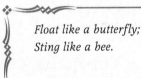

Float like a butterfly;
Sting like a bee.

~ Motto of MUHAMMAD ALI

Social Studies Multicultural Reading Lists

In order to prepare a reading list for the social studies, you need to become acquainted with a variety of multicultural books appropriate for the grade level you teach. A journal published by the American Library Association, *Booklist,* is helpful for high school teachers while their journal, *Book Links,* is designed for K–8 teachers; published monthly, each journal includes annotations for all titles presented.

Students in your class(es) might help you compile a list for those you will teach next year: Books We Recommend by the Class of 2011. Here are a few titles you might explore:

Elementary/Middle School

Lesley M. Blume. *Cornelia and the Audacious Escapades of the Somerset Sisters.* Knopf, 2006.

Diana Cohn. *Si, Se Puede! Yes, We Can! Janitor Strike in L.A.* Cinco Printos, 2002. Eyewitness Guides. Written by different authors on more than 100 varied social studies topics, DK press, varied dates.

Sally Nemeth. *The Heights, the Depths, and Everything in Between.* Knopf, 2006.

Jerdine Nolen. *Pitching in for Eubie.* Illusrated by E. B. Lewis. HarperCollins, 2007. Eubie receives a college scholarship, but her African American family must contribute $3,000 toward her expenses. The whole family pitches in to help Eubie take advantage of this opportunity.

Susan Patron. *The Higher Power of Lucky.* Illustrated by Matt Phelan. Atheneum, 2006. A plucky young girl is afraid she may be sent to an orphanage after her mother dies. This Newbery Award-winning book was controversial in that Patron introduced the word "scrotum," overheard by Lucky, on the very first page!

Jill Wolfson. *Home, and Other Big, Fat Lies.* Holt, 2006.

High School

D. Dina Friedman. *Escaping into the Night.* Simon & Schuster, 2006.

Linzi Glass. *The Year the Gypsies Came.* Viking, 2006.

Alan Gratz. *Samurai Shortstop.* Dial, 2006.

Justina Chen Headley. *Nothing but the Truth (and a Few White Lies).* Little, Brown, 2006.

Kirsten Miller. *Kiki Strike: Inside the Shadow City.* Bloomsbury, 2006.

Mary Beth Miller. *On the Head of a Pin.* Dutton, 2006.

A Thinking + Lesson Plan: A Nation of Immigrants

Follow the directions given in the lesson plan on p. 164. This picture book explains clearly the process that a person wanting to enter the United States had to go through on the West Coast.

This lesson could initiate a full-fledged thematic study titled *A Nation of Immigrants* as students learn about where our ancestors emigrated from originally. Thus, they would better understand why so many diverse peoples make up the U.S. population and recognize that "we are all the children of immigrants."

Acting Out

Search for books that can be used to dramatize history, for example:

Laura Amy Schlitz. *Good Masters! Sweet Ladies! Voices from a Medieval Village.* Illustrated by Robert Byrd. Candlewick, 2007 A collection of seventeen short plays—monologues—so that many people can participate in presenting a bit of history from around 1255, in medieval times. Background topics included are "The Three-Field System," "Falconry," "A Medieval Pilgrimage," "The Crusades," "Jews in Medieval Society," "Towns and Freedom."

Reading Books Aloud in the Classroom

Remember that you can always choose a book to read that would be a bit difficult for students in your class to read independently. They will reach to understand through listening, thus adding to their vocabulary and their knowledge base.

Primary

Trinka H. Noble. Illustrated by Doris Ettlinger. *The Orange Shoes.* Sleeping Bear, 2008. A heartwarming story about a poor family introduces discussion of poverty, bullying, and self-reliance.

THINKING + LESSON PLAN

A Nation of Immigrants: The Ellis Island Experience

Grades 4–10

Expected outcomes

Learners will:

1. Learn about the immigration process.
2. Listen to personal stories of classmates who have immigrated.
3. Recognize the contributions of those who have immigrated.

Teaching/Learning Strategies

Resources Needed

Obtain a copy of *Immigrant Kids* by Russell Freedman (Puffin Books, 1995).

Directions

Step 1: Share this book with your students.

Step 2: Have them select a photo to write about, imagining themselves in the picture and telling about their experiences.

Step 3: Have students research Ellis Island and the entry process that immigrants experienced on the East Coast.

Step 4: Each student should read a novel about an immigrant and write a report about his or her experiences.

Performance Assessment

1. Each student receives + or – depending on class participation and the completion of a novel.
2. Students will prepare written reports about the book they read. These reports will be filed in a class book of IMMIGRANTS WE HAVE KNOWN. Students can refer to these reports in locating another book to read. Reports will receive scores according to this rubric:

   5 Clear report of the person's life; few errors in spelling.

   2 A report that is not as clearly presented.

   0 No report completed.

Susan L. Roth and Greg Mortenson. *Listen to the Wind: The Story of Dr. Greg and Three Cups of Tea.* Dial, 2009. Dr. Greg helped to build schools for children in Pakistan and Afghanistan.

Nancy I. Sanders. Illustrated by E. B. Lewis. *D Is for the Drinking Gourd: An African-American Alphabet.* Sleeping Bear, 2008. Fine watercolors and poetry stimulate classroom discussion.

Elementary/Middle School

Cynthia Kadohata. *Cracker! The Best Dog in Vietnam.* Story of seventeen-year-old Rick and his work with a member of the canine unit during the Vietnam War.

Patrick O'Brien. *The Mutiny on the Bounty.* Walker, 2008. Adventure on the high seas in a retelling for younger students of a classic work.

Doreen Rappaport. Illustrated by Matt Tavares. *Lady Liberty: A Biography.* Candlewick, 2008. Author and illustrator work together to present nicely integrated perspectives of this **great** lady.

High School

Isabel Allende. *Daughter of Fortune.* HarperCollins, 1999. Born in Chile, Eliza follows her lover to the gold fields of California in 1849.

Stephen E. Ambrose. *Nothing Like It in the World.* Simon & Schuster, 2000. The story of those who built the Transcontinental Railroad.

Creating a Fictional Diary

Students can assume the role of an imaginary person living in a specific period of history, participating in the events of that time. For example, Tom might choose to *be* Paul Edwards, a thirteen-year-old boy living outside Philadelphia during the Revolutionary War. His diary entries will reflect things he would be doing, what his family is like, and his reactions to what is happening at that time.

Each day students can take turns sharing their entries. After listening to an entry, students can comment about what they liked best about the writing of the entry, for instance, in writing the journal described above, Tom might tell about an older brother or father who is fighting the British.

You might begin this activity by brainstorming sample names and descriptions of people that someone might choose to personify.

DID YOU KNOW?

—◇—

Comparing Your Life with That of Others

One-third of Pakistan's population lives below the poverty level, according to the World Bank's figures. As prices for basic foods rise, these people become desperate. They will sell anything, even a child!

A healthy child might bring $1,000–$5,000.
A disabled fifteen-year-old might bring $175 to serve as a beggar.

Does this mean that Pakistani mothers and fathers do not love their children?

Social Studies and Science/Mathematics

Social studies covers events, current discoveries, facts about populations, and so forth. Science and mathematics can often, therefore, be linked to geography, economics, civics, and the other social studies. The daily newspaper is a particularly good resource for ideas about fighting in the Middle East, business failures, the ups and downs of the stock market, news about fires, plane accidents, the complexities of preparing a state or federal budget, and so forth.

Maps and Mapping

Talk about maps with students. What are different kinds of maps? What goes into a map? What can maps be used for? In discussions about their neighborhoods, students might talk about places and people of importance to them. Now each student can propose a list of elements to be included on a map of the neighborhood.

Construct a class map on a large sheet of butcher paper. Depending on the level of the students, you may decide to represent only one or two main streets, an interpretation of a larger area (not to scale), or a standard grid map with scale and/or cardinal directions. Students will enjoy developing symbols to use on the map (explained in the *key*) and illustrating or landscaping the map as much as they choose. A more elaborate project would be to create a relief map or three-dimensional model from clay, plaster, or similar material. Such a project will give students a different perspective of the place where all of them live.

Bring in copies of your state or city auto map, enough copies so that students can study the maps in pairs. Ask students to write a set of directions from one specified location to another. After they have written the exact set of directions, have the pairs of students exchange their directions. Then, one student in each pair will read the directions line by line, while the other student moves his "car" on the map exactly as directed. This pair of students will edit any mistakes they find.

Repeat this exercise by changing the locations specified. You might, for example, use a city map and ask students to plan a field trip going from your school to:

- A specific museum
- A park
- A zoo
- The main library
- The airport

Again, exchange the sets of directions and have students test them for accuracy.

Assign one or two students the task of checking each set of directions with a global positioning system to see how their directions compare with the ones the students wrote.

Graphing

Review the various types of graphs that students might use in presenting information that they gather from almanacs, yearbooks, or surveys. Ask students to bring in sample graphs that they see in the newspapers or magazines over a week's period of time. Display these examples on the bulletin board and discuss the information presented. Enlarge several basic types to present on transparencies as you talk about the kinds of information that could be presented using, for example, a pie chart or a bar graph. Discuss the mathematics that a social scientist might need in order to construct a useful graph, for example, percentages.

IDEAS IN ACTION!

Bicycles on the Move

As anxiety about (1) finding replacements for non-renewable energy sources as well as (2) the effect of increasing energy use on climate change rises throughout the world, people are actively investigating ways of reducing our dependence on gasoline-powered automobiles. Everyone is seeking alternate methods of transportation in the United States, for example, the bicycle.

On the Fourth of July in 2008, several city officials in Santa Rosa, California, rode bicycles around their city's streets to find out whether they are effectively encouraging the use of bicycles, for example, to commute to work or to transport family members to city parks for recreation. They were looking for the presence of protected bicycle lanes as well as secure and sufficient parking facilities for bicycles near bus stations, post offices, libraries, parks, and other public destinations.

Promoting bicycle use and bicycle safety is one way for students of all ages and backgrounds to express concern for reducing human impact on the environment. Younger students can discuss bicycle safety, such as the importance of wearing helmets and obeying traffic rules. Upper elementary and middle school students can survey bicycle access between neighborhoods and the school and report obstacles that might impede greater bicycle use. High school students can plan a full campaign, seeking sponsors to participate in a study of bicycle use in your area, presenting their findings to city officials, and recommending ways of connecting the use of bicycles with other forms of transportation, for example, buses or trains.

Encourage students to use maps, graphs, and other visual presentations to support their arguments for expanding facilities for bikers.

Social Studies and the Performing Arts

The arts offer strong support for social studies themes. All cultures, all nations around the globe use the arts for self-expression, so we search out the paintings, the crafts, the dance, and the music for the different groups of people that inhabit the world. Books present a wide variety of the arts for us to explore.

Traveling through Pictures

Pictures in illustrated books offer us a way to travel to other countries.

Elspeth Leacock and Susan Buckley. *Places in Time: A New Atlas of American History.* Illustrated by Randy Jones. Houghton Mifflin, 2001. Here are amazing pictures of places in the United States, including Ellis Island—Doorway to America; Abilene—Cattle Town; Fort Laramie—A Welcome on the Oregon Trail; Gettysburg—Day of Decision.

James Rumford. *Traveling Man: The Journey of Ibn Battuta, 1325–1354.* Houghton Mifflin, 2001. This beautifully-illustrated book describes the historical travels of a

> *Never doubt that a few committed people*
> *can change the world.*
>
> ~ MARGARET MEAD

man when the world was "flat" and Jerusalem was the center of the world. Books allow us to travel not only in space but also in time.

Joan Steiner. *Look-Alikes around the World, An Album of Amazing Postcards.* Little, Brown, 2007. An interesting illustrated book that features famous places in the world.

Creating a Mural

A large mural based on a thematic study is a wonderful culminating activity to which all students can contribute. Use crayons to create figures, appropriately dressed. Watercolors are useful for filling in the background or making hills, desert lands, a wide river, foliage, the sky!

Everyone can discuss what should be in a mural about a thematic study of, perhaps, Native Americans, The Contributions of African Americans to Society, or How Life Has Changed for American Women in the Past Two Hundred Years.

Folk Music as Protest

Pete Seeger is considered the father of the folk music era that peaked in the nineteen-sixties. A confirmed activist even at 90 (in 2009), Seeger continues to make history with his music. He believes in doing whatever you can to correct the wrongs you see in the society around you; for him, participation is a religion. His gifts to the world include such antiwar songs as "Waist Deep in the Big Muddy" and "Where Have All the Flowers Gone?" For seventeen years, branded as a Communist, he was banned from the media, but Seeger prevailed.

DID YOU KNOW?

The image of a tall man wearing red and white pants and a top hat that we call "Uncle Sam" first appeared in a picture in 1852.

This name apparently goes back to the practice of stamping "U.S." on barrels of meat sent to the army in the early eighteen-hundreds. Of course, these letters stood for United States, but the soldiers said they stood for Uncle Sam, the nickname they gave well-known meatpacker Samuel Wilson. The name "Uncle Sam" was later given to a symbol for the United States, depicted as the lanky figure that appears, for example, on many military recruiting posters, pointing a large finger at the viewer and saying, "Uncle Sam wants you!" Look around. You may see Uncle Sam in unexpected places.

Pete Seeger loves to sing to and with young people, and they respond with enthusiasm. Look for recordings of other songs he wrote, for example, "Turn, Turn, Turn," and "If I Had a Hammer . . ." He often sings Woody Guthrie's "This Land Is Your Land," and other singers, for instance, Joan Baez, Bob Dylan, Bonnie Raitt, and Johnny Cash, sing Seeger's songs. There is joy in these folk songs, and there is purpose. Public television offers a wonderful video presentation of Pete Seeger's life called "The Power of Song," and it is worth obtaining a copy for your school.

Invite students to compose original songs about issues that concern them. Provide an opportunity for students to present their songs accompanied by music, perhaps in the lunchroom or at a special assembly following the "Poetry Slam" model.

Collage

Have students create collages about topics they are studying. Students cut words and pictures from magazines and newspapers to organize on a large sheet of paper as a way of presenting a complex topic, for example: "Women's Rights," "The State of Georgia," or "The Civil War." Students can include small realia to provide a 3-D effect, or they can add original art to supply information they want to include but can't find in publications they have access to. Display these collages on the wall in the school hallway so that other students can examine them.

Covers for Reports

After each student has completed a research report, typed it on the computer, and printed it out, findings can be presented formally in booklet form. Creating an attractive cover on a large sheet of 17" × 18" construction paper will enhance each student's presentation, which can be placed in the school library for other students to read. Show students how to create colorful covers by first dropping enamel paint on water in a cookie baking sheet with ½" sides and then laying their paper over the paint floating on the water. The result is a very attractive marbleized design that will dry overnight. The folded sheet provides a suitable front and back cover for a report printed on 8½" × 11" paper.

CONNECTIONS

Our first aim in teaching social studies multiculturally, as is true for teaching any subject, is to (1) support student self-esteem, (2) develop empathy among students, and (3) provide equity for all students in the classroom while they learn social studies content. The learning activities that follow this model provide a foundation for all instruction.

In addition, we find it most effective for multicultural teaching to integrate the social studies with language arts/reading, science/mathematics, and the performing arts. Such integration in an inclusive classroom will invite students to delve into studies that may not have interested them when introduced through the standard social studies textbook.

The social studies offer a wealth of intriguing information about the world and the different people that inhabit it. Let students become actively involved in planning thematic units that particularly interest them. Begin with a list of questions and suggest interactive methods of finding information, for example, conducting *I-Search* Papers or working collaboratively in groups. Students will enjoy working together to present a culminating activity for parents or other students.

GETTING INVOLVED

In this chapter we have suggested a number of learning activities and resources that you will want to explore independently as you plan social studies lessons for the students you teach. Following are additional suggestions of ways to begin your investigations.

Expanding Your Reflective Teaching Portfolio

1. Think back over the chapter you have just completed. Make a list of things you can do immediately to make social studies a more interesting and stimulating subject for the students you teach, for example:

   • Look up the lists of Award Books at the American Library Association website, (www.ala.org), for example, the Coretta Scott King Awards given to Black authors and illustrators of outstanding books created for young people each year.
   • Begin reading a book that you might like to use with students. Take notes about how you might use that book with students in your classroom.

2. Reread the poem presented on page 141. Discuss what the poet is saying. Do you hear assumptions? Do you hear questions? How could you develop a lesson based on this poem?

Working with Your Cooperative Learning Group

1. Develop a thematic study together that will inform students about the Middle East, an area with which we all need to become better acquainted. Explore what your school library and the public library have to offer for such a study, for example:

   Khaled Hosseini. *The Kite Runner.* Riverhead Books, 2003. Story of a young Afghani who flees Afghanistan.

   Philip Wilkinson. *Islam.* DK Publishing, 2002. Part of the EyeWitness Series, which includes information and visual presentations that students find engrossing.

   Draw a map of this area so that you become familiar with the location of each of these countries and the major cities in each one. This map will be useful to share later with students as they, too, get to know this part of the world.

2. Begin sending for free materials that you will find useful as you develop social studies units. A beautiful journal that features the Middle East, *Saudi Aramco World,* is a good resource to request to support the thematic study that your group is working on, (9009 West Loop South, Houston, TX 77096). This free journal features articles about the culture and people of the Middle East. Topics might include "A Community of Arab Music" or "Recipes from Saudi Arabia," and so forth.

Another source is *Understanding Islam and the Muslims,* a small, attractively illustrated booklet available free from:

> The Embassy of Saudi Arabia
> Department of Islamic Affairs
> 601 New Hampshire Ave., NW
> Washington, D.C. 20037
>
> Telephone: 202/342-3700

EXPLORING FURTHER

Gwen Ifill. *The Breakthrough: Politics and Race in the Age of Obama.* Doubleday, 2009. Analysis by an author journalist.

Margaret Mead. *Blackberry Winter: My Earlier Years.* Morrow, 1972. This charming memoir relates the experiences of a well-known anthropologist. Although Mead published widely about her work in the South Seas, in this book she talks about her life as a woman before feminism, influenced by other strong women, married three times, and the mother of a daughter.

Greg Mortenson and David Relin. *Three Cups of Tea: One Man's Mission to Promote Peace . . . One School at a Time.* Viking Penguin, 2006. Mortenson's travels through Pakistani and Afghan villages provide insight into the lives of the Muslims he came to know and love as he helped them build simple schools to educate their children, particularly the girls.

Tanya Shaffer. *Somebody's Heart Is Burning: A Woman Wanderer in Africa.* Random, 2003. Portraits from African and North American cultures come together, told with humor and compassion.

Laurel Schmidt. *Social Studies that Sticks; How to Bring Content and Concepts to Life.* Heinemann, 2007. Lessons about humanity for grades 3–8.

Howard Zinn. *A People's History of the United States: 1492–Present.* Harper, 1995. A moving history told from the point of view of those who have been exploited and largely omitted from most histories.

CHAPTER 6

Multicultural Science

> *Tell me,*
> *I forget.*
>
> *Show me,*
> *I remember.*
>
> *Involve me,*
> *I understand.*
>
> ～ CHINESE PROVERB

Science may often be neglected in the elementary school, as more time is spent on language arts/reading. Integrating these subject areas may serve to see that our younger children are invited to explore the world of science at an early stage in their growth. There is general agreement on the fact that we need to promote science in the United States if we are to continue to hold a leadership position in the world.

As Alan Leshner, head of the American Association for the Advancement of Science, states:

> The purpose of science is to answer our questions about the nature of the world— whether we like the answers or not. Science has discrete limits; it's limited to natural explanations about the natural world.

Noting that people do not have to be able to explain, for example, nuclear fusion, he nevertheless makes clear that citizens do need to have a general understanding of science and its importance in our world in order to function as informed citizens. Many of our decisions regarding the spending of federal monies may be science-related, for instance, matters of health or what we need to do about our impact on climate warming.

He and other scientists argue strongly for the teaching of science effectively throughout the K–12 years. As Laurence Steinberg, Distinguished Professor of Psychology at Temple University, makes clear:

> Too much of today's science education focuses on making students memorize bits of information that will be outdated within a few years. Too little emphasizes how to think like a scientist. And there is no substitute for hands-on research experience.

In order to teach science effectively, teachers need experience with:

- Laboratory skills
- Hands-on learning
- Instructional technology
- Frequent formative assessment

There is a direct correlation between the teacher's knowledge and the students' achievement.

We need students to talk about science, to read about science, and to *do* science. We need to provide better training for teachers, showing them how best to engage students in scientific studies.

❖ Science Activities that Support Esteem, Empathy, and Equity

As we teach science multiculturally, we are concerned for each student's self-esteem, the development of empathy, and providing equity for all students. Organizing our studies around "big ideas" will encourage students of all ability levels to participate in learning concepts within that context. Making sure students understand science activities so that they can succeed will support their feelings of self-worth, and planning small group activities will encourage students to work together amicably as they get to know each other. You can assure, too, that each student has equal access to supplies and equipment needed for specific learning activities and that each has the guidance needed to perform the activities. Following are a few activities selected specifically to support esteem, empathy, and equity, multicultural teaching, in the classroom.

Supporting Self-Esteem

As previously discussed, all students need the chance to succeed. They need to be recognized for what they achieve.

Talking about What We Eat

All students can participate in talking about a subject of great personal interest—what they eat. Have students keep a food log, recording the things they eat for breakfast, lunch, and dinner, plus snacks. Talk about vitamins and minerals that we need to have each day. Discuss which foods contain these vitamins and minerals. Be discreet regarding what families *should* be eating.

Play games with the students, asking such questions as:

1. What vitamin are we getting when we eat carrot sticks? (Vitamin A, which helps our eyes.)
2. What vitamin are we getting when we eat a tomato? (Vitamin C, which builds strong bones and helps us avoid scurvy.)

Such games can be raised while the class is waiting, for example, in the lunch line. Children can generate the questions, too.

Developing a Class Cookbook

Have each student bring in a recipe for a favorite family food. Each can print his or her recipe and directions for preparing the dish. Then, students might decorate the sheet on which the recipe is presented to add to the attractiveness of the publication.

Have an artistic student create a cover for OUR CLASS COOKBOOK. You can use a three-ringed notebook in which to place each sheet. One student can create a table of contents; another might add a short index at the back of the book.

Consider how you might prepare at least one of the recipes in school with the help, perhaps, of lunchroom staff. Your lunch menus may already include enchiladas, Chinese stir-fry, or other ethnic specialties.

Displaying Pictures of Different Foods

Use newspaper food advertisements and magazines that feature foods that are especially appealing to different ethnic groups. Bring in examples of different beans, grains, and so forth so that students can become acquainted with their names. Children who know languages other than English can tell the class what a particular vegetable, for example, is called in Spanish or Vietnamese.

Sharing Science Books

When reading aloud to children, be sure to include interesting nonfiction at times for variety and to add to children's experiential and knowledge base. Reading such books may engage the interest of future scientists. Here are science books for primary grades:

Nic Bishop. *Nic Bishop's Spiders*. Scholastic, 2007. A spectacular photo-essay of spiders—molting, hunting, and even leaping. Bishop also has a book on *Frogs*.

Richard Hilliard. *Godspeed, John Glenn*. Boyds Mills Press, 2006.

Claire Nivola. *Planting the Trees of Kenya: The Story of Wangari Maathai*. Farrar, 2008. The true story of a Nobel Peace Prize winner, a Kenyan woman who urged everyone to replant the forests in Kenya; beautiful watercolors.

David M. Schwartz and Yael Schy. *Where in the Wild? Camouflaged Creatures Concealed . . . and Revealed.* Tricycle, 2007. Poems about animals hiding in plain sight.

Jan Lee Wicker. *Those Excellent Eagles.* Pineapple Press, 2006. Interesting study of our national symbol.

Although older students will also learn much from the picture books, here are several for grades 6–12:

Maxine Anderson. *Amazing Leonardo da Vinci Inventions You Can Build Yourself.* Nomad Press, 2006.

Cheryl Bardoe. *Gregor Mendel: The Friar Who Grew Peas.* Abrams, 2006.

Brian Greene. *Icarus at the Edge of Time.* Knopf, 2008. Includes photos from the Hubble Telescope.

David Macaulay. *Mill.* Houghton Mifflin, 2004.

Don Mitchell. *Liftoff: A Biography of John Glenn.* National Geographic, 2006.

Katherine Pateraon. *Lyddie.* Puffin, 2001.

Joseph B. Treaster. *Hurricane Force: The Path of America's Deadliest Storms.* Kingfisher, 2007.

A Thinking + Lesson Plan: Dealing with Controversy

What is controversy? What kinds of controversial subjects are being presented in today's newspapers and magazines? Let the students get acquainted with the idea of controversy and the fact that it is an important part of daily life in a democracy. Not everyone has the same opinion about how the government should operate. Should we all have the same opinion?

You might read an appropriate Op-Ed piece on a controversial topic that has appeared in your newspaper recently. Let the students voice their opinions, stressing the fact that it is normal for us to disagree at times.

It is important to form opinions based on some evidence or rational reasoning. Why would people sometimes say, "That's just *your* opinion"?

Then follow the directions for the lesson plan on p. 176 about hunting.

Writing an Op-Ed Piece

Scientific topics often invite controversy. Hunting is an excellent topic that students can consider as they listen to the discussion and weigh the arguments, both pro and con. Ask whether viewpoints may have changed overtime. Remind students that Native Americans and early settlers depended on hunting for food.

Refer to the Thinking + Writing Plan on p. 176 as students deal with this topic, and then prepare an Op-Ed piece that they can actually send to your local newspaper.

You might have the class choose the best *Pro* and the best *Con* essay. Submit the two together to your local newspaper accompanied by a cover letter from you explaining the nature of the class assignment.

A THINKING + LESSON PLAN

◄○►

Dealing with Controversy

Grades 6–12

Expected Outcomes

Learners will:

1. Read a book about a controversial subject: hunting.
2. List arguments both pro and con about this topic.
3. Write an Op-Ed piece about this topic.

Teaching/Learning Strategies

Resources Needed

Obtain a copy of *Opening Day* by Susan Bartlett, illustrated by Luanne Wren (Tillbury, 2007). You may also find an earlier book this author wrote, *A Family Goes Hunting* (Clarion, 1991). Few books for children have treated this subject. Collect copies of Op-Ed pieces from the local newspaper as examples of how students might present their ideas.

Directions

Step 1: Read *Opening Day* aloud to the group, showing pictures as you go.

Step 2: Explain that hunting is a controversial (new vocabulary word) topic. Discuss why some people think hunting is bad and should not be allowed while others think hunting is fine and should be permitted.

Step 3: Guide students to organize this thinking into two columns: PRO and CON. Write each reason on the board in the appropriate column.

Step 4: Direct the students to use these arguments in writing an Op-Ed piece that they might submit to your local newspaper. They may choose to present one side of the argument, trying to persuade readers to agree with them, or they may present a balanced viewpoint pointing out both sides.

Step 5: Edit the completed Op-Ed pieces in pairs. Rewrite based on editing.

Performance Assessment

5   Essay completed. Clearly expressed arguments; no obvious errors.
3   Several arguments presented; few errors.
1   Essay incomplete.

You can follow up this activity with a similar one dealing with a different controversial subject, for example:

Teaching evolution in the schools: See: *Abbreviated Guide for Teaching Evolution.* AAAS. (www.aaas.org/news/press_room/evolution)

Reintroducing wolves into Wyoming (or another state): Read: Dorothy Patent. *When the Wolves Returned.* Walker, 2008. A photo-essay about the reintroduction of wolves into Yellowstone National Park and its impact on life there.

Note that less able writers will need support in order to complete this task. A simpler writing task can be substituted for the Op-Ed piece, for example: a paragraph, a short poem, a conversation between two imaginary people.

Talking about Science

What is science? Are there different fields included within the broad term *science*? Begin a list of the different kinds of scientists and their fields of specialization, for example:

Astronomy
Medicine
Physics
Botany
Oceanography
Space
Technology
Climatology
Epidemiology

Continue this list. Develop a display area titled SCIENTISTS AT WORK where students can post pictures and articles.

Invite scientists to visit your class (you may combine several classes for such an event). Be sure to include women as well as men. Perhaps you can arrange a field trip to a laboratory where real scientists are working. We need to expand student interest and their knowledge about the various sciences in which they might become engaged, especially as students move into middle school and then high school where they are seriously considering possible careers.

Developing Science Vocabulary

New words will constantly appear as students are introduced to new processes, for example, *photosynthesis,* or terms for equipment used in the laboratory, for example, *beaker*. At times, too, the meaning of familiar words will be expanded to accommodate new meanings in science, for example, *table*. Remember to include computer-related words that are useful in science studies, too.

Create a Word Wall (or at least a strip) on which new science words can be displayed. Students can challenge each other to read each word in the list. A further challenge will include pronouncing each word and also explaining its scientific meaning.

Such activities encourage the development of scientific and technological literacy.

Developing Empathy

As students learn to collaborate, they can undertake investigations in small groups. Working together helps them learn to respect each other and to make an effort to get along with those who may have differing abilities.

Inventions

Bring in books or tell students stories about inventions that have made a difference in our lives. Have them generate questions that they would like to have answered, for example:

> *How were chopsticks invented?* See: Ying Chang Compestine. *The Story of Chopsticks.* Illustrated by YongSheng Xuan. Holiday House, 2001. Read this funny little story aloud. Is it true? Who knows? We need to investigate further.

> *Who created our popular bluejeans?* See: Doreen Rappaport. *In the Promised Land: Lives of Jewish Americans.* HarperCollins, 2005. Jacob W. Davis first made "waist overalls" to fit a huge miner, but later he went into partnership with Levi Strauss, thus, we have "levis." This is factual.

> *Which came first: the chicken or the egg?* See: Laura V. Seeger. *First the Egg.* Roaring Brook Press, 2007. This question may never be answered. What do you think?

Observing Cycles in Natural Science

Read a book depictiing a cycle (see *First the Egg,* mentioned above). Another good example is:

> Helen Frost. *Monarch and Milkweed.* Illustrated by Leonid Gore. Simon & Schuster, 2008. This picture book describes the migration of the monarch butterfly in detail, including the laying of eggs on the leaves of the milkweed plant. The monarch egg becomes a caterpillar, eventually changing into a lovely butterfly that flies off to Mexico for the winter. The milkweed plant dies, but its seeds emerge as new plants in the spring, in time for the monarchs to return. Thus, the cycle goes on.

Other picture books that portray cycles include:

> Chris Butterworth. *Sea Horse: The Shyest Fish in the Sea.*

> Rick Chrustowski. *Turtle Crossing.*

> Brenda Z. Guiberson. *The Emperor Lays an Egg.*

> April P. Sayre. *Dig, Wait, Listen: A Desert Toad's Tale.*

Hooked on Reading about Science

Many students find nonfiction engrossing, and they will tend to respond to your enthusiasm. Try reading some of these picture books, which are informative and entertaining.

> Jim Aronsky. *Under the Wild Western Sky.* HarperCollins, 2005.

> Jacqueline Briggs Martin and Mary Azarian. *Snowflake Bentley.* Houghton Mifflin, 1998.

> Elaine Scott. *Poles Apart: Why Penguins and Polar Bears Will Never Be Neighbors.* Hyperion, 2004.

Elaine Scott. *When Is a Planet Not a Planet? The Story of Pluto.* Clarion, 2007.

Doug Wechsler. *Frog Heaven: Ecology of a Vernal Pool.* Boyds Mills, 2006.

> *If you ask successful scientists what brought them into science, every one of them says, "A teacher."*

The Green Earth Book Award

This award was founded in 2005 by the Newton Marasco Foundation (NMF) in partnership with Salisbury University. It is awarded annually to books that "inspire a child to grow a deeper appreciation, respect, and responsibility for his or her natural environment." Some of the books that have received this award include:

Primary

Graeme Base. *Uno's Garden.* Abrams, 2006. An attempt to save a garden from urban development.

Peter Farrelly. *Abigaile the Happy Whale.* Illustrated by Jamie Rama. Little, Brown, 2006. Young humpback whales toss trash that humans have dumped in the ocean back on the beach, telling them indirectly to take care of their own trash.

Karen Lynn Williams. *Circles of Hope.* Illustrated by Linda Saport. Eerdmans, 2005. Facile, a young boy in Haiti, plants a mango tree for his baby sister; focuses on deforestation; Creole language included.

Upper Elementary/Middle School

Albert Marrin. *Saving the Buffalo.* Scholastic, 2006. Includes the history of buffalo and the Native Americans as well as current efforts to protect these great American animals.

Rochelle Strauss. *Tree of Life: The Incredible Biodiversity of Life on Earth.* Illustrated by Margot Thompson. Kids Can, 2004. Presents the major categories of life on earth in handsome double-page spreads.

Becoming Responsible Global Citizens

Heifer International, a nonprofit organization that aims to fight world poverty and hunger, offers two "standards-based science education programs."

- **Read to Feed**® A service-learning program that helps foster a love of reading while also helping to end hunger, Grades 3–6.
- **GET IT!**® (Global Education to Improve Tomorrow). Teaches students about sustainable solutions to world hunger and poverty, Grades 6–8.

Leader's Packet available from Heifer International:

Phone: 800/422-0474
(www.HeiferEd.org)

> *Think globally.*
> *Act locally!*
>
> ~ RENÉ DUBOS

Providing Equity

Plan studies in which all students can participate. The studies can range from simple experiments like growing beans to broad thematic studies about multicultural topics. The point is that students of varied abilities can take part in the study and learn to function as scientists do. Here are a few ideas that promote multicultural scientific studies:

Planning for Disabled Students

Studying broad thematic topics enables all students to participate to the best of their abilities. Adapting science instruction to meet diverse abilities will enhance your teaching and make it more effective for all students. Some of the following strategies help students follow through complex studies, as discussed in Chapters 2 and 3:

- Graphic organizers—clustering, Venn diagrams, charts, graphs, outlines.
- Vocabulary study—talking about academic science vocabulary in simpler terms.
- Visual displays—posters, transparencies, video tapes, computer disks.

Students who have physical difficulty with writing may find the computer a useful aid in recording their ideas. They can incorporate checklists, pictures, and text outlines into their work. Take time, as well, to introduce students to the structure of a textbook, noting, for example, the use of boldface headings and sidebars that feature important information.

Developing a Thematic Study: Contributions of African Americans to Science

Africans were first brought to America many years ago. It is interesting to recognize the many contributions they have made to the world, in terms, for example, of science, music, and art. Students can browse through the Internet to begin compiling a list of Black American scientists, noting what each one contributed to society. Here are some names they might include:

George Washington Carver	Daniel Hale Williams
Benjamin Banneker	Zora Neale Hurston
Charles Richard Drew	Perry Lavon Julian
Matthew Alexander Henson	Mae C. Jemison
Norbert Rillieux	Guion Stewart Bluford
Jan Ernst Matzeliger	The Tuskeegee Airmen
Granville Woods	

Many of us have heard of George Washington Carver and his work with the peanut, but how many of you know about Charles Drew's work as a physician who was particularly interested in blood and how we could use it for life-saving transfusions? Many of the people in this list held numerous patents on significant inventions in wide-ranging fields from sugar refining to the third rail used in subways to the gas mask. Jemison and Bluford are astronauts; Bluford went into space three times. Zora Neale Hurston is better known as a writer, but she was also an anthropologist very much interested in the Black culture.

Students can work in groups of two or three to prepare a biography for each of the scientists listed. Add others that you discover. Each biography can be inserted, perhaps in alphabetical order, in a class book entitled *Noted Black American Scientists*. This book can be placed in a local school library.

Look for biographies or autobiographies of these notable African American scientists, for example:

Susan Altman. *Extraordinary African Americans.* Scholastic, 2001. An outstanding collection of short biographies including scientists as well as authors, musicians, and political leaders beginning in the eighteenth century and concluding with contemporary figures, for example, Bill Cosby and Oprah Winfrey.

Carole B. Weatherford. *I, Matthew Henson.* Illustrated by Eric Valasquez. Walker, 2008. A beautiful picture book, told in the first person, records the work of Matthew Henson with Admiral Peary, first in the tropics and later in the Arctic. With five other men he sailed to Greenland, where he learned Inuit and helped Peary chart the way to the North Pole. They made seven trips to the Arctic before standing together at the Pole in 1909.

❖ Integrating Science into Other Curriculum Areas

We may not always think of science as related to other curricular areas of study, but there are always connections to discover. Science, for example, has a history and can become politically controversial, as in the case of evolution versus creationism. The scientist utilizes all of the language skills to communicate with others, and he or she may use artistic abilities in recording details of discoveries. Consider strategies that will integrate science across the curriculum, particularly in the elementary grades where science is sometimes neglected.

Science and Language Arts/Reading

Comparing Books about the Same Topic

Have students locate two or more books that treat the same science topic. Then, they can use a Venn diagram to help them record how the books are alike and how they are different, as in the example (on page 182) that compares two books about the Everglades in Florida:

Jean Craighead George. *Everglades.* HarperCollins, 1995.

Trish Marx. *Everglades Forever: Restoring America's Great Wetland.* Photographs by Cindy Karp. Lee and Low, 2004. A fifth-grade class studies the Everglades.

FIGURE 6.1   Venn Diagram

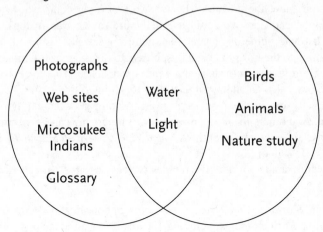

Reading Poetry about Science Topics

Poets have often delighted in writing poems about scientific topics, for example, nature and animals. But they have also written about technology, space science, trucks, museums, and so on. Any topic is fair game for the clever poet. Try some of these books:

Leslie Bulion. *Hey There, Stink Bug!* Charlesbridge, 2006.

Anna Grossnickle Hines. *Winter Lights*. Greenwillow, 2005.

Bobbi Katz. *Trailblazers: Poems of Exploration*. Greenwillow, 2007.

J. Patrick Lewis. *Scien-trickery: Riddles in Science*. Harcourt, 2004.

Judidth Nicholls. *The Sun in Me: Poems about the Planet*. Barefoot, 2003.

Joyce Sidman. *Butterfly Eyes and Other Secrets of the Meadow*. Houghton Mifflin, 2006.

Joyce Sidman. *Song of the Water Boatman and Other Pond Poems*. Houghton Mifflin, 2005.

Marilyn Singer. *Footprints on the Roof: Poems about the Earth*. Knopf, 2002.

Jane Yolen. *Shape Me a Rhyme: Nature's Forms in Poetry*. Boyds Mills, 2007.

Writing Poems about Science

Introduce students to various forms of poetry that they can use to write about science. Elementary school students can compose a five-lined poem, the cinquain, following this form:

Line 1: One word.
Line 2: Two words.
Line 2: Three words.
Line 4: Four words.
Line 5: One word.

For example,

> Sunshine—
> Warm air;
> Flowers nodding lightly;
> Red, Yellow, White, Blue—
> Summer.

Older students might try more complex patterns, for example, an acrostic poem. Notice that the first letters of each line spell a word vertically. Choose the word or words you want to spell first, perhaps SPRING, SEPTEMBER, WONDERS OF NATURE, or PACIFIC OCEAN.

> **D** eep in the forest;
> **E** agles cry,
> **C** rows
> **E** merge,
> **M** ice hide in the grass.
> **B** ears
> **E** at greedily—
> **R** eady for winter.

Students can think about their acrostic poem for several days as they polish up the lines. Encourage them to use a dictionary as they search for just the right word.

Keeping a Science Notebook

Students can keep a notebook in which to record observations, questions that occur to them, facts they come across, or other interesting ideas they may have about life. Read the book *Brendan Buckley's Universe and Everything in It* by Sundee T. Frazier (Delacorte, 2007) to introduce this idea to students in upper elementary and middle school. This book is rich in multicultural ideas, too, for example, a multiracial marriage which created Brendan, who is "milk chocolate." His father is the chocolate, and his mother is the milk. See the Lesson Plan on p. 184.

Students should keep a log as you read this book aloud so they can respond at the end of each chapter. They may be surprised as they record the science facts that they learn through reading fiction. What is a thunder egg? What are the different kinds of quartz? The author had to research information about minerals in order to write this kind of story.

Keeping Science Observation Journals

Bring in examples of journals that scientists, amateur and/or professional, have kept. This provides students with a clear idea of what their journal should consist of, how it might be organized, what kinds of things might be recorded, and so on. Look for some of the following:

Primary

Jim Aronsky. *Beachcombing: Exploring the Seashore.* Dutton, 2004.
Bruce McMillan. *Salmon Summer.* Houghton Mifflin, 1998.

A THINKING + LESSON PLAN

◄○►

The Science Notebook

Grades 5–8

Expected Outcomes

Learners will:

1. Listen to a novel read aloud.
2. Respond in their logs after each chapter is read.
3. Discuss the book in Cooperative Learning Groups.
4. Begin a science notebook of their own.

Teaching/Learning Strategies

Resources Needed

Obtain one or more copies of *Brendan Buckley's Universe and Everything in It*, by Sundee T. Frazier (Delacorte, 2007). You will have one copy at your desk for reading aloud, and another will be available for students who may have missed class to read as they catch up with the class.

Directions

Step 1: Read the first chapter of this book aloud. Talk about that chapter together as students compare notes about their reactions.

Step 2: Have students prepare a log in which they will record their reactions each day.

Step 3: Have students begin collecting science information in their logs. They can include what Brendan shares, but have them also record science information that they have discovered.

Step 4: Give students an opportunity to tell the class what they have discovered. They may display their findings on a special bulletin board.

Step 5: Students will write poems about Brendan's life.

Performance Assessment

1. Use + or – based on students' participation in the discussion.
2. Display the class's poems, giving each one a + or – based on completion of the assignment.

Mary Alice Monroe. *Turtle Summer: A Journal for My Daughter.* Photos by Barbara J. Bergwerf. Sylvan Dell, 2007.

Elementary/Middle School

Sneed B. Collard III. *On the Coral Reefs.* Marshall Cavendish, 2005.

Jennifer Owings Dewey. *Piasano, the Roadrunner.* Photos by Wyman Meinzer. Millbrook, 2002.

Sy Montgomery. *Quest for the Tree Kangaroo: An Expedition to the Cloud Forest of New Guinea.* Photos by Nic Bishop. Houghton Mifflin, 2006.

Sandra Weber. *Two in the Wilderness: Adventures of a Mother and Daughter in the Adirondack Mountains.* Photos by Carl Heilman. Calking Creek, 2005.

After students peruse these journals, they should begin keeping a journal about some area or object of study, for example:

- Life in Central Park
- Birds in Our Back Yard
- Growing Vegetables in Columbus, Ohio

Have the class brainstorm a list of possibilities that reflect your town and its surroundings.

Of course, you can't observe life in Central Park unless you live in New York City! However, creek, river, lake, woods, or park are certainly possible in most areas.

Students should keep the journal for at least six months, recording what they observe every week. At the end of that time, they can summarize their observations and publish their conclusions in book form, much as the writers did in the examples above.

Reading Magazines and Journals

Ask if parents can contribute magazines that students might find interesting. Introduce students in grades 6–12, for example, to *National Geographic, Smithsonian, Reader's Digest, Popular Science, Popular Mechanics, Consumers Reports, Sunset,* and *Fine Gardening.*

Tell students about an article that you have just read. For example, a wonderful article, "Where Food Begins," in *National Geographic* (September, 2008) provides a wealth of information about soil around the world and how the quality of soil directly affects the food supply in every country—China, Norway, Ethiopia, Bolivia, and the United States. The authors emphasize the threat of a worldwide food shortage that can be avoided only by attending to our arable soil. This suggests a great study for upper elementary/middle and high school students. They can conduct research about soil along these lines:

- Search the Internet.
- Invite an expert from the county offices to visit your classroom.
- Examine the soil in several locations near your school.
- Compare different kinds of soil; e.g., loam, sand, clay.
- Interview a local farmer or two.
- Check the local library for books that include information about soil.
- See if there are any relevant films you can borrow.

Ask several students to bring in a soil sample from their own yards (a large mayonnaise jar, half full). Add water to the jar (not quite full). Then, shake the jar vigorously so the soil is thoroughly soaked. Let the jar sit undisturbed overnight. The next day, observe the layers into which the soil has settled. Are all jars of soil identical? What does each layer represent?

Collecting Challenging Quotations

Encourage students to share interesting quotations related to science that they may come across, for example:

> Science and technology, and the various forms of art, all unite humanity in a single and interconnected system.
>
> —Zhores A. Medvedev

> So long as the mother, Ignorance, lives, it is not safe for Science, the offspring, to divulge the hidden causes of things.
>
> —Johannes Kepler

> The sea lies all about us. The commerce of all lands must cross it. The very winds that move over the lands have been cradled on its broad expanse and seek ever to return to it.
>
> —Rachel Carson

> We are an intelligent species and the use of our intelligence quite properly gives us pleasure. In this respect the brain is like a muscle. When it is in use, we feel very good. Understanding is joyous!
>
> —Carl Sagan

> Every great advance in science has issued from a new audacity of imagination.
>
> —John Dewey

> Loveliest of trees, the cherry now
> Is hung with bloom along the bough.
>
> —Alfred E. Housman

> There are two ways of spreading light;
> To be the candle or the mirror that reflects it.
>
> —Edith Wharton

Science and ESL Students

Judith Rosenthal's *Teaching Science to Language Minority Students* (Taylor & Francis, 1996) presents linguistically modified methods of science instruction. The author discusses such topics as diversity of learning styles among ESL students, the many cultures of the science classroom, and pedagogical issues. This book can be ordered from Multilingual Matters Ltd., 1900 Frost Road, #101, Bristol, PA 19007.

A vocabulary game that helps ESL students is the familiar "Categories." Most often used as a unit review, it consists of a word (the topic) written down the left side of a sheet and several categories across the top. Students fill in words under each category that begin with the letters of the topic word (see Table 6.1). For example, after discussing the subject of "space" for several days, give students the challenging exercise on page 187.

IDEAS IN ACTION!

The Edible School Yard

"Give me any kid. In six weeks, they'll be eating chard," says Alice Waters, founder of the pioneering Berkeley restaurant Chez Panisse. Her foundation, which funds community- and youth-oriented projects, has given the Berkeley Unified School District $3.8 million to write a curriculum incorporating food-related lessons in all content areas. Waters has already developed the Edible School Yard, turning a patch of asphalt into a garden at a local middle school.

Since then, every school in Berkeley, California, has its own garden plot. Now Waters wants students to connect gardening with lunch and eating. A long-time promoter of organic, natural produce, she is hoping to make a difference in student consciousness that will lead to better eating habits. In March, 2009, Michelle Obama, the new First Lady, sponsored the establishment of a vegetable garden on the White House lawn. Students from a local elementary school helped to create the garden.

Does your school have a garden? Maybe you could involve students and the community in creating an edible garden where students could learn food-related lessons in math and science and even enjoy the fruits of their labors.

TABLE 6.1 Categories

	Heavenly Bodies	*Colors*	*People/Professions*
S	Saturn	silver	scientist
P	Pluto	purple	pilot
A	Asteroid	azure	astronaut
C	Ceres	cocoa	chemist
E	Earth	emerald	engineer

This game works best if there is more than one possible answer. If you want to make it more difficult, you give points for each letter and reward students who have the longest entries.

Women and Science

Considerable effort has been expended to increase girls' interest in science during the early years with the hope that they will continue with careers in science. Providing experience with science in industry and meeting women scientists who serve as role models are some of the methods used nationwide. The following filmed resources are recommended:

Discovering Women: Six Remarkable Women Scientists (VHS, color, six 1-hour videos).
This outstanding series chronicles the stories of contemporary women scientists and

their efforts to overcome prejudices in male-dominated fields. The scientists include a physicist, an archaeologist, a molecular biologist, a computational neuroscientist, a geophysicist, and a chemist. Encourage your library to order the set from Films for the Humanities and Sciences, Box 2053, Princeton, NJ 08543.

Jane Goodall: A Life in the Wild (VHS, color, 31 min.). Fascinating story of Goodall's life and work studying the chimpanzee. Films for the Humanities and Sciences, 1996, address above.

Evelyn Fox Keller: Science and Gender (VHS, color, 30 min.). Keller's life as a theoretical physicist working in mathematical biology and gender issues throughout the history of science. Films for the Humanities and Sciences, 1996, address above.

Science and Social Studies

The history of our country is inextricably tied up with science. The industrial revolution could not have occurred without inventions that created better machinery and methods of producing goods the nation needed. We would not be traveling into space without new technology and the work of scientists who guide the space station from the Earth.

> *It is good to know that I shall live on even in the minds of many who do not know me and largely through association with things that are beautiful and lovely.*
>
> ～ RACHEL CARSON, *Silent Spring*

Begin Collecting Useful Free Materials

Students can help you write letters requesting free materials that you and they will be interested in reading. Be sure to use school stationery. Here are a few ideas:

- *World Ark,* a journal published by the nonprofit charitable group Heifer International, 1 World Avenue, Little Rock AR 72202. The aim of this group is to end hunger and poverty by giving families livestock—goats, sheep, rabbits, and so on—that provide food and income. Each issue (six per year) features interesting articles, for example: "Why Water Matters," "The Carbon Footprint," "From Farm to Table," and "Healing History."
- State maps and travel information: Each state publishes a vast amount of material about tourist attractions, products, and other information that will attract people to come to their state and to spend their money. Often their advertisements appear in magazines, including an address for requesting materials. You can also search the Internet for information about each state, its capital, and a visitor's center or chamber of commerce for big cities.
- Countries around the world: The Internet will yield a wealth of information about each country and provide addresses where you can obtain samples of brochures, pictures, and other information about each country.

DID YOU KNOW?

—◁○▷—

Sarika Singh, a fourteen-year-old girl in England, was not allowed to go to school because she was wearing a thin, steel bracelet, required as a member of the Sikh religion. She appealed the school's decision and won her case in the British High Court in 2008. The court ruled that the school was not promoting equality when it banned her just for wearing a religious symbol.

Science in the News

Have students bring in copies of the daily newspaper. Working in pairs, they can search out news about science around the world. This news may be in a special section; however, it may also be on the home page or in the business section. Have each pair present one finding to the group until all have been covered. Comment on the different kinds of science represented. Note how our planet depends on science and how interdependent we all are.

A Virtual Fieldtrip

The Africa Trail (CD-ROM for Macintosh and Windows, Teacher's Guide with Educational Version). By the makers of *The Oregon Trail*, this complex simulation program takes students on a bike trek through Africa from Tunisia to South Africa. Although real problems (starvation, ethnic conflicts) and obstacles (rough roads) arise to be solved, the focus is on the people of the continent. The program presents the rich diversity of Africa today. Recommended for grades 6–12. Published by MECC, 1995. (See also *The Amazon Trail*.)

Virginia Walker suggests the following Book Connections:

Nancy Farmer. *A Girl Named Disaster.* Orchard, 1996. Eleven-year-old Nhamo escapes from betrothal to a cruel old man by undertaking a dangerous trek across Mozambique and Zimbabwe.

Beverley Naidoo. *No Turning Back: A Novel of South Africa.* HarperCollins, 1997. A story of homeless young blacks struggling to live in post-apartheid Johannesburg.

A Thinking + Lesson Plan: Dealing with Stereotyped Thinking

A THINKING + LESSON PLAN

—◁○▷—

Dealing with Stereotyped Thinking

Grades 3–8

Expected Outcomes

Learners will:

1. Listen to a novel read aloud by the teacher.
2. Discuss the issues presented by the author.

(continued)

---

3. Analyze the stereotyped thinking presented.
4. Discuss stereotyped thinking and how it can change.

Teaching/Learning Strategies

Resources Needed

Read *There's an Owl in the Shower* by Jean Craighead George to the class over a period of a week or two. This short novel introduces the topic of stereotyped thinking and how it can be changed. Students will investigate this topic.

Directions

Step 1: Read *There's an Owl in the Shower* to the class chapter by chapter. The plot can be summarized as follows:

> One day Borden finds a young owlet blown out of a tree by a gust of wind. Because the owlet is still white, Borden thinks he must be a barred owl, not the protected spotted owl that depends for its existence on the old growth forest in northern California. Loggers like Borden's father hate the spotted owls that prevent them from cutting the big trees. They display such bumper stickers as "I like spotted owls fried" or "The only good owl is a dead owl." The community is divided: loggers versus environmentalists. At a community meeting there is a fistfight between Borden's father, Leon, and his science teacher, who is sympathetic to the plight of the spotted owls.
>
> Borden's father decides to care for the little owl Borden brings home to impress the judge when he appears for a hearing. He builds a box shelter and hunts mice to feed him, even cutting them up to feed this cute elfin baby, which they name Bardy. Feeding the funny little bird nine to ten mice a day, Leon gets hooked on Bardy, even making him a beautiful perch from a redwood sprout, and Bardy imprints on big Leon. The whole family comes to love Bardy, and then Borden notices the spots on Bardy's new feathers. Leon agrees to let Bardy go free when he realizes it is illegal to keep any endangered animal in captivity. He helps the other loggers realize that the owl has told them that they aren't managing the forests right. As Borden notes:
>
> > He came right into our midst and turned us all around. I'll never be able to look at an owl the same way again.

Jean George has presented a perfect example of how stereotyped thinking changes when we get to know an individual.

Step 2: Encourage students to discuss events as they occur in the book. After completing this story, guide students to analyze the thinking exemplified by the various characters created by Jean George. Introduce the concept of "stereotyped thinking." Invite students to identify examples of this kind of thinking that they may have observed.

Ask students to complete the following phrases with the name of an animal:

as fast as a _____
as quiet as a _____
as busy as a _____
as sly as a _____

Point out that these phrases have been used so frequently that they have lost their freshness. They focus on only one characteristic of the animal rather than describing the animal in specific detail. Ask students what would happen if we did this to people.

Another theme in this book that could be developed is that of conflicting interests, in this case, logging as a source of jobs and company income versus the needs of an endangered species. Students could investigate similar situations that involve different issues.

Step 3: Have students work in groups to discover more about animals for which we have stereotyped ideas, for example, wolves, rats, and pigs. They can search out both fiction and nonfiction to provide greater insight into the characteristics of these animals. Each group will then give a class presentation, noting their conclusions about the animal studies. This lesson can also lead to a study of humans, for example, children around the world.

Performance Assessment
Students receive grades of Credit/No Credit based on their participation in a group study and presentation.

Science and Mathematics

Science and math go together like ham and eggs, or so it seems. All scientists use mathematics, but are all mathematicians scientists? That is an interesting question to consider.

Read Biographies
Perhaps biographies will give use a clue, for example:

Don Brown. *Odd Boy Out: Young Albert Einstein.* Houghton Mifflin, 2004. People worried about this baby with the large head who was slow to use language. As a child, he focused on ideas and loved to figure out knotty math problems rather than engaging in sports or playing with other children. Yet he became one of the world's greatest mathematicians.

Kathleen Krull. *Marie Curie.* Illustrated by Boris Kulikov. Viking, 2007. As a woman, Marie Curie had to fight to be recognized as a scientist. She fought prejudice and became a role model for the female scientists that followed her. Part of the Giants of Science series.

Counting Science
Bring in a collection of counting books for students to examine. What are the books teaching besides counting the numbers from 1 to 10 or perhaps, 20? The following example features nature–plants and animals.

Laura Bankin. *Swan Harbor: A Nature Counting Book.* Dial, 2003. Attractive illustrations present different birds, animals, flowers, and so forth as children learn numbers through 20. The author includes a map of the area that shows where each flower, bird, and animal lives.

IDEAS IN ACTION!
The Great Turtle Race

A sixth-grade class in Los Altos, California, sponsored Saphira II, the 1-ton leatherback turtle who finished first as she swam more than 7,500 miles from Monterey Bay to reach her nesting beach in Indonesia. They raised $25,000 to suppport a conservation project led by Stanford's Hopkins Marine Station, called Tracking of Pacific Predators (TOPP). Hopkins biologists had previously tagged forty-six leatherback turtles in order to follow via satelllite their trek from nests in Costa Rica to the feeding grounds around the Galapagos Islands.

So little is understood about this marine species that Saphira II's race was designed to provide information on a different migration route to support preservation plans. The leatherback population is facing extinction after declining more than 90 percent over the past twenty years.

Find a picture of a leatherback turtle. Make a poster drawing of a turtle to show how big it is compared to your classroom. What is their average size, weight, and life span? Why might saving this particular species be important? What kinds of information do scientists need to collect in order to protect it? The TOPP project also tracks other marine life such as sharks, albatross, and different turtles.

Your students can investigate the status of varied sea creatures and select some to support. Depending on students' abilities and grade level, possible activities could range from publicizing the dangers to the preservation of this species to raising money to support conservation and data collection efforts.

Present Science Information in Graphic Form

In an article about water, we learn how much water is used each year by a Chinese person (185,000 gallons), a Saudi (343,400 gallons) an American (660,400 gallons) (*World Ark*, May/June 2008, p. 5).

Challenge a class to see how many different ways they can present this information graphically. Post all presentations on the wall.

For more information about the use of water, a vital resource, see: United Nations, Department of Public Information. *Water for Life Decade: 2005–2015.*

Science and the Arts

All of the arts offer us an opportunity for expressing ideas, for sharing our findings in science as well as any other subject. Through painting and drawing, through music and dance, and through dramatic performance, we can express science through numerous activities such as the following:

Create a Collage

Students can create a collage about a scientific topic that particularly interests them. They will need to collect words and pictures from magazines and newspapers over a period of time to use in this artistic presentation. Students should tell everyone what topic they are presenting so that others may bring in material of interest for each other.

Ask other teachers to contribute magazines you can bring to school so that everyone has access to appropriate resources.

Study Bees

Bees are important to agriculture all over the world. Create a Mason Bee house to encourage the growth of bees to pollinate local fruit trees.

FIGURE 6.2   Mason Bee House

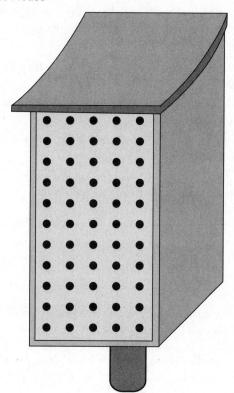

DID YOU KNOW?

The smallest snake in the world is less than four centimeters long, barely covering a quarter. It was discovered in 2008 on an island in the Caribbean, Barbados, and named Leptotyphlops Carlae after the wife of the evolutionary biologist who discovered it. It is not venomous.

Observing the Art of Scientists

When scientists write reports, they often include detailed drawings of something they have developed. When authors write books about science topics, they include photographs, paintings, and line drawings to provide greater understanding of the information they are sharing. Have students examine the different kinds of art used in picture books by talented artists to add to the meaning of the science material presented. Notice that these authors not only wrote the text but also created the illustrations or obtained permission to use pictures from different sources for the following books:

Jim Aronsky. *Field Trips: Bug Hunting, Animal Tracking, Bird-Watching, Shore Walking.* HarperCollins, 2002.

Sy Montgomery and Dianne Taylor-Snow. *Encantado: Pink Dolphin of the Amazon.* Houghton Mifflin, 2002.

Jim Murphy. *An American Plague: The True and Terrifying Story of the Yellow Fever epidemic of 1793.* Clarion, 2003.

Susan E. Quinlan. *The Case of the Monkeys that Fell from the Trees: And Other Mysteries in Tropical Nature.* Boyds Mills Press, 2003.

CONNECTIONS

Science, as we have already noted, covers broad studies from nature, biology, chemistry, geology, medicine, oceanography, physics, technology, and so on. It is important that children at all age levels be actively engaged in science as they extend their knowledge of the world. As they observe the accomplishments and the passions of men and women who are involved in scientific fields, they may begin to see themselves as scientists, too, who can contribute to knowledge in one of these fields.

As we teach science, we will continue supporting student self-esteem, develop empathy through group work, and provide equity for students with different abilities. We will also continue to integrate science with learning in such other areas as language arts/reading, social science, mathematics, and the performing arts. Science adds a wealth of exciting information to studies across the curriculum.

GETTING INVOLVED

Do you know much about science? Perhaps this is the time for you to begin expanding your knowledge about scientists and how much we depend on them.

Expanding Your Reflective Teaching Portfolio

1. Consider how science influences your life. List the many uses of science that you engage in each day, for instance, eating canned food, taking pills, or depending on refrigeration.
2. Scan through the daily newspaper over the period of one week. Clip articles that have something to do with science. Summarize what you have found and what you have learned through reading these articles. Consider how you might use this information in the classroom.

Working with Your Cooperative Learning Group

1. Talk about what you know about science in your CLG. Then, make a list of scientific areas that you think you should know more about, and plan to search the Internet to see what you can discover. Each person will share his or her findings when you next meet.
2. Read a biography of a scientist that is suitable for young readers. Tell your group about this book so that each person can add it to a list of Science Literature for Students that will be useful in teaching.
3. Locate the January, 2007 copy of *Educational Leadership*, published by the Association for Supervision and Curriculum Development (ASCD). This issue focuses entirely on "Science in the Spotlight" and offers broad coverage of science instruction. This journal will be in the Education Library on any college campus that trains teachers.

EXPLORING FURTHER

Karen Rohrich Ansberry and Emily R. Morgan. *More Picture-Perfect Science Lessons: Using Children's Curiosity.* National Science Teachers Association, 2007.

Mary Catherine Bateson. *Peripheral Visions: Learning along the Way.* HarperCollins, 1994. Bateson, a noted anthropologist and the daughter of Margaret Mead, notes: "in our rapidly changing and interdependent world the tasks of learning are never complete." This book offers observations of living in other cultures—Israel, the Philippines, Iran.

Patricia McGlashan et al. *Outdoor Inquiries. Taking Science Investigations Outside the Classroom.* Heinemann, 2007. Detailed lesson plans and suggestions for cross-curricular integration plus ideas for assessment.

Pat Murphy, et al. *Exploratopia: More than 400 Kid-Friendly Experiments and Explorations for Curious Minds.* Illustrated by Jason Gorski. Little Brown, 2006. Includes a companion website, answers, hints, tips, index; for Grades 3–8.

F. Sutman. *The Science Quest.* Jossey-Bass, 2008. Inquiry methods based on National Science Teachers Association (NSTA) standards.

CHAPTER 7

Multicultural Mathematics

> *I've missed over 9,000 shots in my career. I've*
> *lost almost 300 games. Twenty-six times I've been*
> *trusted to take the game-winning shot—and*
> *missed. I've failed over and over and over again*
> *in my life. And that is why I succeed.*
>
> ～ MICHAEL JORDAN

Mathematics is receiving increasing attention across all education levels as we acknowledge the importance of mathematical skill and creative abilities to the future of our country and to the world. It is important that we consider how we can integrate multicultural concepts into the study of mathematics.

We need to engage all students in the possibilities that mathematics has to offer for their lives. As with all subject areas, learning activities should support student self-esteem, and they can also help develop empathy among students. The teacher is responsible for seeing that all students in an inclusive classroom have equitable opportunities to learn math skills and concepts. In this chapter, we explore a number of possibilities for teaching multicultural mathematics. Integrating mathematics into language arts/reading and social studies, where possible, as well as science and even the performing arts, offers more opportunities for making math a real part of our daily lives. We especially want to show diverse students what mathematics has to offer them and why it is important that they continue studying higher mathematics for the intellectual power it gives them.

❖ **Mathematics Activities that Support Esteem, Empathy, and Equity**

In this section we continue emphasizing the model on which we base multicultural education as a way to support students' self-esteem during mathematics activities. We continue to utilize group math activities that develop empathy as students work together, and we also provide equitable access to learning materials and many opportunities to learn mathematics.

Supporting Esteem

Creating a Number Word Wall

Talk about numbers with your students. Depending on the level that you teach, they will have different experience and knowledge about numbers. Engage students with numbers every day beginning with this kind of Number Word Wall:

How do you use numbers every day?

Counting out money for my lunch
Seeing what time it is when the alarm goes off
Watching the clock so I leave for school on time
Getting into my seat in the classroom before the bell rings

Where do you see numbers every day?

On the side of the school bus
Addresses on houses I pass
The door of our classroom
Today's date
The calendar
Watching the clock to see if it's lunchtime yet
Pages in the book I'm reading
Paying for lunch
Math lessons (older students may include chemistry or physics)

DID YOU KNOW?

◄○►

Days in Each Month

Thirty days has September,
April, June, and November.
All the rest have thirty-one
Except February alone,
Which has twenty-eight
Until Leap Year gives it one day more!

Working with Numbers

Aside from the daily math lessons, you can encourage students to play with numbers, which is particularly important in elementary school as children are learning basic mathematical processes.

- Counting from 1–10, 1–100—knowing the number words and concepts.
- Counting by 2s, 3s, 4s, 5s, etc. (helps with addition and multiplication facts).
- Reading the calendar, dates.

Talking about Math Words

Make a Word Wall with words we need to be able to read as well as to write in figures. Begin with columns to list numbers from one to one hundred, thus:

one	ten	twenty	thirty
two	eleven	twenty-one	thirty-one

Continue with words for larger numbers:

thousand	million	billion	trillion

Add words for number processes:

addition	subtraction	multiplication	division
plus	minus	times	divided by

Students need to be able to use such words as part of their working vocabularies.

Increasing Vocabularies

And then there are words that extend the meaning of mathematical relationships. Students can gradually add these words to their active vocabularies.

equal	calculate	estimation
sequence	equality	calculation
predict	sequential	equivalent

Add others as they occur to you.

Developing Empathy

Students seldom have an opportunity to work in groups with mathematics. Here are a few ideas.

Can You Match Me?

Here is a game two or more students can play, a game that challenges their thinking.

They can use the chalkboard to present a mathematical expression, for example:

Given: $\dfrac{5 + 16}{3}$

They then ask, "Can you match me?"

The other students in the group supply any matching statements, for example:

$$10 - 3 \qquad 15 - 8 \qquad \frac{30 + 5}{5} \qquad \frac{21 - 7}{2}$$

Solving Group Problems

Give students math expressions to complete in pairs or small groups, for example:

$$67 \times 589 = \underline{\hspace{1.5cm}}$$
$$\underline{\hspace{1.5cm}} \times 827 = 4962$$

Encourage them to visualize these relationships by drawing pictures or diagrams to help them find different ways of completing these expressions. (See "Singapore Math" on p. 216.)

Doing Math Research in the Classroom

Students can collect math data as they research topics together in the classroom. Two or three students can team together to collect such data as:

Height of students (not weight!)
Number who have brown (dark) eyes
Pages read during a free reading period
Scores on a math test
Scores on a vocabulary test
Favorite color of students
Number of students whose family moved within (last year), (two years), (five years), (never moved)
Favorite book

Each team will plan the research process. Some teams will seek permission to extend their research to include all fifth graders, teachers in the school, etc. They will need to plan any research tools needed, for example, a survey or checklist. Then they will need to schedule the time and method for gathering the data, work together to compile their data, and consider just how they will report their findings. Emphasize that names are omitted in doing research to respect privacy.

Graphs will work nicely for most of the kinds of data that will be reported. With height, however, data might be divided with one graph for everyone, one for boys, and one for girls to provide comparative information. Encourage students to use different kinds of graphs depending on the kinds of data collected (see Figure 7.1).

Providing Equity

It is essential that all students have access to appropriate math instruction. The United States lags behind many countries in student accomplishments in mathematics. What is it that other countries are doing that gives their students such an advantage over our students?

Unfortunately, our emphasis has been on learning facts and following given procedures to solve similar problems rather than on understanding mathematical processes. Students need opportunities to apply mathematical thinking in different situations. They need to see mathematics used in many real-life situations, not just in a mathematics class. Math must become meaningful to all students.

FIGURE 7.1   *Favorite Animals*

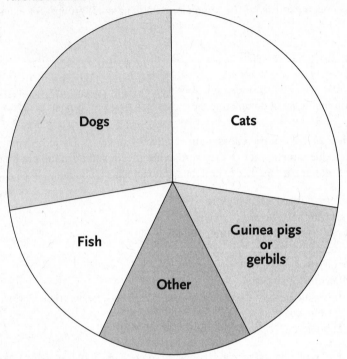

Reading Aloud

David M. Schwartz. *G Is for Googol: A Math Alphabet Book.* Illustrated by Marissa Moss. Tricycle, 1998. Explains the meaning of many interesting math-related words. Add these words to your Math Word Wall. Read one math idea each day.

After reading, have students make Moebius strips. Draw a line down the center of the strip all the way around. Cut along this line to find something surprising. What good is this amazing construction? You can also have students find a pine cone or a sunflower head full of seeds so they can observe Fibonacci numbers.

Caution: Don't confuse *googol* with *google*. Explore the origin of the term *googol*.

Children's Literature That Suggests Math

Explore math concepts with these books after reading them to young children. Use your imagination!

The Wolf's Chicken Stew	Counting
Cook-a-Doodle-Doo	Measuring
Six-Dinner	Patterns, addition

Tikki Tikki Tembo	Counting, graphing
A Chair for My Mother	Costs, purchasing
"The Rule" in *The Stories Huey Tells*	Money, buying a meal
Henry and Mudge: The First Book	Money, savings, weights

Mental Math

My fourth graders in Alaska used to love to play Mental Math while standing in line waiting for lunch. To be sure I had the right answer myself, I kept a small tablet ready in my hand as I called out:

Take six; add five (11); multiply by 3 (33); subtract 6 (27); divide by 3—What's your answer? (9)

Carlos, what did you get? 9? Good! How many people had 9?

OK, take 8; multiply by 2; divide by 4; add 3; multiply by 5. What's your answer?

Frankie, what's your answer? 35? (If Frankie got the wrong answer, I could go over the process with her orally based on the notes on my tablet.)

❖ Integrating Mathematics into Other Curriculum Areas

How does mathematics relate to other subjects of the curriculum? Invite students to consider this question as they develop studies in social studies, science, and the language arts.

DID YOU KNOW?

◀◦▶

In 1992, the popular Barbie doll that many girls wanted was made to say, "Math is tough." This attitude reflected the accepted attitude that girls could not work with mathematics as well as boys. Therefore, girls were not encouraged to take advanced mathematics courses.

In 2008, however, researchers are disproving that statement. University scholars examined the results of required NCLB tests of 7 million students in ten states ranging from grades 2–11. They found no difference in performance between the sexes. Today, girls are encouraged to take mathematics courses that are required for advanced work in science and technology.

In spite of this evidence, in the workplace there is still prejudice that favors men over women in careers that demand high-level mathematics. Also, girls must be encouraged to aspire to work in these fields despite the competition.

Mathematics and Language Arts/Reading

How are mathematics and the study of the English language arts and reading related?

Math as Language

Mathematics is a special kind of language that uses numbers basically, but it also incorporates letters of the alphabet as we move into more advanced expressions of mathematical relationships. Encourage students to create math expressions and to tell a story that goes with a math expression, for example:

The Math Expression: $2\,(6 \times 3) + 2(2) = 40$

The Story:

Six groups of students learned three songs for an assembly that they put on once for the school's students and then later for the PTA. Two students sang solos at each performance. Altogether, the students performed forty songs.

Students can work in pairs or small groups to create math expressions and stories that go with them. The groups can then exchange their work with others as they check to see that each is accurately stated.

Or, groups can challenge each other to provide the math expression, if given the story, and vice versa, to provide a story to explain a given math expression.

Writing Math Messages

Students can learn to write number facts as algebraic expressions, for example:

$$2 + 3 = 5 \qquad a + 3 = 5 \qquad 2\,(a + 3) = 10$$

Students can learn to solve algebraic expressions by explaining what *a* equals. As they gain mathematical skill, they can solve more complex expressions. They can also tell stories that are appropriate for each expression.

Codes

Students can compose simple codes with which to send messages, for example:

A = 1	26 = 1
B = 2	25 = 2
C = 3	24 = 3
D = 4	23 = 4
E = 5	22 = 5
F = 6	21 = 6
G = 7	20 = 7
H = 8	19 = 8
I = 9	18 = 9
J = 10 . . .	17 = 10 . . .

Students can use algebraic expressions to make their codes more complicated:

A = 1 + 7 = 8	or	A = a + 1 = 3
B = 1 + 8 = 9		B = a + 2 = 4
C = 1 + 9 = 10		C = a + 3 = 5

More advanced students can investigate the subject of codes on the Internet. Among other interesting bits of information they may learn about is the use of the Navajo language to send messages during World War II, as a base for codes that no enemy could break.

Number Stories

Challenge students to compose stories around a given set of numbers. Write the numbers 3, 7, and 2 on the board. Each student is to write a story in which these numbers are used, for example:

> Three children went walking. Four other children joined them, so there were seven children walking together. At the swings, five children stopped to play, and two other children continued on their way.

> I had 3 dimes, so I had 30 cents. Mother gave me a nickel and two pennies for taking out the trash, so I had 37 cents. I bought a soda for 35 cents, so I had only two cents left.

Working with Story Problems

Since students often have trouble with "story problems," provide practice in various ways.

1. **Oral Number Stories**
   Tell the class number stories that they are to listen to. The point of this story is not to get the correct answer, but to explain what processes you need to use to solve the problem.

2. You Supply the Numbers
   Display stories like this on a transparency. The students supply the numbers and then solve the story problems.

   > Dick wants to buy a _____. The _____ costs _____. Dick has only _____. How much more money does Dick need in order to buy the _____?

Have students compose similar stories to challenge other members of the class. Those who are more mathematically sophisticated will be able to compose more complicated stories.

Finding Connections between Math and Poetry

Challenge students to find out how many connections they can find between mathematics and poetry. Have students present their discoveries to the class. Then, add each one to a display titled "Math/Poetry Connections." You can begin with the ones presented in this section. Then, ask if anyone can find on the Internet mathematicians who wrote poetry. Remember, too, that mathematics is related to the writing of music, how we keep score in sports, and scientific experimentation. All these topics can be expressed in the form of poetry.

Poetry has often been compared to music, and it is easy to substantiate this comparison. Ask upper elementary and middle school students to help you create a Word Wall of musical/math words. Keep adding to this list as you continue your study of music together:

ballad	rhythm	stanza
lyric	measure	tone

beat	line	mood
song	verse	refrain
theme	pattern	chorus
compose	composer	repetition

Underline the words that are also used in mathematics.

The traditional beat (called meter) of formal poetry can be found in many poems that older students will enjoy. Robert Frost employs the strong beat identified as *iambic* meter in "Stopping by Woods on a Snowy Evening." The poet stops to enjoy looking at the woods as it fills up with snow. Finally he concludes, in the last of four quatrains:

The woods are lovely, dark and deep,
But I have promises to keep,
And miles to go before I sleep,
And miles to go before I sleep.

Beat out the meter as you speak these lines, and you will discover four beats in each line. Have students do this, too, as they become more aware of specific rhythms. Each beat consists of an unaccented syllable followed by an accented syllable as in, for example, "The woods."

There are many creative ways to link poetry with your mathematics curriculum. For instance, the whimsical limerick "Relativity" deals with a mathematics concept:

There once was a lady named Bright,
Who traveled much faster than light.
She set out one day
In a relative way
And returned on the previous night.

Middle school students may be delighted to discover what a famous poet thought about arithmetic. Carl Sandburg presents interesting images of numbers in his poem "Arithmetic." For example, he sees numbers as "pigeons that fly in and out of your head." Students can add lines to go with those of Sandburg as they consider what arithmetic means in our world— buying tickets for a jazz festival, flying an airplane, figuring out temperatures in Fahrenheit and Celsius, and so on. This creates a wonderful listing poem. See the lesson on p. 205.

Making Words Plural in English
Depending on your students' ability levels, you may want to talk about how we form plurals in English, for example:

room	rooms
pencil	pencils
dish	dishes
glass	glasses
fox	foxes

Then there are the words that don't change, no matter how many there are:

deer	deer
sheep	sheep

And, of course, there are such oddities as:

goose   geese
child   children

Groups of Animals

Students will enjoy discovering the many odd expressions that we use for groups of animals, for example:

A pride of lions
A gaggle of geese
A covey of quail
A school of fish

A THINKING + LESSON PLAN

◄◦►

"If I Were King!" Listing Poems

Grades 2–8

Expected Outcomes
Learners will:

1. Listen to a picture book read aloud.
2. Brainstorm ideas around the theme suggested by the book.
3. Write a listing poem about the theme.

Teaching/Learning Strategies

Resources Needed
Obtain a copy of Fred Hiatt's book *If I Were Queen of the World* and/or Judith Viorst's poem "If I Were King."

Directions
Step 1: Read the selected work aloud. Discuss what students would do if they were king (or queen). List ideas on the board.

Step 2: Have students write individual poems titled "If I Were King" or "If I Were Queen" listing all the things they would do.

Step 3: Display the poems on a bulletin board decorated with golden crowns that students cut from construction paper.

Performance Assessment
1. Students will participate in listing ideas after reading the book or poem.
2. Students will produce a short listing poem to display.

Students receive + or − based on their submitting a poem for display.

DID YOU KNOW?

◄○►

Is a Billion a Billion?

Not always—a billion in the United States is not the same as a billion in England! How can this be? The English use the word *milliard* for our billion.

Some authors, particularly poets, have had fun making up interesting, creative names for groups that never were, for example:

A scribble of writers
A chowder of clams
A giggle of girls
A grumbling of buses

If you are intrigued by such wordplay, look for the book *Ounce, Dice, Trice* by Alastair Reid (Little, 1958). Although this is an old book, it has been reissued.

Mathematics and Social Studies

Social scientists use mathematics in their work as it relates to populations, budgets, dates, statistics, and so on. Check on figures presented elsewhere in this text, for example, the population of the United States or important dates associated with civil rights legislation in Chapter 5. The Multicultural Calendar in Chapter 9 is full of such dates, as is the theme on *Time* at the end of that chapter.

Social Studies, Math, and the Newspapers

Arrange to get multiple copies of the local newspaper for a week or more. Have students pore over each issue as they read interesting articles. Have them note the many ways mathematics appears in the daily news—grocery ads, reports on the federal or state budget, reports of student scores on mandated testing, the number of people killed in an accident, the temperature, rainfall, earthquakes, and so forth for a particular day.

Some newspapers make a unit of study about the newspaper available to teachers. Be sure to ask. A member of the paper's staff may also be available for a school visit, or the class could make a field trip to the plant to see how a newspaper is put "to bed" each day, how it is printed, folded, and delivered to those who will drop it off at our homes or at the newsstand.

Dates

Use dates in creating math problems, for example:

Who was older when he was president—George Washington or Thomas Jefferson?

Students will have to do some research. You could add to this process by asking, "How much older?"

How many years ago was Abraham Lincoln assassinated?

Such questions involve two steps: (1) checking the needed dates in a book or on the Internet and (2) solving the math problem.

DID YOU KNOW?

◄◦►

America Is Not the Richest Nation in the World!

In 2008 Switzerland had a higher median household income ($62,000) compared to that of the United States ($48,000).

Our per capita GNP (amount of national income generated per citizen) was $44,000—third in the world.

Luxembourg is first with $78,000.
Norway is second with $52,000.

In 2007, the number of millionaires in China, Russia, and India grew faster than in the United States (Center for American Progress).

Income inequality is also greater in the United States than in other developed nations, which may make us more vulnerable to economic downturns than they are.

However, the United States still has something going for it. College graduates from the United States are not flocking to Luxembourg to earn more money. "People still want to come to the United States more than any other country. They believe there is opportunity here," according to the Hudson Institute.

Post such questions on the board as students arrive in the morning. At the end of the day, see how many students have an answer.

Math Challenges

Give students opportunities to think about math that troubles them, such as fractions. Put challenges on the board, for example:

Which is largest? 2/3, 3/4, 9/10?

Which are the same? 3/4, 12/16, 15/20?

Let students write challenges for other students to answer.

Russian Peasant Multiplication

Here is a tricky method of multiplying larger numbers that students in upper elementary grades will find intriguing. Even older students, who, of course, use calculators, will have fun with it.

~~26 × 33~~   Halve each number on the left side. Double each number on the right side. Discard any halves that remain.

13 × 66

~~6 × 132~~   Cross out any lines that begin with even numbers.

3 × 264

1 × 528   Add the numbers on the right to obtain the right answer.
Check by using your usual method of multiplication.

─────────

858   Why does this strange method of multiplying work?

IDEAS IN ACTION!

Pennies for Peace

In 1993, a mountaineer named Greg Mortenson drifted into an impoverished Pakistan village in the Karakoram mountains after a failed attempt to climb K2, the second-highest mountain in the area after Mt. Everest. Moved by the kindness of the simple village folk who inhabited Korphe, he promised to return and build them a school. Mortenson's story is told in *Three Cups of Tea,* which he and David Relin wrote and published in 2006 (Viking Penguin) after the fateful terrorist attacks on September 11, 2001.

The sincerity of this gentle giant was evident, but his task was not easy because he had no money. Finally, a California businessman, Dr. Jean Hoerni, heard his plea for help and agreed to fund the Central Asian Foundation to support the building of small village schools, which cost only $12,000 each in Pakistan. Mortenson spent months in Pakistan working with the villagers to eventually build and maintain fifty-five schools—especially for girls—in the forbidding terrain where the Taliban came into being.

This humanitarian firmly believes that the way to peace is through education. He feels that mothers who have gone to school will encourage their children also to go to school and aim to improve the lives of their families; their sons will not be tempted to join such terrorist groups as the Taliban or Al Qaeda. As he states, "The enemy is ignorance. The only way to defeat it is to build relationships with these people, to draw them into the modern world with education and business. Otherwise the fight will go on forever."

The nonprofit organization Central Asia Institute, located in Bozeman, Montana (Box 7209, Bozeman MT 59771), was created to raise money to continue making schooling available to the Afghan and Pakistani villagers. One effort that is especially designed to encourage school children to participate in this undertaking is Pennies for Peace (www.penniesforpeace.org). Any school or class can become involved by collecting pennies to buy school supplies for children who have none. Since 1994, more than eight million pennies have been collected to contribute to the work of the Central Asia Institute. It costs the group only $1.00 per month (one hundred pennies) to educate one child in the Middle East; a teacher's salary is about $1.00 per day. Here is a wonderful cause for American children to support as they learn more about these countries and their people.

Comparing Currencies

There used to be far more different coins, the franc or deutchmark, for example, than there are today, since most European countries have joined together to adopt the euro. As you moved from country to country in Europe, you had to change your money into the coins and bills used in the next country.

Many countries still use their individual coinage. The United States, of course, uses the dollar (and larger bill denominations) plus coins—nickels, dimes, quarters, and even pennies.

A Thinking + Lesson Plan: Money Around the World

Help students work with different currencies in the following lesson plan.

A THINKING + LESSON PLAN

-◄○►-

Money around the World

Grades 6–8

Expected Outcomes

Learners will:

1. Learn that different kinds of money are used in various countries.
2. Compare the value of money in other countries to the U.S. dollar.
3. Work at a learning center focusing on Money around the World.

Teaching/Learning Strategies

Resources Needed

Order a class set of newspapers from a major local paper. Be sure that it carries the daily business report and contains a chart of currency values. Set up a learning center—Money around the World—that includes laminated copies of the Task Card presented in Table 7.1. We suggest that you enlarge each part of the card, placing the questions on one side and the currency chart on the other. (See Chapter 3 for suggestions about creating a learning center.) Collect a few coins from different countries. Be aware that many European countries began using the euro in 2002.

Directions

Step 1: Distribute newspapers (at least one per two students). Ask the students to browse through the newspaper to see how many different uses of mathematics they can discover. List these on a large sheet of paper mounted on the wall. The stock prices (decimals) and foreign money values (percents) should be one of the items listed.

Step 2: Point out the daily currency chart. Ask the students what this chart tells us (the value of world coins compared to the U.S. dollar). Show the students a few coins or bills from different countries, telling them the name of each—euro, peso, or krone. Ask them if they have traveled to other countries where they used different coins. Invite them to bring samples to show the class.

Ask students to tell you how many whole yen you would get for one U.S. dollar. Explain that when traveling in Tokyo, for example, you need to quickly translate a price into dollars, so that you know approximately how much you are paying for an item. If you saw a hat on sale for 24 yen, for instance, about how many dollars would you need to buy it? Show the students how to figure the amount exactly through long division.

Step 3: Introduce the learning center you have set up entitled Money around the World. Explain the activities at the center, which they will visit in small groups as assigned. Post assigned times at the center.

Each day bring in the newspaper for this center so students can compare the changing values of certain coins, for example, Mexico's peso.

(continued)

Notice that this math activity challenges student thinking and involves them in reading and math processes. Students might make cardboard euros to use in role-playing purchases made in Paris or Berlin. Encourage students to use a few German or French words in their conversation, such as *Bonjour* (Hello—French) or *Auf wiedersehn* (Goodbye—German).

Performance Assessment
Select several mathematically adept students to serve as consultants to assist students. The activity is graded Credit/No Credit based on a student's completing the questions on the Task Card (even with help). Students may receive extra credit by following the changing values of a specific coin for two weeks and reporting their findings to the class.

Money in the News

Today with the economic downturn experienced in the United States and around the world, we are hearing much about money in the news. Bailouts for large companies are requiring *billions* of dollars from the government. The deficit for the operation of the federal government is expressed in *trillions* of dollars. President Obama has submitted a budget for the coming year that is also in the *trillions*.

Discuss the meaning of these words with students. Talk about other figures that appear in the news, for example, the rising percentage of unemployed people. What do these figures mean? What about "mortgage foreclosure"? Children, especially in the middle school and high school, need an opportunity to talk about such matters which, in many cases, have a direct impact on them.

DID YOU KNOW?

◄○►

High Finance in the United States

With the turmoil in the banking world in 2008 came talk of funds needed to bail out failing businesses. We heard figures beyond millions into billions and trillions bandied about. For most of us it is difficult to comprehend the meaning of such numbers.

In an effort to help us understand the size of the $700 billion the federal government proposed lending institutions to cover their debts, the *New York Times* shared the following comparisons:

- To cover this $700 billion would mean that each man, woman, and child in the United States would have to pay $2,000.
- In terms of 2007 dollars, we spent only $670 billion on the entire Vietnam War.
- The Head Start Program, which serves over 900,000 children from poor families across the country, has an annual budget of $7 billion. The money spent on this $700 billion bailout could fund Head Start for one hundred years!

Just imagine what else we could do with $700 billion—books, libraries, new schools, scholarships, health plans, and on and on. Here is a controversial issue worth discussing.

TABLE 7.1 · Money Around the World Task Card

SIDE ONE
Money from Other Countries

Country	Currency	Worth in dollars*
Australia	dollar	1.2994
Austria	euro	.7664
Belgium	euro	.7664
Great Britain	pound	.5321
Canada	dollar	1.1244
China	yuan	8.2781
Denmark	krone	6.27
France	euro	.7664
Germany	euro	.7664
Hong Kong	dollar	7.7979
Israel	shekel	4.37
Italy	euro	.7664
Japan	yen	102.72
Mexico	peso	11.233
Netherlands	euro	.7664
Norway	krone	6.27
Russia	ruble	.00349
Sweden	krone	6.27
Switzerland	euro	.7664

*January 25, 2005.

SIDE TWO
Money around the World

Have you ever heard of a yuan?
In which country would you find this coin?
  (Look at the chart on the other side of this card.)
How much is a yuan worth compared with our dollar?

Do other countries use dollars besides the United States?
Which countries use dollars?
Are these "dollars" worth the same amount?
Which "dollar" is worth the most?

Every day this list of currencies appears in the newspaper. See if you can find it in the financial or business section. Compare the values for each coin to see how it has changed since this list was published.
Why might values of coins or bills go up or down?
See if you can find information about what determines the value of a piece of currency.

Pretend you are traveling to several different countries. As you enter each country, you exchange $10 for the currency of that country.
How many pesos would you get in Mexico?
How many euros would you get in France?
How many pounds would you get in Great Britain?

Find pictures of some of these coins. Perhaps someone you know has money from different countries.

Women in Mathematics

Students working in small groups can focus a special unit of study on the achievements of women in mathematics. Invite female mathematicians to visit your classroom. Discuss math anxiety and how students can overcome it. Have students search for additional information about women mathematicians. Teri Perl presents a summary of women's achievements in *Math Equals: Biographies of Women Mathematicians,* which students might update.

A Learning Center: Inventing Tomorrow

A LEARNING CENTER PROJECT

◄○►

How to Invent the Year 2050!

Solve this problem:

Begin with the year 2050.
Subtract the current year.
Answer (years until 2050): _____

Now, add your age.
Answer (your age in 2050 A.D.): _____

IMAGINE! You are _____ years old. Look around you. What is life like at this time? Complete the following sentences:

1. In 2050, I will be living in:

   _____

   _____

2. In 2050, I will be spending most of my time:

   _____

   _____

3. In 2050, my most significant relationship will be with:

   _____

   _____

4. In 2050, the newspapers will be featuring:

   _____

   _____

5. In 2050, our people's most serious problems are:

_____

_____

6. In 2050 the world's most serious problems are:

_____

_____

Have a small group of advanced students search for copies of Alvin Toffler's book *Future Shock*, which was very popular in the last decades of the twentieth century. See what he was predicting for the twenty-first century. Compare his ideas with those students are predicting for 2050.

Ask students to write on the following topic: Would you like to know exactly what is going to happen in the future? How would this be an advantage? How would it be a disadvantage?

Developing a Thematic Study: A Global Village

The label "a global village" seems an increasingly accurate description of the way we live today. We can't isolate ourselves from the beliefs and actions of people who may be very different from us, whether they live nearby or far away, because all of us are interrelated. The activities in this section will enable students to appreciate the interesting diversity as well as the overriding commonalities of human experience.

This broad theme encompasses everything from communications to food to racial and ethnic backgrounds to religions and more. You might open up a discussion of what the concept "a global village" means by introducing the demographics shared by the United Nations, as shown in Figure 7.2.

You might present this information on a large poster so that the information could be readily available during the class study. Later, provide a copy for each student to place in his or her Learning Log, which will be kept throughout the study of the Global Village.

Read the information on the poster aloud to focus everyone's attention on the ideas presented and to see that they can all read the words. Ask students to think about why this information was shared with the public. What did the people who created this poster want to convey? Have several students record the answers students give on the chalkboard for later reference.

Then, lead a discussion about the information presented, beginning with the first section about population. What do these figures tell us? Then discuss the rest of the information item by item as each topic is summarized. Take plenty of time with this kind of discussion, probably at least forty-five minutes to cover the full poster. Be aware that this poster covers a wide breadth of major topics: total world population, religions, wealth and lifestyle, literacy, food, housing, and education.

This is an interesting way of beginning a study of what's going on with our planet and the people who live on it. This study could easily last a full year, if that much time

FIGURE 7.2 A Village of 100

If we could, at this very moment, shrink the world's population to a village of exactly 100 people, and all existing human ratios remained the same, the people in the village would be:

57 Asians

21 Europeans

14 North, Central, and South Americans

8 Africans

Of those people:

70 would be non-Christians; 30 would be Christian.

6 people would hold 50% of the wealth of the village; these 6 people would all be from the United States.

70 of the people would be unable to read.

50 would suffer from malnutrition.

80 would live in substandard housing.

Only 1 person would have a university education.

United Nations, 1990

were available. You can also see how readily the study crosses the full curriculum. The first math project would be to update the figures presented using data from the latest census.

One way to move forward with this study is to have students identify the general topics presented on the poster as you write each one on the chalkboard. Suggesting that the class needs to find out what lies behind each summarizing statement presented, ask students to sign up to investigate the topic that interests them the most. Limit the number of signups for each topic to the first five so that one study does not become overloaded. Students will then form Cooperative Learning Groups and begin to brainstorm the questions they need to answer about each topic.

This study leads naturally to the use of the computer and Internet. A final class project might well be a multimedia presentation that the whole class can present to other groups of students as well as to parents.

A Learning Center: Using the Computer

Software can help engage students with math across cultures, too. *Maya Math,* for example, a CD-ROM program, was designed by Bank Street College of Education and published by Sunburst Communications (Box 100, Pleasantville, NY 10570; Phone: 800-321-7511). Appropriate for grades 4 through 8, it helps students discover the importance of place value and zero by deciphering the Mayan base-20 number system. They learn to convert Mayan dates to contemporary dates.

The above program has been integrated with social studies in *The Second Voyage of Mimi.* This program engages students in discovering a lost Mayan city.

Recommended Resources

Material is constantly being published to help teachers connect math and multicultural education, for example:

The Multicultural Math Classroom: Bringing in the World by Claudia Zaslavsky (Heinemann, 1996). It presents a short history of mathematics, then suggests activities for grades K–8, beginning with finger counting and simple games and moving to geometry in architecture and art, data analysis, and probability theory.

Math across Cultures is a fifty-page publication available from the San Francisco Exploratorium Order Department, 3601 Lyon Street, San Francisco, CA 94123 (Phone: 800-359-9899). Appropriate for grades 4 through 12, it includes many multicultural activities and resources. A small group of students might, for example, follow directions for unraveling and counting the Incan Quipu knots and then present a report and demonstration to the class. Another group could learn to play Madagascar solitaire, offering to teach others who were interested.

Cynthia Manthey's *Pre-K Math: Concepts from Global Sources* (Humanics Learning, ISBN 0-89334-240-8). Appropriate for ages two to five, this 160-page book helps children learn to count in different languages and play number games. Sketches and detailed instructions help teachers share ideas from such countries as Brazil, Congo, Cuba, India, and Thailand.

Cultures of the World series from Marshall Cavendish. Includes countries such as Mongolia, Ghana, Barbados.

Enchantment of the World series from Children's Book Press. Includes countries such as Serbia, Japan, Colombia.

Beatrice Hollyer. *Wake Up, World! A Day in the Life of Children around the World.* Holt, 1999. Follow eight children from eight countries as they go through their daily routines.

IDEAS IN ACTION!

A Picture Worth a Thousand Words

The Nature Conservancy, since 2001, has provided more than 220 people in sixty-one remote villages in China with inexpensive cameras with film included so that the Chinese villagers can capture pictures of their daily lives to share with the world. They talked with oral historians to record the stories that go with each picture. This project is called Photovoice.

Isn't this a great idea! You can do it, too. Watch for sales of these handy cameras so you can give them to your students. They can picture their lives by shooting scenes from their family life and activities to share with their classmates. The twenty-four or more pictures they take will provide a wealth of information about which they can talk and write for at least a semester. Of course, they will publish their work!

David Wallechinsky. *The Complete Book of the Summer Olympics: Sydney 2000 Edition* and *The Complete Book of the Winter Olympics* (1998 Edition). Overlook, 1998. History and statistics of the Olympic Games.

Older students can explore issues relating sports and politics. Many people believe that sports are about merit and, therefore, are not biased. Find a book such as the following to discuss this issue.

Susan D. Bachrach. *The Nazi Olympics: Berlin 1936.* Little, Brown, 1999. Shows how sports have been used for propaganda purposes.

Human Needs

Looking at other cultures can help students learn more about themselves and their culture. After you have been studying a particular group of people or reading tales from several cultures, ask students to list the most basic needs they think are common to all cultures. Focus on the fundamental human needs for love, food, and shelter. Relate these to students' lives. How are these provided for in their lives? How do different groups satisfy them?

Students can brainstorm examples of how different people respond to one need, such as *love.* Then they can write personal responses, completing the sentence "Love is . . ." and illustrating their ideas. As a class, students can prepare a collage for the bulletin board, showing how different needs are met in different cultures, based on their own illustrations or examples they have found.

For a graphic representation of the global family, see *Material World: A Global Family Portrait* by Peter Menzel. Thirty families, from countries such as Bosnia, Mali, Haiti, India, and Japan, were asked to display all their possessions and tell how they live. The striking disparities as well as similarities among the families will stimulate student interest and discussion.

Singapore Math

Why do students from Singapore typically score high on international math exams? They have been taught to use a bar model to visualize math problems, which tells them graphically (symbolically) what they know as well as what they need to find out. They can literally see what process to use.

Given the problem—Zula read 248 pages last week. Zendra read 202 pages (see Figure 7.3). How many pages did they read? Who read more pages? How many more pages?—students would draw the following bar:

FIGURE 7.3 Bar Graph

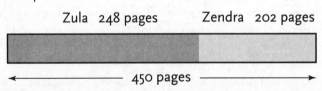

Zula 248 pages   Zendra 202 pages

←——————————— 450 pages ———————————→

Mathematics and Science

Scientists use math in making important discoveries. People who want to become scientists need to know advanced ways of using mathematics, advanced ways of thinking.

Observation

Students who work with science need to observe even minute changes. They need to learn to define terms and then to use those terms accurately. They need to observe with their eyes and ears, with all of their senses.

Following is a humorous poem that clearly illustrates how important accurate observations can be.

The Blind Men and the Elephant

It was six men of Hindostan,
To learning much inclined,
Who went to see the elephant,
(Though all of them were blind);
That each by observation
Might satisfy his mind.

The first approached the elephant,
And happening to fall
Against his broad and sturdy side,
At once began to bawl,
"Bless me, it seems the elephant
Is very like a wall."

The second, feeling of his tusk,
Cried, "Ho! What have we here
So very round and smooth and sharp?
To me 'tis mighty clear
This wonder of an elephant
Is very like a spear."

The third approached the animal,
And happening to take
The squirming trunk within his hands,
Then boldly up and spake;
"I see," quoth he, "the elephant
Is very like a snake."

The fourth stretched out his eager hand
And felt about the knee,
"What most this mighty beast is like
Is mighty plain," quoth he;
"'Tis clear enough the elephant
Is very like a tree."

The fifth who chanced to touch the ear
Said, "Even the blindest man

Can tell what this resembles most;
Deny the fact who can,
This marvel of an elephant
Is very like a fan."

The sixth no sooner had begun
About the beast to grope
Than, seizing on the swinging tail
That fell within his scope,
"I see," cried he, "the elephant
Is very like a rope."

And so these men of Hindostan
Disputed loud and long,
Each of his own opinion
Exceeding stiff and strong,
Though each was partly in the right,
And all were in the wrong!
—John Godfrey Saxe

Problems with a Catch: Stimulate Student Thinking

Print one of these problems on the board. Add the note: "DON'T TELL ANYONE YOUR ANSWER—IT'S A SECRET!" At the end of the day write the answer on the board. Ask how many got the "right" answer. And, have a good laugh together.

(Adjust these instructions for older students who are in a science class.)

- How much dirt is there in a hole 3½ feet by 4¼ feet wide and 24 inches deep?

  Answer: There is no dirt in a hole of any size, only air.

- Multiply $9 \times 999 \times 0$. What's the answer?

  Answer: How many people worked to multiply 9×999? The answer is 0.

- A butcher is 33 years old. He is 6' 2" tall. He wears a size 12 shoe. What does he weigh?

  He weighs meat.

Geometric Shapes

Teach students to observe life around them carefully. Ask students to search out the following shapes:

Where can you find triangles?

The roof of a gabled house.
The letters V, W, M, N, A.
A musical instrument, the Triangle.
The number 4.

Try other shapes, for example, cone, cylinder, cube, to encourage observation of life around us.

Groupings

Which number does not belong in each group? Why?

3/7 4/8 2/5 4/9, 10/11   (4/8, can be reduced)

236 279 837 21   (21, not in hundreds)

2 9 7 5 21 13   (2, not an odd number)

Challenge students to create other similar lists of numbers.

Counting Triangles

Have each student draw a large star like this:

FIGURE 7.4   Counting Triangles

How many triangles are in this drawing?

Mathematics and the Arts

Does an artist need to know anything about mathematics? How about measuring and perspective? What about the temperature for firing pottery or how to work with blowing glass? Even artists have to pay bills or figure out the cost of creating the costumes for presenting a play. Math is related to writing a symphony, and it comes into use as we choreograph a dance routine. We just can't get along without mathematics!

Mixing Colors

Students can experiment with mixing colors. Talk about the color wheel (see Figure 7.5). Introduce the concept of primary colors, secondary colors, and tertiary colors.

FIGURE 7.5 The Color Wheel

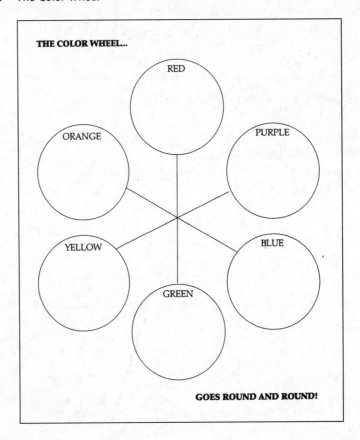

Students begin with any of the three primary colors—red, yellow, or blue. Suppose they choose yellow. What happens when they add a little of one of the other primary colors, for instance, blue? Of course, they get green (the secondary color that falls between yellow and blue on the color wheel). Add a little more blue, and the green color deepens; keep adding blue to get blue-green.

Then, start again with yellow, add a little bit of red, the other primary color. This time, the paint gradually turns orange. Add more red to achieve red-orange.

Students can work out a mathematical formula to achieve a pure secondary color each time, for example:

2 parts yellow + 2 parts red = orange

2 parts yellow + 2 parts blue = green

Tangrams

Tangrams (or seven ingenious pieces) originated in China many years ago. Early forms consisted of seven pieces—two larger triangles, one medium triangle, two small triangles, one square, and one parallelogram—arranged to form a large square. Many figures—animals, human figures, landscapes—could be formed by rearranging these seven pieces.

In 1862, a scholar named Tong Xiengeng created a more elaborate tangram composed of fifteen pieces (enhancing intelligent pieces) which could also be arranged into a square. Tangrams are supposed to have philosophical and mathematical implications.

A third kind of Chinese puzzle is the nine-linked rings. It takes 341 moves to unlink these rings, so it's far from a snap.

These puzzles are sometimes on display at the Chinese Cultural Center in San Francisco, California. Meanwhile, they offer a research challenge to motivated students. Students may want to search local libraries and/or the Internet for more information about these famous Chinese puzzles, many of which were lost during the Cultural Revolution in China. Search for local Chinese connections to discover whether someone has an example they can show the class. There are modern reproductions.

Perspective

Introduce the vocabulary word *perspective*. In art, perspective means that things look smaller when they are farther away. Thus, a road or a path will almost disappear in a picture as it moves away from the foreground. The back of a barn appears smaller than the front of the barn, so the lines draw closer together as they move away from the viewer. Perspective will be used as students work together on a large mural depicting, for example, "Life in Rural America" or "Going up the Amazon by Boat."

Have students look up other meanings of the useful word perspective. They can add it to their vocabulary.

Proportion: Making Masks

Students can make simple masks to hold before their faces as they perform a skit. Begin by folding a large sheet of paper in half, then cutting out the outline of a face, including an ear. Unfold the paper to produce a simple mask shape that can be decorated appropriately by drawing eyes and adding hair, as desired. The emphasis in this activity is on using the mask rather than constructing it.

Students might portray a group of Indians meeting in a council to discuss the coming of the White men and what it means for their people.

Or, students might play the roles of a book the class has just read, for example, *Elijah of Buxton* (see the lesson on p. 146).

CONNECTIONS

More and more, we are realizing how important it is that students learn mathematics and mathematical ways of thinking, for example, prediction, estimation, approximation, and equivalencies, processes we all engage in every day. We have learned that both boys and girls can engage in using such processes with equal success and that girls can become skillful mathematicians if they so desire. Providing many opportunities for their use of mathematical ways of thinking will engage students in more advanced thinking skills as they move beyond facts to evaluation and on to creativity! The future of our country depends on seeing that young people acknowledge the importance of mathematics as we advance technologically and as we move out into space. We need to encourage students to become involved in these exciting adventures.

GETTING INVOLVED

Expanding Your Reflective Teaching Portfolio

1. How do you feel about mathematics yourself?
2. How can you bring math into your classroom no matter what you teach?
3. Begin collecting quotations about mathematics that you can display in your classroom.

Working with Your Cooperative Learning Group

1. Turn to the description of Russian Peasant Math on p. 207. Work several of these problems together following the directions.

    Examine these problems and the effects of each operation. Why and how does this method of multiplying work? Can your group provide an explanation?
2. Try several algebraic math expressions using Singapore Math methods. Can you see that this kind of visualization would be helpful to students?
3. In the college library, locate the November 2007, issue of *Educational Leadership*, the journal published by the American Association of Curriculum Development (ASCD). Read the articles in this issue, which focused on math instruction at K–12 levels.

EXPLORING FURTHER

Jean d'Amico and Kate Gallaway. *Differentiated Instruction for the Middle School Math Teacher.* Jossey-Bass, 2008.

Susan M. Brookhart. *Exploring Formative Assessment.* ASCD, 2009.

Ellen Fogelberg, et al. *Integrating Literacy and Math: Strategies for K–6 Teachers.* Guidford, 2008.

Eric Gutstein and Bob Peterson. *Rethinking Mathematics: Teaching Social Justice by the Numbers.* Rethinking Schools, 2005.

Darrell Huff. *How to Lie with Statistics.* Norton, 1954.

Judith Muschia. *Hands-On Math Projects with Real-Life Applications.* Jossey-Bass, 2002.

Multicultural Arts

> *Be like the bird,*
> *Halting in his flight*
> *On limb too slight,*
> *Feels it give way beneath him,*
> *Yet sings,*
> *Knowing he hath wings.*
>
> ~ VICTOR HUGO

The arts may be neglected as teachers strive to keep up with standards and the demands of No Child Left Behind (NCLB), particularly in reading and mathematics. However, the arts stimulate creativity and offer much in terms of multicultural understandings. They stimulate a different kind of intelligence and offer different methods of expressing meaning. Therefore, it seems to us to be especially important that we plan for integrating the arts into the mainstream curriculum as students use painting, dancing, and singing as ways of expressing ideas related to social studies, language arts/reading, science, and mathematics.

The arts are essential, too, as we support esteem, develop empathy, and provide equity for all students. Often these activities engage students in learning and remaining in school in a way that more academic pursuits do not. The quotation above makes it clear that the arts may provide "the wings" a student needs.

❖ Performing Arts Activities that Support Esteem, Empathy, and Equity

Multicultural art activities engage students in learning more effectively than any textbook, no matter how clearly it is written. Students respond to the arts in a much more personal manner that enables them to use abilities that have not often been exercised. They begin to express ideas and feelings, they respond to others, and they develop a sense of belonging to a group that strengthens their sense of self-worth. Involvement in the performing arts reaches a different kind of intelligence than that touched by more academic studies.

Supporting Esteem

Most students enjoy experimenting with different forms of art. In this section, we have included relatively easy techniques that all students can perform. In each activity they will produce an attractive work of art that they can be proud of, or they will participate in singing songs, dancing, or acting out something they enjoy.

Making "Butterfeet"

This activity is pure fun! Prepare a shallow cookie pan filled with a thick mixture of watercolor paint—blue, red, or orange. The student who is ready to create a "butterfeet" removes his or her shoes and socks, then steps into the paint pan with both feet. Then he or she steps onto a large sheet of paper, making sure that the feet touch each other. After pressing firmly on the paper to create two good prints, the student steps into a pan of warm sudsy water in order to clean off the paint. Have several large towels laid out so that wet feet can be dried. (If you hesitate to use paint, students can simply draw around each other's feet to achieve a similar effect.)

Students will be surprised and pleased to see how the two footprints together form a butterfly shape. When the paint is dry, students can use crayons with which to add spots of contrasting color, using black to create antennae. The completed butterflies are cut out and displayed all over the wall for a gorgeous, colorful array.

Marbleized Book Covers

Older students will be pleased to create attractive panels or booklet covers from large sheets of marbleized paper. To create the marbleized effect that Ezra Jack Keats used to create fabric in *The Snowy Day,* prepare several shallow baking pans almost filled with water. You also need several small cans of colored enamel paint—red, yellow, and blue. (The enamel won't mix with water; don't buy water soluble paint.)

The students then drip various colors of enamel on the water where it floats and mixes to make gorgeous colored patterns. The enamel can be stirred carefully with a wooden coffee stirrer to mix the colors and to create interesting patterns.

The student then lays a clean 12" × 24" paper gently over the paint, which attaches to the paper as it is lifted and laid aside to dry overnight. The result is beautiful shiny marbleized sheets that can be used to create placemats, frames for the student's artwork, or, folded in half, to create attractive portfolios or booklet covers for written work. Every sheet is lovely, so every student is pleased to see the result of his or her efforts.

Singing Favorite Songs

Particularly in the elementary school, students like to sing together. Songs may be familiar camp songs, for example, "I've Been Working on the Railroad," or they may be related to social studies, as in "The Erie Canal" or songs cowboys might sing.

Children can be introduced to singing in parts by guiding them to sing rounds in three parts; an easy one to begin with is "Row, Row, Row Your Boat." Gradually, students can work up to more complicated songs like "White Coral Bells," which is presented below. If you hesitate to teach such singing, ask a colleague or a music specialist to help you.

Reading Books Aloud

Choose a variety of attractive picture books. Look for books illustrated by these well-known artists.

Chris Van Allsburg. *The Polar Express*. Houghton Mifflin, 1985. This popular book is illustrated with soft colors in full-page pictures; it was made into a film that is still available. Van Allsburg wrote and illustrated other books, for example, one that is intriguing but quite different, *Two Bad Ants* (Houghton Mifflin, 1988). Older students will be delighted by the *antics* of these two as they sneak into a kitchen to steal sugar for their queen.

Jan Brett. *Annie and the Wild Animals*. Houghton Mifflin, 1985. Brett uses softer colors, and in this book frames each picture with intricate drawings.

Brian Wildsmith. *Brian Wildsmith's ABC*. Oxford University Press, 1962. Wildsmith uses bold colors to produce vibrant art to create animals that appeal to primary grade children.

Virtual Field Trip: Visiting Art Museums

For students in the United States, *The Louvre* (Windows and Macintosh), a CD-ROM for all ages, provides the experience of going to this famous museum in Paris and viewing more than 150 representations of the art displayed there. The program is user-friendly and includes games and activities to help reinforce learning. (See also *With Open Eyes,* a similar visit to Chicago's Art Institute.) Virginia Walker suggests the following Book Connections:

Elaine Konigsburg's classic, *From the Mixed-up Files of Mrs. Basil E. Frankweiler.* Atheneum, 1967. Favorite story set in the Metropolitan Museum of Art.

Peggy Thomson. *The Nine-Ton Cat: Behind the Scenes at an Art Museum.* Houghton, 1997. Information about backstage work at the National Gallery of Art.

Internet connections include:

Fine Arts Museums of San Francisco. (www.thinker.org/index.shtml) Virtual visits to the DeYoung and the Legion of Honor; includes 60,000 item database.

WebMuseum. (www.watt.emf.net/louvre//) A stunning collection of famous paintings, including some items too fragile to be viewed in person.

Suggest artists that students might research, for example, Diego Rivera, Frida Kahlo, R. C. Gorman, Maya Lin, and Faith Ringgold. Also suggest questions to guide their research, for instance: Which women artists are included? or What kinds of art are presented?

Playing Circle Games

Children who go outdoors for recess love to participate in circle games, some of which include songs or dances, for example:

A 'Tisket, A 'Tasket, A Green and Yellow Basket!
The Hokey Pokey
Dodge Ball

Almost everyone can play such games. If one circle gets too big, the leader just makes another circle. Make it clear that any student who wants to can join the game. Just open the circle and make room!

Developing Empathy

Petite Performances

Getting acquainted through small group activities moves students toward feelings of empathy. Working to perform a skit for another class or to participate in presenting Mother Goose rhymes to kindergarten children adds to feelings of empathy as students share problems that occur and work to help each other succeed as they plan their performance together.

Brainstorm a variety of *petite performances* that students can sign up to work on, for example:

Singing a selection of folksongs
Putting on a puppet show
Dramatizing Mother Goose rhymes
Dramatizing a fairytale
Playing group games with primary grade children

Creating a Self-Portrait Collage

Each student prepares a large collage that tells something about, for example, José García—his life, his family, what he likes to do after school, and what he would like to be doing when he is twenty.

Each student presents his or her collage, saying, for instance:

My name is Carlie Johnson. I live in an apartment on Harley Street with my family. I have one sister named Donna and a brother, Fred. My mother is Elena, and my father is Henry Johnson. He runs a shoe repair shop around the corner from our apartment. Because we live near Greenbriar Park, I usually go there after school to play softball. Some other girls in the room are also on that team, and we're pretty good. We practice on Monday, Wednesday, and Thursday afternoons at three-thirty. You ought to come see us play!

Reading about Music in the Lives of Young People

Students may be interested in reading stories that tell of young people who have musical talent. Some examples include:

Bruce Brooks. *Midnight Hour Encores.* Harper, 1986. Cellist.

Gillian Cross. *Chartbreaker.* Holiday House, 1987. Rock band.

Gavin Curtis. *The Bat Boy and His Violin.* Simon & Schuster, 1998.

Amy Littlesugar. *Marie in Fourth Position.* Philomel, 1996. Ballet.

Suzanne Newton. *I Will Call It Georgie's Blues.* Viking, 1983. Jazz piano.

Reading about Real Musicians

Students may select autobiographies, biographies, or fiction for reports required in the social studies, for example:

Pete Fornatale. *The Story of Rock 'n' Roll.* Morrow, 1987.

Robert Love. *Elvis Presley.* Watts, 1986.

Susan Saunders. *Dolly Parton: Country Goin' to Town.* Viking, 1985.

Catherine Scheader. *Contributions of Women: Music.* Dillon, 1985. Beverly Sills and four other women.

Jeanette Winter. *Sebastian, A Book about Bach.* Harcourt, 1999.

Challenge students to locate additional information about diverse persons who have made a contribution to the musical world.

An audio presentation, *Lives of the Musicians* (Audio Bookshelf, 1996), presents interesting facts about the lives of well-known musicians. Recommended for grades 4 through 8, the information is well-read and amusing.

A Thinking + Lesson Plan: U.S. Folk Music from Every Region

A THINKING + LESSON PLAN
◄○►

U.S. Folk Music from Every Region

Grades 3–8

Expected Outcomes

Learners will:

1. Identify folk songs representative of different regions in the United States.
2. Integrate music into social studies activities.
3. Present a program for other classes in the school.

Teaching/Learning Strategies

Resources Needed

This lesson ties in with studies of individual states and/or regions of the United States. It also fits with studies of different groups that live in this country, and it could be adapted to studies of other countries.

Check the catalogs of your school district or the public library to locate recordings of regional folk music. Songbooks may also include examples that you can use. Begin playing a song or two each day to students. Share the information provided about each song. Teach them the words to some of the songs to add to their singing repertoire.

Directions

Step 1: Teach the class the following Pennsylvania Dutch folksong:

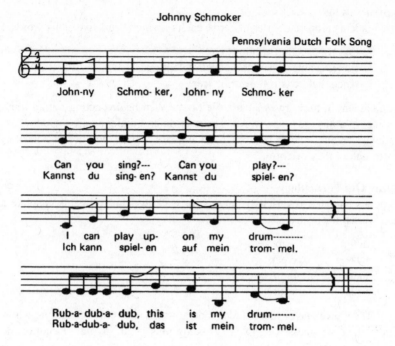

Johnny Schmoker

Pennsylvania Dutch Folk Song

John-ny Schmo-ker, John-ny Schmo-ker

Can   you   sing?---   Can you   play?---
Kannst du   sing-en? Kannst du   spiel-en?

I   can   play up-   on   my   drum----------
Ich kann   spiel-en   auf mein   trom-mel.

Rub-a-dub-a-dub, this   is   my   drum----------
Rub-a-dub-a-dub, das   ist   mein   trom-mel.

Explain that this song (with words in German) was sung by people of German ancestry who settled in what is now Pennsylvania. These people were called Pennsylvania Dutch because their name *Deutsch* (German) sounded like *Dutch*. You might also like to show students examples or pictures of their distinctive art. Then suggest that each group find a song that is typical of the state or region that they are researching. They should plan to incorporate the song into their report. They might plan to teach the song to the rest of the class.

Step 2:   Each group will plan to participate in an assembly to be attended by other classes. Each group will first point out on a large map the location of the area they studied. Group members will contribute to the presentation with information about the people who live there, how they live, and any distinctive contributions they have made.

Step 3:   Each group will submit a brief description of what they plan to contribute to the assembly. Two volunteers will prepare a printed program to send to the classes who are invited to attend their assembly. The groups will practice their presentations. The class will present the assembly.

Performance Assessment
The success of the total project will be assessed by each group. They will look at their individual presentations to decide what was particularly effective and also how it might have been improved. The responses from the other classes will add to the assessment process.

Improvisations

Have students prepare a series of cards, each of which bears five or six words, for example:

1. fox, rope, cabin, window, river
2. stone, candle, flashlight, pencil, telephone
3. fence, bell, chair, flowerpot, tree

Each student in turn draws a card. He or she then begins acting out an improvised story that incorporates the given words. Description and dialogue are included, as appropriate. Students can also engage in this activity in pairs or trios, but they will need a little time to confer before they perform.

Acting Out Vocabulary

Introduce students to varied synonyms for walking. Have students generate a long list of such words, for instance:

tramp	leap
stalk	creep
saunter	prance
stroll	strut

Then have one or more students demonstrate one way of walking while other members of the class guess which word is being illustrated, saying: "Kendra is demonstrating how she can stroll."

Providing Equity

Talk about art with your students. There are many forms of art to explore as they discuss "What is art?"—a subject that can prove controversial, especially among more conservative adults.

Developing a Word Wall about the Performing Arts

Encourage students to brainstorm words about art as they share what they know about the arts. They can discuss different categories of art, for example, painting (with varied media), crafts, sculpture, cartoons, and then into music, dance, and drama. This Word Wall may extend around the room as students in grades 5–12 develop long lists under such categories as shown here in Table 8.1:

TABLE 8.1   Performing Arts Word Wall

Art on the Wall	*Dance*	*Outdoor Art*	*Dramatic Performance*
impressionism	ballet	architecture	pantomime
surrealism	tap dancing	sculpture	poetry slam
renaissance	ballroom	photography	play
tapestry	hip-hop	walls	documentary

As you can see, the minute you try to categorize, the more you have to add new lists, as in the grouping developed above under "Art on the Wall." Students will be motivated to investigate further as they probe into the topics suggested.

Experiencing Different Kinds of Art

Pore over children's literature to discover the wide variety of art techniques used by the illustrators of picture books. Bring in a selection to share with students as they experiment with collage, mixed media, oil painting, water color, stitchery, and so forth. The following are a few books to look for:

Stitchery

Esther N. Krinitz and Bernice Steinhardt. *Memories of Survival.* Hyperion, 2005. Intricate stitchery panels tell the story of Esther's childhood in Poland and her flight with her little sister from the Nazis. Each of Esther's beautiful panels is accompanied by her own words explaining the picture as well as a history written by Bernice of what happened to the two Jewish girls, who were the only family members to survive the war.

Quilted Art Forms

Arthur Dorros. *Tonight Is Carnaval.* Dutton, 1991. *Arpilleras*, a native South American art form, decorates this picture book. The pictures are photographs of work by members of the Club de Madres Virgen del Carmen of Lima, Peru.

Oil Painting

Joseph Bruchac and Jonathan London. *Thirteen Moons on Turtle's Back: A Native American Year of Moons.* Illustrated by Thomas Locker. Philomel, 1992. Locker uses oils to create handsome art to accompany each piece in this beautiful collection of poetry. Although it is not likely that younger students will use oils to create paintings, it is interesting for them to notice the different media that artists use.

Cut Paper

A number of artists have used cut paper to create illustrations for children's books. Featured here are several examples that students can compare to note the varied ways of using cut paper to illustrate children's books.

Eric Carle. *Animals, Animals.* Scholastic, 1989. Carle creates all kinds of impressive animals with cut paper in bold colors to accompany a collection of poetry that any elementary teacher would find useful. Children might enjoy making animals following Carle's examples to accompany original poems they have written. Another favorite book by Eric Carle is *The Very Hungry Caterpillar.*

Lois Ehlert. *Oodles of Animals.* Harcourt, 2008. This talented artist presents simple texts that provide information in different written forms (here, it's poetry) accompanied by cut paper animals; their bodies are formed with nine basic shapes that students might enjoy emulating. Ehlert has created numerous books; a favorite is an early one, *Feathers for Lunch*, about a cat who tries to catch a robin, a cardinal, and so forth, but ends up with only "feathers for lunch."

Taback Simms. *Joseph Had a Little Overcoat*. Viking, 1977. Based on a Yiddish folksong, this book won the annual Caldecott Award for art in children's books. Simms uses an unusual kind of *peep hole* in his illustrations.

A Writing + Lesson Plan: Cut Paper Art
Follow the directions given below for making tissue paper decorations to celebrate The Day of the Dead.

A THINKING + LESSON PLAN
◄◇►

Cut Paper Art

Grades 1–8
Expected Outcomes
Learners will:

1. Examine examples of cut paper art.
2. Read and study books that use cut paper in the illustrations.
3. Make cut paper designs to decorate the classroom.

Teaching/Learning Strategies

Resources Needed
Ask the librarian to assist you in locating examples of cut paper art—Chinese, Mexican, Pennsylvania Dutch, and so on. An excellent resource is *Making Magic Windows: Creating Papel Picado/Cut-Paper Art with Carmen Lomas Garza* (Children's Press, 1999) in which the artist provides specific instructions for introducing students to both beginning and more advanced techniques. Collect the necessary materials for a beginning experience in paper cutting: scissors, paper (tissue and others), string, and glue. (Older, more expert students might use a box-cutter knife as Garza also describes.)

Directions
Step 1: This activity can be done at any time of year, but it is especially appropriate near November 2, *Día de los Muertos* (Day of the Dead). Discuss the display of banners and cut tissue designs to honor the dead who, according to Mexican tradition, are permitted to return to earth to visit on this one day each year. Challenge students to investigate this holiday. Many Mexican Americans observe the autumn holiday, which coincides with Halloween or All Saints Day.

Students can also research the topic of cut paper as an art form that is said to have begun in ancient China.

Step 2: Write the words *papel picado* on the chalkboard, saying, "Today we are going to make papel picado." Explain that *papel* means "paper" in Spanish and *picado* means "cut." Point out how in Spanish adjectives follow the noun described. In English adjectives precede the nouns. Spanish-speaking students might supply other examples of this grammatical feature.

Students will make cut paper hangings (papel picado) to decorate the room following the directions in Figure 8.1. Each can then take the decoration home to share with family members. Each hanging will be different, as shown in Figure 8.2

FIGURE 8.1   Directions For Cutting Paper

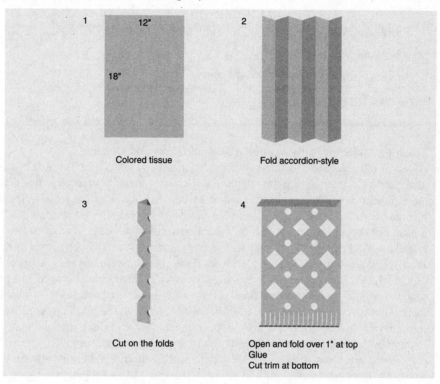

1   12"

18"

Colored tissue

2

Fold accordion-style

3

Cut on the folds

4

Open and fold over 1" at top
Glue
Cut trim at bottom

FIGURE 8.2   Thread Cut Paper On Heavy Cord

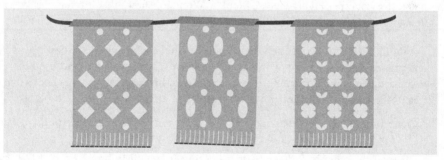

Step 3:   Place the tissue paper decorations on a cord hung across the windows so that light can come through each individual creation. If there is air blowing anywhere in the classroom, the hangings will blow gently in the breeze.

Performance Assessment
Students receive credit for following directions and completing the task.

Exploring Other Media

Murals

George Ancona. *Murals: Walls That Sing.* Marshall Cavendish, 2003.

Scrapbooking

Pam Price. *Cool Scrapbooks.* Abdo, 2005.

Decorating Eggs

Jane Pollak. *Decorating Eggs: Exquisite Designs with Wax and Dye.* Sterling, 1996.

Teaching Multiculturally Around a Theme: Quilts and Quilting

A quilt is often defined as a three-layer sandwich, composed of a top (created by piecing or appliqué), a filling or batting (for warmth), and a back (sometimes pieced as well). There are three distinct processes usually referred to by the term "quilting." *Patchwork* traditionally incorporates leftover scraps of material or pieces of old clothing. The scraps are "pieced" together into special patterns, often with attention to color and design, and then sewn together to make a block. These blocks may have colorful names, such as Rocky Road to Kansas or Jacob's Ladder. A special kind of patchwork is the crazy quilt. In this version, special pieces of fabric (often velvet or silk) are sewn together in a pleasing fashion but without a fixed pattern. In *appliqué,* a design (often floral) is cut out from material and sewn onto background fabric in blocks or for a whole quilt. *Quilting* itself refers to the stitching (done by hand or machine) that holds the three layers together. Sometimes the quilting stitches create a design in themselves. Quilts may also be held together by knots tied at intervals.

What are some of the names for patchwork patterns? Where do the names come from? Students can learn about the different patterns and investigate what they mean by reading Ann Whitford Paul's *Eight Hands Round: A Patchwork Alphabet,* illustrated by Jeanette Winter (Harcourt, 1966). This ABC book explains the origin of the interesting names for patterns (Flying Geese, Monkey Wrench), shows the different designs, and tells the story of the people behind the quilts.

Quilts in History.   Quilts kept log cabins warm, accompanied families in wagon trains, and preserved the memory of friends and relatives. Women (and men) used their needles to make quilts that reflected passages in their lives. Investigate the many books that tell stories of these early quilts and provide examples of quilt blocks.

Jane Bolton. *My Grandmother's Patchwork Quilt: A Book and Portfolio of Patchwork Pieces.* Doubleday, 1994.

Mary Cobb. *The Quilt Block History of Pioneer Days.* Millbrook Press, 1995. Examples of projects for children using paper and cut magazines.

Eleanor Coerr. *The Josefina Story Quilt.* Harper, 1989. When Faith's family sets out for California in 1850, she brings along the old hen Josefina. After Josefina rescues them from trouble, Faith sews a quilt to commemorate the trip. Also available in Spanish.

Valerie Flournoy. *The Patchwork Quilt.* Illustrated by Jerry Pinkney. Dial, 1985. When Tanya's grandmother gets too sick to work on her quilt, telling stories of family history, Tanya decides to help her finish it. African American family.

Ellen Howard. *The Log Cabin Quilt.* Holiday, 1996. Quilt scraps warm a family by providing chinking for their new cabin in Michigan.

Ann Whitford Paul. *The Seasons Sewn: A Year in Patchwork.* Harcourt, 1996.

Patricia Polacco. *The Keeping Quilt.* Simon & Schuster, 1988. Polacco traces her family's Jewish heritage through a quilt made from relatives' clothing and passed down through generations to celebrate births, marriages, and deaths. In each shape she can see the stories she's been told of her family.

Ask students if they have any quilts. Who made these quilts? What designs were used? What do these quilts mean to them? Share books with students that reflect how quilts can preserve people's heritage and help them make connections with others.

Underground Quilts. Quilts may even have been used historically to carry secret information. In the same way that scraps of cloth were pieced together to keep memories alive, slaves may have sewn essential information into the quilts they made. Although it would be difficult to prove this actually took place, students can imagine how important it was to preserve knowledge when slaves couldn't read or write. These books give us a picture of what quilts might have meant to the enslaved Africans at that time.

Dennis Brindell Fradin. *Bound for the North Star: True Stories of Fugitive Slaves.* Clarion, 2000. In 1850, the Fugitive Slave Act set free states against slave states because it compelled people to catch and return runaway slaves to their owners. The cover of this book shows a quilt representing the flight to freedom.

Deborah Hopkinson. *Sweet Clara and the Freedom Quilt.* Illustrated by James Ransome. Knopf, 1993. As a slave, Clara is not allowed to read or write, so she carefully stitches into the quilt the information she needs for her escape.

Alice McGill, coll. *In the Hollow of Your Hand: Slave Lullabies.* Illustrated by Michael Cummings. Houghton Mifflin, 2000. Despite their wretched conditions, slaves managed to express love for their children, through lullabies, for example. The quilt illustrations convey comfort. Includes a CD.

Hmong Traditions. Investigate other quilting-like traditions with students. Perhaps students know of the Hmong stitchery called pa'ndau (story cloth). These intricate designs are passed on through generations. The Hmong come from Southeast Asia and are known for their colorful clothing. Show students examples in books such as:

Dia Cha. *Dia's Story Cloth: The Hmong People's Journey of Freedom.* Stitched by Chue and Nhia Thao Cha. Lee and Low, 1996. This story cloth, made by the author's aunt and uncle, chronicles Hmong life, past and present.

Pegi Deitz Shea. *The Whispering Cloth: A Refugee's Story.* Illustrated by Anita Riggio, stitched by Yon Yang. Boyds Mills, 1995. A Hmong family in a refugee camp in Thailand makes story cloths to earn money.

Amish Quilts. The Amish, fleeing religious persecution and now living in small communities in Pennsylvania and other parts of the Midwest, are known for their quilts featuring solid colors and strong, simple, symmetrical designs. These quilts are representative of the Amish culture and beliefs, which include self-sufficiency, plain clothing, farming without machinery, and horse-driven buggies for transportation. Use a study of Amish quilts as a point of entry into this interesting culture and the choices that Amish people have made to live a simple life without modern technology.

> Richard Ammon. *An Amish Year.* Illustrated by Pamela Patrick. Atheneum, 2000. Amish life through eyes of fourth-grader Anna.

> Doris Faber. *The Amish.* Illustrated by Michael Erkel. Doubleday, 1991. Nonfiction.

> Patricia Polacco. *Just Plain Fancy.* Bantam, 1990. A story about the Amish in Lancaster County, Pennsylvania.

Hawai'ian Quilts. Hawai'ians are another group with a distinctive quilting tradition. The native Hawai'ians sewed *tapa cloth* (made from bark) before the European arrival. When they began to make quilts, they adapted many of the same techniques to sewing cotton. Traditional Hawai'ian quilts are made of a single large appliqué design (based on local flowers, trees, animals, or birds) sewn onto a solid background of a contrasting color. While in traditional European quilting everyone may use the same patterns to make very different quilts, Hawai'ian quilters believe that every quilter should make her own pattern and not borrow another's without permission.

Students can experience the effect of a Hawai'ian-style quilt by folding a square piece of paper into eighths (like a snowflake design). Show your students how to cut out a design, making sure that they keep the paper connected along the folded side. Students may want to plan their design on paper first. They can draw designs based on animals, plants, or other familiar objects. When they unfold their design, notice how symmetrical it appears. Point out the axes of symmetry—vertical, horizontal, other.

Share the following book with students to introduce Hawai'ian quilting.

> Georgia Guback. *Luka's Quilt.* Greenwillow, 1994. Luka wants to make her own pattern, not the traditional Hawai'ian one.

Quilt Quotes. Include quotes about quilting as you discuss social studies, history, art, or other topics. Place quotes on the bulletin board for students to read. Students can write responses to these quotes. What do these quotes tell us about people's lives? About the importance of beauty in utilitarian objects? About our connection with the generations before us?

> My husband tells about the time he got sick with the measles. He was six years old. His mother set him to piecing a quilt and every other block he set in red polka-dot pattern. Said it was his measles quilt. (Patricia Cooper and Norma Bradley Allen. *The Quilters: Women and Domestic Art.* Anchor, 1989, p. 39.)

> In the summers we'd put up the frame on the screened porch, and when the work was done, Mama would say, "O.K., girls, let's go to it." That was the signal for good times and laughin'. We'd pull up our chairs around the frame and anyone that dropped in would do the same, even if they couldn't stitch straight. Course we'd take out their stitches later if they was really bad. But it was for talking and visiting that we put in quilts in the summer. (Patricia Cooper and Norma Bradley Allen. *The Quilters: Women and Domestic Art.* Anchor, 1989, p. 76.)

You can give the same kind of pieces to two persons, and one'll make a "nine-patch" and one'll make a "wild goose chase," and there'll be two quilts made out of the same kind of pieces, and just as different as they can be. And that's just the way with the living. The Lord sends us the pieces, but we can cut them out and put them together pretty much to suit ourselves, and there's a heap more in the cutting out and the sewing than there is in the calico. (*A Quilter's Wisdom: Conversations with Aunt Jane,* based on a text by Eliza Calvert Hall. Chronicle, 1994, pp. 37–38.)

Everyone put their hand to piecing in the winter. All my boys pieced right along with the girls. It was work that had to be done. (Patricia Cooper and Norma Bradley Allen. *The Quilters: Women and Domestic Art.* Anchor, 1989, p. 154.)

Nine-Patch Math.   A nine-patch square is the basis for many quilt designs. Provide students with an 8- or 9-inch square. Have them divide it into thirds along each side, making nine equal spaces. Then ask them to divide some of those spaces in half. What are some different ways to do this? Can they divide the spaces into thirds or quarters? What different patterns can they make in their squares? Have students color in their designs. Show them how the same pattern can come out looking different depending on the arrangement of colors.

Figure 8.3 shows two examples of nine-patch patterns. Students can choose one to color. Assemble the student squares into a paper quilt. Are there alternative ways to put the quilt blocks together? Can students see larger patterns in the class quilt?

Faith Ringgold's Story Quilts.   Sometimes quilts are used to tell a story. The story quilts of Faith Ringgold, an African American artist, are an example of stitched work based on a theme of pride in one's heritage. Her works assemble words and images in fabric in a revolutionary technique to create a narrative through a kind of collage. Investigate her work

FIGURE 8.3   Quilt Patterns

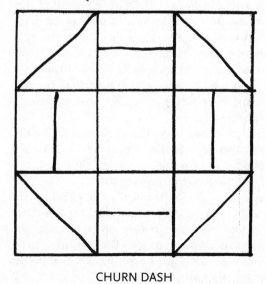

CHURN DASH

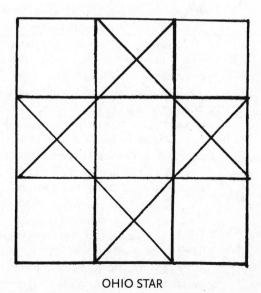

OHIO STAR

with students to show them how a person's own life and experience can be reflected in art. She has turned some of her quilts into children's picture books. Look at examples of her books and read about her life.

Faith Ringgold. *The Last Story Quilt.* Video, 1991. Ringgold talks about her life and shows her artwork.

Faith Ringgold. *Tar Beach.* Crown, 1991. This story of a girl's dreams as she lies on her city rooftop is framed by pieces of Ringgold's story quilts.

Faith Ringgold. *We Flew over the Bridge: The Memoirs of Faith Ringgold.* Little, Brown, 1995.

Robyn Montana Turner. *Faith Ringgold.* Little, Brown, 1993. From her childhood in Harlem in the 1930s to her status as an artist today, this detailed biography follows Ringgold's life and development, setting it in the context of African American experience.

Another famous story quilter is Harriet Powers, who worked in the nineteenth century. Her work links the quilting traditions of slaves with that of contemporary artists. Read about her surprisingly modern images in:

Mary E. Lyons. *Stitching the Stars: The Story Quilts of Harriet Powers.* Scribner's, 1993. African American artist's Bible-based quilts.

Students Make Friendship Quilts.   Students may be motivated to make quilts for many different reasons: to express their creativity, to distribute to the homeless, or to raise money. For example, they can select one of the many attractive Amish designs to cut out and sew, using solid colors. The drafting of the patterns for cutting will involve use of basic geometric shapes. Students in fourth grade and up can handle a sewing machine or a needle and thread with some adult assistance. Students can also make a crazy quilt, using donated scraps of fabric. Have each student assemble the odd-sized pieces on a foundation block of a fixed size so that the quilt can be assembled easily. Another popular theme for student quilts is "Our Neighborhood." Each student can make a block representing a house, embellishing each house differently with items such as trim and buttons. Or they can make individual blocks for particular features of the community—special buildings, sights, people. Students can also make an international quilt, showing children from many different countries and different backgrounds. In an *album* quilt, each student makes a block with his or her name in it, as a present for someone.

Primary students can draw on fabric with fabric crayons that become permanent after ironing. One kindergarten class made an alphabet quilt. For students who were unable to draw a letter, the teacher outlined large letters and the students colored them in. Later, students pierced layers with yarn and tied knots to hold the quilt together.

Students can also adapt quilt techniques to paper. Collect supplies of colorful paper such as wrapping paper, magazines, or catalogs. Have students cut long strips of equal width. They can sew or glue these strips together lengthwise to make a band of six inches. Then cut across the strips every six inches so that you have squares. These squares can be assembled into the Rail Fence pattern. Encourage students to experiment with different possibilities for arranging their squares in a pleasing pattern.

Sources for Further Study

Raymond Bial. *With Needle and Thread: A Book about Quilts.* Houghton Mifflin, 1996. A social history of quilting.

Patricia Cooper and Norma Bradley Allen. *The Quilters: Women and Domestic Art, An Oral History.* Anchor, 1989. Collections of quilters' stories and memories. Also a play.

Roland Freeman. *A Communion of the Spirits: African American Quilters, Preservers, and Their Stories.* Rutledge Hill Press, 1996.

Eliza Calvert Hall. *A Quilter's Wisdom: Conversations with Aunt Jane.* Chronicle Books, 1994. Reprint of traditional comments, ascribed to "Aunt Jane."

Eli Leon. *Who'd a Thought It: Improvisation in African-American Quiltmaking.* San Francisco Craft and Folk Museum, 1990. Shows the connections between contemporary quilting and African traditions.

Jacqueline L. Tobin and Raymond G. Dobard. *Hidden in Plain View: A Secret Story of Quilts and the Underground Railroad.* Anchor, 2000. Intriguing book makes argument that some quilt patterns served as codes for slaves to escape by the Underground Railroad.

❖ Integrating the Arts into Other Curriculum Areas

Including multicultural arts in studies across the curriculum enhances teaching at all levels. In the elementary school, the arts slide nicely into almost any study, particularly a broad thematic study, for instance, "Chinese Americans and Their Contributions to the United States" or "How African Americans Gained Their Freedom." Studies will tend to be more focused with older students, perhaps based on a literature selection and its links or on the lives of different peoples, for example, the Mayans. In any case, the various performing arts offer diverse ways for students to express their ideas. The arts draw on different kinds of intelligence.

Multicultural Arts and Language Arts/Reading

The various performing arts have many links to studies of language and literature, and of course, we use language skills to express ideas about creating a painting, or in the lyrics that we sing. These expressive arts are inextricably intertwined in human activity. Students will be interested in observing how this occurs in their own lives as well as in the lives of people in other times and places they may be studying.

Music: A Universal Language

Brain research shows that music is truly universal. All humans seem to have music programmed in their brains just like language.

Savion Glover and Bruce Weber. *Savion! My Life in Tap.* Morrow, 2000. Biography of noted tap dance artist.

Matthew Gollub. *The Jazz Fly.* Illustrated by Karen Hanke. Tortuga Press, 2000. Experience the joy of improvisation, hear the "sound" of jazz, and learn to communicate in the "language" of music.

Deborah Hopkinson. *A Band of Angels.* Illustrated by Raúl Colón. Atheneum, 1999. Fictionalized account of Jubilee Singers, keeping traditional Black songs alive.

Toyomi Igus. *i see the rhythm.* Illustrated by Michele Wood. Children's Book Press, 1998. Poetry and images convey the history of Black music, from forbidden drums to today.

Isaac Millman. *Moses Goes to a Concert.* Farrar, Straus & Giroux, 1998. Moses is deaf but he can "hear" the rhythm with his bare feet.

Ken Nordine. *Colors.* Illustrated by Henrik Drescher. Harcourt, 2000. Radio commentator's "word jazz" poems about colors.

Maria Diaz Strom. *Rainbow Joe and Me.* Lee & Low, 1999. Although Joe is blind, he portrays colors through music.

Picture Books

Illustrated books, most commonly referred to as "picture books" are usually intended for primary grade readers. These books, however, offer a rich resource for teachers of older students. There are biographies, for example, that share the lives of talented musicians, scientists, politicians, and so on. There is nonfiction reporting information about animals, religions, travel, or almost any subject that interests you. This sampling gives you an idea of what you might find.

Carmen T. Bernier-Grand. *Frida: ¡Viva la vida! Long Live Life!* Marshall Cavendish, 2007. Poetry interspersed with examples of Frida Kahlo's paintings, including a wedding portrait of Frida and Diego Rivera.

Maya Christina Gonzalez. *My Colors, My World/Mis colores, mi mundo.* Children's Book Press, 2007. The little girl is Maya herself, author/illustrator of this Spanish and English story. Simple text includes the color words in Spanish that all students can learn.

Sandra L. Pinkney. *Read and Rise.* Photos by Myles C. Pinkney. Scholastic, 2006. Foreword by famed poet Maya Angelou. Message: "Learn to Read"—with a flashlight under the covers, on the couch beside a sister—read everywhere! This book would be a good model for older students who are creating original children's books.

Exploring Biography

The lives of artists have been featured in attractive picture book biographies that students will enjoy reading. Here is a sampling to delve into:

Pat Cummings. *Talking with Artists: Conversations with Victoria Chess, Pat Cummings, Leo and Diane Dillon, Richard Egielski, Lois Ehlert, Lisa Campbell Ernst, Tom Feelings, Steven Kellogg, Jerry Pinkney, Amy Schwartz, Lane Smith, Chris Van Allsburg, and David Wiesner.* Bradbury, 1992. Biographies of fourteen different artists who have illustrated prize-winning children's books.

Dean Engel and Florence B. Freeman. *Ezra Jack Keats: A Biography with Illustrations.* Silver Moon Press, 1995. The authors present the illustrator and author of *The Snowy Day,* winner of the Caldecott Award, Ezra Jack Keats. It is fascinating that a Jewish man chose to make a small Black child, Peter, the main character in his prize-winning picture book. Keats noticed that Black children were never portrayed in children's literature. He said: "So I resolved that, when I had the confidence to do my own work, my hero would be a black child." This biography is a joy to read; it would be terrific to read aloud.

Jan Greenberg. *Romare Bearden: Collage of Memories*. Abrams, 2003. Full-page reproductions of Bearden's work accompany the story of his life. Chiefly, he used collage in color and in black and white, and he combined this technique with other media, for example, watercolor. His art is rooted in the African American culture, but as the biographer notes, "His work speaks to everyone."

Susanna Reich. *Painting the Wild Frontier: The Art and Adventures of George Catlin*. Clarion, 2008. A well-known American painter, George Catlin painted many portraits of Native Americans, developing an "Indian Gallery" with which he toured the United States. Included in this book are many archival prints as well as an eight-page color insert.

Leslie Sills. *Inspirations: Stories about Women Artists*. Whitman, 1989. The lives of several noted women artists—Georgia O'Keeffe, Frida Kahlo, Alice Need, and Faith Ringgold—are presented.

Comparing Fairy Tales

You can find many versions of Cinderella rewritten to reflect different cultures. Artists have also enjoyed rendering new interpretations of other familiar tales.

Ed Young. *Lon Po Po*. Philomel, 1989. An illustrator/author, who was born in China and brought up in Shanghai, specializes in Chinese tales, his version of "Red Riding Hood" won the Caldecott Award for illustration of children's literature in 1989. His art shows eastern influences that are appealing. He also retold and illustrated *Yeh Shen, A Cinderella Story from China*.

A Thinking + Lesson Plan: Beautiful Writing

Follow the Lesson Plan on p. 242.

Reading Beautifully Illustrated, Touching, Multicultural Stories Aloud

These books are examples of warm, multicultural stories that are enhanced by the work of talented artists.

Ann Grifalconi. *Ain't Nobody a Stranger to Me*. Illustrated by Jerry Pinkney. Hyperion, 2007. A beautifully illustrated story of a Black American who knows what the "sad, old days of slavery" were like. He tells his granddaughter how he always "carried apple seeds in his pockets, so that when freedom came, he could plant them in his own soil." He tells the little girl the story of his determination to be free and how it drove him and his wife to strike out for freedom with their little baby, the girl's mother. Close to the Ohio River, a White man and his wife fed them and helped them cross the river to freedom. There, they worked hard, saving their money to buy a farm where he could plant those apple seeds! Finally he is happy, because "both me and my heart is free."

A THINKING + LESSON PLAN

◄○►

Beautiful Writing

Grades 4–12

Expected Outcomes

Learners will:

1. Learn an interesting art form.
2. Select quotations from diverse cultures.
3. Create an attractive display.

Teaching/Learning Strategies

Resources Needed

Collect examples of quotations presented in calligraphy. Some are presented at the beginning of chapters in this text. Bring in books of quotations that students can use as resources.

Directions

Step 1:   Show students examples of quotations presented in calligraphy. Explain the history of calligraphy. Teach students the rudiments of italic calligraphy, which is not unlike the manuscript or D'Nelian handwriting that they may have used in primary grades.

Step 2:   Have students select and print a quotation or saying they like from a specific culture.

Step 3:   Have each student frame the quotation. Framing can be done by mounting the quotation on a sheet of 9" × 12" red construction paper, or you may prefer to frame the quotations in simple black wooden frames that can be made or purchased. Older students may explore Chinese calligraphy following this experience.

Performance Assessment

Students should display their work in the classroom, the library, or another more public place where other students can view the art and the wise words depicted. No grades should be assigned for this project. Give credit or no credit for completing the task.

William Miller. *Richard Wright and the Library Card*. Illustrated by Gregory Christie. Lee & Low, 1997. Although Richard's mother had taught him to read the newspaper, he was not allowed to enter the library to read the books he craved so badly. Why? Because he had dark skin. At last he meets a friendly White co-worker who lends Richard his library card. In order to use the card, of course, Richard had to say the books were for the owner of the card, Jim Falk, and he kept the books hidden from the other workers. He read powerful books, full of ideas, which changed his world.

Students will enjoy reading and/or listening to Richard Wright's autobiography, *Black Boy*, which inspired Miller's story. Miller wrote two other outstanding picture book biographies of African American authors: *Zora Hurston and the Chinaberry Tree* and *Frederick Douglass: The Last Day of Slavery*—to form a kind of trilogy.

Claire A. Nivola. *Planting the Trees of Kenya.* Farrar, 2008. Lovely watercolors depict the land that Wangari Maathai knew so well—the fig trees, crotons, and flame trees. When the opportunity came, she went to college to study biology in America, returning to her homeland at last to apply what she learned. During the five years she was gone, Kenya had lost almost all its trees! The place was taken over by large tea plantations. She was determined to replant the trees in Kenya and to take care of the land. She organized the Kenyan women who began collecting tree seeds and nurturing young seedlings. Gradually, the woods began to appear again—in thirty years over thirty million trees were planted, and the planting never stopped. Wangari Maathai received the Nobel Peace Prize in 2004 for her leadership, which produced the Green Belt Movement. As she said, "I always felt that our work was not simply about planting trees. It was about inspiring people to take charge of their environment, the system that governed them, their lives and their future."

Coleen M. Paratore. *Catching the Sun.* Illustrated by Peter Catalanotto. Charlesbridge, 2008. A warm story of a pregnant mother and her five-year-old boy, Dylan, who share a birthday tradition of rising early on the morning of Dylan's birthday in order to "catch the sun" just as it rises. Dylan's mother teaches him that no matter what happens, he can always recapture that moment by closing his eyes and remembering.

A Thinking + Lesson Plan: Illustrating a Poem
Follow the directions given on p. 244.

Gorgeous Art in Picture Books
These picture books are especially valuable for the fantastic art they include. Notice that these artists chose to retell folktales and to embellish the tales with strong, vibrant art.

Demi. *The Firebird.* Holt, 1994. Demi has presented a Russian folktale using flamboyant golds and reds that are truly amazing. As in most fairytales, a poor boy is turned magically into a prince, marries the princess, and they live happily ever after.

Gerald McDermott. *Musicians of the Sun.* Aladdin, 1997. This book relates a lost tale of the Aztecs. The Lord of the Night thought people were too unhappy, so he sent the wind to free the Musicians of the Sun. Although they were afraid of the powerful sun, they flew down to Earth with the wind, bringing the joy of sound and color to the people, who began to sing and dance. Even the Sun was impressed, so he continued to shine down kindly on the happy people.

Drama and Movement
- Read about performing artists, for example, dancer Alvin Ailey, actor Sidney Poitier, singer Lena Horne, or ballerina Maria Tallchief.
- Write responses to multicultural literature, for example, biographies of performing artists, poetry by Langston Hughes, a novel by Virginia Hamilton.
- Listen to the teacher reading a story that could be acted out—*Amazing Grace; Let the Circle Be Unbroken; Bud, Not Buddy.*

A THINKING + LESSON PLAN
◄○►

Illustrating a Poem

Grades 3–12

Expected Outcomes

Learners will:

1. Select a favorite poem to copy using the computer.
2. Illustrate the poem.
3. Place the poem in a class collection of favorites to place in the school library.

Teaching/Learning Strategies

Resources Needed

Bring in a large collection of poetry books from the library. Also, have various art supplies available.

Directions

Step 1: Students will spend time browsing through poetry books to select a favorite poem. They should be prepared to tell why they chose a particular poem.

Step 2: Take the class to the computer lab (or schedule time in the classroom) so students can copy the poem they select. Show them how to select an interesting font to use. Encourage them to try more than one font so they compare to choose one they like best.

Step 3: Have students illustrate their poems. Then, collect the poems in a volume titled *Our Favorite Poems.*

Performance Assessment

1. Students will select poems to present using the computer. Each will then copy and illustrate one poem.
2. Each student will share the poem he or she selected with the class either by reading it aloud or recording it for the listening center.
3. Students will produce a class publication that can be placed in the school library.

Music

Ann Hayes. *Meet the Orchestra.* Illustrated by Karmen Thompson. Harcourt, 1991. Funny animals perform with each instrument.

Janet Nichols. *Women Music Makers: An Introduction to Women Composers.* Walker, 1992.

Bob Spitz. *Yeah! Yeah! Yeah! The Beatles, Beatlemania and the Music That Changed the World.* Little, Brown, 2007.

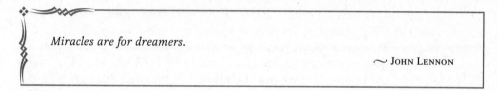

Miracles are for dreamers.

~ JOHN LENNON

The Arts and Social Studies

Many aspects of the performing arts are associated with the history of people and their lands. The performing arts offered a kind of communication and sharing long before forms of writing were developed. The pictographs of early people in the United States, France, and China reveal how they lived. Almost every group of people employ some kind of music—drumbeats, chants, songs—to express happiness or celebrations; they dress in colorful attire and dance to the music. Storytelling and acting out are part of ancient traditions as well as our contemporary lives. The performing arts enhance thematic studies and encourage students to explore their various kinds of intelligence. They offer students different ways of becoming involved in learning.

Music for the Soul

Black Americans are revered for giving us jazz, an original American art form, which they contributed to the music of the world. Give students a chance to explore this popular music and those who create it by sharing such books as the following:

Ashley Bryant. *Let It Shine: Three Favorite Spirituals.* Atheneum, 2007. African Americans also contributed a wealth of folk music. Bryant gives us wonderful, vibrant art to accompany the words of three well-known spirituals: "This Little Light of Mine," "He's Got the Whole World in His Hands," and "When the Saints Go Marching In!" The melody for each one is included to encourage us all to sing joyfully. Students of all ages will be happy to accept this illustrator's invitation "to lift their voices" together.

Leo and Diane Dillon. *Jazz on a Saturday Night.* Scholastic, 2007. These noted illustrators provide simple, poetic commentary as Miles Davis, John Coltrane, Ella Fitzgerald, and other jazz greats play while the people dance through the lively illustrations. A CD included with the book lets us hear the music, including the classic "Jazz on a Saturday Night." Short biographies and recommended recordings are provided for each musician mentioned in the book.

Leslie Gourse. *Sophisticated Ladies: The Great Women of Jazz.* Illustrated by Martin French. Dutton Children's Books, 2007. The lives of fourteen fabulous women, including Bessie Smith, Ethel Waters, Peggy Lee, Sarah Vaughan, and Rosemary Clooney, are presented. The illustrator provides splashy portraits of each.

Folksongs

Every country has folk music, songs that are familiar to most people, songs that originated long ago. Pete Seeger and Woody Guthrie are known for making music that touches the heart. They both sang simple songs that spoke of the people they knew and the problems almost everyone in America faced during the Great Depression and into the1960s.

One of Woody Guthrie's popular songs is "This Land Is Your Land," which he wrote and recorded in 1940. A beautiful picture book by the same title was published by Little, Brown in 1998. Illustrated with oil paintings by Kathy Jakobsen, the book invites the reader to take a journey across the United States, especially on Route 66, with families fleeing the Dust Bowl as they traveled toward California. A folded double-page map provides a detailed study of America's diversity and the country that Guthrie extoled. The music and words for this song are included at the back of the book so that everyone can join in singing with Woody. Invite student guitarists to play as the class (or the whole school) sings: "This land is your land, this land is my land; from California to the New York island . . . this land was made for you and me." This single book is a wonderful expression of our multicultural world.

Illustrated History and Geography

The Alphabet Atlas by Arthur Yorinks (Winslow, 1999), focuses on geography. The book is illustrated by his wife, Adrienne, who works with textiles and quilts. Her quilted art in this book is rich and explicit, with a full-page presentation for each place. Each letter of the alphabet, representing geographic locations, for example, Australia, New Zealand, or Denmark, is decorated by artist Jeanyee Wong, who also collaborated on this book.

This geographic ABC book suggests a class project in which each student provides a page of art and a short typed text to accompany the description of a place he or she chooses to feature. Yorinks chose Brazil, for example, for his book, but students will have fun poring over atlases to find other alphabetical possibilities. For example, B could be Bolivia, Bermuda, or Burma. As the pages are completed, each is placed in order to complete a class-made book. The class can present their pages in order before an audience of parents or other students.

The Great Migration (HarperCollins, 1992) is a collection of African American artist Jacob Lawrence's portrayals of the stories of Blacks in the United States. Lawrence was part of that great migration during World War II of Blacks from farms in the South to the large industrial cities of the North—Cleveland, Detroit, Chicago, and Harlem, the new home of many Blacks, in New York City. This collection of paintings was exhibited widely across the United States and viewed by thousands of interested people. Lawrence's simple text accompanies each picture with the refrain, "And the migrants kept coming."

A legend set "when monsters and giants and fairy folk lived in England," Margaret Hodges's retelling of *Saint George and the Dragon* (Little, Brown, 1984) was illustrated by a talented artist, Trina Schart Hyman, who won the Caldecott Award for this beautifully illustrated work.

Developing a Thematic Study: Everyone Is Special

The integrated learning activities that are inherent in a thematic study allow for the full use of diverse intelligences. Activities that permit children to dramatize scenes from history or to create original songs to share the information they have gathered on the Internet will serve to make such a study exciting and involving. Following are resources to help you develop a study focusing on Everyone Is Special! The intent of the thematic studies included throughout this chapter is to infuse the performing arts into academic learning so that students experience a varied approach to education that is truly multicultural and engages multiple intelligences.

A THINKING + LESSON PLAN

Acting Out Scenes from *Morning Girl*

Grades 4–8

Expected Outcomes
Learners will:

1. Listen to the teacher's reading of a short book.
2. Identify important scenes in the book.
3. Act out these scenes for an audience.

Teaching/Learning Strategies

Resources Needed
Obtain a copy of *Morning Girl* by Michael Dorris. To encourage students to read, try to obtain multiple copies of this book.

Directions

Step 1: Read this short book aloud to the class, reading a chapter a day over a week's time. Take time to discuss the happenings in the story.

Step 2: Display a map of the southeastern portion of the United States and the Caribbean. Locate the setting of this book.

Step 3: Assign two advanced students to research the Taino Indians and to report their findings to the class.

Step 4: Review the story. Have students identify significant scenes that tell the story. Choose students to play the roles of the native boy and girl, other Indians, White explorers. Other students can assume various roles, for example, narrators, a chorus, a director and assistant.

Performance Assessment
Practice the performance. Invite another class to serve as the audience. Invite parents to come, too.

Each student brings a unique perspective to the classroom. Unfortunately, these differences can be experienced as problems rather than assets to benefit everyone. Focus on students as individuals who all have strengths and weaknesses. Show the students that they don't have to listen to people who make fun of them.

Special Days. Students' birthdays offer an opportunity to recognize students as individuals. On your class calendar, list the birthdays that will occur each month. Let the birthday student do something special that day, for example:

- Wear a special hat
- Choose a game for everyone to play
- Teach the class a poem
- Distribute papers or books for the teacher
- Use a favorite color on the bulletin board

Another way of recognizing a student is to have the rest of the class brainstorm what they like about that person. These comments can be written down and collected in a book for the student to take home. The students can also make up a song about that person and sing it, perhaps to the tune of "Happy Birthday."

Decide how to schedule celebrations for students with summer birthdays. You might ask students to select from open dates. An alternative would be to celebrate "unbirthdays."

Ask students how birthdays are celebrated in their families. Do they have any special customs or ceremonies? Suggest that there are many different ways to honor people on their special day.

Although many students enjoy being the center of attention for a day, others may be shy or embarrassed by the publicity. Monitor your birthday activities to make sure that the student feels like an important part of the class and not singled out for uncomfortable attention.

Some books to share about birthdays are:

Eve Feldman. *Birthdays, Birthdays, Birthdays! Celebrating Life around the World.* Bridgewater, 1996.

Elisa Kleven. *Hooray, a Piñata!* Dutton, 1996. Clara chooses a dog piñata for her birthday party but can't face breaking it. Her friend Samson helps solve the dilemma. Multiethnic neighborhood, detailed illustrations.

The "Me" Collage.   Collage comes from the French word *coller,* meaning "to stick together." When you make a collage, you assemble many different items, often overlapping, from different media, to create an image (see Figure 8.4).

Ask students to bring in materials for everyone to share as they make a collage. Have magazines, newspapers, pictures, paints, and pens on hand. Students can cut out pictures and words, illustrating their ideas through a variety of media, to prepare a collage poster that expresses who they are and what they are like. Talk about the topics they might include, for example:

- Hobbies
- Birthplace—picture, part of a map
- Baby pictures
- Things they like—food, sports
- Their family—people, pets
- Where they have lived or traveled

Provide large pieces of cardboard on which students can mount their collages. Display the collage posters for everyone to appreciate.

After they have thought about how to represent themselves through collage, ask the students to write something to accompany their work. They can write a short description or a series of phrases, perhaps a poem.

Students will be interested to see how illustrators of children's books have used the collage technique. Share books illustrated by collage artists/authors such as Ezra Jack Keats, Christopher Myers, and Simms Taback, as well as the following:

Andrew Clements. *Workshop.* Illustrated by David Wisniewski. Clarion, 1999. The collage illustrations of woodworking tools, with their three-dimensional effect, encourage a second look.

FIGURE 8.4 "Me" Collage

Source: Tiedt, Tiedt, and Tiedt, *Language Arts Activities* (3rd ed.). Allyn and Bacon, 2001.

Steve Jenkins. *The Top of the World: Climbing Mount Everest.* Illustrated by the author. Houghton Mifflin, 1999. Cut and crushed paper collage adds a realistic effect to an informational book.

We All Belong to Many Groups.   Each student possesses multiple identities because each one belongs to many different groups. Discuss possible groupings with students and write their suggestions on the board. They might mention grouping by family background, language, country of origin, geography, religion, interests, and gender, for example. Point out

FIGURE 8.5   Groups I Belong To

I am . . .
a girl
a daughter
a member of the Wong family
a Californian
a member of this class
a twelve-year-old
a Chinese American
a U.S. citizen
an athlete

that some of these are groups you are born into (gender and race), some you learn (language and culture), some you have chosen (education and activities), and some that change (age and interests).

After students have had the opportunity to share their ideas, have them make individual lists. They can draw a picture of themselves and write their lists alongside (see Figure 8.5).

Display these pictures on the wall. Later they can be bound as a class book: Room 15, the Class of 2014.

Not Like Everyone Else.   Everyone is familiar with the fear of standing out from others and the pressure to conform. Yet we need to help students recognize that each of them differs from every other student and provide safe places for the discussion of these differences. Open this sensitive topic by reading *The Straight Line Wonder* by Mem Fox, illustrated by Marc Rosenthal. This short book tells the story of a "straight line" whose desire to dance, jump, and twirl isn't understood by the other "straight lines." The humorous message will appeal to all students, from preschoolers to teenagers. Invite students to take different sides of the issue in role-play, act or write out a different ending, or tell the story in the first person from the perspective of another character.

Other books you might use to address this concern are:

Katie Couric. *The Brand New Kid.* Illustrated by Marjorie Priceman. Doubleday, 2000. Lazlo's second-grade classmates mock him because he speaks with an accent.

Pat Mora. *The Rainbow Tulip.* Illustrated by Elizabeth Sayles. Viking, 1999. Although Estrelita (called Stella in class) wishes her Mexican American family weren't so different from the other students' families, she learns that sometimes there are advantages in standing out from the others.

Christopher Myers. *Wings.* Scholastic, 2000. The new kid in school isn't accepted by the others because he has wings.

Journals for Personal Writing.   An excellent way to promote the kind of writing that supports students' self-esteem and self-discovery is to encourage students to write frequently in a journal. Journals can be spiral-bound notebooks or sheets of composition paper stapled together. Students can individualize the cover with drawings or a collage and also use simple binding techniques to make their own books.

Schedule a specific time for writing in students' journals, and continue this writing for at least three weeks. The journals should be kept in the classroom so that all students have their journals on hand at the scheduled time. We recommend that you, too, write in a journal, both to demonstrate the value of the activity and to share entries periodically. Personal writing should never be graded or corrected. Students may select an entry to share if they wish, but the students' privacy must be protected.

Stimulate student imagination by providing some examples of personal journals from children's literature, such as:

Marissa Moss. *The All-New Amelia Series.* Pleasant, 1999.

At all times, students should feel free to write about subjects important to them. However, you may want to provide a stimulus each day for those who need an idea. Select a quote, read a short poem, or use one of the following topics:

- Friends are important because . . .
- If I were a superhero, I would be able to . . .
- I felt sad when . . .
- The bravest thing I ever did was . . .
- One characteristic I would like to change about myself is . . .
- Some of my favorite activities are . . .

Before you embark on this activity, recognize that students may write about painful, intimate, or uncomfortable topics. Decide in advance how you will handle the vulnerabilities that students expose, while acknowledging their concerns. If you share writing with the class or in small groups, talk with the students about treating each other's contributions with respect.

The following resources will help you set up a journal writing program.

Lucy Calkins and Shelley Harwayne. *Living between the Lines.* Heinemann, 1991.

Lorraine M. Dahlstrom. *Writing down the Days: 365 Creative Journaling Ideas for Young People.* Free Spirit, 1990.

Donald Murray. *Write to Learn,* 3rd ed. Holt, Rinehart, and Winston, 1990.

J. A. Senn. *325 Creative Prompts for Personal Journals.* Scholastic, 1992.

Death and Grieving. Well-written literature can help children learn how to manage the emotional and practical aspects of loss. Reading about other children who have gone through similar experiences, from the upheaval of change to the loss of a loved one, will provide models of coping strategies, language to organize and process their experience, and a safe setting in which to express their emotions. Select stories that demonstrate the variety of approaches people have used to confront these problems. Also note the cultural influences in attitudes toward death, grieving, and funerals.

T. A. Barron. *Where Is Grandpa?* Illustrated by Chris K. Soentpiet. Philomel, 2000. Members of a family try to make sense of their loss, but a young boy just wants to know where Grandpa is.

Pat Brisson. *Sky Memories.* Illustrated by Wendell Minor. Delacorte, 1999. Girl and her mother prepare for the mother's death from cancer by developing a ritual to help her grieve.

Eve Bunting. *The Happy Funeral.* Illustrated by Mai Vo-Dinh. Harper and Row, 1982. Chinese American girl's grandfather dies.

Eve Bunting. *Rudi's Pond.* Illustrated by Ronald Himler. Clarion, 1999. When another child dies, a girl and her classmates create a special place where they can remember him and feel close to him.

Lucille Clifton. *Everett Anderson's Goodbye.* Holt, 1983. In one of many picture books about Everett Anderson, an African American boy, his father dies.

Audrey Couloumbis. *Getting Near to Baby.* Putnam, 1999. Relatives' misguided attempts to help family get over baby sister's death are countered by warmth and humor of two sisters.

Bruce Coville. *My Grandfather's House.* Illustrated by Henri Sorenson. Bridgewater, 1996. A boy can't understand where his grandfather has gone when he dies.

Paul Goble. *Beyond the Ridge.* Aladdin, 1993. This picture book shows an old woman confronting death according to the beliefs of the Plains Indians. Death may seem like an end, but it is not.

Kevin Henkes. *Sun and Spoon.* Greenwillow, 1997. A ten-year-old boy lists fifty-two special things about his late grandmother.

Cynthia Rylant. *Missing May.* Orchard, 1992. In this extraordinarily sensitive novel, winner of the Newbery Award, twelve-year-old Summer grieves for her Aunt May, who took her in when no one else in the family wanted her.

Personality Prints.   Another way to feature students as individuals in the primary grades is to make handprints. Have each student place his or her hand on a piece of paper and draw around it with a thick colored pen. Then each student writes something about him- or herself on each finger—for example, writing his or her name on the thumb, a descriptive adjective on the next finger, then a favorite activity, a favorite color, and finally a favorite book. Post these "prints" on the wall to affirm the students' diverse personalities.

My Lifeline.   Have students draw a series of mountain peaks across a sheet of paper. Tell them that this line represents their life. What are the big peaks in their life? What are the smaller peaks? What are the valleys? Have them label the peaks and valleys that they have experienced in their lifetime so far.

Older students can make this a timeline by adding the years and sequencing the events in chronological order. This idea can be extended by describing their usual daily existence across the base of the mountains. A few fantasies can be added on clouds: "Someday I'd like to . . ."

African American History

The story of African Americans should be a part of the history that all of us learn. Unfortunately, presentations that focus on African Americans tend to occur in clumps in

February during Black History Month and remain rare the rest of the year. Spread discussion of African American history throughout the curriculum with books that make Black people more visible and help Black students find their lives in history.

Michael L. Cooper. *The Double V Campaign: African Americans and World War II.* Lodestar, 1998. African Americans fought on two fronts—against Germans and against racism.

Jeri Ferris. *With Open Hands: A Story about Biddy Mason.* Lerner, 1999. Born a slave, she won her freedom and became one of the richest women in Los Angeles.

Ayanna Hart and Earl Spangler. *Africans in America.* Lerner, 1995. This history shows the continuity of African traditions and values.

James Haskins and Kathleen Benson. *Out of the Darkness: The Story of Blacks Moving North 1890–1940.* Benchmark, 2000. Uses two historical figures to explain this period.

Dorothy Hoobler and Thomas Hoobler. *The African American Family Album.* Oxford University Press, 1995. This social and cultural history, part of the *American Family Album* series, is full of project ideas.

Deborah Hopkinson. *A Band of Angels: A Story Inspired by the Jubilee Singers.* Illustrated by Raúl Colón. Atheneum, 1999. Ella Sheppard, born a slave, toured with the Jubilee Singers to raise money for Fisk University and keep the traditional songs alive.

Jacob Lawrence. *The Great Migration: An American Story.* HarperCollins, 1993. Sixty paintings by the famous artist Jacob Lawrence, accompanied by explanatory text, show the movement of Blacks from the rural South to the urban North. Lawrence also painted sequences of the lives of Harriet Tubman and Frederick Douglass. The epilogue is a poem by Walter Dean Myers.

Osceola Mays. *Osceola: Memories of a Sharecropper's Daughter.* Disney Press, 2000. Outstanding oral history.

Positive Images of Black Families in Literature.   Students need to see realistic yet positive images of the lives of people like themselves. Well-written children's books can give students a mirror against which to measure themselves as well as a chance to imagine a better world. The following books acknowledge the problems and conflicts typical of African American children's lives and at the same time offer hope. In addition, the quality of the writing ensures that children from other racial backgrounds will appreciate the stories, too.

Marie Bradby. *Momma, Where Are You From?* Illustrated by Chris K. Soentpiet. Orchard, 2000. Realistic pictures as girl's mother reminisces about her hard childhood.

Lucille Clifton. *Some of the Days of Everett Anderson.* Illustrated by Evaline Ness. Henry Holt, 1987. The famous Black poet has written a series of picture books about lively Everett, with warm pictures of family life in an apartment in the city.

Monica Gunning. *Under the Breadfruit Tree.* Illustrated by Fabricio Ven den Broeck. Boyds Mills, 1998. Author's childhood in Jamaica.

Lorri Hewett. *Dancer.* Dutton, 1999. Black sixteen-year-old girl wonders whether to follow her dream to be a ballerina or go to college.

Mary Hoffman. *Amazing Grace.* Illustrated by Caroline Binch. Dial, 1991. Grace likes to act out characters from stories she reads. Her grandmother tells Grace she can be anyone she wants to be.

Elizabeth Fitzgerald Howard. *Virgie Goes to School with Us Boys.* Illustrated by E. B. Lewis. Simon & Schuster, 2000. Virginia wants to go to school to learn to read like her older brothers. Based on family's story.

Phil Mendez. *The Black Snowman.* Illustrated by Carole Byard. Scholastic, 1989. Jacob learns pride and bravery from a snowman that he builds with his younger brother.

Margaree King Mitchell. *Uncle Jed's Barbershop.* Illustrated by James Ransome. Simon & Schuster, 1993. A Black man dreams of owning his own barbershop, not an easy goal in the 1920s.

Gloria Pinkney. *Back Home.* Illustrated by Jerry Pinkney. Dial, 1992. Eight-year-old Ernestine from the city visits relatives on a farm in North Carolina. She's eager to fit in, but the country ways are different. This story of a Black family presents universal themes of home, family, and belonging.

Faith Ringgold. *Tar Beach.* Crown, 1991. Cassie and BeBe in Brooklyn dream of flying away from the pressures of the world.

Mildred Taylor. *Roll of Thunder, Hear My Cry.* Phyllis Fogelson, 2001. Classic story of a southern Black family maintaining its pride and its land despite the humiliations of racial prejudice. A Newbery Award winner, it is especially noteworthy for its acknowledgment of the complexity of Black–White relations.

Virginia Euwer Wolff. *True Believer.* Atheneum, 2001. In this novel, teenager LaVaughn struggles to achieve her goals despite the limitations of her situation.

Jacqueline Woodson. *Maizon at Blue Hill.* Delacorte, 1993. When Maizon is accepted at Blue Hill, an elite, mostly White boarding school, she has to leave behind her grandmother, her best friend, and her familiar neighborhood. She struggles to find her own place despite the barriers. Look for other stories about Maizon.

Questions of Identity.   One of the issues confronting us as we teach multiculturally is how to define who is an African American. In the time of slavery, the answer was simple: People known to have even a drop of "African blood" were considered Black, even if they came from primarily White ancestry. The label of African American has always included people of many different racial and ethnic backgrounds. Today, however, increasing attention has been drawn to the recognition of *multiracial* heritage. For the first time, respondents to the U.S. Census were allowed to identify themselves as members of more than one racial or ethnic group. One advantage to this change is that children who have parents from different racial groups are no longer forced to select an identity that excludes one parent. On the other hand, how do we count the African American population? From 29 million people in 1990, the number of blacks in 2000 has increased to 34 million (if you count the people who checked only one box) or 35 million (if you count the people who checked at least this race). The difference of one million people is a substantial one. In that case, what does it mean to be an African American? Should "multiracial" be considered a separate identity in the multicultural curriculum?

One person who has faced this question is the popular golf star Tiger Woods. He has been called African American because his father is Black, Afro-Asian because his mother is from Thailand, and simply multiracial in honor of his diverse heritage. Students can select one of the many biographies of this outstanding individual and then discuss the challenge of labeling people. What would they prefer to be called?

Carl Emerson. *Tiger Woods.* Child's World, 2000. Part of the *Sports Superstars* series. Good photographs.

Libby Hughes. *Tiger Woods: A Biography for Kids.* Genesis, 2000. For primary grades.

Paul Joseph. *Tiger Woods.* Abdo & Daughters, 2000. Part of the *Awesome Athletes* series.

Elizabeth Sirimarco. *Tiger Woods.* Capstone, 2001. Part of the *Sports Heroes* series, for intermediate grades.

Mark Stewart. *Tiger Woods: Drive to Greatness.* Millbrook, 2001. For intermediate grades.

A Thinking + Lesson Plan: Reading and Writing Haiku
Follow directions given below.

A THINKING + LESSON PLAN

Reading and Writing Haiku

Grades 3–12
Expected Outcomes
Learners will:

1. Read examples of haiku poetry.
2. Identify the characteristics of haiku.
3. Write original haiku.
4. Publish a collection of haiku.

Teaching/Learning Strategies

Resources Needed
Collect books of poetry related to social studies to read aloud to students. Students will write haiku poems about selected social studies topics. They will then contribute their best haiku to a class publication.

Directions
Poetry is especially suitable for enhancing a social studies lesson. Your own enthusiasm will be contagious as students listen to you read (or recite) a favorite poem related to the current study. A wonderful collection of poems about people in history is *The Book of Americans* by Rosemary and

(continued)

Stephen Vincent Benet. *Bronzeville Boys and Girls* is a collection by Pulitzer Prize winner Gwendolyn Brooks. Sample the work of Black poet Langston Hughes; the composer of outstanding free verse, Carl Sandburg; and the well-polished haiku written by Japanese poets of the thirteenth century. Give students a sheet on which you have typed three to eight examples of classic haiku. Have them identify the characteristics of these poems before they try writing their own haiku.

Step 1: Writing poetry is a way for students to express their ideas and feelings. Have students write haiku as part of a study of Japan. Here are two examples of haiku translated from the original Japanese:

First cold showers fall.　　　　All sky disappears
Even little monkey wants　　　 The earth's land has gone away;
A wee coat of straw.　　　　　Still the snowflakes fall.
　　　—*Bashō*　　　　　　　　　—*Hashin*

An excellent source of information for the teacher who wants to know more about haiku is *An Introduction to Haiku* by Harold Anderson. Children are most successful with this brief verse form if emphasis is rightly placed on the thoughts they are expressing rather than on the confining form, for example:

The sun shines brightly.　　　　The old cypress tree,
With its glowing flames shooting　So beautiful by the rocks,
It goes down at night.　　　　　Has been there for years.
　　　—*Ricky*　　　　　　　　　—*Marjorie*

After first thinking about an idea they wish to express, the students are encouraged to write it on paper. They can then examine their own written thought to determine how it can be divided into three parts. Experimentation with word arrangement, imagery, changing the order of the lines, and choice of words used should be encouraged as the poem is developed.

Step 2: Print out haiku written by a class with a computer using two long columns so that the folded sheets will produce two long, slim pages. Cut the sheets to form pages of an attractive booklet and make a decorative cover, as shown in Figure 8.6.

Step 3: A rewarding art experience that correlates well with the writing of haiku is blowing ink with a straw. Washable black ink is applied in a swath near the bottom of an unlined file card (or any nonabsorbent paper). The wet ink is then blown with a straw to direct the ink in the desired direction. Blowing across the ink causes it to branch attractively. When the ink is dry, tiny dabs of bright tempera may be applied with a toothpick to add spring blossoms to the bare branch. The student then writes a haiku on the card below the flowering branch, and the card is used for display or as a gift for parents.

　　For an authentic presentation of haiku, use rice paper (or thin onion skin or tissue paper) mounted inside colored paper. The poem is written (a felt pen will write on thin paper) along with a Japanese design—reeds, moon over water, flowering branch—and the author's name.

FIGURE 8.6   Haiku Booklet

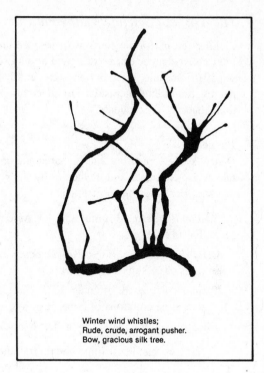

Winter wind whistles;
Rude, crude, arrogant pusher.
Bow, gracious silk tree.

The cover is folded so that the front flaps overlap slightly, as in the sketch. A ribbon is then tied around the folder, which is ready for presentation as a gift (see Figure 8.7).

Performance Assessment
Students will receive grades of Credit/No Credit based on their completing at least one haiku. Each student should have one haiku included in a class publication.

FIGURE 8.7   Haiku Gift

Folded slightly overlapping . . .
. . . tied with ribbon

The Arts and Science/Mathematics

Linking the performing arts with science and mathematics may require real ingenuity. Interpretive dances can be designed around scientific studies as well as the lives of noted scientists, and the lyrics of songs can extol their contributions. Both science and mathematics studies lend themselves to the creation of books with attractive covers and illustrations made by the students.

Dance

Dance is also something that is shared and understood around the world. Demonstrate the universality of dance and its themes by showing videos of dancing performed by different cultures. Here are a few examples:

> *African Rhythms.* 13 minutes, color. Associated Film, Inc., 1621 Dragon Street, Dallas, TX 75207.

> Betty Casey. *International Folk Dancing.* Doubleday, 1992. Includes directions and pictures of costumes for students.

> *Dancer's World.* 30 minutes. NET. Martha Graham discusses dancing as her students dance the emotions of hope, fear, joy, and love.

> *The Strollers.* 6 minutes, color. The Moiseyev Dance Company in a Russian folk dance.

> Students can learn some simple folk dances to perform.

Making Counting Books

Before beginning this project have the group brainstorm topics that would work well in counting from one to ten. Consider the audience—preschool and first grade children—and what would interest them.

Older students can create counting books around various themes, for example, the cheetah, elephants, grizzly bears or perhaps "Going to the Zoo," where children might count: 1 tiger, 2 giraffes, 3 pandas, and so on, thus learning the names of different animals as well as the numbers in order. To provide accurate pictures of each animal and their typical habitats, each student will need to use the library and Internet to research the required information. Students who don't draw well might use stick figures or cut pictures from magazines.

Creating Bilingual Books for Young Children

Students who know a language other than English might use it to prepare a counting book in, for example, Vietnamese, Arabic, or French. Making these books bilingual with the English words included might be especially helpful for children who are learning English. Such books can be donated to the school library so that children who speak these languages can check them out for use at home. Parents can learn from them, too.

Students can choose different science or mathematics topics to present in a picture book with a simple text. Information about birds or animals with just a line or two of text would be appropriate, for example, a picture of a crow with the text: *A crow is black. A crow says "caw."*

Numbers in Our Language

Have students brainstorm "numbers" and how we use them in our language, for example:

One—

    You are *the* one!
    He's Number One!
    He's Numero Uno!
    Right answer
    Trunk on an elephant
    The clock struck "one"

Two—

    A pair
    Twins
    Eyes
    Ears
    Parents
    Teams competing
    Duet

Three—

    Three's a crowd!
    Three strikes; you're out!
    Triplets
    Trio
    Three blind mice

Four—

    Four and twenty blackbirds
    Quadruplets
    Downs in football
    Legs on a horse

Five—

    Basketball team
    Quintuplets
    Fingers on one hand
    Toes on your foot
    Five cards in a straight

Six—

    Sextet
    Half a dozen

Seven—

    Seven come eleven
    Seven dwarves

Eight—

    Octet
    Octuplets

Nine—
    A baseball team
    Cat o'nine tails
    A cat has nine lives

Ten—
    Fingers on two hands
    Toes on both feet

Have students develop a large collage that includes the numbers 1–10 and the associations brainstormed by the class for each.

Finding Numbers All Around You

Students could take photographs of numbers they observe around town. If cameras are not available, students can sketch a replica of the number and the environs in which it appears, for example, a house with a numbered address near its front door. Other kinds of numbers that students will find include:

- Numbers on buses
- A price on an advertisement
- Numbers on a tee-shirt
- The numbers on a car's license plate
- The numbers for floors in an elevator

A Thinking + Lesson Plan: Depicting Sports Through Mixed Media

---

A THINKING + LESSON PLAN

◄◌►

Depicting Sports through Mixed Media

Grades 4–12

Expected Outcomes

Learners will:

1. Select one sport to research.
2. Collect information about this sport and the players.
3. Create a display depicting the sport.
4. Report on the sport and share your art.

Teaching/Learning Strategies

Resources Needed

Brainstorm a list of sports played around the world. Students will choose one sport to study, working individually or in groups of two to three students. All students will be encouraged to contribute information or clippings that other students can use. Representative players of

---

different sports will be invited to the classroom to be interviewed by class members. Students will create collages and report on their study.

Directions

Step 1: Challenge students to see how many different sports they can name. Print their contributions on a large sheet of paper where they can remain for a few weeks. Tell students to talk with their parents or siblings about this list to see if they can suggest additional sports. You may need to define games versus sports.

Step 2: Have students choose one sport to research, for example, soccer, lacrosse, lawn bowling, or bocce ball. Students can work individually or in small groups, if several are interested in the same sport. Limit the number studying one sport to three so that more sports will receive attention. Students will visit the library to locate informative nonfiction or biographies, for example:

Crystal Bowman. *Ivan and the Dynamos.* Eerdmans Books, 1997. Fiction; hockey.
Kristin S. Fehr. *Monica Seles: Returning Champion.* Lerner, 1997. Biography; tennis.
Stew Thornley. *Deion Sanders: Prime Time Player.* Lerner, 1997. Biography; football.

Students can also invite high school or college players to come to the school for interviews and to demonstrate aspects of their sport. Have students bring in newspapers and magazines to use for information and to clip as they collect material for their collages. Criteria for making reports and creating an effective collage should be discussed in order for students to do a good job.

Step 3: A few at a time, students will present their studies and their collages to the class.

Performance Assessment

Reports and collages will be judged based on the criteria established. Five students can be selected as the judges to place ribbons on the collages: Blue for Outstanding; Red for Good; White for Incomplete. The class can select the best five collages to be displayed in the hall near the principal's office, where they can be seen by parents and other students.

Women Who Made a Difference

Ruth Ashby and Deborah Ohrm, eds. *History: Women Who Changed the World.* Viking, 1995.

Tanya Bolden. *Portraits of African American Heroes.* Dutton, 2003. Includes both men and women—dancers, writers, politicians, etc.

Penny Colman. *Adventurous Women: Eight True Stories about Women Who Made a Difference.* Holt, 2006.

Joy Paige. *Ellen Ochoa, The First Hispanic Woman in Space.* Roaring, 2004.

Melissa Schwarz. *Wilma Mankiller: Principal Chief of the Cherokees.* Chelsea, 1994. Part of Series: *Native American Indians of Achievement.*

The Work of Noted Artists

Some picture books introduce and explain the work of artists whose paintings are hung in museums around the world.

> Marie Sellier. *My Little Picasso*. Translation by Isabel Ollivier. Réunion des musées nationaux, 2002. Here is a selection of Picasso's art explained by the author with reproductions from the museum. See also *My Little Orsay; My Little Louvre*, which introduces two famous art museums in Paris; originally published in French.

CONNECTIONS

The performing arts—painting, singing, dancing, acting, and so forth—offer students an opportunity to use different kinds of creative abilities. Including such activities in the classroom enhances instruction and serves to engage student interest in what he or she is learning in school.

Including all of the performing arts in some way as we teach subjects across the curriculum invites students to use various forms of intelligence as they learn new information, new ways of looking at the world. Providing opportunities for students to build on their strengths supports their individual self-esteem and promotes feelings of empathy as they share their contributions.

Integrating the performing arts across the curriculum makes learning more inviting and allows students to increase their knowledge as they deal with information in different ways. Acting out scenes from history, for example, makes it more likely that students will remember the information with which they are dealing.

GETTING INVOLVED

Expanding Your Reflective Teaching Portfolio

1. Select a number of activities from this chapter to use as models for enhancing learning in the social studies and/or science, subjects that could well benefit from added appeal and time spent on each subject. Then, plan a lesson for each of the two subjects following these models.
2. Survey your own interests and abilities as you consider what you can do to engage students more actively in learning. Can you sing, dance, or play an instrument? Is there something that you would like to learn to do? It's never too late to learn a new skill—crafts, dancing, acting, whatever appeals to you.

Working with Your Cooperative Learning Group

1. Plan a short play demonstrating how the arts were an integral part of the lives of members of a specific ethnic group.
2. Learn how to make a specific art form, for example, "ojos de dios," or felted animals. Offer to teach other students who are interested how to make these figures.

EXPLORING FURTHER

Woody Guthrie. *This Land Is Your Land*. Illustrated by Kathy Jacobsen. Little, Brown, 1998. A wonderful portrayal of the diversity in this country, from California to the New York island, in a folksong; includes the last two verses usually omitted and the history of song.

Helen Hume. *The Art Teacher's Survival Guide for Elementary and Middle School*. Jossey-Bass, 2008, 2nd ed. Effective art instruction, including art appreciation.

Kenneth Koch and Kate Farrell. *Talking to the Sun: An Illustrated Anthology of Poems for Young People*. Metropolitan Museum of Art, 1985. A carefully chosen selection of poetry plus pictures of varied art taken in a museum.

B. Shannon. *The Power of Pictures: Creating Pathways to Literacy through Art*. Wiley, 2008.

CHAPTER 9

Multicultural Ideas for Every Day of the Year

> *Education is an important element in the struggle for Human Rights. It is the means to help our children and our people rediscover their identity and thereby increase their self-respect.*
> **Education is our passport to the future,**
> *for tomorrow belongs to the people who prepare for it today.*
>
> ～ MALCOLM X

"It takes a village," as the saying goes, and so it does, requiring the efforts of every person to save this planet. We must work together to relieve the effects of poverty and hunger. We must join hands and look into each other's eyes as we acknowledge the presence of children who need health care, mothers and fathers who are in desperate straits as they struggle to feed their families, and poor countries that are unable to provide schools for their young people.

Multiculturalism is with us every day, so it behooves us to recognize this fact and to make it explicit in our classrooms. In this chapter, we present a Multicultural Calendar, which we have developed in great detail. Our aim is to provide every teacher with a powerful tool that will enable each student to focus attention on the contributions every American offers as we strive to improve our world, to reach out to those who are in need, and to support efforts to move toward a peaceful world.

Used in conjunction with the lessons, thematic studies, and ideas for differentiated instruction that permeate this book, the calendar presents hundreds of suggestions for enhancing the curriculum at all levels of schooling throughout the United States. The calendar is meant to recognize the contributions made by many ethnic groups, different races, speakers of diverse languages, and those who espouse varied religious faiths. It presents a myriad of people to whom we owe a word of thanks in appreciation for what they have done for us and our country.

There are those who will choose to label this multicultural calendar derisively as "a heroes and holidays approach," implying that this wealth of information is less useful because of the format in which it is presented. That criticism is akin to saying, "Let's not celebrate Easter because some people come to church only on that Sunday." Rather, the calendar makes it clear that we should celebrate multiculturalism every day, not just for one week during a unit of study at one grade level. Multiculturalism is far too complex and evolutionary a subject to even think of tying it up in one neat little package. We must instead see that it is integrated into all areas of education. If we open our eyes, we will see that the possibilities for engaging even young children in dealing with controversy, talking about the importance of friendship, love, and trust, and engaging in issues of the real world are exhilarating!

This chapter includes an introductory section, "Displaying the Multicultural Calendar," and a final section that develops the intriguing theme, "Time." The bulk of the chapter, however, is devoted to the series of twelve calendars. Included with each month's calendar is a treasurehouse of relevant information about people born in that month and about events that occur on a day in the month, a week, or even the whole month. No one expects students to know who was born on February 3rd or October 16th, but we do want younger students to begin recognizing the names of such people as Martin Luther King, Jr., and his contribution to our country's growth. We'd like them to recognize the reason that somebody decided to designate one day as Presidents' Day or another as Veterans' Day. This is part of being an American patriot.

❖ Displaying the Multicultural Calendar

You can install the calendar directly on a large bulletin board. Divide the display space into squares or rectangles using thick colored yarn or strips of colored paper. Students can select distinctive colors and pictures for each month.

Make the spaces as large as possible. Challenge several students to solve this measurement problem. Print large block letters for the days of the week and the names of the month. Also print a set of numbers from 1 to 31. Computer graphics will give students multiple options for font style and size. Print on colored paper for variety.

Developing the Calendar

Older students can write or print out events, names, and dates on slips of colored construction paper or unlined file cards to mount in the appropriate block for each month. Be sure that they check the current calendar so that the number 1 is placed under the correct day of the week; the rest of the dates will then fall in place accordingly. Add events that are celebrated locally or dates of personal interest to your students, such as birthdays. Include pictures and quotations wherever possible.

Quotations are of special interest for the multicultural calendar. Find as many as possible for people whose names appear for that month. Begin with the quotations presented throughout this book. Additional sources of quotations include:

Ella Mazel. *"And Don't Call Me a Racist!" A Treasury of Quotes on the Past, Present, and Future of the Color Line in America.* Argonaut Press, 1998.

Richard Newman. *African American Quotations.* Facts on File, 2000.

The Quotable Woman: The First 4000 Years. Facts on File, 2001.

J. A. Senn, comp. and ed. *Quotations for Kids.* Illustrated by Steve Pica. Millbrook Press, 1999. Includes the words of celebrities, historical figures, and fictional characters.

Pictures add a special dimension to the calendar. Have students search for varied multiethnic pictures for this purpose. If you have a large bulletin board on which to display the calendar, you might place a ring of pictures around the calendar. Ask students if they can identify the people and events pictured.

Encourage students to continue adding to the calendar. As they read, they can take notes on information to include in the calendar. They can search the Internet, newspapers, their textbooks, library reference books, and fiction. Students can become "investigators" as each one takes responsibility for exploring a specific topic.

Students can also decorate the bulletin board by adding seasonal designs, symbols, or illustrations. Snowflakes for the winter months, leaves for the fall, and flowers for the spring add interest and individuality to the calendar. Other possible motifs include pumpkins, kites, butterflies, and hearts. Avoid popular symbols that reinforce stereotypes, such as shamrocks or Indian headdresses.

Strategies for Using the Calendar

Often a more extensive unit of study is triggered by a single historical event or a series of dates on the calendar. Thematic units cross subject areas as well as periods of time and allow students to express their ideas in a variety of formats—spoken, written, drawn, performed, for example:

- Muslims in the United States
- Religions around the World
- Japanese Americans in Our Community
- Holidays and Celebrations
- Women in Sports

Almost any subject presented in an elementary, middle school, or high school classroom will lend itself to a multicultural approach. As you introduce each topic and discuss it with students, point to the contributions of various groups—ethnic, religious, racial, young and old, male and female—as important threads woven into the quilt of our society.

Letters
Encourage students to express their ideas about people and issues in the form of letters. They can write letters to the local newspaper about an issue on which they have an opinion. They can also write letters to people from whom they would like information— members of Congress, authors of articles or books, leaders of groups or movements, and so on. Letters to parents can explain what the class is doing. Letters to different media can be used to inform the public of important events or activities.

Great Interviews
Students practice significant skills as they role-play an interview of a personality from the past or present. Two or more students will need to develop this activity together as they plan the best questions and appropriate responses. Students can also interview several people, perhaps from different times. They will need to investigate a variety of sources to play these roles as realistically as possible.

Multimedia Presentation
Students select a person or topic from the calendar to research. They can present their findings in a speech to the class, using notes and appropriate visual and/or auditory aids, such as graphics imported from CD-ROMs or the Internet, pertinent newspaper items mounted on posters, audio or video recordings of speeches, overhead transparencies for new vocabulary, a time line displayed on the wall, and props or artifacts to share with the class. Older students can develop a PowerPoint® presentation about the topic they choose.

The Time Machine
Ask students whom they would like to invite from the past to visit their community. For example, how would W. E. B. Dubois or Frederick Douglass respond to the problems of people today? What would they think of your town? Would they be impressed or disappointed? How might they react to meeting people such as U.S. Supreme Court Justices Clarence Thomas or Ruth Bader Ginsburg? Students can then write an imaginary diary for their visitor from the past, recording such reactions.

❖ The Months of the Year

In this section, we present ideas for celebrating multicultural understandings every day of the year. The activities in this section provide opportunities for students to ask and answer questions, to discuss fundamental issues such as race and identity, and to develop skills and information essential to living in a complex world.

Each calendar includes:

- Birthdays of historical and contemporary Americans from major ethnic groups
- Important dates in the history of different groups
- Religious and cultural holidays and festivals

The individuals mentioned here are the exceptional few whose achievements have been recognized by history. We want to honor them without limiting ourselves to their example. In every community there are people who have made significant contributions to the welfare of society. One way to acknowledge and appreciate their efforts is to include them on the multicultural calendar as it is created by your class.

Following each month is a short list of suggested activities for incorporating the calendar information into your everyday teaching.

To facilitate presentation, we have not prepared the calendar for one specific year. You will need to make slight adaptations to correct the dates accordingly. For each month, too, there are certain special weeks or holidays that occur on variable dates. The months of July and August are included so that you have the option of presenting this information at other times during the school year.

September Activities

Our calendar (see Table 9.1) begins with September and the traditional opening of the school year. From September 15 to October 15 the contributions of Americans of Latino heritage are highlighted. What events occur during this time that are particularly associated with Latinos? Local celebrations will give you an excellent opportunity to collect ideas and materials that you can use in the classroom now and throughout the year, because your inclusion of Latinos will not be limited to this month.

The fourth week of the month is Banned Book Week and Religious Freedom Week as well. The activities suggested for this section will enable students to explore issues of citizenship, literacy, and freedom of speech.

September 8

On International Literacy Day (sponsored by UNESCO since 1965), focus student attention on the importance of reading. Ask students if they have library cards. Have they ever been to the library? Provide information for students who aren't familiar with the library. For more information on this day, consult (www.nifl.gov/celebrate).

Discuss "literacy" with students. What does it mean to be "literate"? Why is literacy important? Dictators traditionally control access to literacy for fear that knowing how to read and write will encourage people to seek their freedom. Share with students powerful tales of the importance of literacy. When Blacks were enslaved, it was illegal to teach them to read and write. A fictional account, *Nightjohn* by Gary Paulsen (also available on video), describes the obstacles encountered by Black slaves attempting to become literate. Read *Richard Wright and the Library Card* by William Miller, illustrated by Gregory Christie, to learn more about this writer and how he had to sneak books out of the library.

September 16

Prepare the class for Mexican Independence Day by featuring Mexico in the classroom. Use all available materials to create an atmosphere of Mexico. Travel posters, clothes, and objects from Mexico will contribute a festive appearance. Display books about Mexico. Older students can write reports on different aspects of Mexico to put around the room. Use a map of Mexico as a focus for featuring facts about Mexico. Have students research information to construct a time line of significant events in Mexican history. Why is Mexican Independence Day important? What other historic dates celebrated in Mexico are

TABLE 9.1 September

1	2	3	4	5	6	7
International Literacy Day	Liliuokalani, 1838–1917, last sovereign of Hawai'i	Prudence Crandall, 1803–?, first to admit Black girls to her school	Richard Wright, 1908–1960, Black author; Geronimo surrenders 1886	Harriet E. Wilson published first novel by Black American		Artist Jacob Lawrence 1917–2000
8	**9** Ellis Island Museum of Immigration opened 1990; Sarah Douglass, 1806–1882, Black teacher and abolitionist	**10** Alice Davis, 1852–1935, Seminole tribal leader	**11**	**12** Mae Jemison, first Black woman in space, 1992	**13** Maria Baldwin, 1856–1922, Black educator and civic leader; Aloha Festivals, Hawai'i	**14**
15 Porfirio Díaz, President of Mexico, 1830–1915; Latin American Independence Day, 1821	**16** Mexican Independence Day, 1821; Mayflower Day (Pilgrims left England, 1620)	**17** Citizenship Day; International Day of Peace	**18** Québec surrendered to English, 1759	**19** Lajos Kossuth, Hungarian patriot, 1802–1915; Booker T. Washington founded Tuskegee Institute, 1881	**20**	**21** Sandra Day O'Connor, first woman confirmed as Supreme Court Justice, 1981; Autumnal Equinox
22 Martha Corey hung as a witch, Salem, 1692; Andrea Bocelli, 1958–, Italian tenor	**23**	**24** Francis Watkins Harper, 1825–1911, Black author and reformer; Federal troops enforce desegregation Little Rock, 1957	**25** Balboa "discovered" Pacific Ocean, 1513; Columbus began second trip to America, 1493; Howard University founded, 1867, first all-Black university	**26**	**27** Native American Day	**28** Confucius' birthday (National holiday, Taiwan)
29 Elie Wiesel 1928–	**30** Bryant Gumbel 1948–					

Sept. 15–Oct. 15—Latino Heritage Month
4th week—Banned Books Week
4th week—Religious Freedom Week

. . . why I swore never to be silent whenever and wherever human beings endure suffering and humiliation. We must always take sides. Neutrality helps the oppressor, never the victim. Silence encourages the tormentor, never the tormented.

—*Elie Wiesel*

FIGURE 9.1　A Learning Center

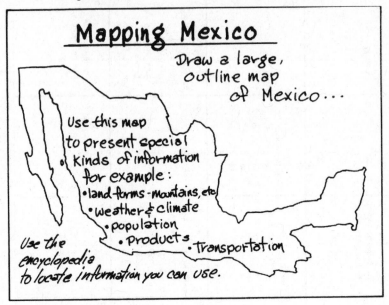

important to people living in the United States? Create a Learning Center focusing on Mexico and Mexican Americans. Include a map of Mexico like Figure 9.1, shown here.

Read students the Mexican tale *The Woman Who Outshone the Sun/La mujer que brillaba aún más que el sol,* from a poem by Alejandro Cruz Martínez. Provide colored pens for students to illustrate the story. Students can also compare the English and Spanish texts in this bilingual book. Perhaps a Spanish speaker can read the Spanish version aloud or on an audiorecording so that all students can hear how it sounds.

Other books to share with students include:

Antonio Hernández Madrigal. *Blanca's Feather.* Illustrated by Gerardo Suzán. Rising Moon, 2000. Simple story conveys the atmosphere of rural Mexico.

Naomi Shihab Nye, coll. *The Tree Is Older Than You Are: A Bilingual Gathering of Poems and Stories from Mexico.* Illustrated by various Mexican artists. Simon & Schuster, 1995. Includes works by children and adults; provides insight into contemporary Mexican cultures as well as universal concerns.

Jonah Winter. *Diego.* Illustrated by Jeannette Winter. Knopf, 1991. Biography of Diego Rivera, Mexican mural artist; for students of all ages.

September 17
The importance of citizenship is recognized on the anniversary of the signing of the Constitution (1787). Do students know what it means to be a citizen of a country? While people who are born in the United States are automatically U.S. citizens, legal immigrants must pass a test to become citizens. Once they are citizens they gain the right to vote, to

hold public office, and to serve on juries. This process is called *naturalization.* About one million *aliens* (people from other countries) applied for citizenship in 1996. Conditions for naturalization are:

- Living in the United States for five years.
- No convictions for serious crimes.
- Ability to read, write, and speak basic English.
- Passing grade on U.S. history and civics test. (They have to be able to answer such questions as: What does the Constitution do? What is one thing Benjamin Franklin is known for?)

Discuss these requirements with students. Should all people who want to be citizens have to pass a test? Why do people want to become citizens? Invite an immigration lawyer or naturalization advisor to the class to explain the naturalization process. Discover what countries the new citizens come from.

Who Belongs Here: An Immigration Story, by Margy Burns Knight and Anne Sibley O'Brien, will spark student discussion of the issues of immigration and citizenship. A teacher's guide is also available.

Fourth Week in September
Banned Books Week is sponsored by the American Library Association. The goal of the program is to highlight the importance of the First Amendment and the power of literature and to celebrate the freedom to read. Ask students what they would do if someone took their books away. Why is reading important? Have each student complete the sentence: Reading is important to me because . . .

For more information on censorship and challenges to books, contact the ALA, 50 E. Huron, Chicago, IL 60611 or (www.ala.org/bbooks). They publish *The Banned Books Resource Guide.* The National Organization of Teachers of English (NCTE) also offers assistance to teachers concerned about issues of censorship. Contact them at SLATE, NCTE, 1111 W. Kenyon Road, Urbana, IL 61801-1096 or visit (www.ncte.org/censorship/).

October Activities

October is National UNICEF Month. Latino Heritage Month also continues until October 15. The third week is Black Poetry Week, and the fourth is United Nations Week. In this month (see Table 9.2) dominated by the presence of Christopher Columbus and the implications of his voyages, we must aim for a balanced perspective by pointing out the substantial presence of Native Americans and the impact his arrival had on them.

October 12
Columbus Day commemorates the landing of Christopher Columbus at San Sálvador in 1492. Locate San Sálvador on the map. Trace Columbus's journey from Spain to the "New World."

Columbus may not have been the first European to land on the continent. There is evidence of Viking settlements and perhaps other voyagers landed here. Should we celebrate Viking Day instead? Discuss with students. Why has Columbus become the symbol of all European contact and colonization?

TABLE 9.2 October

1	2	3	4	5	6	7
Jimmy Carter, 1924–, 39th U.S. president; Thurgood Marshall, first Black Supreme Court Justice, 1967; International Day for the Elderly; James Meredith first Black student at U Miss, 1962	Mohandas K. Gandhi, 1869–1948; First Pan American Conference—Washington, DC, 1889		Tecumseh (Shawnee) died, 1813; Child Health Day	Author/artist Faith Ringgold, 1930–; Fannie Lou Hamer 1917–1977, Black Civil Rights leader	Imanu Amiri Baraka (LeRoi Jones), 1934–; Marian Anderson, first Black hired by Metropolitan Opera, 1954	
8	**9**	**10**	**11**	**12**	**13**	**14**
Jesse Jackson, 1941–	Leif Erikson Day; Mary Shadd Cary, 1823–1893, Black teacher, journalist, lawyer	Shawnees defeated in Battle of Point Pleasant (WV), 1774, ends Lord Dunmore's War; Chinese Revolution began, 1911	Eleanor Roosevelt, 1884–1962; Casimir Pulaski Memorial Day; National Coming Out Day	Columbus lands at San Sálvador, 1492; Día de la Raza (Latin America); Indigenous People Day	Margaret Thatcher, 1913–, British prime minister	Eamon de Valera, Irish president, 1882–1975; William Penn, 1644–1718; National Children's Day
15	**16**	**17**	**18**	**19**	**20**	**21**
World Poetry Day	Sarah Winnemucca died, 1891, Paiute Indian leader; Alaska Day Festival; John Brown's Raid, 1859	Albert Einstein came to U.S., 1933	First Chinese opera performed in U.S.—San Francisco, 1852; Helen Hunt Jackson, 1831–1885, author of *Ramona*			Alfred Nobel, 1833–1896
22	**23**	**24**	**25**	**26**	**27**	**28**
	Hungarian Freedom Day, 1956; Pélé, Brazilian Soccer star, born, 1940	United Nations Day; Kweisi Mfume, 1948–		Mahalia Jackson, 1911–1972; Hillary Clinton, 1947–, First Lady	Ah Nam, first Chinese in California, baptized, 1815	Statue of Liberty Day, dedicated 1886
29	**30**	**31**				
		Black Hawk died, 1838, Sauk Indian leader; Roberta Lawson, 1878–1940, Delaware civic leader				

National UNICEF Month

Sept. 15–Oct 15—Latino Heritage Month
3rd week—Black Poetry Week
4th week—United Nations Week

There is a sufficiency in the world for man's need but not for man's greed.
—*Mohandas Gandhi*

Encourage students to look at Columbus's voyages from different perspectives. How did the Native Americans perceive his arrival? Read *Encounter,* written by Jane Yolen and beautifully illustrated by David Shannon. This encounter with Columbus is told from the point of view of a Taino boy on San Sálvador. An excellent book to read with older students is *Morning Girl* by Michael Dorris. A Taino boy and girl tell of their life in the West Indies, little dreaming of how it will change with the arrival of "strange visitors." After studying the many rich civilizations of the Native Americans before First Contact, students can write their own accounts of how they might have reacted upon first meeting the European explorers with their strange skin, language, clothing, and customs.

Students can also imagine what it was like to travel with Christopher Columbus. Share the excitement and adventure through the following books:

Pam Conrad. *Pedro's Journal: A Voyage with Christopher Columbus: August 3, 1492– February 14, 1493.* Illustrated by Peter Koeppen. St. Martin's, 1991.

Susan Martin. *I Sailed with Columbus: The Adventures of a Ship's Boy.* Overlook Press, 1991.

Miriam Schlein. *I Sailed with Columbus.* HarperCollins, 1991.

Have students work in Cooperative Learning Groups as they prepare to accompany Columbus on his expedition. They will need to research the period in order to decide what to bring along and what to expect during the trip. How long will they be gone? How will they react to the people whom they encounter?

October 24

United Nations Day was first observed in 1948, three years after the creation of the United Nations. Fifty countries signed the charter in 1945. Large numbers of countries joined in the 1950s and 1960s as African colonies became independent and in the 1980s and 1990s as the Soviet Union broke up. Have students look into the history of the United Nations and the League of Nations that preceded it. What are the advantages and disadvantages of such an organization? What power does the UN actually have? How are UN peacekeeping forces constituted and where are they sent? For more information, write the United Nations Information Center, 1889 F Street NW, Washington, DC 20006 or visit (www.un.org).

October 31—Halloween

Popular customs for this time of year draw on many of the world's cultures. In ancient Egypt they used to set out oil lamps and delicacies in honor of Osiris, the god of the dead. The Romans established November 1 and 2 for similar rituals. October 31, All Hallows Eve, became a Christian holiday in 1006. In the British Isles, Samhain (the Celtic festival of the dead) meant candles lit in carved turnips. For the autumn festival of Bon, the Japanese dress up in disguise and hang paper lanterns to guide the spirits of their ancestors home. In Mexico, November 2, El día de los muertos (the Day of the Dead) is celebrated with special sweets to feed the spirits and with masks and skeletons to scare them away.

How is Halloween celebrated in different communities in the United States? Read about the Day of the Dead in George Ancona's *Fiesta USA* (also available in Spanish). His photos document the inclusive spirit of the ritual as celebrated by a Latino community in

San Francisco. *Day of the Dead* by Diane Hoyt-Goldsmith, with photographs by Lawrence Migdale, shows a Mexican American family in Sacramento, California. How does this celebration compare with the one in your community?

Have students prepare favorite mysterious stories for Readers' Theater or storytelling to present to other classes. (Check the index for folklore resources.) Independent readers will enjoy Brian Selznick's *The Boy of a Thousand Faces,* a scary story about Alonzo King, born on Halloween, who loves monsters. Or share a read-aloud such as *Celie and the Harvest Fiddler,* by Vanessa and Valerie Flournoy, illustrated by James Ransome, set in the 1870s in the South. *The Halloween Book,* from DK Ink, offers a guide to varied projects students can make for this holiday.

National UNICEF Month
Previously UNICEF Day, the U.S. Committee for UNICEF (now called the United Nations Children's Fund) has expanded its focus, working in partnership with schools and communities in order to understand global diversity better. For more information, write UNICEF, 331 East 38th Street, New York, NY 10016 or visit (www.unicef.org).

An excellent resource for introducing global diversity is *Children Just Like Me: A Unique Celebration of Children around the World,* by Barnabas and Anabel Kindersley. Included are pictures and information about individual children, ages 6 to 12, from a variety of backgrounds. Representing the United States are an Acoma Pueblo boy and a Yu'pik Eskimo boy. How are these children like the ones your students know? How are they different? What more would students like to know about these children? Information about a penpal club is provided if students want to explore further.

November Activities

In November we celebrate Native American Heritage Month (see Table 9.3). Watch for new and interesting material about Native Americans, historic and current, that you will be able to use throughout the year to appear during this month. In addition to the seasonal focus on Indians and Pilgrims, the activities in this section also look at the position of African Americans and whether it has changed much since slavery.

U.S. Election Day
Election Day, November 4, 2008, was truly historic for the United States as Barack Obama was chosen to be the forty-fourth president, becoming our country's first Black president. Black Americans, who represent 12 percent of the U.S. population, are gradually moving into leadership positions. (See page 287 for information about the achievements of Black Americans.)

Edward Brooke was elected to the Senate in 1966 and Shirley Chisholm to the House of Representatives in 1968. They were the first Blacks in Congress since Reconstruction. Have students investigate and discuss these questions. How many African American men and women serve in the U.S. Congress now? How many African Americans (or women or people from other historically underrepresented groups) are in your state legislature? What about city mayors or state governors? What factors, such as racial prejudice or lack of financial support, affect the presence of African Americans in politics today? Why should

TABLE 9.3 November

1	2	3	4	5	6	7
National Family Literacy Day Sholem Asch, 1880–1957 Seminole War began FL, 1835 El Día del Todos los Santos (All Saint's Day)	Haile Selassie crowned Emperor of Ethiopia, 1930 El Día de los Muertos (Day of the Dead)	U.S. Election Day	Barack Obama, first Black American elected 44th president of U.S., 2008	Shirley Chisholm, first Black woman elected to House of Representatives (NY), 1968 Guy Fawkes Day (Canada)		L. Douglas Wilder, 1st Black governor since Reconstruction (VA) elected 1989 Alabama repeals anti-miscegenation law, 2000
8	**9**	**10**	**11**	**12**	**13**	**14**
Edward Brooke, first Black U.S. senator, elected (MA), 1966 First Women's College, Mt. Holyoke, 1837	Kristallnacht, 1938 W. C. Handy, 1873–1958 Benjamin Banneker, 1731–1806 Berlin Wall torn down, 1989		Remembrance Day (Canada) Veterans' Day	Dr. Sun Yat-sen, 1866–1925 Baha'u'llah birthday, 1817, founder of Baha'i faith	Supreme Court upheld segregated buses illegal, 1956	Freedom for Philippines, 1935 Jawaharlal Nehru, 1889–1964
15	**16**	**17**	**18**	**19**	**20**	**21**
	Louis Riel hanged (Canada) 1885 Chinua Achebe, 1930– Brother and Sister Day (India, Nepal) W. C. Handy, Father of the Blues, 1873–1958		First Thanksgiving, Pilgrims and Massasoit, Chief of Wampanoags, 1777	Indira Gandhi, 1917–1984 Christopher Columbus landed, Puerto Rico, 1493 Día del Descubrimiento (Puerto Rico)	Atahualpa, Inca of Peru, filled room with gold for Pizarro, 1532 Transgender Remembrance Day	
22	**23**	**24**	**25**	**26**	**27**	**28**
Nation of Islam (U.S.) founded, 1930			St. Catherine's Day (Canada) Religious Liberty Day	Sojourner Truth died, 1883		
29	**30**					
	Shirley Chisholm, 1924–2005	Native American Heritage Month				

To understand is hard. Once one understands, action is easy.

—*Sun Yat-sen*

minority groups be represented among our lawmakers? Shirley Chisholm, who ran for the presidential nomination in 1972, stated:

> I don't want to be remembered necessarily as the first black woman to have made a bid for the presidency. Or even the first black woman elected to the U.S. Congress. I would rather be remembered as a daring, determined woman who happened to be black and was a catalyst for change in the 20th century.

Thanksgiving

While November has traditionally been the month for activities featuring Pilgrims (hats) and Indians (headdresses), we can help students comprehend the one-sidedness of that perspective. From the perspective of Native Americans, Thanksgiving is a national day of mourning. Make it possible for students to understand this point of view by sharing several books such as the following:

Joseph Bruchac. *Squanto's Journey: The Story of the First Thanksgiving.* Illustrated by Greg Shed. Harcourt, 2000. Historically accurate, Squanto tells his version of helping the Plymouth colony survive and the circumstances of the Thanksgiving feast.

Michael Dorris. *Guests.* Hyperion, 1994. Moss is confused by the strange White visitors his father has invited to the feast.

Marcia Sewall. *People of the Breaking Day.* Atheneum, 1990. The Wampanoag were a tribe in what is now Massachusetts when the Pilgrims arrived.

Instead of reinforcing the stereotype of the first Thanksgiving, consider ways to promote multicultural understanding. Celebrate the season with a harvest festival, featuring the food of cultures from around the world, to learn about the sources of our food as well as issues of hunger and famine. For example, why do we have turkey at this time of year? Do other people eat turkey as well? The turkey we eat comes originally from Mexico, where the Aztecs called it *uexolotl,* and it was brought to Europe in the 1500s. What are some of the dishes at your holiday feast? Where do they come from? Discuss differences in family rituals. Students can write short poems, modeled on *Thanksgiving Day at Our House* by Nancy White Carlstom and illustrated by R. W. Alley, about their favorite activities. This collection of poetry can also be used to motivate oral presentations.

A Holiday of Arrival.   Because we all, including Native Americans, came from some other place, make Thanksgiving a holiday of arrival, a day to honor the many immigrants to this country. How and why did the students, their parents, or their ancestors come to this country? By choice, by force, or by migration? To seek better jobs, to flee religious or political persecution, for educational opportunities? How has each group of newcomers been treated by the previous inhabitants of this country?

Read *Coming to America,* by Eve Bunting, a picture book about a family forced to flee their country for the United States and freedom. When they arrive, they find that everyone is celebrating Thanksgiving and they join in gratefully. As the author notes, whether you arrive by boat or by airplane, you share the pain of leaving the familiar and the challenge of making a home in the new land.

Molly's Pilgrim by Barbara Cohen, a book for intermediate-level students, teaches everyone a lesson about diversity when a simple assignment to dress a doll like a Pilgrim has unexpected consequences. Molly's mother doesn't know the story of the Pilgrims, but she does understand religious freedom. As a result, she dresses the doll to represent herself, a Russian Jewish immigrant woman. Molly is embarrassed in front of her classmates because her doll looks "different." But the teacher explains how Molly's "Pilgrim" fits the true spirit of Thanksgiving.

November 26

In 1851, Sojourner Truth said:

> The man over there says women need to be helped into carriages and lifted over ditches, and to have the best place everywhere. Nobody ever helps me into carriages or over puddles or gives me the best place . . . ain't I a woman? Look at my arm! I have ploughed and planted and gathered into barns and no man could head me—ain't I a woman? I could work as much and eat as much as a man—when I could get it—and bear the lash as well! And ain't I a woman? I have born 13 children and seen most of 'em sold into slavery, and when I cried out with my mother's grief, none but Jesus heard me . . . and ain't I a woman?

Who was Sojourner Truth? Investigate her life with the class. She was born a slave in the late 1790s and won her freedom in 1827 when all the slaves in New York were freed. Look for information on the life of women and of African Americans at that time. Why did Sojourner Truth, a Black woman, fight for the women's movement and women's right to vote? What might she say to women today? A biography for young students is *A Picture Book of Sojourner Truth* by David Adler and illustrated by Gershom Griffith. Older students will appreciate *Sojourner Truth: Ain't I a Woman* by the award-winning African American author, Patricia McKissack.

December Activities

Many cultures, ancient and modern, celebrate the end of darkness and the return of the sun, or the winter solstice, on December 21. Instead of restricting December festivities to Christmas and Santa Claus, which can exclude many students, a multicultural approach to this month would be to study the variety of winter celebrations around the world and the cultural origin of specific customs such as lighting candles, burning the Yule log, and decorating a tree (see Table 9.4). Students can learn the Hanukkah dreidl song, reenact the Posadas, interpret the seven principles of Kwanzaa, make snowflakes, and write their updated version of *'Twas the Night before Christmas.* (See *'Twas the Night b'fore Christmas,* by Melodye Rosales, for a southern African American retelling.)

Include books in your classroom that reflect diverse perspectives on this time of year, such as the following:

Marc Brown. *Arthur's Perfect Christmas.* Little, Brown, 1999. Arthur's expectations of a perfect holiday are all broken.

Lulu Delacre. *Las Navidades: Popular Christmas Songs from Latin America.* Scholastic, 1990. This collection of songs and music for Christmas to Epiphany includes information on the origins of the songs and descriptions of the traditions.

TABLE 9.4 December

1	2	3	4	5	6	7
Rosa Parks arrested, 1955, refused to give up seat on bus	Monroe Doctrine, 1823 World AIDS Day	Myrtilla Miner opened first Colored Girls School, Washington DC, 1851 International Day of Disabled Persons	Phillis Wheatley died, 1784, Black poet	Feast of St. Nicholas Columbus landed, Haiti, 1492		Bombing of Pearl Harbor by Japanese, 1941 La Gritería (Nicaragua)
8	9	10	11	12	13	14
Diego Rivera, 1886–1957		Red Cloud died, 1909 U.S. acquired Cuba, Guam, Puerto Rico, Philippines, 1898 Human Rights Day, Universal Declaration of Human Rights ratified, 1948	Aleksandr Solzhenitsyn, 1918–2008	Día de la Virgen de Guadalupe	Yehudi Menuhin makes NY debut, 1927	
15	16	17	18	19	20	21
Bill of Rights Day, Bill of Rights ratified, 1791 Sitting Bull killed, 1890	Las Posadas begin	Maria Stewart died, 1879, Black teacher and lecturer	Ratification of 13th Amendment ended slavery, 1865	Bernice Pauahi Bishop, 1831–1884, Hawai'ian leader	Cherokees forced off their land in Georgia because of gold strike, 1835 Sacajawea died, 1812, Shoshoni interpreter	María Cadilla de Martínez, 1886–?, early Puerto Rican feminist Pilgrims landed at Plymouth (MA), 1620 Winter solstice
22	23	24	25	26	27	28
Teresa Carreño, 1853–1917, Venezuelan American concert pianist	Akihito, 1944–, Emperor, Japan Madame C. J. Walker, 1867–1919, Black businesswoman	Nochebuena	Christmas Day	Kwanzaa begins		
29	30	31				
Wounded Knee massacre 1890	Pocahontas rescued Captain John Smith, 1607 Gadsden Purchase signed with Mexico, 1853	New Year's Eve	2nd week—Human Rights Week			

We didn't have any of what they called Civil Rights back then. It was just a matter of survival—existing from day to day.

—*Rosa Parks*

Gail Gibbons. *Santa Who?* Morrow, 1999. History of the famous symbol, from an original bishop who gave to the poor to today's bringer of gifts.

Mary Hoffman. *An Angel Just Like Me.* Illustrated by Cornelius Van Wright and Ying-Hwa Hu. Dial, 1997. Tyler's African American family looks for an angel that represents them.

Cynthia Rylant. *Silver Packages.* Illustrated by Chris K. Soentpiet. Orchard, 1997. A rich man tosses packages to poor children in Appalachia for Christmas.

December 10 and 15

Human Rights Day celebrates the proclamation of the Universal Declaration of Human Rights by the United Nations (1948). Ask each student to complete this sentence: Every human being has the right to . . .

Related to human rights is the Bill of Rights, the first ten amendments to the U.S. Constitution (see Figure 9.2). Groups of students can present the Bill of Rights as a series of short skits, acting out the meaning of each amendment. Enlarge the copy of the Bill of Rights to display on a bulletin board. Copy it on a transparency for use in classroom discussions.

December 16

Latino communities hold several distinctive celebrations at this time of year. Las Posadas, a nine-day ritual commemorating the journey of the Holy Family in search of lodging, and the lighting of luminarias are customs characteristic in New Mexico. Students can decorate the classroom with "papel picado," as shown in Chapter 8. Two books to share with the class are:

Rudolfo Anaya. *Farolitos for Abuelo.* Illustrated by Edward Gonzales. Hyperion, 1998.

Diane Hoyt-Goldsmith. *Las Posadas: An Hispanic Christmas Celebration.* Holiday, 1999.

In Spanish Catholic tradition, children receive their gifts from the Three Kings on January 6, El Día de los Reyes, or Epiphany. This custom is maintained in communities such as Puerto Ricans in New York City. George Ancona's book *Fiesta USA* includes photographs of the festive Puerto Rican parade as well as Las Posadas in Albuquerque, New Mexico.

December 18

The ratification of the Thirteenth Amendment meant the official end of slavery. "Neither slavery nor involuntary servitude, except as a punishment for crime whereof the party shall have been duly convicted, shall exist within the United States, or any place subject to their jurisdiction."

Begin reading a book such as *The Slave Dancer* by Paula Fox, which won the Newbery Award in 1974, an excellent historical novel for grades 5–9. A book for younger students, *The Freedom Riddle* by Angela Shelf Medearis and illustrated by John Ward, tells the story of a slave named Jim who composes a riddle in order to win his freedom one Christmas.

FIGURE 9.2   United States Bill of Rights

Amendment 1
Congress shall make no law respecting an establishment of religion, or prohibiting the free exercise thereof; or abridging the freedom of speech, or of the press; or the right of the people peaceably to assemble, and to petition the government for a redress of grievances.

Amendment 2
A well-regulated militia being necessary to the security of a free State, the right of the people to keep and bear arms shall not be infringed.

Amendment 3
No soldier shall, in time of peace, be quartered in any house without the consent of the owner; nor in time of war but in a manner to be prescribed by law.

Amendment 4
The right of the people to be secure in their persons, houses, papers and effects, against unreasonable searches and seizures, shall not be violated, and no warrants shall issue but upon probable cause, supported by oath or affirmation, and particularly described the place to be searched, and the persons or things to be seized.

Amendment 5
No person shall be held to answer for a capital or otherwise infamous crime, unless on a presentment or indictment of a grand jury, except in cases arising in the land or naval forces, or in the militia, when in actual service in time of war or public danger; nor shall any person be subject for the same offense to be twice put in jeopardy of life or limb; nor shall be compelled in any criminal case to be witness against himself, nor be deprived of life, liberty, or property, without due process of law; nor shall private property be taken for public use, without just compensation.

Amendment 6
In all criminal prosecutions the accused shall enjoy the right to a speedy and public trial, by an impartial jury of the State and district wherein the crime shall have been committed, which district shall have been previously ascertained by law, and to be informed of the nature and cause of the accusation; to be confronted with the witnesses against him; to have compulsory process for obtaining witnesses in his favor, and to have the assistance of counsel for his defense.

Amendment 7
In suits at common law, where the value in controversy shall exceed twenty dollars, the right of trial by jury shall be preserved, and no fact tried by a jury shall be otherwise reexamined in any court of the United States than according to the rules of the common law.

Amendment 8
Excessive bail shall not be required, nor excessive fines imposed, nor cruel and unusual punishments inflicted.

Amendment 9
The enumeration in the Constitution of certain rights shall not be construed to deny or disparage others retained by the people.

Amendment 10
The powers not delegated to the United States by the Constitution, nor prohibited by it to the States, are reserved to the States respectively, or to the people.

Mr. Lincoln had told our race we were free, but mentally we were still enslaved.

—*Mary McLeod Bethune*

Discuss this quote. What does *mentally enslaved* mean? Is it possible to change people's thinking by passing a law? What factors made it difficult to change? (education, jobs)

December 26–January 1

Begun in 1966, Kwanzaa (Swahili for "first fruits of the harvest") is a nonreligious celebration of African American culture, community, and family that lasts seven days. Each day participants light a candle and discuss one of the seven principles to live by all year: Umoja (unity), Kujichagulia (self-determination), Ujima (collective work and responsibility), Ujamma (cooperative economics), Nia (purpose), Kuumba (creativity), and Imani (faith).

The Seven Days of Kwanzaa: How to Celebrate Them, by Angela Shelf Medearis, includes all the instructions students need for this holiday, such as ideas for gifts to make, African foods, and stories of inspirational African Americans. Another rich source of information is *Celebrating Kwanzaa* by Diane Hoyt-Goldsmith, with photographs and text showing how thirteen-year-old Andy's family celebrates African American history and traditions.

See also:

Denise Burden-Patmon. *Imani's Gift at Kwanzaa.* Illustrated by Floyd Cooper. Simon & Schuster, 1992.

Andrea Davis Pinkney. *Seven Candles for Kwanzaa.* Illustrated by Brian Pinkney. Dial, 1993.

Donna L. Washington. *The Story of Kwanzaa.* Illustrated by Stephen Taylor. HarperCollins, 1996.

January Activities

The name of this month comes from the Roman god Janus, who had two faces and could look back into the past and as well as forward into the future. Janus was the spirit of doorways and the god of beginnings, also represented as two sides of the same coin. It is very appropriate, therefore, to take time now to consider where we have been and where we are going (see Figure 9.3). (See also Table 9.5.) Talk with the class about the history of this

FIGURE 9.3   Looking to the Past and Future

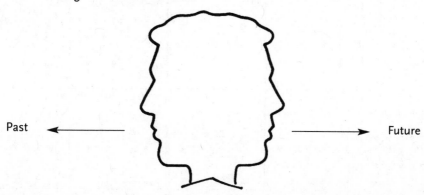

Past ←   → Future

TABLE 9.5 January

1	2	3	4	5	6	7
Emancipation Proclamation, 1863; Commonwealth of Australia established, 1901; Ellis Island opened, 1892; New Year's Day	Emma, 1836–1885 Queen of Hawai'i		Louis Braille, 1809–1852; Selena Sloan Butler, 1872, founded first Black PTA in country	Sissieretta Jones, 1869–1933, Black singer	Celebration of King's Day—Pueblo Dances; Lucy Laney, school for Negro children, 1886; Día de los Reyes (Epiphany)	Harlem Globetrotters played first game (Illinois), 1927
8	**9**	**10**	**11**	**12**	**13**	**14**
	Joan Baez, 1941– Latina singer	League of Nations founded, 1920; Geneva; George Washington Carver, 1864–1943, Black scientist	Eugenio de Hostos, 1839–1903, Puerto Rican patriot	Adah Thomas, 1863–1943, Black nursing leader	Charlotte Ray, 1850–1911, first Black woman lawyer; First Black Cabinet member, Robert Weaver, becomes Secretary of HUD, 1966	Carlos Romulo, Philippine leader, 1901–?; Albert Schweitzer, 1875–1965
15	**16**	**17**	**18**	**19**	**20**	**21**
Martin Luther King, Jr., 1929–1968, Black minister and civil rights leader; Human Relations Day; MLK Day	Religious Freedom Day				Martin Luther King, Jr., holiday began 1986; Edwin "Buzz" Aldrin, 1930–, second on moon; Inauguration of Barack Obama, 2009	Fanny Jackson-Coppin died, 1913, Black educator; Eliza Snow (Smith), 1804–1887, "Mother of Mormonism"
22	**23**	**24**	**25**	**26**	**27**	**28**
Sam Cooke, 1932–1964; Roe v. Wade decision, 1973	Antonio Villaraigosa, 1953–, first Latino mayor L.A.; 24th Amendment barred poll tax in federal elections, 1964; Amanda Smith, 1837–1915, Black evangelist; Elizabeth Blackwell, first woman to receive U.S. medical degree, 1849	Eva del Vakis Bowles, 1875–1943, Black youth group leader	Florence Mills, 1895–1927, Black singer and dancer	Bessie Coleman, 1892–1926, Black aviator; Republic Day (India); Liberation of Auschwitz	Vietnam War ended, 1973	Louis Brandeis, first appointment of American Jew for U.S. Supreme Court, 1916; Zora Neal Hurston died, 1960
29	**30**	**31**				
	Mohandas Gandhi (India) assassinated, 1948	Jackie Robinson, 1919–1972				

It may be true that the law cannot make a man love me, but it can keep him from lynching me, and I think that's pretty important....

—*Martin Luther King, Jr.*

country. Have them list ways in which the country has changed: inventions, attitudes, and people. Then ask them to face forward and think about what might change in the future. What would they like to see happen in their lifetime? Use the excitement of speculating about the future to show the importance of finding the roots of the future in the past.

January 1

Although the Emancipation Proclamation was supposed to free the slaves, it had little impact in the South since the Confederate States would not be bound by it until the war was over. It did, however, enable Blacks to join the Union forces. The Massachusetts 54th Colored Infantry was the first officially sanctioned regiment of Black soldiers. These heroic soldiers fought in the front lines despite knowing that, if captured by the Confederate forces, they would be treated as slaves and not military prisoners. Have students investigate the word "emancipation." What does it mean? What other words contain the root word "manu"? How many synonyms for "emancipation" can students list?

January 15

Discuss with students the quotation by Martin Luther King, Jr., featured on the calendar. What does lynching mean? Martin Luther King, Jr., is known as a leader in the civil rights movement for African Americans. What are civil rights? In 1964, he received the Nobel Prize for Peace, an international award in recognition of his work for human relations. Why would people in other countries think that his work was important?

Happy Birthday, Dr. King, written by Kathryn Jones and illustrated by Floyd Cooper, features a boy puzzled by a school assignment to celebrate King's birthday. But after talking with his family, he learns about the civil rights movement and King's achievements.

Ask students what they would do if they wanted to change someone's behavior or opinion. What methods work best, and when? Do any laws protect them from other people? What about classroom rules—do they protect anyone? Discuss problems the students might have with a bully or a liar. Have them write or act out possible strategies to resolve a conflict.

Students can find out more about the life of Martin Luther King, Jr., and his most famous speech, "I Have a Dream," in these books:

Rosemary Bray. *Martin Luther King, Jr.* Greenwillow, 1995.

Margaret Davidson. *I Have a Dream, the Story of Martin Luther King.* Scholastic, 1991.

King was only 39 when he was assassinated in 1968, yet he continues to be a hero to many people. His birthday became a national holiday in 1986. Martin Luther King, Jr.'s vision of an inclusive society is an inspiration for all Americans, not only African Americans. How should we celebrate this holiday? Involve students in planning and carrying out an appropriate celebration. They might read excerpts from his speeches or prepare a skit dramatizing an important event in his life. Check your library for audiorecordings or videos to illustrate the power of King's words. Other resources are:

I Have a Dream: Dr. Martin Luther King. An Illustrated Edition. Scholastic, 1997. The text of King's speech, given August 28, 1963, in Washington, DC, is accompanied by paintings from noted Black children's book artists such as Leo and Diane Dillon,

Floyd Cooper, James Ransome, Jan Spivey Gilchrist, Brian Pinkney, Jerry Pinkney, and Tom Feelings.

Martin Luther King, Jr. *Wisdom of Martin Luther King, Jr.* Meridian, 1993.

January 20
Inauguration of president in U.S.; 2009 first Black president, Barack Obama.

January 30
Although Gandhi lived in India, his successful use of nonviolent protest to overthrow the British imperial rule has had a major impact on many people throughout the world, from Martin Luther King, Jr., in the United States to Nelson Mandela in South Africa. Feature several quotations from this influential philosopher/activist.

> *Ahimsa* ("harmlessness" or nonviolence) means the largest love. It is the supreme law. By it alone can mankind be saved. He who believes in nonviolence believes in a living God.
>
> All humanity is one undivided and indivisible family, and each one of us is responsible for the misdeeds of all the others. I cannot detach myself from the wickedest soul.
>
> All amassing of wealth or hoarding of wealth above and beyond one's legitimate needs is theft. There would be no occasion for theft and no thieves if there were wise regulations of wealth and social justice.
>
> My nationalism is intense internationalism. I am sick of the strife between nations or religions.

A biography to share with students is John Severance's *Gandhi: Great Soul.*

February Activities

February is African American History Month so you can look forward to programs, articles, speeches, and discussions about the history and current status of African Americans (see Table 9.6). Formerly Negro History Week, this celebration was sponsored by the Association for the Study of AfroAmerican Life and History, founded by historian Carter G. Woodson. The week was first observed in 1926 and it included the birthdays of Abraham Lincoln (12th) and Frederick Douglass (14th). However, the celebration was expanded in 1976, in honor of the bicentennial, because the whole month is rich in the birthdays of exceptional African Americans. Request from the association a publication list of materials to be used at this time: Mrs. Irena Webster, Executive Director, 7961 Eastern Avenue, Suite 301, Silver Springs MD 20910 or at (www.artnoir.com).

As the calendar quotation illustrates, Carter G. Woodson was concerned about promoting the history of underrepresented groups. The National Council for the Social Studies presents the Carter G. Woodson Book Award annually for the most distinguished social studies book for young readers that depicts ethnicity in the United States, to encourage writers and readers of literature that treats multicultural subjects sensitively and accurately. The winners for 2000 were (elementary) Ruby Bridges, *Through My Eyes,* and (secondary) Sharon Linnea, *Princess Ka'iulani: Hope of a Nation, Heart of a People.* Honors went to Carmen Lopez Garza, *Magic Windows,* and Frank Staub, *Children of the*

TABLE 9.6   February

1	2	3	4	5	6	7
Langston Hughes, 1902–1967 National Freedom Day Treaty of Guadalupe Hidalgo, 1848	Día de la Candelaria	15th Amendment (right to vote) ratified, 1870	Liberia founded, 1822 home for freed slaves Apache Wars begin, 1861 Rosa Parks, 1913–2005	Constitution Day (Mexico)	Senate ratified treaty ending Spanish-American War, 1899	
8	**9**	**10**	**11**	**12**	**13**	**14**
Alice Walker, 1944–		Leontyne Price, 1927– End of French and Indian War, 1763	Nelson Mandela released from prison, 1990 Vermont abolished slavery, 1777	NAACP begun, 1909 Fannie Williams, 1855–1944, Black lecturer, civic leader Thaddeus Kosciusko, Polish patriot, 1746–1817 Abraham Lincoln, 1809–1865 Chinese Republic, 1912		Frederick Douglass, 1817–1895 Valentine's Day
15	**16**	**17**	**18**	**19**	**20**	**21**
Galileo Galilei, 1564–1642 Susan B. Anthony, 1820–1906 SBA Day		Chaim Potok, 1929–	Toni Morrison, 1931–	Amy Tan, 1952– Executive Order signed, 1942, Japanese-Americans sent to camps	Buffy Saint-Marie, 1942–	Malcolm X Day, assassinated, 1925–1965 Barbara Jordan, 1931–1996
22	**23**	**24**	**25**	**26**	**27**	**28**
W. E. B. Du Bois, 1868–1963	Gertrude Bonnin, 1876–1938, Sioux author and reformer Ishmael Reed, 1938–	Mardi Gras	First Black in Congress, Hiram Revels (MS), 1870 José de San Martín (the great liberator), 1778–1850		Marian Anderson, 1902–1993	
29						
Emmeline Wells, 1828–1921, Mormon leader and feminist Mother Ann Lee, 1736–1784, founder of the Shakers	African American History Month Week of 3rd Monday: Brotherhood/Sisterhood Week					

If a race has no history, if it has no worthwhile tradition, it becomes a negligible factor in the thoughts of the world and it stands in danger of being exterminated.

—*Carter G. Woodson*

Tlingit (for elementary), Richard Wormser, *The Rise and Fall of Jim Crow: The African American Struggle against Discrimination 1865–1954,* and Patricia and Frederick McKissack, *Black Hands, White Sails: The Story of African American Whalers* (for secondary). For more information, contact the Council at (www.ncss.org/awards).

Students can learn the lyrics of James Weldon Johnson's song, also known as the African American National Anthem, presented in *Lift Ev'ry Voice and Sing* (Scholastic, 1995), illustrated by Jan Spivey Gilchrist. James Weldon Johnson, a school principal, wrote the poem and his brother, J. Rosamond Johnson, composed the music in 1900 to celebrate Abraham Lincoln's birthday. James Weldon Johnson also became the first African American director of the NAACP, in 1920.

Lift every voice and sing
Till earth and heaven ring.
Ring with the harmonies of Liberty;
Let our rejoicing rise
High as the listening skies,
Let it resound loud as the rolling seas.
Sing a song full of the faith that the dark past has taught us,
Sing a song full of the hope that the present has brought us,
Facing the rising sun of our new day begun,
Let us march on 'til victory is won.

Students can also prepare their own book of illustrations and writing about this song as a special project for African American History Month.

Another activity for this month is to feature "Celebrating African Americans" as shown in Figure 9.4. You can challenge students to create their own acrostics using the names of historic or contemporary African Americans.

African American Read-In Chain
In 2000, the eleventh year of this international celebration promoting literacy, it is estimated that more than one million people participated. As part of Black History Month, this read-in brings schools, libraries, and communities as well as students and parents together with the goal of reading books by African American writers. To find out more about creating or joining African American Read-In events in your community, contact NCTE, 1111 W. Kenyon Drive, Urbana, IL 61801-1096 or at (www.ncte.org/special/aa-read-in.shtml).

February 1
Introduce students to the poetry of Langston Hughes. An attractive collection is *The Dreamkeepers and Other Poems,* illustrated by Brian Pinkney. Langston Hughes's poetry lends itself to graphic presentation. Have students create posters featuring a selection from a poem. Encourage them to use calligraphy and art on the poster in order to celebrate the poem. *The Collected Poems of Langston Hughes* is available from Knopf. Play the recording *Langston Hughes Reads and Talks about His Poems* for students or read aloud Floyd Cooper's biography for younger students, *Coming Home: From the Life of Langston Hughes.*

Students can learn a poem or tell a story. "Thank You, Ma'am," a short story by Langston Hughes, is included in *Jump up and Say! A Collection of Black Storytelling*

FIGURE 9.4   Celebrating African Americans

Fill in the last names of these famous African Americans to solve this puzzle. Their occupations are given as clues.

```
_ _ B _ _ _ _ _            baseball player
_ _ _ _ L _                Secretary of State under Pres. G.W. Bush
_ _ _ _ _ A _              children's advocate
_ _ C _ _ _ _              ran for president
_ _ _ K _ _                author, poet

      H _ _ _ _ _          poet, leader in Harlem Renaissance
    _ I _ _ _ _ _          talk show/book club host
    _ S _ _                tennis champion
    _ _ T _ _              educator
_ _ _ _ _ O _ _            artist, quilter
    _ _ R _ _ _ _ _        former Supreme Court justice
  _ _ _ _ Y                comedian, actor

      M _ _ _ _ _ _ _      won Nobel Literature Prize
  _ _ _ _ O _ _            astronaut
    _ N _ _ _ _ _          writer, poet, dancer
  _ _ _ _ T _ _            writer, folklorist
  _ _ _ _ _ _ H            Olympic star runner
```

1. Choose one name and find out why that person is famous.
2. List five other famous African Americans in the same field.

Answers to "Celebrating African Americans": Jackie Robinson, Colin Powell, Marian Wright Edelman, Jesse Jackson, Alice Walker, Langston Hughes, Oprah Winfrey, Arthur Ashe, Mary McLeod Bethune, Faith Ringgold, Thurgood Marshall, Bill Cosby, Toni Morrison, Guion Bluford, Maya Angelou, Zora Neale Hurston, Wilma Rudolph.

(Linda Goss and Clay Goss). *The Sweet and Sour Animal Book* is an alphabet book of poems by Langston Hughes illustrated by students from the Harlem School of the Arts. Students will enjoy these humorous poems that offer playful language.

February 12
Have students prepare a bulletin board display about Abraham Lincoln, a president who has become a folk hero. He symbolizes the poor boy who rose to leadership, the president who freed the slaves. Feature quotations by Lincoln around his picture, for instance:

The ballot is stronger than the bullet.

Any people anywhere, being inclined and having the power, have the right to rise up and shake off the existing government, and form a new one that suits them better.

> This is the most valuable, a most sacred right—a right which we hope and believe is to liberate the world.

> A house divided against itself cannot stand. I believe this government cannot endure, permanently half *slave* and half *free.*

> As I would not be a *slave,* so I would not be a *master.* This expresses my idea of democracy. Whatever differs from this, to the extent of the difference, is no democracy.

A group of students can prepare "The Gettysburg Address" for choric speaking. Plan a short program using this address, quotations, and poetry about Lincoln. One or two students might tell a story about Abe.

The following books illustrate a range of approaches to this man who is everyone's hero.

Harold Holzer. *Abraham Lincoln the Writer: A Treasury of His Greatest Speeches and Letters.* Boyds Mills, 2000. Examples of his powerful writing put in historical context, with time line and photographs.

Elizabeth Van Steenwyk. *When Abraham Talked to the Trees.* Illustrated by Bill Farnsworth. Eerdmans, 2000. Fictionalized account of young Abraham practicing his speaking where no one could hear him.

Presidents' Day
The creation of the Presidents' Day holiday as a replacement for Lincoln's and Washington's birthdays provides an opportunity for students to look more closely at those who have been president in the past and perhaps speculate on possible presidents of the future. What are the qualifications for President? Can anyone grow up to be President? Have students discuss the following comment:

> The time has come to change America. Someday, somewhere, somehow, someone other than a white male could be President.
>
> —Shirley Chisholm

We have an African American (male) president (2008). Could a woman be elected president? These books will answer students' questions and encourage them to explore the topic further.

Kathleen Karr. *It Happened in the White House.* Illustrated by Paul Meisel. Hyperion, 2000. A humorous look at the White House from a child's point of view, including such information as presidential pets.

Judith St. George. *So You Want to be President?* Illustrated by David Small. Philomel, 2000. Rather than follow the typical time line or repeat the tired stories, this book addresses what being president is really like. The presidents are shown as similar in many ways and yet diverse.

George Washington. *George-isms.* Atheneum, 2000. When he was young, Washington copied out a series of maxims to live by. Students will enjoy comparing their paraphrase of the original words that Washington wanted to remember with the translation that accompanies them.

ABRAHAM LINCOLN'S 200ᵀᴴ BIRTHDAY!

—◀○▶—

February 12, 2009

Primary Grades

Robert Burleigh. *Abraham Lincoln Comes Home*. Illustrated by Wendell Minor. Holt, 2008.

Deborah Hopkinson. *Abe Lincoln Crosses a Creek: A Tall, Thin Tale: Introducing His Forgotten Frontier Friend*. Illustrated by John Hendrix. Random, 2008.

Ellen Jackson. *Abe Lincoln Loved Animals*. Illustrated by Doris Ettlinger. Whitman, 2008.

Staton Rabin. *Mr. Lincoln's Boys: Being the Mostly True Adventures of Abraham Lincoln's Trouble-making Sons. Tad and Willie*. Illustrated by Bagram Ibatoulline. Viking, 2008.

Elementary/Middle School

Nikki Giovanni. *Lincoln and Douglass: An American Friendship*. Illustrated by Bryan Collier. Holt, 2008.

Doreen Rappaport. *Abe's Honest Words: The Life of Abraham Lincoln*. Illustrated by Kadir Nelson. Hyperion, 2008.

Judith St. George. *Stand Tall, Abe Lincoln*. Illustrated by Matt Faulkner. Philomel, 2008.

Sarah L. Thomson. *What Lincoln Said*. Illustrated by James E. Ransome. HarperCollins, 2009.

Rosemary Wells. *Lincoln and His Boys*. Illustrated by P. J. Lynch. Candlewick, 2009.

Older Students

Barry Denenberg. *Lincoln Shot: A President's Life Remembered*. Illustrated by Christopher Bing. Feiwel and Friends, 2008.

Candace Fleming. *The Lincolns: A Scrapbook Look at Abraham and Mary*. Random, 2008.

Martin Sandler. *Lincoln through the Lens: How Photography Revealed and Shaped an Extraordinary Life*. Walker, 2008.

March Activities

Women's history is celebrated this month on March 8 (see Table 9.7), along with International Women's Day. This holiday commemorates the beginning of a strike by women garment workers in New York City in 1908, which resulted in the eight-hour work day.

On March 8, 2009, President Barack Obama signed the Ledbetter Bill which guarantees "equal pay for equal work" for women as well as men.

As you collect materials for use in the classroom this month and throughout the year, aim for a diverse perspective: women of the past and women of today, women who represent different ethnic and other groups, stories of both women and men who have actively combated stereotypes about both sexes. The National Women's History Project (7738 Bell Road, Windsor, CA 95492-8518) offers books, posters, and other resources for the classroom.

TABLE 9.7 March

1	2	3	4	5	6	7
Ralph Ellison, 1914–1994, Black author; Peace Corps est., 1961; St. David's Day (Wales)	Texas declares independence from Mexico, 1836; Puerto Rico became territory, 1917	Doll Festival (Japan); Indian Appropriations Act, 1885	Knute Rockne, 1888–1931	Crispus Attucks Day	Fall of the Alamo, 1836	Thomás Masaryk (Czech patriot), 1850–1937; First Selma (Alabama) civil rights march, 1965—Bloody Sunday
8 International Women's Day; Women garment workers began strike, New York, 1908	**9** Amerigo Vespucci, 1451–1512, Italian navigator; Antonia Novello, first woman, first Latina surgeon general, 1990	**10** Harriet Tubman's death, 1913; Hallie Q. Brown, 1850–1949, Black teacher and women's leader	**11**	**12** Gabriele d' Annunzio, 1863–1938	**13**	**14** Albert Einstein, 1879–1955; Albert II, 1958–, ruler of Monaco
15 Eugene Marino, first Black Archbishop, appointed 1988; Ruth Bader Ginsburg 1933–	**16** *Freedom's Journal*, first Black newspaper in United States, 1827	**17** St. Patrick's Day; Myrlie Evers-Williams, 1933–	**18** Hawaii admitted to Union, 1959 (50th state)	**19** St. Joseph's Day (Italy)	**20** Harriet Beecher Stowe's *Uncle Tom's Cabin* published, 1852; Spike Lee, 1957–; Vernal equinox	**21** Benito Juárez, Mexican leader, 1806–1872; Namibia became independent, 1990; New Year (India)
22 Emancipation Day (Puerto Rico)	**23**	**24** Canada gives Blacks right to vote, 1837	**25** Seward's Day (Alaska); Gloria Steinem 1934–, noted feminist	**26** Kuhio Day (Hawaii); Sandra Day O'Connor, 1930–, first woman on Supreme Court; Nancy Pelosi, 1940, first female Speaker of House	**27** Marconi sends first international wireless message, 1899; First Mormon temple dedicated, 1836	**28**
29	**30** U.S. purchased Alaska from Russia, 1867	**31** First treaty U.S.–Japan, 1854; U.S. took possession of Virgin Islands from Denmark, 1917; César Chávez, 1927–1993				

Women's History Month
Irish American Heritage Month
3rd Saturday—Día de los Compadres (Mexico)

My spirit was never in jail.
—*César Chávez*

March 10

Harriet Tubman led an active and dangerous life. Despite not knowing how to read or write, she was able to escape slavery and flee to the North where she was free. Instead of remaining safe in the North, however, she returned to slave-holding territory many times to guide other slaves to freedom. Read about her exploits and have students choose several crucial events to dramatize. They can prepare a play by writing dialogue and narration and using a few props. This play can be presented for other classes to watch. There are many biographies of Harriet Tubman. A book for primary students is *Minty: The Story of Young Harriet Tubman* by Alan Schroeder and illustrated by Jerry Pinkney. This fictionalized account focuses on her childhood.

Harriet Tubman is not just a figure from the past but has come to symbolize freedom and strength for today. For example, in Faith Ringgold's book *Aunt Harriet's Underground Railroad in the Sky,* Harriet is the "conductor" for a modern, liberating trip through the skies of New York. Talk with students about the importance of symbols. Why was the organization that helped slaves to freedom called the "underground railroad"? Slaves were "packages," helped from "station" to "station" by "conductors."

March 17

March is also Irish American Heritage Month. Although highly stereotyped because of the association with shamrocks and leprechauns, St. Patrick's Day offers an opportunity to recognize Irish Americans and their history. Two books provide accurate information on Ireland and the Irish immigrants.

> Eve Bunting. *St. Patrick's Day in the Morning.* Clarion, 1993. Set in Ireland, this book is about a boy who wants to prove he is big enough to march in the parade.

> Steven Kroll. *Mary McLean and the St. Patrick's Day Parade.* Illustrated by Michael Dooling. Scholastic, 1991. Story of Irish immigrants in New York in 1850. Includes information on Irish traditions and St. Patrick.

Ask students what they think of when they hear the word *Ireland.* If a shamrock or a leprechaun is all they know, have students look into Irish folklore and historical traditions. They can report their findings to the class.

Read aloud Irish tales such as the following:

> Sheila MacGill-Callahan. *The Last Snake in Ireland.* Illustrated by Will Hillenbrand. Holiday House, 1999. Retelling of legend of St. Patrick and the snake with a surprise ending.

Some students will be aware of the ongoing conflict in Northern Ireland. Older students can discuss how they might feel if they lived under those conditions. Share books such as the following to give them a clear picture of that world.

> Patricia McMahon. *One Belfast Boy.* Houghton Mifflin, 1999. Photos show life of an eleven-year-old Catholic boy in Northern Ireland.

March 22

Emancipation Day. Puerto Rico is a part of the United States but it is not a state. As a result, Puerto Ricans cannot vote for representation in Congress. Have students investigate the history of Puerto Rico's relationship to the United States. What is Puerto Rico like? One way to explore Puerto Rico is through its traditional folklore.

Jan Mike. *Juan Bobo and the Horse of Seven Colors: A Puerto Rican Legend.* Troll, 1995. A traditional tale with a foolish folk hero; includes information about Puerto Rico.

Nicholasa Mohr. *Old Letivia and the Mountain of Sorrows.* Illustrated by Rudy Gutierrez. Viking Penguin, 1996. This tale, meant to be read aloud, features a curandera (healer) in the Puerto Rican rain forest.

Nicholasa Mohr and Antonio Martorell. *The Song of El Coquí: And Other Tales of Puerto Rico.* Viking, 1995. This collection includes stories from the three strands of Puerto Rican heritage—Taino (native), African, and Spanish. A good resource for storytelling, it includes Spanish vocabulary in context and a glossary.

April Activities

Because April includes many birthdays of jazz (and blues) musicians such as Duke Ellington and Ella Fitzgerald, you might choose to focus this month on jazz, America's "classical" music. Jazz, with its roots in African rhythms and the Black church and interwoven with Latin traditions, has become an international language (see Table 9.8). Introduce students to the special magic of jazz through these books, suitable for a variety of grade levels:

Debbi Chocolate. *The Piano Man.* Illustrated by Eric Velasquez. Walker, 1998. A young African American girl recalls the life of her grandfather in vaudeville.

Linda England. *The Old Cotton Blues.* Illustrated by Teresa Flavin. McElderry, 1998. A city boy living with his mother wants to play the clarinet but has no money for an instrument.

Matthew Gollub. *The Jazz Fly.* Illustrated by Karen Hanke. Tortuga Press, 2000. Introducing students to the art of improvisation, it includes a CD.

National Poetry Month

April is also National Poetry Month. Post the following quote as a theme for this month and invite students to respond:

It is difficult
to get the news from poems
yet men die miserably every day
for lack
of what is found there.
—William Carlos Williams

Keep a collection of poetry beside you so that you can easily read a short poem when you have the chance. In addition, provide a variety of poetry collections in the classroom for students to investigate. They are often drawn in by the beautiful illustrations. Make sure that students see poetry that is written by and about people just like them, such as:

Davida Adedjouma, ed. *The Palm of My Heart: Poetry by African American Children.* Illustrated by Gregorie Christie. Lee & Low, 1997. Coretta Scott King Honor book for illustration.

TABLE 9.8 April

1	2	3	4	5	6	7
Spring Corn Dances (Pueblos) Telugu New Year (India)	Ponce de León landed in Florida, 1513 International Children's Book Day Hans Christian Andersen, born 1805, Denmark	Jane Goodall, 1934–, primatologist	Martin Luther King, Jr., assassinated, 1968 Henry Cisneros elected mayor of San Antonio, 1981, first Hispanic mayor of a large city Maya Angelou, 1928–, Black American poet	Booker T. Washington, 1856–1915 Pocahontas married John Rolfe, 1614 Colin Powell, 1937–, Black Sec'y of State	Peary and Henson reached North Pole, 1909 John Smith founded Mormon Church, 1830 Alexander Herzen, 1812–1870	Billie Holiday, 1915–1959
8	9	10	11	12	13	14
First synagogue in America founded in NYC, 1730 Buddha's birthday (Japan), 563–483 BC	Civil War ended, Treaty of Appomattox, 1865 African Methodist Episcopal Church established, 1816	Joseph Pulitzer, 1847–1911 Dolores Huerta, 1930– Buchenwald Liberation Day, 1945		Civil War began, 1861, Ft. Sumter Yuri Gargarin, Russian cosmonaut, first person to orbit earth, 1961	Lucy Laney, 1854–1933, Black educator Tamil New Year	Pan American Day Abraham Lincoln assassinated, 1865 Carlos Romulo, Philippine leader, 1899–1985 First U.S. abolition society (PA), 1775
15	16	17	18	19	20	21
Bessie Smith, 1894–1937, Black blues singer Jackie Robinson signed by Brooklyn Dodgers, 1947	Mary Eliza Mahoney, 1845–1926, first Black nurse	World Health Day Giovanni Verrazano entered NY harbor, 1524		Revolutionary War began, 1775		Spanish-American War began, 1898
22	23	24	25	26	27	28
Earth Day U.S. Holocaust Memorial Museum opened, 1993			Ella Fitzgerald, 1918–1996 UN founded, 1945	Gertrude (Ma) Rainey, 1886–1939, Black blues singer Syngman Rhee, 1875–1965 First democratic elections South Africa, 1994	Coretta Scott King, 1927–2006 Eritrea becomes independent from Ethiopia, 1993 August Wilson, 1945–2005	Canada/U.S. Goodwill treaty signed, 1817 Equal Pay Day
29	30					
Emperor's birthday (Japan) Duke Ellington, 1899–1974 St. Catherine (Italy)	Louisiana Territory purchased, 1803 Loyalists and Blacks attacked Shrewsbury, NJ, 1780 Día del Niño (Day of the Children)					

National Poetry Month

You can't hold a man down without staying down with him.
—*Booker T. Washington*

Nikki Grimes. *Shoe Magic.* Illustrated by Terry Widener. Orchard, 2000. Sixteen poems in which different kinds of shoes spark kids' imaginations.

Neil Philip, ed. *It's a Woman's World: A Century of Women's Voices in Poetry.* Dutton, 2000.

For more information about poetry-related activities in April, visit the Children's Book Council website (www.cbcbooks.org) or the Academy of American Poets website (www.poets.org).

April 14—Pan American Day

On this day, we remember that "America" includes many countries besides the United States. James Blaine, the U.S. Secretary of State under President Benjamin Harrison, called for an international conference of North and South American countries. The group met April 14, 1890, to form the Pan American Union, now the Organization of American States. In recognition, President Hoover established Pan American Day in 1931.

Display a map of North, Central, and South America, showing the names of the countries and their capitals. Illustrate it with the flags of the different countries. Discuss what these countries have in common. For example, all the countries of the Americas have great ethnic, linguistic, and racial diversity, as well as substantial immigrant populations. What are the major languages spoken in each country? Note that the people in these countries are "Americans" too.

April 15

On this date in 1947, Jackie Robinson broke the colorline. He became the first Black big league baseball player. Before this date, Blacks played in the Negro Baseball League and only Whites could play in the major leagues. Why was Jackie Robinson's achievement significant? Have racial barriers to equitable treatment in sports been eliminated?

Students can investigate the position of Black athletes then and now. Read about Jackie Robinson, the problems he faced, and how he handled them.

Peter Golenbock. *Teammates.* Harcourt Brace Jovanovich, 1990. Racial prejudice experienced by Jackie Robinson, first Black player in major league baseball.

Kenneth Rudeen. *Jackie Robinson.* HarperCollins, 1996. Easy-to-read biography.

Interview adults who remember Jackie Robinson's career. How did they feel about his success? Compare Jackie Robinson to the Black athletes of today. How do they continue to struggle against racial stereotypes and prejudice?

After learning about Jackie Robinson's experience, students will be able to formulate more complex questions about the historical context for his achievements. Have them brainstorm a list of questions raised by their study, such as:

- What was it like playing in the segregated leagues?
- Were there other players as good as Jackie Robinson?
- Would Black players prefer to play in the major leagues?
- Who supported these changes?

They can find out more about the Negro Baseball Leagues in the following books:

Patricia McKissack and Frederick McKissack. *Black Diamond: The Story of the Negro Baseball Leagues.* Scholastic, 1994.

Jonah Winter. *FairBall! Fourteen Great Stars from Baseball's Negro Leagues.* Scholastic, 1999.

April 22

The U.S. Holocaust Memorial Museum in Washington, DC, opened on this date in 1993, keeps alive public awareness of the immensity of this tragedy in which 6 million men, women, and children were killed simply because they were Jewish. What does the word *holocaust* mean? Talk about *genocide.* Analyze the parts of this word. Can students apply this understanding to similar words such as suicide, patricide, fratricide, homicide? What other words does the morpheme *gen-* appear in?

Many people believe that this tragedy could never happen again. Yet large groups of people around the world are still being killed because of their religion, ethnic background, or race. What lesson does the Holocaust have for those of us living today? How can students respond to the genocide occurring even now around the world? Discuss the following quotes:

Forgiveness is the key to action and freedom.

—Hannah Arendt

The motto should not be: Forgive one another; rather, Understand one another.

—Emma Goldman

The Holocaust Day of Remembrance (Yom Hashoah) is celebrated on the 27th day of Nisan according to the Jewish calendar and falls in March, April, or May.

April 26

In 1994, the Black population in South Africa, long a majority in the country, was finally allowed to vote. Locate South Africa on the map. Who lives here? The population includes colonial groups of English and Boer (Dutch) settlers and varied African tribal groups such as Xhosa. Sanctions, or penalties, by many nations against the White government for its system of *apartheid* (racial separation) helped force South Africa to hold democratic elections.

Who is Nelson Mandela, the former political prisoner who was elected president in this first free election? Share a biography with students, such as Jack L. Roberts's *Nelson Mandela: Determined to Be Free.*

How did it feel to be able to vote? Find out by reading:

Elinor Batezat Sisulu. *The Day Gogo Went to Vote: South Africa, April 1994.* Illustrated by Sharon Wilson. Little, Brown, 1996. A six-year-old Thembi girl accompanies her 100-year-old grandmother who is determined to vote for the first time.

How would students feel if their families were not allowed to vote? Why is being able to vote important, especially for groups that have experienced discrimination? When did African Americans receive the right to vote? When were women allowed to vote? Compare these dates to 1924, when Native Americans were granted citizenship. What is required in order to vote in the United States today? The last major change in voting requirements was the lowering of the age limit from 21 to 18. Students can debate the question: Should teenagers be allowed to vote?

May Activities

This month has been selected to recognize the contributions made by people of Asian and Pacific Islander heritage. During this month, we can acknowledge the diversity of Asian and Pacific Island immigrants and the rich cultural and linguistic heritage that they hope to maintain (see Table 9.9).

How many groups of Asian and Pacific Islanders can students name? Which groups are represented in your class? In your community? Locate their place of origin on the map. Note that this category includes such diverse groups as Koreans, Hmong, Hawai'ians, Samoans, and Filipinos.

May 5

This day is the Children's Festival in Japan and Japanese children fly carp kites. Students can make their own gaily decorated fish to hang like streamers. Students can draw their own, or you can provide one for everyone to trace onto construction paper. (Enlarge model below.) They should have two fish shapes, one right side and one reversed. After the children color and cut out the fish, they glue the two pieces together around the edges (except for the mouth) and gently stuff with tissue paper for a three-dimensional effect. These fish can be hung around the room with thread tied to the back, or attached to a stick (fishing

| ichi—one | san—three | go—five | shichi—seven | ku—nine |
| ni—two | shi—four | roku—six | hachi—eight | ju—ten |

One, two, three,
  (echo)
Listen to me,
  (echo)
I can count to ten,
  (echo)
In Japanese,
  (echo)
Ichi, ni, san, shi, go
  (echo)
I can count to five
  (echo)
Let's try four more.
  (echo)
Roku, shichi, hachi, ku,
  (echo)
I can count to nine,
  (echo)
Let's try one more,
  (echo)
(together) JU!

TABLE 9.9 May

1 Lei Day (Hawai'i) Agrippa Hull, free Black, began six years of army service, 1777	**2**	**3** Golda Meir, 1898–1978 World Press Freedom Day	**4**	**5** Children's Festival (Japan) Gwendolyn Brooks won Pulitzer Prize for Poetry, 1950 Cinco de Mayo	**6** Chinese Exclusion Act passed, 1882 Rudolph Valentino, 1895–1926	**7** Rabindranath Tagore, 1861–1941
8 Mother's Day Joan of Arc Day (France) Teacher's Day (U.S.)	**9**	**10** Chinese labor helped complete Transcontinental Railroad, Utah, 1869 Nelson Mandela inaugurated president of South Africa, 1994	**11**	**12**	**13** Joe Louis, 1914–1972 Congress declared war on Mexico, 1846	**14** Jamestown established, 1607
15 Día del Maestro (Mexico) Madeleine Albright 1951–, first female Sec'y of State	**16**	**17** Supreme Court declared racial segregation in schools unconstitutional, 1954, *Brown v. Topeka*	**18** Hispanic Society of America founded, 1904 Supreme Court affirmed separate but equal laws, 1896, *Plessy v. Ferguson*	**19** Malcolm X, 1925–1965 Lorraine Hansberry, 1930–1965	**20** Cher, 1946–	**21** Amelia Earhart completed solo flight across Atlantic, 1932
22	**23** Emilio Aguinaldo, Philippine independence leader, captured, 1901	**24** Ynés Mexia, 1870–1938, Mexican American botanical explorer	**25** African Freedom Day	**26** Susette LaFlesche Tibbles died, 1903, Omaha Indian rights advocate Sally Ride, 1951–, first female astronaut	**27** Victoria Matthews 1861–1907, Black author and social worker Buddha's birthday (China)	**28** Jim Thorpe, 1888–1953 Equal Pay Act passed, 1963
29 Baha'u'llah Ascension Day	**30** Hernando de Soto landed in Florida, 1539 Countee Cullen, 1903–1946 Memorial Day					

Asian and Pacific Islander Heritage Month

I have fought against white domination, and I have fought against black domination. I have cherished the ideal of a democratic and free society in which all persons live together in harmony and with equal opportunities. It is an ideal which I hope to live for and to achieve. But if needs be, it is an ideal for which I am prepared to die.

—*Nelson Mandela*

pole) by the mouth. If you have Japanese-speaking children in the class, this is a good opportunity to have them teach the class how to count in Japanese.

Count Your Way through Japan by Jim Haskins is a good book with numbers in Japanese accompanied by pictures of the country. Provide a variety of other books on Japan so that students can explore this country.

> John Langone. *In the Shogun's Shadow: Understanding a Changing Japan.* Little, Brown, 1994. Covers history and culture, including information on United States–Japan relations.

> Richard Tames. *Exploration into Japan.* New Discovery Books, 1995.

May 5

Cinco de Mayo marks the victory of Mexican forces over the French at Puebla, Mexico, on May 5, 1862. While not a major holiday in Mexico, it is celebrated today in Latino communities in the United States as the occasion for a fiesta, with a parade, dancing, and other activities. You can plan a fiesta in your room. Bring recordings of Mexican popular music, folk songs, or Mexican Indian music. Let the students prepare food such as tortillas, guacamole, or buñelos. Students can decorate the room appropriately by using poster paint or felt pens to create murals that evoke Mexico and Mexican American life. Possible subjects include food, sports, clothing, arts and crafts, and historical figures.

Create a learning center on Mexico. Have students contribute ideas. Explore your library for nonfiction and fiction about Mexico as well as stories about Mexican Americans/Chicanos. Develop activity cards that focus on Mexico for reading in the content areas. Use a biography such as *¡Viva México! A Story of Benito Juárez* and *Cinco de Mayo* by Argentina Palacios and illustrated by Howard Berelson. This volume in the *Stories of America* series tells of the Mexican hero of the battle of Puebla. Although born a poor Zapotec Indian in Oaxaca, he grew up to be compared to Abraham Lincoln.

May 25

African Freedom Day offers an opportunity to present information about the great cultural and racial diversity of Africa as well as to discuss the origins of African Americans. Explore books such as the following:

Picture Books

> Muriel Feelings. *Jambo Means Hello; A Swahili Alphabet Book.* Dial, 1974.

> Xan Hopcraft and Carol C. Hopcraft. *How It Was with Dooms: A True Story of Africa.* McElderry, 1997. A boy and his pet cheetah in Kenya.

> Ifeoma Onyefulu. *A Triangle for Adaora: An African Book of Shapes.* Penguin, 1999. Fascinating search for shapes in an African village.

For Independent Readers

> Ashley Bryan. *Lion and the Ostrich Chicks, and Other African Tales.* Atheneum, 1986.

> Eric Campbell. *The Story of the Leopard Song.* Harcourt, 1992. Animal life on the Serengeti Plain in Africa.

Jason Lauré. *Botswana.* Children's Press, 1993. *Enchantment of the World* series. Describes country and people of Botswana.

Beverly Naidoo. *No Turning Back.* Harper, 1997. Sipho's life with a gang in urban Johannesburg.

June Activities

See calendar of activities and events in Table 9.10.

June 11

Discover Hawai'i, the fiftieth state, with your students. One of the state's assets is its multicultural, multilingual heritage. Investigate the history of Hawai'i. How and when did it become a state? People from many different countries are represented in Hawai'i. What are some of them? Who are the native Hawai'ians? Point out the different spellings for this state: *Hawaii* and *Hawai'i.* Many people prefer the form *Hawai'i* because it reflects the native pronunciation. The superscript symbol represents a unique sound in the Hawai'ian language and so this form is considered more respectful.

Ask students to find examples of unusual facts about Hawai'i, for example, words for different foods. Here are a few words used commonly in Hawai'i:

ae	(eye)	yes
aloha	(ah *loh* hah)	hello/goodbye
haole	(*how* lay)	foreigner (White person)
hula	(*hoo* lah)	dance
lani	(*lah* nee)	sky
lei	(lay)	wreath
luau	(loo ah oo)	feast
mahalo	(mah *hah* loh)	thanks
mauna	(*mou* nah)	mountain
moana	(moh *ah* nah)	ocean

Following are examples of books about the multicultural heritage of Hawai'i:

Roy Kakulu Alameida. *Stories of Old Hawai'i.* The Bess Press, 1997.

Sharon Linnea. *Princess Kai'ulani: Hope of a Nation, Heart of a People.* Eerdmans, 1999. Biography of a princess.

Emily McAuliffe. *Hawai'i Facts and Symbols.* Capstone, 2000.

June 14—Flag Day

On this day in 1777, the U.S. flag was adopted. In 1877, Congress declared the flag should be flown on this day. In 1916, President Woodrow Wilson proclaimed Flag Day. The first flag, "Old Glory," had thirteen stars and thirteen stripes. How is today's flag different? A flag is a symbol. Ask students what symbols represent the United States to them. What would they put on an American flag if they designed a new one? Students can discuss different kinds of flags and banners—for countries, states, organizations—and work together on creating a banner to represent their classroom or school.

TABLE 9.10 June

1	2	3	4	5	6	7
Brigham Young, 1801–1877 International Children's Day	Congress granted American Indians citizenship, 1924	DeSoto claimed Florida for Spain, 1539 Roland Hayes, 1887–1977		World Environment Day English colonists massacre Pequot village in Pequot War, 1637 Kaahumanu died, 1832, Hawai'ian ruler	Marian Wright Edelman, 1939– Evacuation of Japanese Americans into concentration camps completed, 1942 Sarah Remond, 1826–1887?, Black lecturer and physician	Gwendolyn Brooks, 1917–, Black poet Nikki Giovanni, 1943–
8	**9**	**10**	**11**	**12**	**13**	**14**
			Kamehameha Day (Hawai'i) Addie W. Hunton, 1875–1943, Black youth group leader Henry Cisneros, 1947–	G.H. Bush, 1924 41st U.S. Pres. Philippine Independence Day Anne Frank Day Girls allowed to play Little League baseball, 1974	St. Anthony (Portugal, Brazil) Thurgood Marshall appointed 1967, first Black Supreme Court judge	Hawai'i organized as territory, 1900 Harriet Beecher Stowe, 1811–1896 Flag Day
15	**16**	**17**	**18**	**19**	**20**	**21**
	Flight of Valentina Tereshkova (first woman in space), 1963 Soweto Day	Susan LaFlesche Picotte, 1865–1915, Omaha physician James Weldon Johnson, 1871–1938 Sweden-America Day	War of 1812 declared against Great Britain, 1812 Sally Ride, first U.S. woman in space, 1983	Statue of Liberty arrived in New York Harbor, 1885 Juneteenth— Emancipation reaches Texas, 1865	Start of French Revolution, 1789 Announced purchase of Alaska from Russia, 1867	Summer Solstice
22	**23**	**24**	**25**	**26**	**27**	**28**
Slavery abolished in Great Britain, 1772 Joe Louis (Brown Bomber) defeated Max Schmeling, 1938	William Penn signed treaty with Indians, 1683 Wilma Rudolph, 1940–1994	San Juan Day (Puerto Rico)	Crazy Horse (Sioux) defeated Custer— Battle of the Little Bighorn, 1876	Pearl S. Buck, 1892–1973 UN Charter signed, 1945	Paul Dunbar, 1872–1906, Black writer Joseph Smith, Mormon prophet, killed, 1844 Helen Keller, 1880–1968	Treaty of Versailles ended World War I
29	**30**					
First African church in the U.S. (Philadelphia), 1794 Azalia Hackley, 1867–1922, Black singer José Rizal, 1861–1896	Korean War began 1950 NOW founded 1966					

LGBT Month

We could never learn to be brave and patient, if there were only joy in the world.
—Helen Keller

June 19—Juneteenth

News of the 1863 Emancipation Proclamation freeing the slaves did not reach African Americans in Texas until June 1865, more than two months after the end of the Civil War. As a result, *Juneteenth* (June 19) has become a community celebration of African American heritage, featuring picnics and music.

In Carole Boston Weatherford's *Juneteenth Jamboree,* illustrated by Yvonne Buchanan, Cassandra, who has just moved to Texas, learns about the history of this celebration and the end of slavery.

June 20

Investigate Alaska, the forty-ninth state. Only a little more than half a million people (670,053 estimated in 2006) inhabit this huge area (571,951 square miles). That's about one person for every square mile. Alaska is the first of the fifty states in size but forty-eighth in population. (Only Vermont and Wyoming have fewer inhabitants.) Compare Alaska's population and area to that of Hawai'i, which had 1,288,198 people in 2008 (estimate) in only 6,423 square miles. How do these figures compare with your state? See the Alaska Learning Center on page 78 for more ideas.

Who lives in Alaska? Read about this unusual land in the following books:

Ruth Crisman. *Racing the Iditarod Trail.* Silver Burdett, 1993. The famous Alaska dogsled race.

Jean Craighead George. *Snow Bear.* Illustrated by Wendell Minor. Hyperion, 1999. Polar bear cub and Eskimo child play together briefly.

Carolyn Meyer. *In a Different Light: Growing Up in a Yu'pik Eskimo Village in Alaska.* Simon & Schuster, 1996.

Debbie S. Miller. *A Caribou Journey.* Illustrated by Jon Van Zyle. Turtleback Books, 2000. Nonfiction, shows life of caribou mother and her calf, in-depth coverage in a picture book.

Debbie S. Miller. *River of Life.* Illustrated by Jon Van Zyle. Clarion, 2000. How an Alaskan river changes through the seasons.

Claire Rudolf Murphy. *A Child's Alaska.* Alaska Northwest Press, 1994. Many different people live in Alaska, including Eskimos, Indians, and Aleuts.

Lori Yanuchi. *Running with the Big Dogs: A Sled Dog Puppy Grows up in Denali National Park Alaska.* Illustrated by Wendy Brown. Ridge Rock Press, 1999. First year of training for puppy to work with rangers in park.

July Activities

See Table 9.11 for this month's events and activities.

July 1 and 3

Recognize Canada on Canada Day, celebrating the Confederation in 1867. Display its symbol, the maple leaf, with pictures of Canada from travel folders. Can students name some

TABLE 9.11 July

1	2	3	4	5	6	7
Canada Day Thurgood Marshall, 1908–1993 Civil Rights Act of 1964 Voting Rights Act became law, 1964	Champlain founded Québec, 1608		Edmonia Lewis, 1845–?, Black-Cherokee sculptor Lucy Stowe, 1885–1937, Black teacher and administrator Giuseppe Garibaldi, 1807–1882		Cecil Poole, first Black U.S. attorney, 1961	
8	**9** Dr. Daniel Hale Williams, Black doctor, performed first open heart surgery, 1893	**10** Mary McLeod Bethune, 1875–1955 Arthur Ashe, 1943–1993, Black tennis star	**11**	**12**	**13** Wole Soyinka, 1934–	**14** Bastille Day (France), 1789 George Washington Carver monument dedicated, 1951
15 Maggie Walker, 1867–1934, Black insurance and banking executive Ch'iu Chin, 1875–1907	**16** Ida Wells-Barnett 1862–1931, Black journalist and civic leader Mary Baker Eddy, 1821–1910, founder, Christian Science	**17** Spain transferred Florida to U.S., 1821 S. Y. Agnon, 1888–1970 Angela Merkel, 1954–, first female chancellor of Germany	**18** Nelson Mandela, 1918–, president of South Africa Miguel Hidalgo, 1753–1811, Father of Mexican independence	**19** Alice Dunbar Nelson, 1875–1935, Black author, teacher	**20** Seneca Falls Convention (NY) launched women's suffrage movement, 1848	**21** First daily Black newspaper, New Orleans Tribune, 1864 National Women's Hall of Fame dedicated, 1979
22	**23** Pham Tuan, first non-Caucasian in space, 1980	**24** Simón Bolívar, 1783–1830 Mormons settled Salt Lake City, 1847 Pioneer Day	**25** Puerto Rico became a commonwealth, 1952 (Constitution Day) Saint James (Spain)	**26** Americans with Disabilities Act signed, 1990	**27** Korean War ended, 1953	**28** Senator Hiram Fong (HI) and Rep. Daniel Inouye (HI) first Asian Americans in Congress, 1959
29	**30**	**31** Sarah Garnet, 1831–1911, Black educator and civic worker				

I did not equate my self-worth with my wins and losses.
—Arthur Ashe

famous Canadians? Display a map of Canada. Look at the names of the provinces. What do they indicate about the ethnic influences in Canada and where the early settlers came from? How is the history of Canada different from that of the United States? How is it similar?

Ted Harrison. *O Canada.* Tickner and Fields, 1993. Book by noted Canadian artist, based on national anthem.

Lawrence Jackson. *Newfoundland & Labrador.* Fitzhenry, 1999. Part of *Hello Canada* series.

Bobbie Kalman. *Canada: The Culture.* Crabtree, 1993. Part of the *Lands, Peoples, and Cultures* series.

Include books set in Canada in your library such as the following:

Dave Bouchard. *If You're Not from the Prairie* . . . Illustrated by Henry Ripplinger. Aladdin, 1998. A poem describing the world of children who live on the Canadian prairie.

Jonathan London. *The Sugaring-Off Party.* Illustrated by Gilles Pelletier. Dutton, 1995. Paul's grandmère describes the French-Canadian custom.

Gary Paulsen. *Hatchet.* Aladdin, 1999. Thirteen-year-old Brian must learn how to survive alone when his plane crashes in Canadian wilderness.

July 4—Independence Day

Independence Day for the United States can be recognized in many ways. Prepare a program that includes poetry and prose representing the many voices of America—people of different colors, languages, and religions united in their celebration of U.S. independence. *Celebrating America: A Collection of Poems and Images of the American Spirit,* poetry compiled by Laura Whipple with art from the Art Institute of Chicago, is an excellent example of a multicultural sampler.

A book to share with students is *Celebration!* by Jane Resh Thomas, illustrated by Raúl Colón, about an African American extended family gathered for the Fourth of July. Rich with description of food and games, this story will stimulate student discussion of their family get-togethers. They can compare the foods they eat and the activities they engage in with those described in this book.

Younger students can talk about words associated with the Fourth of July, such as democracy, independence, equality, liberty, and fraternity.

July 10

Mary McLeod Bethune, known as The Great Educator, was born in South Carolina and grew up working in the cotton fields. In an age when the education of Black children was not considered terribly important, she graduated from college and became a teacher. When she heard that the town of Daytona Beach in Florida didn't have a school for Blacks, she established one for young Black women that is now the Bethune-Cookman College. She also founded the National Council of Negro Women. In 1935, President Franklin Roosevelt appointed her administrator of the new Office of Minority Affairs.

Challenge students to find out more about this amazing woman. Read a biography such as *Mary McLeod Bethune* by noted poet Eloise Greenfield, illustrated by Jerry Pinkney or *Mary McLeod Bethune* by Patricia McKissack.

Provide the following quote for discussion:

> I am my mother's daughter, and the drums of Africa still beat in my heart. They will not let me rest while there is a single Negro boy or girl without a chance to prove his worth.
>
> —Mary McLeod Bethune

August Activities

In this month that includes the bombing of Hiroshima and Nagasaki, the fall of the Aztec Empire to the Spanish conquerors, and the violence accompanying Indian and Pakistani independence, we focus on the need for world peace and justice (see Table 9.12). Talk with students about the need to resolve differences peacefully, without resorting to violence, on a personal level as well as an international level.

First Sunday in August—Celebration of Peace Day

How can we help students appreciate peace without their having to endure the horrors of war? Stories of what people have experienced in war and how they survived offer students an opportunity to empathize yet not be overwhelmed. Two books for young children tell of life in times of war:

Haemi Balgassi. *Peacebound Trains.* Illustrated by Chris K. Soentpiet. Clarion, 1996. A young girl's grandmother tells her of life during the Korean War. Although she was forced to flee Seoul by train with her children, the trains also bring people home from war.

Rosemary Breckler. *Sweet Dried Apples: A Vietnamese Wartime Childhood.* Illustrated by Deborah Kogan Ray. Houghton Mifflin, 1996. Two children living in the countryside are forced out of their village by the war.

August 6—Hiroshima Day

Hiroshima Day marks the anniversary of the dropping of the atomic bomb on Japan, resulting in Japan's surrender, ending World War II. Although the war was over, the effects of radiation from the bomb lingered long afterward. Explore the impact of the bomb on the Japanese people and the implications of this event for world peace.

Eleanor Coerr's *Sadako,* illlustrated by Ed Young, is a picture book suitable for all students; it's a rewrite of the author's famous earlier book *Sadako and the Thousand Cranes,* the true story of a Japanese girl who suffered from radiation poisoning. Sadako attempted to ward off death by folding a thousand origami cranes. Although she was not successful, Japanese schoolchildren still fold paper cranes in her memory, united in their desire for world peace. Today a statue of Sadako holding a golden crane in outstretched hands stands in Hiroshima Peace Park. Inscribed below are the words: "This is our cry, this is our prayer: Peace in the world."

Other books to support student study of this period are:

Tatsuharu Kodama. *Shin's Tricycle.* Illustrated by Noriyuki Ando. Translated by Kazuko Hokumen-Jones. Walker, 1995. Shin dreamed of having a tricycle but the war meant that metal was scarce. He never had the chance to enjoy the tricycle he received for

TABLE 9.12 August

1	2	3	4	5	6	7
Maria Mitchell, 1818–1889, astronomer	Friendship Day James Baldwin, 1924–1987 Isabel Allende, 1942–, Chilean writer	Columbus started first voyage, 1492	Barack Obama, 1961–, 44th U.S. President Anne Frank captured, 1944 Freedom of the Press Day Zwenger acquitted, 1735	Neal Armstrong, 1930–, first on moon	Hiroshima Day (U.S. bombed Hiroshima, Japan, 1945) President Johnson signed Voting Rights Act, 1965	Ralph Bunche, 1904–1971 Congress authorized Vietnam War, 1964
8	9	10	11	12	13	14
Roberto Clemente, 1934–1973	Janie Porter Barrett, 1865–1948, Black social welfare leader U.S. bombed Nagasaki, Japan, 1945		Alex Haley, 1921–1992 Watts Riots (CA), 1965	U.S. annexed Hawai'i, 1898 King Philip's War ended, first Indian War, 1676	Cortez conquered Aztecs, 1521 Fidel Castro, 1926–, Cuban leader	Japan surrendered, World War II, 1945 Pakistan became independent, 1947
15	16	17	18	19	20	21
India became independent, 1947	Carol Moseley-Braun, 1947–	Charlotte Forten (Grimke), 1837–1914, Black teacher and author V. S. Naipaul, 1932–	19th Amendment ratified 1920, women's right to vote	Mammy Pleasant, 1814–1904, Black California pioneer	Bernardo O'Higgins, Chilean patriot, 1778–1842 First African slaves arrived in U.S., 1619	
22	23	24	25	26	27	28
	Farsi New Year Sacco and Vanzetti electrocuted, 1927	Lucy Moten died, 1933, Black educator Amelia Earhart flew nonstop across U.S., 1932		Women's Equality Day Women's Suffrage 19th Amendment certified, 1920	Rose McClendon, 1884–1936, Black actress	Martin Luther King, Jr., gave "I Have a Dream" speech, Washington, DC, 1963
29	30	31				
	Guion Bluford, first Black astronaut, flew 1983 Saint Rose of Lima (Americas)	Josephine Ruffin, 1842–1924, Black leader				

The wonder is not that so many Negro boys and girls are ruined but that so many survive.

—*James Baldwin*

his fourth birthday because he was killed in Hiroshima. His tricycle is displayed at the Hiroshima Peace Museum.

Laurence Yep. *Hiroshima.* Scholastic, 1995. This book juxtaposes the flight of the *Enola Gay,* the airplane delivering the bomb, with the story of two Japanese sisters taking a walk in their city. Includes accounts of survivors.

August 7

I was offered the ambassadorship of Liberia once, when the post was earmarked for a Negro. I told them I wouldn't take a Jim Crow job.

—Ralph Bunche

Ralph Bunche was a famous diplomat and in 1950 the first African American to win the Nobel Peace Prize, in recognition of his role as United Nations mediator in the Palestine armistice. Ask students whether they know what a "Jim Crow" job is. Can they guess? Why would the ambassador to a country such as Liberia be expected to be Black? Find out more about this early peacemaker in a biography:

Anne E. Schraff. *Ralph Bunche: Winner of the Nobel Peace Prize.* Enslow, 1999.

Martin Luther King, Jr., is another African American who was awarded a Nobel Peace Prize. What other famous people have received this award? How are the recipients chosen? Students can investigate the lives and achievements of the following men and women from diverse backgrounds who have won this international recognition for their efforts on behalf of peace and justice.

2006	Muhammed Yunus, Grameen Bank (Bangladesh)
2005	Mohammed El Bardee (Egypt) and International Atomic Energy Agency (Austria)
2004	Wangari Maathai (Kenya)
2003	Shiren Ebadi (Iran)
2002	Jimmy Carter (United States)
2001	Kofi Annan (Ghana), UN
2000	President Kin Dae Jung (South Korea)
1999	Doctors without Borders
1998	John Hume and David Trimble (for Northern Ireland)
1997	Jody Williams (U.S.) and International Campaign to Ban Land Mines
1996	Bishop Carlos Ximenes and Jose Ramos-Horta (Timor)
1994	Yasir Arafat (Palestine), Shimon Peres, and Yitzhak Rabin (Israel)
1993	Frederik de Klerk, Nelson Mandela (South Africa)
1992	Rigoberta Menchú (Guatemala)
1991	Aung San Suu Kyi (Myanmar, formerly Burma)

Read a biography to students such as the following:

Caroline Lazo. *Rigoberta Menchú.* Dillon, 1994. Tells how a poor Mayan Indian woman from Guatemala came to world attention for her philosophy of nonviolence and her ability to bring groups together. Part of the *Peacemakers* series.

August 13

Who were the Aztecs and how did the Spanish conquer them? Pose such questions to the students and have them search for the answers. The Aztec civilization is particularly interesting because it was so advanced, and yet we know very little about it because the Spanish destroyed most of the records. Investigate the Spanish treatment of the Aztecs. (See information on the Aztec calendar later in this chapter.)

The following books are a starting point for student research.

John Bierhorst. *The Hungry Woman: Myths and Legends of the Aztecs.* Morrow, 1993.

Johanna Defrates. *What Do We Know about the Aztecs?* Bedrick Books, 1993.

Andrea Guardiano. *Azteca: The Story of a Jaguar Warrior.* Rinehart, 1992.

❖ Movable Holidays

Listed here are holidays or events that fall on different dates each year. Students can determine the particular dates and add them to the calendar.

United States Holidays or Special Days

Note that many holidays are celebrated on a Monday or Friday to provide a holiday weekend.

Commonwealth Day (Canada)	second Monday in March
Memorial Day	last Monday in May
Labor Day	first Monday in September
Canadian Thanksgiving	second Monday in October
Election Day	first Tuesday after first Monday in November
Veterans' Day	fourth Monday in October
Thanksgiving Day	fourth Thursday in November

Jewish Feasts and Festivals

Because the Jewish calendar (described later in this chapter) is lunar (based on the moon's cycles), the (Gregorian) dates that Jewish holidays fall on will vary each year. Table 9.13 gives the names and dates for the holidays by year and shows the corresponding Jewish

TABLE 9.13 Jewish Holidays

(Gregorian) Year	Purim (Feast of Lots)	Pesach (Festival of Freedom)	Shavuot (Feast of Weeks)	Rosh Hashanah (New Year)	Yom Kippur (Day of Atonement)	Succot (Feast of Tabernacles)	Hanukkah (Feast of Dedication)
2004–5	Mar. 7	Apr. 6	May 26	Sept. 16 (5765)	Sept. 25	Sept. 30	Dec. 8
2005–6	Mar. 25	Apr. 24	June 13	Oct. 4 (5766)	Oct. 13	Oct. 16	Dec. 26
2006–7	Mar. 14	Apr. 13	June 2	Sept. 23 (5767)	Oct. 2	Oct. 7	Dec. 16
2007–8	Mar. 21	Apr. 20	May 9	Sept. 13 (5768)	Sept. 22	Sept. 27	Dec. 5

TABLE 9.14 Islamic Celebrations

New Year: Muharram 1	Ashura: Muharram 10	Mawlid: Rabi'l 12	Ramadan: Ramadan 1	Eid al-Fitr: Shawwal	al-Adha: Zulhijjan 10
2004–5 March 4 (1425)	Mar. 31	May 13	Oct. 26	Nov. 25	Feb. 1
2005–6 Feb. 20 (1426)	Feb. 19	Apr. 21	Oct. 4	Nov. 3	Jan. 10
2006–7 Jan. 30 (1427)	Feb. 8	Apr. 10	Sept. 23	Oct. 23	Dec. 30
2007–8 Jan. 20 (1428)	Jan. 29	Mar. 31	Sept. 12	Oct. 12	Dec. 20

calendar year under Rosh Hashanah, when the new year begins. Note that each holiday actually begins at sundown on the preceding day.

Islamic Holidays

Table 9.14 shows the dates of the major Islamic celebrations. See more information on the Islamic calendar later in this chapter.

❖ Variable Holidays and Activities

Divali

Divali, the Hindu New Year celebration in October or November, lasts five days. Like Hanukkah, Divali is known as the Festival of Lights, because South Asians light oil lamps and set off fireworks, symbolizing the triumph of good over evil. Divali has become a chance to celebrate Hindu culture as well as religion. At this time of year, Hindus give thanks for life's bounty with special foods, gifts, and cleaning the house. The holiday commemorates the return of Lord Rama after fourteen years of exile and his victory over Ravan, the demon king. See the following books:

Rachna Gilmore. *Lights for Gita.* Illustrated by Alice Priestley. Tilbury House, 1995. Gita, a recent immigrant from New Delhi, is looking forward to celebrating Divali in Canada, her new country. At first disappointed because the weather is not like at home, she learns the true meaning of the holiday.

Dilip Kadodwala. *Divali.* SteckVaughn, 1998. Describes the activities of each day in detail, including the third day, the last day of the old year, and the fourth day, the first day of the new year. The fifth day is known as Sister's Day. (*A World of Holidays* series)

Dianne M. MacMillan. *Divali: Hindu Festival of Lights.* Enslow, 1997. Shows celebrations of South Asians in United States and Canada with photographs. Includes a glossary.

Asian New Year

According to the lunar calendar used by Chinese, Koreans, Vietnamese, Tibetans, and Hmong, the New Year falls in January or February. For many Asian Americans, this is the

FIGURE 9.5 Happy New Year (Chinese)

biggest holiday of the year (see Figure 9.5). Chinese American families give children red (lucky) envelopes containing money and hold large family banquets. Firecrackers and a parade also herald the New Year. Korean Americans pay homage to their ancestors and feast on special dishes. The Vietnamese Americans celebrate with firecrackers, incense, food, and an exchange of gifts. Tet, the Vietnamese New Year, is also the advent of spring. Ask Asian American students in your class to describe how their families plan to celebrate the holiday. Share the following books with your students to dispel misinformation and introduce students to the Chinese New Year celebrations:

Karen Chinn. *Sam and the Lucky Money.* Illustrated by Cornelius Van Wright. Lee & Low, 1995. After receiving his lucky money envelope, Sam and his mother go to Chinatown (New York) to spend it. The book shows Chinatown alive with preparations for the holidays—the reader sees firecrackers, red lanterns, bakery tarts, and a Chinese lion dancing in the street.

Demi. *Happy New Year: Kung-Hsi Fa-Ts'Ai!* Dragonfly, 1999. How the New Year is celebrated in China.

Diane Hoyt-Goldsmith. *Celebrating Chinese New Year.* Illustrated by Lawrence Migdale. Holiday House, 1998. Photos of community enjoying parade, food, music.

Ramadan

Muslims throughout the world celebrate God's delivery of the Koran, Islam's holy book, to Muhammed by fasting for the month of Ramadan. For twenty-nine or thirty days, Muslims are forbidden to eat, drink, or smoke from sunrise to sunset. The fast ends with the three-day feast of Eid al-Fitr. Because many students are unaware of Muslim observances or have stereotyped preconceptions, share books such as the following:

Suhaib Hamid Ghazi. *Ramadan.* Illustrated by Omar Rayyan. Holiday House, 1996. Hakeem, an elementary school student, shows how Muslims celebrate Ramadan. Includes information on Islamic history and customs.

Mary Matthews. *Magid Fasts for Ramadan.* Illustrated by E. B. Lewis. Houghton Mifflin, 2000. Eight-year-old Muslim wants to celebrate Ramadan by fasting.

Hanukkah—The Festival of Lights

On this eight-night Jewish holiday, candles are lit in a menorah to commemorate the survival of the Jews in the second century B.C. Non-Jewish students may have heard about Hanukkah but be confused about the meaning of this holiday. Books to help primary students understand the holiday are:

Linda Glaser. *The Borrowed Hanukkah Latkes.* Illustrated by Nancy Cole. Whitman, 1997. Rachel solves the problem of getting an elderly neighbor to join the celebration.

Fran Manushkin. *Latkes and Applesauce: A Hanukkah Story.* Illustrated by Robin Spowart. Scholastic, 1990. A poor family saves a starving cat and dog, which then help the family find food.

Intermediate students will appreciate *Celebrating Hanukkah* by Diane Hoyt-Goldsmith, with photos by Lawrence Migdale. This book explains and illustrates the distinctive features of the holiday. It also includes instructions for playing the dreidl (a top to spin), a recipe for making latkes (potato pancakes), and information about the Hebrew calendar.

❖ Teaching Multiculturally around a Theme: Time

The study of time is fascinating to students. They are often surprised to find all the different ways that humans have counted time, in the past as well as today, because they tend to assume that "time" is a fixed concept that can be viewed in only one way. In addition, different cultures have contributed to our understanding and measurement of time, leading students to observe that even a "scientific" topic such as time is subject to social forces and political considerations. This unit suggests activities that unite the study of time with the language arts, social studies, math, science, and the arts.

Marking Time

What is a day? One idea of day is a 24-hour period that includes both light and darkness. Is it not strange that we count a day from the middle of a night to the middle of the next night? In some cultures there is no word that means just that. Many ancient cultures recognized a single event such as dawn, the rising of the sun, and spoke of so many dawns or suns. Other cultures used the night and spoke of "sleeps." Gradually the light period was broken up with terms related to the sun: daybreak, sunrise, noon, afternoon, twilight, and sunset. The crowing of cocks, the yoking of oxen, and the siesta are other examples of ways of marking the time of day. Italians in the seventeenth century counted the hours from 1 to 24, beginning at sunset, so that the hours of the day varied according to the season. For some peoples day begins with dawn, but, for example, Hebrew days begin at sundown. Dividing the day into equal hours is a modern concept brought about by industrialization.

Folklore provides a wealth of information related to these concepts of time. Encourage students to search out such ideas. They might begin with expressions or beliefs related to time; for example, Friday is a bad day, and Friday the thirteenth is the worst of all days! *Blue Monday and Friday the Thirteenth* by Lila Perl explores the origins of many beliefs. Students can pursue the study of cultural beliefs and superstitions in such books as *Cross Your Fingers, Spit in Your Hat* by Alvin Schwartz.

How Calendars Developed

Encourage students to investigate the history of calendars. They can learn, for example, the origins of the word, which goes back to the Latin *calendarium,* which means *account book.* Calendars are associated, therefore, with the payment of debts, marking times when payments were due. A calendar, as generally used, is a system for recording the passage of time. Congress, for example, has a calendar, or schedule of events.

The first calendars, created by the Babylonians, were based on moons. Twelve moons make a 354-day year. When it was observed that every four years the year needed an adjustment to make the calendar fit the seasons, the Babylonians added another moon, or month. This calendar was adapted by the Egyptians, Semites, and Greeks.

The Egyptians modified this calendar by basing their calculations on the regular rising of the Nile River, which occurred each year just after Sirius, the Dog Star, appeared. They developed a calendar that more nearly matched the solar year, using 365 days, which was still a little off from the $365\frac{1}{4}$ days we now consider accurate. Considering that they created this system around 4000 B.C., however, they were amazingly exact. They worked with 12 months of 30 days each and simply added 5 days at the end of the year.

Plot some of these different calendars on a time line. Show students what calendars (Julian, Gregorian) were in use in different parts of the world at the same time.

The Christian Church Calendar

On this calendar there are certain fixed dates, such as December 25, Christmas, based on the solar year. Movable feast days include Easter and Palm Sunday, based on the lunar calendar (see Table 9.15).

Eastern Orthodox Christians—such as Greeks, Syrians, Ethiopians, Eritreans, Bulgarians, Russians, and Serbs—celebrate Easter and other holidays according to a different formula.

TABLE 9.15   Christian Holidays

	Ash Wednesday	Easter Sunday
2004	February 25	April 11
2005	February 5	March 27
2006	March 1	April 16
2007	February 7	April 8
2008	February 8	March 23
2009	February 9	April 12
2010	February 17	April 4

TABLE 9.16   Months in the Hebrew Calendar

Tishri	Nisan
Heshvan	Iyar
Kislev	Sivan
Tevet	Tammuz
Shevat	Av
Adar	Elul

Note: Veadar added in leap years and one day added to Adar.

The Hebrew Calendar

Another calendar that is widely used today is the Hebrew, or Jewish, calendar, based on the Creation, which preceded the birth of Christ by 3760 years and 3 months. The Hebrew year begins in September rather than January. From the fall of 2002 to the fall of 2003, therefore, the Hebrew year was 5763.

Based on the moon, the Hebrew year usually contains 12 months, alternately 30 and 29 days long. Seven times during every 19-year period, an extra month of 29 days is inserted to adjust this calendar, as shown in Table 9.16.

The Jewish New Year, Rosh Hashanah, begins on the first day of Tishri. Students can learn more about the Jewish calendar from books like *Annie's Shabbat* by Sarah Marwil Lamstein, illustrated by Cecily Lang, and *Milk and Honey: A Year of Jewish Holidays* by Jane Yolen, illustrated by Louise Anjust.

The Islamic Calendar

Also based on the moon, the Islamic calendar dates from Mohammed's flight from Mecca, the Hegira, in 622 A.D. The year has only 354 days so that its New Year moves with respect to the seasons. It makes a full cycle every 32½ years. The twelve Islamic months are:

Muharram	Rabi II	Rajab	Shawwal
Safar	Jumada I	Shaban	Zulkadah
Rabi I	Jumada II	Ramadan	Zulhijjah

Muharram 1 is the New Year. The months begin with the sighting of the new moon. A book such as *Id-Ul-Fitr* by Kerena Marchant will help students appreciate the Islamic calendar.

The Chinese Calendar

One of the oldest calendars still used, the Chinese lunar calendar (see p. 84) is said to have been invented by Emperor Huangdi in 2637 B.C. By 350 B.C., the Chinese were able to calculate the solar year. Years are counted in cycles of 60. The years within each cycle are divided into repeating 12-year cycles. Each of these 12 years is named after an animal. The year 2002 in the Gregorian calendar was the year of the horse, the 19th year in the 78th cycle. The Chinese New Year starts at the second new moon after the beginning of winter. Another important celebration in the Chinese calendar is the Moon Festival in mid-autumn. Share *Moon Festival* by Ching Yeung Russell, illustrated by Christopher Zhong-Yuan Zhang, in which she recalls the joys of family and tradition when she was a child in China.

The Aztec Calendar

The Aztecs flourished in the Valley of Mexico from 1215 to 1521. Although they had no horses and no wheels, they possessed sophisticated astronomical knowledge and built a vast, powerful nation. Because the Spanish conquest destroyed most of their culture, we know very little about them. They counted using a base 20 system. The Aztecs had two calendars, adopted from the Mayans. One was for sacred or ritual purposes and had 20 days

FIGURE 9.6   The Aztec Day Signs

1 Crocodile	2 Wind	3 House	4 Lizard
5 Serpent	6 Death's-head	7 Deer	8 Rabbit
9 Water	10 Dog	11 Monkey	12 Grass
13 Reed	14 Ocelot	15 Eagle	16 Vulture
17 Motion	18 Flint knife	19 Rain	20 Flower

that combined with the numbers 1 to 13 to yield 260 days. The day names and numbers told a person's fortune (see Figure 9.6).

The other calendar represented the solar year and had 18 months of 20 days each to make 360 days. To this were added five empty or unlucky days to complete the year. Children born during this time received names meaning "worthless." The two calendars meshed every 52 years, which was a time of celebration.

How Music Came to the World, retold by Hal Ober and illustrated by Carol Ober, is a source of pictures and other information on the Aztecs and their calendar.

CONNECTIONS

In this chapter we have presented a detailed Multicultural Calendar that covers the full twelve months of the year. We began with a discussion of how to display and how to use the calendar in the classroom. Then, beginning with September and the school year, we presented birthdays of famous people, significant events, recognized weeks and months, and so forth on each calendar, together with numerous activities that teachers might use during each month. Then we presented information about movable holidays. Finally, we included an interesting thematic study about *Time* and how "marking time" and various calendars evolved from ancient times. This chapter has much to offer for all of the preceding five curriculum chapters.

GETTING INVOLVED

Expanding Your Reflective Teaching Portfolio

1. Many people find the designation of February as "African American History Month" a degrading practice. Others argue that at least we do recognize the contributions of Black Americans at that special time. How can we keep from reducing multicultural education to the simplest of "heroes and holidays" levels? In your journal respond to this issue. What do you think and why? How would you answer critics of using the calendar as presented in this chapter?
2. Make a list of learning activities that you might use as a way of introducing information presented on the calendar each month. Review the calendars from September through June for ideas.

Working with Your Cooperative Learning Group

1. Discuss the different ethnic/religious/racial groups who live in your community or your part of the country. Select one of these groups and plan for your CLG to become "experts" on that group. Collect such information as important celebrations or facts about the group's history, and influential leaders, past or present, who represent that culture. Plan a presentation for parents or another class that will enable you to share the information you have gathered. Each CLG will make a presentation.

2. Following the Jigsaw learning model, have all CLGs break up and regroup so that each group is comprised of persons from each CLG. Discuss the following questions:

   - How do the different groups in your community get along?
   - What opportunities are there for interaction?
   - How can teachers promote greater empathy among these groups?
   - Are there additional questions you should address?
   - Return to your original groups and go over the same questions, sharing what you learned from other groups.

3. April 2, 2005, marks the 200th anniversary of the birthdate of Hans Christian Andersen, whom many consider the originator of the fairy tale, which all of us have enjoyed through the years. Check the Internet to find out what you can about this famous Dane. You will find the following books particularly informative and entertaining as you learn about this man's childhood and his later accomplishments:

   H. C. Andersen. *The Fairy Tale of My Life: An Autobiography.* Reissued. Cooper Square, 2000. Originally published in 1871, this readable story of his life reveals interesting understandings about this writer's life and how such stories as "The Princess and the Pea" came to be written.

   Jackie Wullschlager. *Hans Christian Andersen: The Life of a Storyteller.* Knopf, 2000. A well-documented biography.

   Andersen is said to have written more than 150 fairytales. Look for some of these picture books that can be used with any age level:

   Thumbelina. Retold and illustrated by Brad Sneed. Dial, 2004. (Compare other presentations of this story.)

   The Emperor's New Clothes. Retold by Marcus Sedgwick and illustrated by Alison Jay. Chronicle, 2004.

   The Wild Swans. Translated by Naomi Lewis and illustrated by Anne Yvonne Gilbert. Barefoot, 2005.

   Brainstorm how you can present these tales in a classroom activity.

EXPLORING FURTHER

Byrd Baylor. *I'm in Charge of Celebrations!* Illustrated by Peter Parnell. Scribner's, 1986. Useful for initiating discussion and writing, also for introducing a thematic study: Celebrations! Available in paperback.

Franklyn M. Branley. *Keeping Time: From the Beginning and into the 21st Century.* Illustrated by Jill Weber. Houghton Mifflin, 1993. Clock time and calendar time.

David Ewing Duncan. *Calendar: Humanity's Epic Struggle to Determine a True and Accurate Year.* Avon Books, 1998.

Leonard Everett Fisher. *Calendar Art: Thirteen Days, Weeks, Months, and Years from around the World.* Four Winds Press, 1987. How various civilizations have measured time, including Aztec, Babylonian, and Roman.

Betsy Maestro. *The Story of Clocks and Calendars: Marking a Millennium.* Illustrated by Giulio Maestro. Lothrop, Lee, Shepherd, 1999. From prehistory to the atomic clock, shows sociocultural influences on calendar.

E. G. Richards. *Mapping Time: The Calendar and Its History.* Oxford University Press, 1999. Theory of clocks, calendars, and numbers.

Jane Yolen. *The Perfect Wizard: Hans Christian Andersen.* Dutton, 2005.

Jane Breskin Zalben. *To Every Season: A Family Holiday Cookbook.* Simon & Schuster, 1999.

PART III

Continuing the Journey toward Multicultural Competency

In the first three chapters of *Multicultural Teaching*, we endeavored to provide you with a strong foundation for multicultural education in general and for multicultural teaching, with specific attention to our model that stresses Esteem, Empathy, and Equity for each learner. We followed that with a series of chapters that addressed multicultural teaching across the curriculum, including actitivities and resources selected to carry out this model in each subject area as taught in levels Pre-K through high school. We expect that by now you are beginning to realize your potential as a multiculturally competent teacher.

However, this journey toward multicultural competency has only just begun. It will continue throughout your professional life. In this final section of *Multicultural Teaching*, we guide you to address the larger socioeconomic factors that affect the teaching/learning process, factors that you cannot fully control; for example, poverty, social class, peer influences, learned powerlessness, academic tracking, and the conflict between long-term and short-term goals. At this point in your development, we invite you to join us in examining more deeply important aspects of multicultural education that are directly affected by the factors enumerated above.

Chapter 10 presents language as an integral part of culture and communication. As individuals, we use language as a lens through which we take in information and through which we organize the world as well as a channel through which we communicate with others. Teachers need to expand their knowledge about what human language is and how it works, such as the difference between dialects and standard forms of languages, in order to promote language development for all students.

Chapter 11 addresses students' special needs as we consider how to provide the education that will enable each student to reach his or her greatest potential. We can work to identify and to alleviate negative effects of recognized social factors that may affect student learning. In particular, we examine the education provided in the early years, reviewing the strengths and weaknesses of our accomplishments. We evaluate diverse programs to maintain high expectations for all children who enter our classrooms, helping them move confidently into the future.

At last, in Chapter 12, we turn back to focus on you, as teachers continuing on your path toward achieving multicultural competency. New students will continue to appear in your classroom looking to you for validation and reassurance about their growing identities. We present ways to help you develop the skills needed to respond to that challenge.

We close here with the inspiring words of then-Senator Robert F. Kennedy, spoken in 1966 in South Africa:

> Few will have the greatness to bend history, but each of us can work to change a small portion of the events, and in the total of all these acts will be written the history of this generation. Each time a person stands up for an ideal or acts to improve the lot of others or strikes out against injustice he sends forth a tiny ripple of hope, and crossing each other from a million different centers of energy those ripples build a current which can sweep down the mightiest walls of oppression and resistance.

CHAPTER 10

Language: Communication and Culture

FRIENDSHIP FOREVER

In this chapter we present some of the fundamental concepts about language that you need to understand as part of the process of developing your competencies. Language is a basic part of our social identity. We think with language, we communicate with others through language, and we use language for many different functions, from persuading and ordering to playing with language and composing poetry.

The first section of this chapter builds a broad picture of languages in the world, how they vary, and how they have developed. We then focus on the English language and its place in the context of world languages. In order to understand how English has come to be the language we know today, we show its historical development from what we call "Old English" through "Middle English" into "Modern English." The second section looks at language from the perspective of the social context in which it is used. In the last section of the chapter, we describe how any classroom can foster multilingualism and show how teachers can support students in their class who are learning English as an additional language.

❖ The Nature of Language

A teacher's multicultural competence in language includes some of these following concepts:

- All human languages have complex structures and are equally capable of expressing complex information or being used to fulfill multiple functions.
- The language we speak affects how we see the world.
- Knowledge of more than one language is a cognitive and cultural asset; it does not limit one's ability in any single language.
- Many language communities exist in the United States, and many people speak other languages as proficiently as they speak English.
- Because language is closely associated with culture, many communities are actively working to maintain their language of identity so that its unique attributes are not lost.
- All healthy children are born equally capable of learning any of the languages spoken in the world.
- All living languages are constantly changing, with the result that no one can point to a particular grammatical usage and claim that this form is "better" than any other grammatical form.

Languages Around the World

The largest group of language belongs to what we call the Indo–European language family which includes languages that have spread across Europe, India, and much of Asia. If you look at a map of Europe, most of the languages you find will be part of the Indo–European family, such as Spanish, Serbo–Croatian, Icelandic, and Greek. Non-Indo European languages include isolates like Basque and small families like Finno-Ugric (Finnish, Hungarian, Estonian, and Lappish). Looking at South Asia, again you find many Indo–European family members, such as Persian (Farsi), Sanskrit, Bengali, Hindi, and Nepali. Some languages concentrated in the southern Indian peninsula are members of the Dravidian family. Their location suggests that they were older languages replaced by an influx of Indo–European language speakers. Despite the geographical proximity, these families have developed separately.

The region of Asia includes several distinct language families. The Korean and Japanese languages are related to each other, but many people are surprised to find that

---

IDEAS IN ACTION!

A Book in the Hand

Five thousand third graders around the San Francisco (California) Bay Area have something to celebrate. On "Dictionary Day," they each received their very own brand-new dictionary, thanks to the California Dictionary Project, which aims to put just such a treasure in the hands of every third grader in the state. As students at Cleveland Elementary School (in San Francisco) excitedly thumbed through the pages of their personal copy, perhaps the first dictionary some had ever seen, they located some familiar words ("tricycle") and tried to look up other words ("cool").

Students found that their new books were amazing. The dictionaries didn't just list words; they also included lots of bonus information, such as the population of the country called Kazakhstan (15.3 million), the distance to the planet Neptune (2.8 billion miles), and what they claimed was the longest word in the English language, the name of an exzyme (1,909 letters long). Naturally, one of the students had to check for himself, so he spent his recess counting up the letters.

You can't assume that all of your students have access to a dictionary, particularly one that they can consult whenever they want. Brainstorm ideas for a campaign to put a dictionary into the hands of every student in your classroom, school, or grade level. Review the various editions available to determine which one is most useful for your students. What service organizations might be interested in funding such a project? How might students go about raising the money themselves?

Chinese is not part of that family. The languages appear similar on the surface because Japanese speakers adopted some Chinese characters for their written alphabet. When we use the label "Chinese," we refer to a large family of many languages. Speakers of one language cannot understand speakers of another language within the same "Chinese" family. However, because the Chinese use an "ideographic" writing system, representing ideas instead of sounds, they can communicate in writing rather than speech. Modern China is in the process of developing a single standard language based on Mandarin, one of the eight major languages included in "Chinese." However, most of the Chinese immigrants to the United States came from other regions where they spoke Cantonese, so they have to learn the new standard Chinese as a new language. Without this standardization, none of the speakers of the eight forms could understand each other. They are as different from each other as any of the languages in Europe.

The spread of Islam, a religion based on the Holy Book, the Koran which was written in Arabic, brought the Arabic language to many countries in the Near East. Not all of these countries espoused the Arabic culture. For example, Iraqis speak Arabic, but Iranians speak Farsi, which is Indo-European. Arabic, like Hebrew, is part of the Semitic language family. Because Arabic spread widely as the language people used in religious studies and higher education, it often differed from the language that the same people learned as children, speaking with family. Such multilingualism, in which people use different languages for different purposes or in different contexts, is common around the world.

Focusing on English

Students need to know more about the English language in order to understand it as a living, growing entity and to recognize how the elements that they find irregular and confusing have an explanation in the historical development of the language. The more they learn about the background of the English language, the more they will appreciate its diversity. In addition, learning about English cannot be separated from learning about other languages, as English has been influenced by many languages, is intertwined with related languages, and illustrates interesting similarities and differences in the way that languages operate.

There is no one story of English, no place that you can point to as the beginning of the language, the middle stage, or the end, because the story doesn't end. English is classified as a member of the Germanic family, which means it descended from the Gothic language, as did German and Dutch, among many others. When comparing these languages, it may be difficult to see a family resemblance. The Germanic languages are just one branch of the Indo–European language family. We study the history of these languages, just looking at patterns of similarities and differences in words and comparing them to develop a picture of a hypothetical single parent language called "Proto-Indo-European."

The Indo-European Language Tree

Prepare a bulletin board display to show the family of Indo-European languages and the relationship of English to other languages in this family. Construct a large tree out of construction paper, with eight branches representing the main groups (see Figure 10.1):

- Albanian
- Armenian
- Balto-Slavic: Russian, Polish, Serbian, Croatian, Czech, Ukrainian, Bulgarian, Lithuanian
- Celtic: Irish, Scots, Gaelic, Welsh, Breton
- Greek
- Indo-Iranian: Hindi, Urdu, Bengali, Persian
- Romance: French, Italian, Spanish, Portuguese, Romanian
- Germanic: German, English, Dutch, Danish, Norwegian, Swedish

Have students research the differences in the languages that belong to each branch. How many people speak each language? Compare these figures with the number who speak Chinese or a language in another family. In what countries are these languages spoken?

When the language tree is constructed and the branches labeled, students can add life

FIGURE 10.1   The Language Tree

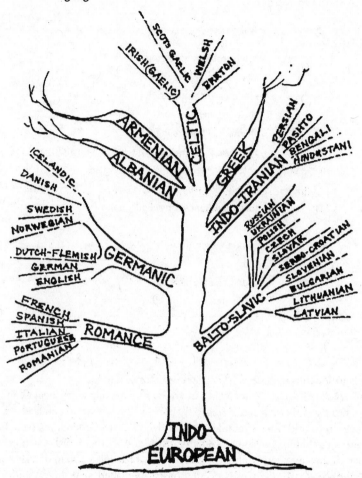

to the tree by discovering words in different languages. Provide "leaves" cut out of construction paper on which to write words to place on the tree according to the appropriate "branch."

Exercises such as looking up the word for *ten* in many languages will help demonstrate to students the relationship among languages that appear to be very different. Here are some examples to begin with:

English	ten	German	zehn
French	dix	Dutch	tien
Italian	dieci	Swedish	tio
Spanish	diez	Danish	ti
Portuguese	dez	Norwegian	ti
Romanian	zece		

TABLE 10.1   Borrowed Words

Language	Word
Malay	ketchup, batik, orangutan
Arabic	alcohol, syrup, algebra
German	kindergarten, sauerkraut
French	souvenir, menu, encore
Hindi	shampoo, khaki, bungalow
Spanish	bonanza, mosquito, tamale, cargo, alligator
Dutch	cole slaw, sleigh, boss, yacht, cruise
Tagalog	boondocks
Italian	macaroni, piano, crescendo, cello
Yiddish	kosher
Japanese	kimono, bonsai
Bantu	tote
Persian (Farsi)	bazaar, caravan, sugar
Russian	samovar, steppe

Other words to look up include *mother* and *cook,* for example.

The English that we speak today is a mixture of many languages, heavily influenced by long-term contact with French and enriched by borrowed words from contact with many languages around the world. List a number of borrowed words for students (see Table 10.1). Can they guess the language each word came from or why that word was borrowed?

Prepare a display showing the origins of the words. Use a map of the world pinned to the bulletin board with the words printed on cards placed near their country of origin. Discuss how the display shows which languages have contributed most to the English language. Why are some languages represented more than others? Speculate on why these words might have been borrowed.

In their study of the influence of different languages, students will notice the extensive body of English vocabulary that comes from the French language. For the study of French words, place a map or outline of France on the bulletin board. As students discover words of French origin, they can write each example on a card and attach it to the map with string or yarn. Possible words to begin this study include:

chic	compliment	ennui
cuisine	liqueur	ballet
embarrass	azure	

Have students investigate the kinds of English words that come from French. They can explore what the topics illustrate about the prestige of using the French language.

Other resources for further study of borrowed words include:

Philip Gooden. *Faux Pas? A No-Nonsense Guide to Words and Phrases from Other Languages*. Walker, 2005. Describes English as a "free market" language and explains the historical context for the presence of so many borrowed words from other languages.

Guy Deutscher. *The Unfolding of Language: An Evolutionary Tour of Mankind's Greatest Invention*. Holt, 2005.

David Crystal. *Words, Words, Words*. Oxford University Press, 2005.

The Development of English

We can divide the development of English into three stages that occur over a period of centuries. Around 1000 AD, the language we now call "Old English" looked much more like today's German and is the language of *Beowulf* and other sagas. We can't read Old English without translation, as if it were a foreign language. The period we call "Middle English" (about 500 years ago) includes the language we find in the work of such writers as Chaucer. Although spelling was extremely varied, the language begins to look familiar to speakers of English, and we can read and understand most of the written language. However, the English language spoken in Shakespeare's time would have been surprisingly difficult for us to understand, and forms of written and spoken English were extremely divergent. The spellings that seem so strange today reflect the pronunciation that was actually used at that time. For example, the word "name" was pronounced with two syllables, as in NAH-muh, and all the consonants in a word like "knight" were fully pronounced. "Modern English," the language that we recognize today, conserves the older pronunciation in its written form, while spoken English continues to develop new forms, leading to the confusing spelling rules that children must learn, such as the effect of the silent *e* which makes no sense to language speakers. For this reason we look to the spoken form of a language as the form we study, rather than the arbitrary conventions of written language. Spellings continued to be erratic until the appearance of dictionaries promoted the concept of standardized spelling as a sign of a proper education.

When the English-speaking colonists arrived on the East Coast of North America, they encountered a New World that required new words. At that time there were an estimated 2 million indigenous people living in North America, comprising about 6 distinct groups based on culture, and speaking perhaps as many as 500 different languages. Colonists encountering new plants, animals, and aspects of landscape did not hesitate to adopt words freely from the local languages. Most of the borrowed words came from the languages of the Iroquois Confederacy (a sophisticated political organization uniting Mohawk, Cherokee, Oneida, Seneca, Delaware, and Huron tribes) or the widespread Algonquian language family (about 50 languages including Cree, Illinois, Ojibwa, and Penobscot). Examples of the more than 100 words adopted at this time include:

Raccoon	Hickory
Caribou	Powwow
Opossum	Wigwam

As English speakers spread and continued to encounter different native languages, the variety of words they borrowed, as shown below, illustrated their awareness of local culture and flexibility in communicating with new people.

Toboggan	Hammock
Maize	Barbecue
Bayou	Catalpa
Teepee	Tupelo
Kiva	Kachina

Older students can explore the complex interaction of English and Native American languages in Charles L. Cutler's *Tracks That Speak: The Legacy of Native American Words in North American Culture* (Houghton Mifflin, 2002).

❖ Language in Social Context

Language is an essential part of one's culture and the language that students bring to school is as significant as any other aspect of their culture to their identity. Says the Chicana poet Gloria Anzaldúa: "If you want to really hurt me, talk badly about my language. Ethnic identity is twin skin to linguistic identity—I am my language." In addition, language is an important part of the way we categorize other people as "like us" or "not like us." We can also look at language as an example of social behavior as we use language to persuade others, to socialize children through stories, and to explain our inner selves to other people.

How We Use English

The language that we use every day is dynamic and constantly changing. It is alive in a way that textbook descriptions of English grammar and usage are not. We vary our speech depending on the many aspects of the social context within which it is used, for example, the audience, the setting, and the topic or purpose. We know that we speak differently with children than we do with adults. We speak differently with close friends than we do with strangers. We adapt our speech to how we assess the formality of an occasion. Speech that you might use in addressing a crowd of 500 would sound pompous and out-of-place in the intimate setting of chatting with friends over a cup of coffee. We also use language to achieve different goals or effects. Consider the language that you would use to persuade a friend to do you a favor, and compare that to how you would speak when asking your boss for a raise.

In addition, we use certain kinds of speech to show that we belong to a particular *speech community*. Teenage slang is an excellent example. Teenagers deliberately use special language to identify who belongs to their group, language that is meant to be incomprehensible to persons outside the group, such people as their parents and other adults.

Our knowledge of the great variety of speech choices available to us and our proficiency in employing these varieties of speech appropriately is called *communicative competence*. The development of communicative competence in students should be the aim of our language program. However, programs that focus on identifying usage errors or inappropriate grammatical constructions reveal all too clearly our narrow conceptualization of the nature of language. We must create, instead, programs based on achieving communicative competence, engaging students in realistic, challenging language experiences that will prepare them to function effectively in the world of the future, in ever-changing multicultural settings.

Regional and Social Dialects

Linguists recording features of language variation onto maps find geographical patterns of language use that we call regional dialects. Thus we can refer to the speech associated with a particular area of the country as the New England dialect or the Southern dialect. Complex social groupings such as are found in major urban areas also exhibit patterns of language use organized according to social class and economic status. We can talk, for example, about the different social dialects of New York City. Dialects are distinguished from each other by such features as syntax (word order), vocabulary, and pronunciation ("accent").

From this perspective any language can be considered as composed of a bundle of different dialects that vary in prestige. Over time one particular dialect may acquire such standing that it becomes thought of as the "standard" form or the most prestigious form, that is, the norm for that language. As a result, this dialect is the form taught in schools, used in formal settings, and codified in dictionaries. Note that no single dialect is intrinsically better or more qualified to be thought of as "the language," a fact acknowledged by the linguist's definition of a language as "a dialect with an army," that is, the particular dialect whose only qualification is that it is used by those possessing political power.

Because English is spoken in so many places throughout the world, there are many versions of "standard English" or "Englishes." Robert MacNeill traveled all over the United States, asking people, "Do you speak American?" People responded according to the speech community with which they identified, illustrating the impossibility of establishing a single definition for English, and particularly for "American English."

The more we communicate with others around the world, the more we are concerned to make sure that ALL students, no matter what dialect of English or other language they speak, have equal access to learning the language forms that will provide the greatest access to the most opportunities. Whatever variety of English these students have learned at home, they are just as capable of learning the variety that is considered more prestigious.

Black English: A Special Case

A dialect that continues to stir up controversy in education is the variety of English used by many speakers to identify themselves as part of an African American speech community. Black English, also referred to as *ebonics* or *Black English Vernacular*, has its roots in the language originally used by enslaved Africans to communicate with each other since they were lacking a shared native language. Children who come from communities where Black English is the normal variety of spoken English often encounter extremely negative attitudes about their home language when they enter schools where another dialect is enforced as the norm. Prejudice against speakers of Black English is usually based on the stereotyped perceptions, for example, that Black English is "lazy" speech, used only by uneducated people, reflecting poor grammar, and evidence of an inability to learn "proper" English.

Despite years of evidence that speaking Black English does not prevent people from learning to use other dialects, or that knowledge of Black English is an asset for those operating in African American communities where Black English is used, educators continue to experience difficulties understanding what role this dialect should play in the classroom. Several key points need to be made:

- As with all dialects, speakers of Black English vary in the ease with which they can switch among various dialects. Nor are all African Americans necessarily equally proficient at using Black English.
- Speaking Black English doesn't prevent students from being able to do well in school. At the same time, students who come to school speaking only BE will benefit from access to the language of wider communication, in this case, Standard English. Reassure students that they can learn to use Standard English without losing their familiar language that connects them to family and community.
- Varied models for the teaching of Standard English to speakers of Black English have been based on bilingual education or the teaching of (Standard) English as a second language. We would like to suggest a model of "code switching." All speakers switch among various "codes" of their language (or languages), using specific forms for different purposes and in different contexts. To be an effective communicator, a speaker of Black English needs to be able to use that form in casual talk, perhaps with peers in the African American community, and at the same time be able to switch to a more formal style when needed, as when applying for a job. Typical code-switchers are bilingual, with equal levels of proficiency in more than one language, participating in speech communities where such bilingualism is the norm.

What can teachers and students do to learn more about Standard English and to master the skill of code switching between different forms as appropriate? For example, students can:

- Develop role-play exercises, setting up different situations that might require using different speech forms.
- Analyze the way Black characters deliberately vary speech patterns on television programs or other media.
- Read and retell stories in both Black English and other varieties of English.

Throughout these activities, establish shared goals with students. Your aim is to increase their exposure to Standard English as necessary, to permit them to practice using Standard English in safe, playful environments, and to direct their conscious awareness to the differences between Black English and Standard English.

Discussion of the usefulness of knowing more than one variety of English and the practical application of being able to use them as appropriate is an important aspect of

---

DID YOU KNOW?

◄◌►

The Ladies Professional Golf Association (LPGA), the premier circuit in women's golf, with 121 players from twenty-six countries, has implemented a new policy. As of August, 2008, their members must be able to speak English (defined as "able to converse effectively") or risk suspension. There will be an oral evaluation in 2009 and new players will have two years to demonstrate their English skills. What does speaking English have to do with playing golf?

Since this is an international organization, with forty-five members from South Korea alone, four of whom are ranked among the top twelve golfers in the world, several members expressed concern that this policy discriminated against Koreans. However, organization staffers insisted that the new policy, the evaluation of English-speaking ability, would be applied equally to everyone, native English speakers as well as English language learners.

When questioned about this sudden concern over members' ability to speak English and its relationship to promoting professional golf, the LPGA responded that speaking English is part of the members' professional duties, one aspect of its history of offering assistance to bridge cultural differences, which is intended to expand the sports' popularity.

However, the thinking that tied English-speaking and athletic ability together was exposed when the LPGA admitted that its interest extended beyond the golf course and into the world of "sports as entertainment." They didn't just want good players; they wanted representatives who would look good in the media events (interviews, speeches, and relations with other players) expected of modern athletes and project a "proper" image, which naturally was associated with speaking English well.

---

communicative competence. Raising student awareness of language use in social context, or *metalinguistic knowledge,* is a fundamental element in this process.

❖ Students Learning English

Monolingualism has been a major stumbling block for the many teachers whose classes include students learning English. Teachers who have limited experience with languages other than English are more likely to express negative attitudes toward language learners or lack knowledge of the complexities of the language learning process. Such attitudes hamper students' self-esteem as language learners and limit their opportunities for success in school. All teachers must, therefore, learn more about languages in general and become familiar with problems faced by language learners in order to support learning for every student in their class. Knowing more than one language is a competency expected of people living in today's multicultural world.

By making our value for students' languages clear, we are consciously building each individual student's sense of *esteem*. Speakers of every language have a contribution to make to the classroom. As we talk about language diversity, and have students give examples of words from the languages they know, such as Amharic, Spanish, Gujarati, or Russian, we are helping all students develop their *empathy* for others. We can introduce the major languages spoken in the world and in the countries of origin for many students who may come to be U.S. citizens. By offering positive feedback and assistance to students who are learning English as an additional language instead of regarding them as deficient, we strive to create *equity* in the classroom.

Assisting Students Learning English

Although a monolingual teacher cannot actually "teach" students' native languages, that teacher can foster *multiliteracy* in the classroom. Forbidding use of children's home languages denies the children the opportunity to learn their native languages well. Allowing the home language usually means restricting usage to specific times or settings, such as recess or after school. This option reinforces the subordinate position of the child's home language. The third option, maintenance, is associated with weekend schools or extracurricular programs, often taught by native speakers but not necessarily experienced teachers. Fostering multiliteracy in the school setting, on the other hand, is the multicultural option. This either takes the form of dual language/bilingual programs and/or monolingual teachers fostering multiliteracy within any regular classroom. In classes where there is a diversity of languages, the following practices will promote multiliteracy to meet the needs of all children:

- Create a multiliterate print environment.
- Use literature in students' native languages.
- Invite community members to share their native languages.
- Create curricular language centers with the help of community members.
- Assess students' literacy in their first languages.
- Start learning some words in the students' languages as well as your own heritage language.
- Create audio recordings for a Listening Center.
- Involve community members as active participants in the class.
- Translate environmental print as well as letters sent to parents so that students see purposeful and authentic uses of their native languages.
- Use the students' culture and background as a resource, inviting students to share their knowledge with others.

The instructional choices we make reflect our knowledge that children acquire a first language by being biologically attuned to language as a system. By the age of six or seven, children already possess a fundamental knowledge of the grammar of their childhood language. Children who have grown up with two languages will have the basics of both languages on which to build as they increase their knowledge of vocabulary and sentence structure. But the framework is already in place. Now imagine these children attending school for the first time. The experience of school is a new one for everyone, but the degree of unfamiliarity can vary radically. Some children have attended preschool or day care where they have encountered lessons and other school-like patterns. Other children may have trouble adjusting to taking turns, listening to the teacher, and raising a hand when you wish to speak—expectations of a typical classroom. Still other students may lack any bridge to comprehending this new experience because they do not speak the language used in school by the teachers and others. However, students of all ages and backgrounds benefit from instructional support in this area— providing English labels for objects in the classroom, teaching English through content lessons while doing experiments, and rewarding students for recognizing words and letters in different contexts, for example. Older students learning English as an additional language learn best when they have good reasons to communicate. Pairing a student with an English-speaking buddy will ensure that explanations of classwork will occur, through some combination of words and acting out. And the teaching of routines such as passing in assignments or organized playground games will enable the student to find his or her place in the group.

As you prepare your lessons for students learning English as a second language, keep these factors in mind:

1. Proficiency in English does not develop automatically.
2. Primary language literacy facilitates literacy development in English.
3. Oral language development is the foundation for literacy development in English.
4. The primary purpose for assessing the language and literacy development of English language learners is to inform instruction.
5. No single instructional approach will meet the needs of all English language learners.
6. Meaningful reading instruction should integrate thinking, listening, speaking, reading, and writing.
7. Students should have access to literacy that includes a variety of genres, interests, levels, and cultural perspectives.
8. Language learning is facilitated by providing oral practice, developing a literacy base, and teaching vocabulary in context as needed.

Developing a Literacy Base

Students who come to school with little or no English-speaking proficiency need a solid foundation in basic areas to achieve literacy in either or both of their languages. In any program that starts with the student's first language and gradually introduces English in order to develop literacy skills, successful instruction will incorporate these principles:

1. *Read aloud to students.* Students need to hear the special kind of language used in books. Have them respond by writing in the language they choose.
2. *Give students time to write every day.* Beginning writers need frequent practice to develop fluency. "Invented" spelling and grammatical mistakes are evidence that students are applying hypotheses about how each language works.
3. *Publish some student writing.* This gives students an incentive to polish some of their pieces. As they revise and edit, they learn the conventions of written lan-

guage. Use teacher-student writing conferences to focus attention on aspects of form and content.

4. *Provide many books and printed materials, particularly in languages other than English.* Students can transfer their literacy skills from one language to another. The more they read, the more they will learn about language.

Remember that students who don't know any English still want to communicate. Provide them with varied media and nonjudgmental opportunities to express themselves.

With this technique, even students with limited English vocabulary can write their own stories. Introduce students to the language experience approach (LEA) by composing a story as a group. After an experience shared by the class, begin writing about it on a chart. As students make comments, write down the sentences they contribute. Prompt them to include more information if necessary. After the story is completed, read it back to the class so that they can see it is *their* story. Create a class collection of Big Books that students can read later. Or students can copy the class story and read it themselves.

The same technique can be used for individuals. Students can dictate a story to the teacher or an aide, or write it themselves, in their own fashion, to read back later. ESL students can dictate stories into an audio recorder. After these stories are transcribed and typed, they can be read back to the students, showing the relation between the spoken and written language.

Another technique to provide practice in reading and writing stories is the use of books with illustrations but no words. Wordless books can be used with students of all ages. Students can ask each other questions, describe the action taking place, and make predictions about what will happen. Because each student can create a text at his or her own level, these books can be used again and again.

Lewis Trendheim. *Happy Halloween.* Scholastic, 2003. Halloween monsters create havoc for everyone.

Gabrielle Vincent. *A Day, a Dog.* Front Street, 2000. Minimal illustrations of eventful day in the life of a dog allow space for multiple interpretations.

David Wiesner. *Sector 7.* Clarion, 1999. On a class field trip to the Empire State Building, a boy is carried off by a cloud and becomes a "cloud architect."

Recording Class Activities

All students can participate in recording class activities and other information on a daily basis. They can make weather observations, write about special events, and note birthdays and other news. Students can take turns being secretary, making entries in a class log or diary by copying information off the board or from weather instruments. This is useful to refer to later and it is interesting to show to visitors as a record of the class year.

October 3

It was 76 degrees outside and partly cloudy at 10 A.M. Today a woman from the Police Department came to talk to us about bicycle safety. She gave us a list of rules and taught us how to lock up our bikes. We saw a film about life in the ocean. My favorite part was how the hermit crab lives in other shells.

Older students can benefit from the challenge of producing a "newspaper" for the class or school. The variety of language activities required (writing short fiction, interviewing, persuasive advertising, argument, expository writing, and editing) is especially appropriate for a class with mixed English language abilities.

Andrews Clements. *The Landry News.* Simon & Schuster, 1999. Fifth graders learn the power of the printed word.

English as the Official Language of the United States

Should we designate English, by law or by amendment, as the official language of the United States (or of individual states)? Perhaps this question appears superfluous because, as we all know, English has been assumed to be the language of commerce, and it is used for all official purposes. However, the question is more complex than it would first appear because it raises a number of related issues, for example:

- Should English be the *only* language permitted in the United States?
- Does English as the official language mean English *only*?
- Is education considered an official use of language?
- Is the nurturing of a child's home language permissible in public schools?
- Are fully bilingual programs to be promoted?
- Should we promote the learning of additional languages in schools?

Debate: Do People Discriminate against Speakers of other Languages? Use this proposal to initiate a class discussion. Have students collect data to support their position.

Welcoming Limited-English-Speaking Students

Your English-speaking students can help you enormously to integrate the student with limited English skills into the class. Assign a "buddy" to each student. This buddy can show the student where to go and what to do, as well as help explain what the teacher wants. Most significantly, the buddy, by speaking lots of English, provides important vocabulary and grammar input for the English language learner. And both participants in the pair receive rewards. Peer tutoring, using a student in the same class, and cross-age tutoring, when a student in the upper grades helps a student in the lower grades, have also proved helpful for language development of ESL students.

Encourage older ESL students to prepare a guide to the school. It could include information useful for other ESL students as well as any new students. Have students take pictures of classrooms, student activities, and other important elements of school life. They can prepare captions ranging from a few words to a longer description of what is expected of a student. If you work with one particular language group, you might consider having the guide translated and sent out to incoming families as a bilingual introduction to the U.S. school system.

Bringing Other Languages into the Classroom

Within the United States, many, usually monolingual, speakers of English decry the need to address languages in our schools. They see no need for learning *foreign languages.* Yet,

FIGURE 10.2   Excerpt from Local Telephone Instructions

Para obtener más información sobre los dos cargos adicionales nuevos en su factura, por favor llame al 1-800-573-7847 y oprima el número 1 en su teléfono de botones.

Muốn biết chi tiết về hai khoản bội phí mới trong hóa đơn của quý vị, xin gọi số 1-800-573-8828 và bấm số 1 trên điện thoại bấm số của quý vị.

有關您的帳單上兩項新的附加費之資料，請電1-800-570-8868（粵語），或1-800-303-8788（國語），並請在您的按鍵式電話上按1。

귀하의 전화 요금 청구서에 있는 두 가지의 새로운 부과세에 관한 정보를 원하시면 1-800-560-8878로 전화를 거신 다음, 터치톤 전화기 번호판에서 1번을 누르십시오.

Para sa impormasyon tungkol sa mga bagong surcharges sa inyong bill, tumawag sa 1-800-404-1212, pagkatapos ay pindutin ang number 1 sa inyong touch-tone phone.

the reality of the diversity in our population and the trend for large companies and our government to work around the world demands that we acknowledge the presence of languages other than English (see Figure 10.2).

Encourage students to begin a collection of different languages that they see in print. The newspapers and magazines often have examples of the languages in local communities. Check labels in grocery stores as well.

At least one in five of U.S. residents over the age of 5 in Arizona, California, Texas, and New Mexico spoke Spanish at home in 2007. This represented a 35 percent increase over the figures from the 1980 census. Contrary to popular perception, however, 80 percent of these people spoke English fluently as well. Determine what languages are represented in your classroom. Ask students to bring in examples of their language and put them on the wall. Perhaps you might ask them how to say *thank you, please, hello,* or *goodbye.*

Bilingualism in the Schools

An early significant legal case initiating standards for multicultural/bilingual education was *Lau v. Nichols,* a Supreme Court decision that required all school districts to provide for linguistic and cultural diversity. In 1974, it charged a school district as follows:

> The failure of the San Francisco school system to provide English language instruction to approximately 1,800 students of Chinese ancestry who do not speak English, or to provide them with other adequate instructional procedures, denies them a meaningful opportunity to participate in the public educational program and thus violates . . . the Civil Rights Act of 1964.

This class-action suit against the San Francisco Unified School District led to a decision that school districts must provide education in languages that meet the needs of students who attend the school. Thus began plans to teach students in their native language, whether it be Yupik or Tagalog, and to provide English as a second language programs specifically designed for each group. In 1999, however, the pendulum suddenly swung to the opposite

TABLE 10.2   Ten States with Highest Population Speaking Language Other than English at Home

State	Speaking Language Other than English at Home	Percent of Population over 5 Years of Age	Number Reporting Spoke English Less than "Very Well"
California	12,401,756	39.5%	6,277,779
Texas	6,010,753	31.2%	2,669,603
New York	4,962,921	28.0%	2,310,256
Florida	3,473,864	23.1%	1,554,865
The Commonwealth of Puerto Rico	3,008,567	85.6%	2,527,156
Illinois	2,220,719	19.2%	1,054,722
New Jersey	2,001,690	25.5%	873,088
Arizona	1,229,237	25.9%	539,937
Massachusetts	1,115,570	18.7%	459,073
Pennsylvania	972,484	8.4%	368,257

Source: www.census.gov. Based on U.S. 2000 Census.

side of the spectrum, with bilingual methods and materials viewed as handicapping students and emphasis placed on learning English as soon as possible. This movement is aligned with earlier efforts to declare English the "official language" of the United States. Table 10.2 shows the diversity of languages in ten states.

Bilingual Books

Many books are available with the text in English and a second language, such as Spanish or Vietnamese. Having bilingual books in the classroom supports students who speak another language. Reading these stories aloud also helps other students learn more about a culture and language that may be unfamiliar to them. Encourage your students to learn some vocabulary from another language.

Several books in Spanish and English demonstrate the range of bilingual books to use with students. *This House Is Made of Mud/Esta Casa Está Hecha de Lodo,* written by Ken Buchanan and illustrated by Libba Tracy (Rising Moon, 1991), tells a simple story about living in the southwestern desert. See also:

Lee Merrill Byrd. *The Treasure on Gold Street/El Tesoro en la Calle Oro.* Cinco Puntos Press, 2004.

Other books are useful to expand student awareness of the many different languages in the world. Some suggestions are:

Jan C. Hafer. *Come Sign with Us: Sign Language Activities for Children.* Gallaudet, 1996.

Charlotte Pomerantz. *If I Had a Paka.* Illustrated by Nancy Tafuri. Mulberry, 1998. A book of poetry which includes examples of words from such languages as Swahili, Vietnamese, Samoan, and Spanish.

Dana M. Rau. *Secret Code* Illustrated by Bari Weissman. Children's Press, 1998. A story about a blind boy who reads Braille.

Claudia Schwalm. *Being Bilingual Is Fun!* Cultural Connections, 1998. Examples of three families where more than one language is spoken. Includes Spanish, Hmong, and Tagalog.

Chamroeun Yin. *In My Heart I Am a Dancer.* Philadephia Folklore Project, 1996. In Cambodian and English.

What can students learn about other languages by investigating these books?

Spanish Is All Around Us

In 2007, the Hispanic population of the United States was estimated to be 45.5 million, which made them the largest ethnic or racial minority in the country. Hispanics (the term preferred to Latinos by the U.S. Census Bureau) made up 15 percent of the nation's total population. In addition, there are about 3.9 million Hispanics in Puerto Rico, also part of the United States (see Table 10.3). The Hispanic population of the United States is larger than that of Spain (40.4 million). Only Mexico (108.7 million) had a larger Hispanic population than the United States. California and Texas have the highest Hispanic populations of the fifty states but there are sixteen additional states with a Hispanic population of at least half a million.

Students may be surprised to see how many Spanish words they know. If Spanish is frequently used in the community, students should have no trouble recalling words seen on signs and heard in conversations. Have students list words they know as you write them on the board. Do they know what the words mean? They might suggest the following words:

amigos	fiesta	siesta
adiós	tortilla	piñata

TABLE 10.3   Hispanic Population

Country of Origin	Percentage of U.S. Population (2006)
Mexico	64
Puerto Rico (U.S. citizens)	9
Cuba	3.4
El Salvador	3.1
Dominican Republic	2.8
Other Latin America, other countries	17.7

Source: www.census.gov.

Do any stores in the community have signs in Spanish? Where do the children hear Spanish spoken? What does "Aquí se habla español" mean? ("Spanish is spoken here") Are there any Spanish place names or street names in the community?

English has borrowed extensively from Spanish, particularly in the Southwest. List examples of borrowings on the board. Do students know what these words mean? What kinds of words have been borrowed? Discuss why borrowings might take place. The following are examples of borrowings from Spanish:

arroyo	burro	avocado	plaza
bronco	canyon	vanilla	stampede
rodeo	lasso	adobe	mesa
sombrero	chili	mustang	sierra

Older students will enjoy exploring this topic independently. They might consult *Spanish Word Histories and Mysteries: English Words that Come from Spanish,* from the editors of the *American Heritage Dictionary* (Houghton Mifflin, 2007), a compilation of words and their stories.

Students will become more aware of the Spanish influence in the United States when they explore place names on a map. Project a copy of a U.S. map on the wall so that all the students can see the names marked on the map. Have students find examples of Spanish place names. Talk about how you can tell whether a name is Spanish or not. If the first word is *San* or *Santa* the name is probably a Spanish saint name. What would these names be in English? (San Francisco-Saint Francis, San Antonio-Saint Anthony, for example.)

Books in Spanish and English
Bring books in Spanish into the classroom. Display book covers on the wall and prop books open to colorful illustrations on shelves around the room. Students will enjoy exploring bilingual books, where they can compare stories in Spanish and English, as well as books in Spanish alone. Perhaps children who read Spanish can tell the other students about these books. Show students that knowing another language, such as Spanish, can be an asset. Students can make recordings when they read books in Spanish and include them in the Spanish Learning Center.

Alma Flor Ada. *Gathering the Sun.* Illustrated by Simon Silva. Lothrop, 1997. Bilingual poems in Spanish and English honor farm workers in this ABC book.

Francisco Alarcón. *Laughing Tomatoes and Other Spring Poems/Jitomates risueños y otras poemas de primavera.* Illustrated by Maya Christina Gonzales. Children's Book Press, 1997. Twenty poems in Spanish and English in a colorful book for intermediate students.

Julia Alvarez. *A Cafecito Story/El Cuento del Cafecito.* Illustrated by Belkis Ramirez. Chelsea Green, 2004.

George Ancona. *Somos Latinos/We Are Latinos.* Children's Book Press, 2004. This six-book bilingual series includes titles such as *Mi Casa/My House, Mi Barrio/My Neighborhood,* and *Mis Amigos/My Friends.*

Gloria Anzaldúa. *Prietita and the Ghost Woman/Prietita y la llorona.* Illustrated by Christina Gonzalez. Children's Book Press, 1996. A fanciful encounter of a young girl with the ghost woman on the King Ranch in Texas.

Lois Ehlert. *Cuckoo/Cucú: A Mexican Folktale/Un cuento folklórico mexicano.* Harcourt, 1997. A bilingual tale illustrated with examples from Mexican folk art.

Juan Felipe Herrera. *The Upside Down Boy/El Niño de Cabeza.* Children's Book Press, 1999. Memories of poet's childhood.

Tish Hinojosa. *Cada Niño/Every Child: A Bilingual Songbook for Kids.* Illustrated by Lucia Angela Perez. Cinco Puntos, 2002.

Susan Kuklin. *How My Family Lives in America.* Bradbury, 1992. The story of three families from different cultures. Eric's family comes from Puerto Rico.

Peter Laufer. *Made in Mexico.* National Geographic, 2000. Illustrated by Susan Roth. Life in a small Mexican village where great guitars are made.

Bobbi Salinas. *Three Pigs/Los tres cerdos: Nacho, Tito Y Miguel.* Children's Book Press, 1999. Bilingual story, not the usual tale of the wolf and the three little pigs.

Gary Soto. *The Cat's Meow.* Strawberry Hill Press, 1987. Nicol is "part Mexican." She is fluent in English and understands some Spanish. Her cat Pip, however, speaks Spanish.

Nancy Tabor. *El Gusto del Mercado Mexicano/A Taste of the Mexican Market.* Charlesbridge, 1996. Readers learn counting skills and information about the Mexican culture.

This list of fiction and nonfiction, poetry and folklore, picture books and novels includes examples that can be used at all grade levels. They lend themselves to reading aloud, having students act out stories, and students writing their own stories.

Latino Folklore

An important aspect of studying Latino language and culture is Latino folklore. This folklore reflects Spanish, English, African American, and Indian influences and is an important part of the American experience. Folklore includes stories *(cuentos),* sayings *(dichos),* songs, music, legends *(leyendas),* and drama. Special types of songs are *corridos, mañanitas,* and *rancheros.* Many legends center around *La Bruja* (the Witch) and *La Curandera* (the Healer).

Provide examples of different kinds of folklore and discuss the ritualized characteristics of each form. Encourage students to research more examples. Because all of the stories and songs are short, they are particularly suitable for presenting in front of the class. Several students can take turns telling stories that are spooky or humorous. You can also obtain records of traditional ballads and songs to play.

Alma Flor Ada. *The Three Golden Oranges.* Illustrated by Reg Cartwright. Atheneum, 1999. Traditional tale of Blancaflor, about the value of working together.

Pura Belpré. *Perez and Martina.* Viking, 1991. From the Puerto Rican storyteller, the tale of Perez the mouse and Martina the cockroach.

Gerald McDermott. *Papagayo the Mischief Maker.* Harcourt Brace Jovanovich, 1992. Papagayo the parrot is the traditional trickster hero of the Amazon rain forest.

The Pura Belpré Award, established in 1996, is given by the American Library Association and its affiliate, REFORMA, to honor Latino writers and illustrators whose work best portrays and celebrates the Latino culture experience in an outstanding work of literature for children and youth. This award is named for Pura Belpré, the first Latina librarian at the New York Public Library. As a children's librarian, storyteller, and author, she enriched the lives of Puerto Rican children in the United States through her pioneering work of preserving and disseminating Puerto Rican folklore. The awards are given biennially.

Yuyi Morales has received the Pura Belpré award for several books. After winning for *Los Gatos Black on Halloween,* she called it "un regalo" (a gift). She added, "The Pura Belpré Award is also joyful. Just come one day to the award ceremony, see the colorful decorations, take a look at the pages of the winning books, tap your feet to the rhythm of the salsa dancers, listen to the speakers, and then, at the end, when everybody at the podium and in the audience are holding hands and singing together, you will know that every time a Pura Belpré Medal is awarded, the regalo is given to all."

A Thinking + Lesson Plan: Latina Author Pat Mora

Pat Mora has written over thirty books, including picture books, poetry, nonfiction, travel essays, and memoirs, which appeal to all ages. She calls her commitment to sharing books with children "BookJoy" and she was responsible for creating the celebration "El día de los niños/El día de los libros, Children's Day/Book Day (held on April 30) to make family reading time fun for everyone. She lives in Santa Fe, New Mexico, and many of her picture books show her love for the landscape of that particular region.

The following lesson plan uses Mora's poetry to introduce her work to students. Here are some suggested titles:

Pat Mora. *Join Hands: The Ways We Celebrate Life.* Charlesbridge, 2008. In this picture book, Mora uses the repeating lines of a Malaysian poetic form, the pantoum, to show how joy brings people together. Accompanied by George Ancona's photographs of diverse communities.

Pat Mora. *Adobe Odes.* University of Arizona Press, 2006. Collection of her poems for adults.

Pat Mora, comp. *My Own True Name: New and Selected Poems for Young Adults.* Piñata, 2000. Award-winning collection of diverse poems.

Other books by Pat Mora to share include:

Pat Mora. *This Big Sky.* Illustrated by Steve Jenkins. Scholastic, 1998. Poems about the landscape of the Southwest.

Pat Mora. *A Library for Juana: The World of Sor Juana Inés.* Illustrated by Beatriz Vidal. Knopf, 2002. Story of the noted seventeenth-century poet and scholar.

A THINKING + LESSON PLAN

◄◦►

Introducing Pat Mora

Grades 3–8, adjusted for ability levels

Expected Outcomes

Learners will:

1. Read poetry and stories written by Pat Mora.
2. Learn about the life and work of this poet.
3. Illustrate one of her poems.

Teaching/Learning Strategies

Resources

Collect copies of the many books for young people written by Pat Mora. Check her website for updated information: (www.patmora.com). Have art supplies available.

Directions

Step 1: Share information about Pat Mora and read one of her books aloud to the students. Share several of her poems. Emphasize the fact that she writes for young people and that many of her works are presented in both English and Spanish.

Step 2: Display as many books as you can collect from local libraries. Provide time for students to read Mora's stories and poems. Direct students to select one poem that they would especially like to illustrate. Older students can read entries about this author in such library references as *Contemporary Authors*.

Step 3: Have each student copy a poem using interesting fonts on a computer. After printing their poem on a sheet of paper, have students decorate the presentation of the poem. Students should then punch holes at the left side of the page and put their poem into a class publication titled *Presenting Poetry by Pat Mora*.

Performance Assessment

1. Students will participate in this class activity.
2. Students will receive Pass/Fail evaluations based on their placing a page in the class poetry book.

Setting Up a Language Learning Center

Designate an area where you and the students will collect books, materials, task cards, and other activities that they can participate in. You might include a book introducing students to Spanish such as *Say Hola to Spanish*, by Susan Middleton Elya and illustrated by Loretta Lopez (Lothrop & Low, 1998).

FIGURE 10.3   Spanish Color Wheel

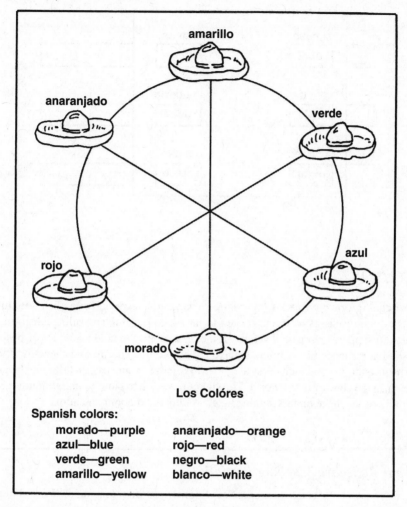

amarillo

anaranjado

verde

azul

rojo

morado

Los Colóres

Spanish colors:

morado—purple	anaranjado—orange
azul—blue	rojo—red
verde—green	negro—black
amarillo—yellow	blanco—white

A color wheel is helpful to show students the names for colors in another language. Make a large poster to display on the wall like that shown in Figure 10.3. Students can supply examples from languages they know. Prepare a variety of displays similar to the color wheel showing basic vocabulary. Include numbers, days of the week, and words used in the classroom.

Help students review vocabulary they have learned in other languages by preparing slip charts (see Figure 10.4). Construct a chart with common words written on the front. Students read the word, say it aloud, give the English equivalent, and check their response by pulling the tab that shows the English word below. These are especially useful for practicing limited sets of words such as numbers and days of the week.

FIGURE 10.4 Slip Chart

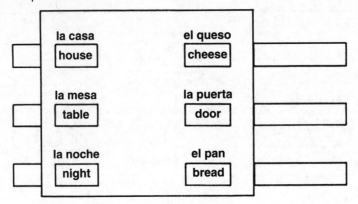

CONNECTIONS

This chapter presents information about the nature of language, especially English—its history, structure, and use—and discusses concepts related to language learning and bilingualism in order to enable teachers to support linguistic diversity in the classroom. We note examples of best practices, promote the maintenance of the home language, and provide special assistance for students learning English. In addition, we include strategies to promote awareness of different languages spoken by students in the class or in the world. Throughout, we aim to build your multicultural competence in the study of language and its significance in culture and communication.

GETTING INVOLVED

Expanding Your Reflective Teaching Portfolio

1. Consider your own language heritage. Was English your first language? What about your parents? How far back in generations do you have to go to find the closest ancestors that didn't know English? Do you have any family stories about learning English? If other languages were present, how were they used and for how long? Reflect on your family's experience, educationally and emotionally.

2. How might you assess an English language learner's proficiency in English? Consider factors such as oral and written, formal and informal, and appropriate use of language in social settings.

3. Generate several strategies that you might use to make your classroom a more welcoming environment for students with limited English skills.

Working with Your Cooperative Learning Group

1. Have each group select a common phrase or word in English and create a poster showing how it is translated in several languages.

2. Brainstorm how to communicate with parents and keep them involved if they are not comfortable using English in school settings.

3. Learn a song in another language and teach it to the other students. A good example would be "Las Mañanitas," a beautiful song that Spanish speakers sing to celebrate a birthday.

EXPLORING FURTHER

Carolyn Temple Adger, Catherine Snow, and Donna Christian, eds. *What Teachers Need to Know about Language.* Center for Applied Linguistics, 2002.

Lisa Delpit and Joanne Kilgour Doudy, eds. *The Skin That We Speak: Thoughts on Language and Culture in the Classroom.* New Press, 2002.

Robert MacNeil and William Cram. *The Story of English.* Penguin, 2003.

Geoffrey Nunberg. *The Way We Talk Now: Commentaries on Language and Culture from NPR's Fresh Air.* Houghton Mifflin, 2001.

Patricia O'Connor. *Woe Is I: The Grammarphobe's Guide to Better English in Plain English,* 2nd ed. Riverhead, 2003. Full of humor and very user-friendly.

Lynne Truss. *Eats, Shoots & Leaves: The Zero Tolerance Approach to Punctuation.* Gotham, 2003. This classic is witty and very British. It includes stories and explanations of how correctness has changed.

Charles Harrington Elster. *What in the Word? Wordplay, Wordlore, and Answers to Your Peskiest Questions about Language.* Harcourt, 2005. Structured around questions and answers about correctness.

C H A P T E R   1 1

Identifying External Socioeconomic Factors that Affect Student Learning

> *It takes a whole village to raise a child.*
>
> ～ AFRICAN PROVERB

Education has long been considered the key to advancement in the United States. An educated citizenry, furthermore, is also seen as the foundation for a sound democracy. Throughout our history, therefore, efforts have consistently been made to improve our public schools and the curriculum offered in them across the nation.

Slowly, progress has been made over the years. The number of students attending school and the number who graduate from high school have steadily increased. Teacher preparation and teacher pay have improved. The curriculum has also become more demanding. The quality of education is far better today than it was more than fifty years ago when the U.S. Supreme Court first declared segregated schools as unequal and therefore illegal.

More and more we find ourselves focusing attention on the student as we endeavor to improve the teaching/learning process, and our goal remains on enabling every child to achieve to his or her greatest possible potential. In this chapter we will address the following:

- Recognizing How Socioeconomic Factors Affect Student Learning
- Supporting Education during the Early Years
- Engaging Teenage Students in the Learning Process
- Gender-Fair Education
- Investigating the Achievement Gap

❖ Recognizing How Socioeconomic Factors Affect Student Learning

Although we cannot eliminate them, we do need to recognize the many social factors that may block student learning, for example, peer influences, social class, parental education, learned powerlessness, and most important, the socioeconomic effects of poverty. Once we recognize that social factors do affect students' lives, we may be able to alleviate some of the negative effects they may have on students' learning experiences.

In this section we will examine poverty/social class in some detail, noting the broad effects that lack of sufficient money has on a family's needs, for instance, health care, nutrition, preventive medicine, availability of reading material, poor housing, and so forth as displayed in the web of linked effects shown on the next page.

There were 35.9 million Americans living in poverty in 2004, representing a 1.3 million increase over the previous year. One in ten U.S. households experienced hunger or the risk of hunger. Over the past twenty years, the poverty rate among working families has increased by almost 50 percent. In addition, nearly one in five of all Americans 65 and older live in poverty or near poverty. In such states as California, the cost of living is so high that even families that earn more than the poverty rate have trouble paying their rent, buying food, and obtaining health insurance.

Poverty, poor health, disease, death around the world—the facts appear daily in our newspapers. Access to safe drinking water and sanitation are important worldwide concerns and a top priority for the United Nations. "The hardest hit by bad sanitation are the rural poor and the residents of slums in fast-growing cities, mostly in Africa and Asia, but the quality of drinking water and sanitation facilities also has dropped in some industrialized nations, particularly the former Soviet republics," according to a 2004 UNICEF report. "About 2.4 billion people are likely to face the risk of needless disease and death by 2015." Leaders at a 2000 summit adopted the Millennium Goals and pledged to:

- Cut in half the number of people living on less than $1 a day.
- Reduce child mortality.
- Provide universal primary school education by 2015.
- Promote gender equality and empowerment of women.
- Improve the lives of slum dwellers.
- Improve maternal health.
- Halt or reverse the spread of HIV-AIDS, malaria, and other diseases.
- Close the so-called digital divide between the poor and the wealthy.
- Work to improve environmental sustainability.
- Establish a global partnership for development.

Mark Malloch Brown, Head of the UN Development Program, said: "The world is doing so poorly in meeting the poverty-reduction targets that it will take African countries almost 150 years to achieve them."

No wonder so many persons want to emigrate to the United States, where they are happy to work in low-paying sweatshops in Los Angeles or as farm workers in North

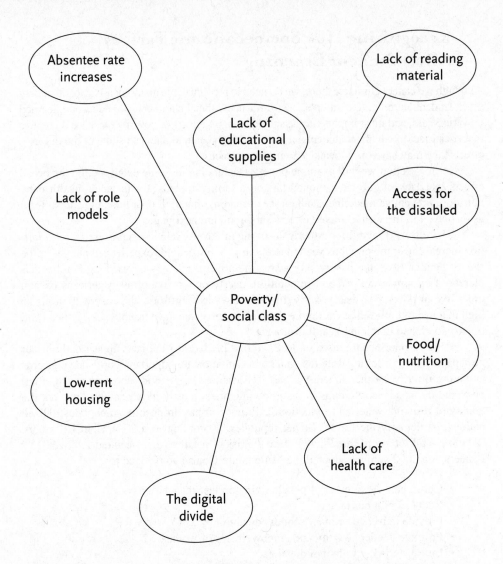

Carolina. Once in the United States, however, they find themselves in a vicious cycle of poverty again, where "poverty leads to health and housing problems. Poor health and housing lead to cognitive deficiencies and school problems. Educational failure leads to poverty," as David Shipler states in his 2004 book, *The Working Poor.* The wealthy continue to acquire wealth on the backs of the poor. Is there any way out?

Selected Resources

Barbara Ehrenreich. *Nickel and Dimed.* Holt, 2002. Author attempts to live on low-wage jobs.

Sharon Hays. *Flat Broke with Children: Women in the Age of Welfare Reform.* Oxford University Press, 2004.

Mike Rose. *The Mind at Work: Valuing the Intelligence of the American Worker.* Viking, 2004.

David K. Shipler. *The Working Poor: Invisible in America.* Knopf, 2004.

Let's examine several of the factors that are directly affected by poverty to see just how this in turn affects what happens in a classroom. The digital divide is an obvious result of poverty, which places the child who does not have access to a computer at home at a definite disadvantage in school. Also important are concern for the disabled and the lack of health care beginning at birth and continuing throughout a child's life.

The Digital Divide

A household income of $50,000 or above is a key predictor of Internet use, according to a Pew study called "Internet and the American Life" in 2003. That puts families below the poverty line at a disadvantage. Statistics from the Department of Education confirm this, showing that 77 percent of Whites used computers at home in 2001, compared to 41 percent of Blacks and Hispanics. Although research shows that this digital divide between rich and poor children over access to key computer skills may be shrinking, "the kids who are left behind are in even deeper trouble than those in previous years. Their lack of knowledge is almost akin to not knowing how to use the telephone." "Their peers are absolutely surrounded by digital media. It's one of the basic ways in which kids communicate and find out about the outside world, form community and engage in social relationships."

"Literacy alone is no longer our business. Literacy and technology are," says Cynthia Selfe of her work on computers and education. She claims that we have to pay attention to the technology that the students are picking up and learning to use so that we can help them direct their attention to critical thinking and exploring the world. However, we can't help them become literate in the Internet unless we have some experience ourselves. Then we can show students how to navigate the Internet, how to evaluate the information they obtain, and what to do with the information once they've retrieved it. The understandings involved are not so far removed from those we are familiar with from teaching reading comprehension and reading in the content areas—critical analysis, paraphrasing, summarizing, separating fact from opinion.

Selected Resources

Lauren Myracle. *ttyl.* A novel in text message from (www.ncte.org/collections/weblit/strategies)

Nancy Patterson. "Becoming Literate in the Ways of the Web: Evaluating Internet Resources." *Voices in the Middle,* March 2003.

Cynthia Selfe. *Technology and Literacy in the Twenty-First Century.* Southern Illinois University Press, 1999.

Access for the Disabled

Noreen Grice, astronomer, was working as an intern while at Boston University when students from nearby Perkins School for the Blind were visiting and she helped them to seats in the planetarium. Afterwards, she asked how they liked the show. "That stunk!" said one.

Like most planetarium shows, it had been a visual show of the night sky with no explanation to help those who couldn't see it for themselves to know what it was all about. Grice asked, "Why does it have to be that way?" Writing a brochure in Braille wasn't the answer; what was missing were the pictures. So she went to Perkins and looked at their astronomy books. There were no pictures because the only tactile illustrations available were made by an expensive labor-intensive process.

Finally, technology caught up and she could use a VersaPoint machine to make bas-relief pictures to hand to visually impaired visitors—constellations and phases of the moon. She published a book of astronomical diagrams, *Touch the Stars*.

Bernhard Beck-Winchatz, astronomer and associate director of NASA Space Science Center for Education, proposed a similar book of tactile Hubble Space Telescope images. *Touch the Universe* (Joseph Henry Press, 2002) was tested on astronomy students at the Colorado School for the Deaf and Blind in Colorado Springs. The book includes fourteen pictures taken by Hubble—images of planets, stars and galaxies—in full color for sighted, but with contours of Saturn's rings, the swirl of Jupiter's red spot, brilliant color of inter-stellar gas clouds conveyed by ridges and bumps embossed on images for the visually impaired.

Is there any point in giving this information to people who will never see the sky? Ask Kent Cullers, radio astronomer with SETI (Search for Extraterrestrial Intelligence) who is totally blind. Blindness doesn't inhibit his ability to handle information. Although he lacked the ability to see the constellations, he could still read the scientific data off the computer.

Learning disabilities raise other problems of access. When the mayor of San Francisco, Gavin Newsom, came out about his dyslexia, it was front page news in the local newspaper. This often misunderstood disability appears to be at least twice as common in boys as in girls, claims Dr. Michael Rutter, of King's College, London. However, others suggest that girls' reading problems are more likely to go unnoticed by teachers.

Nearly 3 million children in the United States have learning disabilities, and about 80 percent of them are dyslexic. Their dyslexia does not affect their intelligence, only their ability to read and identify words, numbers, and sounds. More than a half a million three- to five-year-olds received special education services in 2003, and that number may grow as toddlers are diagnosed even earlier.

A public preschool in New Jersey designed for the benefit of special education students that invites children of typical abilities to attend is currently overwhelmed by applications from parents of non-special education children. This "reverse mainstreaming" approach is proving popular because it provides a rich setting in which all can learn. The advantage of the special education focus is a "very individualized education that looks at a child from many points of view, delivered by a team in a familiar and supportive environment," says Rick De Matteo, director of personnel and special services in Waterford, Connecticut. In addition, the teachers use different strategies and techniques to reach different students in different ways. This kind of education is not only appropriate for those students who need special services, but for all students, and is a model for multicultural education.

Selected Resources

Susan Burch. *Signs of Resistance: American Deaf Cultural History 1900–World War II.* New York University Press, 2004.

David Chandler. "To Touch the Heavens." *Smithsonian Magazine,* August 2003.

Paul Longmore and Lauri Umansky, eds. *The New Disability History: American Perspectives.* New York University Press, 2003.

Steven Noll and James W. Trent, Jr., eds. *Mental Retardation in America.* New York University Press, 2004.

Lack of Health Care

It is common for a poor girl (married or not) who becomes pregnant to resist going to a doctor or even a clinic for prenatal care. Therefore, the baby may not receive appropriate nutrition and care, while yet a fetus, as the child is developing both physically and mentally. Thus, the child may be at a disadvantage from birth.

The poor, especially the unemployed, cannot afford insurance premiums. Consequently, they seldom take children to the doctor for regular checkups, shots, or antibiotics when they are sick. They are less likely to have checkups for hearing or vision, and they seldom have dental coverage to care for problems with children's teeth.

Related to health care, of course, is good nutrition, based on eating several healthy meals each day. Children who begin the day without a good breakfast come to school hungry. Their ability to pay attention to lessons in school is understandably greatly diminished.

For this reason, many school districts offer breakfast for qualified children. The problem with this approach is that the time spent eating breakfast at school comes out of the time allocated for covering the mainline curriculum. Children may be eating breakfast while their fellow students are learning how to read.

Children who do not have regular health checkups tend also to become ill more frequently. Therefore, they often miss school days and valuable learning time.

❖ Supporting Education during the Early Years

Learning begins in the home, so we continue to stress what parents can do to stimulate the learning process for their young children. The school and community offer support through parks and recreation, literacy programs, and social events that include the whole family. Building a fund of knowledge and experiences ensures that young children are ready to participate in more formal schooling.

Young children, particularly if they have no older siblings, experience an unusual learning job in just getting to know how to adjust to the school culture. Taking turns, working with other children in groups, listening to the teacher—all are behaviors that are foreign to a child who has been at home with his or her mother and perhaps a baby or two.

What is the best kind of education to provide our youngest children? That continues to be the question.

IDEAS IN ACTION!

Teaching for Tolerance

When Matthew Shepard, a young gay man, was brutally beaten and killed in Laramie, Wyoming, in 1998 because of his homosexuality, his mother decided to get involved. She set up the Matthew Shepard Foundation and began to accept speaking engagements around the country. Her message was always the same: tolerance. All of the people who had been outraged by the story of Matthew's death and engaged in national soul-searching and discussion of homophobia and anti-gay violence now had a focus for their energies.

Below is a selection of ideas from the pamphlet "101 Tools for Tolerance" (www. tolerance.org), 400 Washington Avenue, Montgomery, AL 36104.

- Help an adult learn to read.
- Speak up when you hear slurs.
- Participate in a diversity program different from your own.
- Learn sign language.
- Go to an ethnic restaurant. Learn about more than the food.
- Donate acceptance-related books, films, magazines, and other materials to local and school libraries.
- Ask school counselors what resources they have for supporting gay and lesbian youth. Offer additional materials if necessary.
- Seek out co-workers from different backgrounds, different departments, and at different levels in the company. (Seek out students of backgrounds, cliques, social-economic groups, or interest groups different from your own.)
- Advocate for domestic partnership benefits.
- Frequent minority-owned businesses and get to know the proprietors.
- Make sure that anti-discrimination protection in your community extends to gay and lesbian people.
- Be an educated voter. Know who your representatives are and where they stand on issues important to you—and VOTE. It is your privilege and your responsibility.

What can you do in your community to foster tolerance? What groups are victims of intolerance in your area—how could you find out? Invite students to prepare a handout for other people of the same age. What activities can they suggest to help spread an attitude of tolerance? What strategies can they pursue when they come across an example of intolerance?

Supporting Early Learning

In general, people are more worried about the well-being of children than the war in Iraq or the local high cost of living, according to Field Research, a study commissioned by the Lucille Packard Foundation for Children's Health. Their primary concerns are: obesity and unhealthy eating habits, the influence of media and the Internet, and the quality of education. Children's issues cut across all demographic groups, according to a Foundation spokesperson.

Stanford University brought together six experts in fields related to childhood and education to comment on assumptions related to "Childhood Today" published in *Stanford Magazine* (July, 2006). Some of this panel's comments include:

> The time we allocate for childhood is really preparation for adulthood. It doesn't give the child time to enjoy the intrinsic pleasure of being a child. Parents of preschoolers are already angling for advantages for their boy or girl. Competition begins in preschool. Some kids respond positively to being pushed. Some poor kids, however, can't compete in the same way; they don't have the support.
>
> There is a diminishing number of positive opportunities for kids after school. Many have been dropped because of budget shortages—sports, playgrounds, art, something positive to do—then they wouldn't get in trouble. What are adults saying and what kind of guidance are they giving? Are adults available to interact with kids?
>
> Technology can become a problem because it is sedentary. It can also be socially isolating. What does this involvement do for a child's self-esteem, learning how to deal with frustration, learning values, and getting along with others? Like watching television, technology can involve a passive process of thinking.
>
> We may be failing students in many respects. It's a real problem when we don't have enough adult resources to help kids sort out their futures. Families can't always supply this resource. Extended families are disappearing; nuclear families are in the minority. Only about 25 percent of kids are raised by a traditional two-parent family. Certainly single parents can raise kids, but they need extra resources.
>
> Social mechanisms that nurture and respect children's friendships are very important. Other children help shape a child's sense of ethics, a sense of fairness and loyalty. Enabling interactions among children is essential.
>
> Some kids will do very well despite lack of resources, so poverty is not determinative. Kids growing up in affluent homes may end up drifting or getting into drugs. If they are getting guidance, they may not be taking advantage of it.

A final statement made by one panelist summarizes the attitude of the public toward overcoming the problems faced by young children and their parents:

> By and large we have left the responsibility for providing the needed resources for each student to the teachers with whom he or her she interacts. They must be trusted to help each student reach his or her greatest potential.

On the other hand, however, we have made some effort at the federal level to alleviate deficits noted for children from poor families by developing such programs as Head Start.

The Head Start Program

Head Start is an outstanding example of a successful federal endeavor that provides enrichment experiences for preschool children. It was designed to enhance the experiential level with which children from low socioeconomic homes enter kindergarten in the public schools.

Head Start schools across the nation receive federal funding, which has been slowly increased over the years. These schools may be located in churches, in elementary schools, or in any other suitable space that is available. The curriculum addresses the needs of the whole child, emphasizing health, emotional and social development, motor skills, and an appropriate academic program.

This program was created especially to help four- and five-year-old children in lower socioeconomic neighborhoods by providing learning experiences beyond what the home can. Typical learning activities might include:

- Listening to books read aloud by the teacher.
- Singing and playing games.
- Counting and math manipulative activities.
- Taking a fieldtrip to the library or the zoo.
- Art activities: clay, crayons, paints, cut paper.

Emphasis is on language and concept development. Children are learning to adjust to the school culture, working together with other students, acquiring the habit of learning and performing successfully. Millions of Black and Latino children have benefitted from this program over a period of some forty years.

Assessment of Head Start and its results is an important aspect of this program. In 2004, a proposed new test, Head Start National Reporting System, was criticized by such organizations as The National Black Child Development Institute and The National Council of La Raza. These organizations are concerned that assessment is being too narrowly defined, focusing only on the children's language and mathematical ability rather than looking at the broader educational aims for which Head Start is noted, as noted above. Early childhood educators will be keeping their eye on how the assessment of Head Start progresses in the near future.

❖ Engaging Teenage Students in the Learning Process

As students move into the teenage years, problems increase. Students move into the streets and encounter the influences of drugs; they attain puberty; they are heavily influenced by their peers. Life becomes much more complex, and there are factors competing for the time spent in school.

More and more we are learning to invite students to participate actively in making decisions about what happens in the classroom. We are offering them more choices, encouraging them to brainstorm possibilities, guiding them to wider exploratory ventures. There is greater stress on inquiry by students, less on lectures by the teacher. The teacher becomes more of a coach.

Coaching

John McPhee, a noted football coach, says, "First of all, let them play." We found the following poem in his comments about working with kids who are learning a sport.

Sports is—
Children and joy,

> Teaching and teamwork.
> The channeled grace
> And gift of our bodies,
> The subtle education
> And epiphany
> That sports offers
> For the young of
> Our peculiar species.

In an interview published in *Stanford Magazine,* Coach McPhee offers these basic principles that he follows when coaching kids, which suggest positive guidelines for all teachers:

- No shouting, no embarrassment, no humiliation. Be the same to every kid. Respect them. No berating, no browbeating. Don't treat the star any different than the kid just learning the game. Be a model, be an example. Kids are enormously, exquisitely sensitive, and you never know what slight or what quiet compliment, will linger in their souls.
- Second, don't talk too much. Give them the rules and tools and let them learn the game themselves. Kids learn by seeing and doing, not by listening. Scrimmages teach more than sermons.
- Scores don't matter. You're not coaching to win games. They're not playing to win games. You're all in it, at that level, to learn the language, the rules, the discipline, the fun of it.
- Everyone gets equal playing time. Period. No exceptions. One thing I hate about bad coaching is seeing kids who never get off the bench. That's insulting. That's terrible coaching when kids are young.
- Finally, most important of all, the whole point of coaching, the whole point of kids in organized sport: teach them to *love* the game, to *love* to play. The only measure of success for a coach is if the kids come back to play a second season. If they don't return for a second season, you weren't a good enough coach, period.

"One more question, Coach McPhee," asks the interviewer, "What's the bone of sport, the koan, the holy of it? And out of his mouth pops a single word like a talisman, a prayer, a lodestar—*joy!*" (Reported by Brian Doyle in "Good Sports," *Stanford Magazine,* July, 2008.)

Could *joy* be our key to working with teenagers in the classroom? Most of McPhee's advice fits in any classroom. What might be comparable to a "scrimmage" in your classroom? How might you share the "joy of learning" with your students?

Working with Students at Risk

Many children are at risk of not succeeding in the schools today. We recognize that "school people did not create or cause most of the problems that confront young people today, nor can they solve the problems by themselves." On the other hand, educators have a responsibility for not only alleviating but actively counteracting the conditions that place some students at risk and helping them overcome obstacles that impede successful achievement in school. For too long we have failed to solve the problem of reaching diverse students, intervening in the early years, providing models with whom they can identify. For example, our teaching has often failed to recognize that "at-risk students need to learn higher order thinking such as problem solving, not just basic skills that may keep them dependent thinkers all their lives." Multicultural approaches to education may offer all students something special as we deliberately select literature with which they can find a common bond and make a sincere effort to provide equitable opportunities for successful learning experiences, beginning in the primary grades.

Phi Delta Kappa, an educational honor society, sponsored extensive research of at-risk students. Begun in 1988, the study was based on reports from almost 22,000 elementary, middle school, and high school students, including about 30 percent African American, Latino, Native American, and Asian students. Researchers identified thirty-four indicators of risk, which were grouped into the following five categories or factors:

- Personal pain (drugs, abuse, suspension, suicide)
- Academic failure (low grades, failure, absences, low self-esteem)
- Family tragedy (parent illness or death, health problems)
- Family socioeconomic situation (low-level income, negativism, lack of education)
- Family instability (moving, divorce)

These factors are not limited to minority students or students from low-income families, but appear across the whole group of students. Researchers addressed four major questions:

- Who is at risk? Only one in five of students interviewed had no risk factors; one out of four had three or more risk items evident. Older students are more at risk than younger; African Americans are more at risk than Whites; Latinos are more at risk than Asians; and boys are more at risk than girls.
- What factors put them at risk? "Most of the risk factors are beyond the sphere of influence of the school." If one risk factor is present, usually there are others. More than half of students who were retained came from broken homes. One-third of them had low grades and 17 percent had fathers who had not graduated from high school.
- What are schools doing to help these students? Nearly one-fourth of the 9,700 teachers interviewed say they spend more than 50 percent of their time with at-risk students. Strategies used by more than 75 percent of teachers include individualized scheduling, conferences with parents, more time on basic skills, emphasis on thinking skills, and notification of parents.

    The following practices were judged to be at least 75 percent effective: special teachers, smaller classes, special education, individualized scheduling, conferences with parents, more time on basic skills, peer tutoring, vocational courses (in high school), special study skills, emphasis on coping skills, emphasis on thinking skills, notification of parents, and teacher aides. In addition, "teachers and principals provide students who are at-risk with more instructional efforts than students who are not at-risk, and teachers are committed to and are concerned with helping students who have special problems, whatever those problems might be."
- How effective are the schools' efforts? Although teachers and principals considered their efforts only 71 to 75 percent productive, principals reported that their

schools had a great deal of influence over students' reading comprehension, math, writing, and listening skills; daily attendance, general behavior, and attitude toward school; completion of homework, attention in class, and higher order thinking skills.

Yale professor James Comer, author of *Beyond Black and White,* supports these recommendations, noting: "Black children need somebody to care about them, first of all. They need somebody who wants them to learn, who believes they can learn, and who gives them the kind of experiences that enable them to learn. That's what all children need." Comer also stresses the importance of emphasizing relationship issues and the social condition—"interaction between teacher and student, between parent and student, between parent and teacher." In carrying out his School Development Program, he argues for providing support for "the kind of development that all children need."

Selected Resources

Robert D. Barr and William H. Parrett. *Hope at Last for At-Risk Youth.* Allyn and Bacon, 1995.

Annie Boule. *After-School Success: Academic Enrichment with Urban Youth.* Teachers College Press, 2006.

Gloria Ladson-Billings. *The Dreamkeepers: Successful Teachers of African-American Children.* Jossey-Bass, 1994.

David L. Marcus. *What It Takes to Pull Me Through.* Houghton, 2005.

❖ Gender-Fair Education

The Bush administration announced plans in March 2004 to allow public schools to educate boys and girls separately, a loosening of restrictions that could lead to the most dramatic shakeup of the coed system in more than thirty years. The proposed changes would let school districts offer classes, grade levels, or entire schools to just boys or girls. Federal regulations currently prohibit single-sex education in public schools except in sex education classes and PE classes involving body contact. Single-sex schools or classes would rely on voluntary enrollment and could be offered only if "opportunities for both sexes are substantially equal," according to the U.S. Department of Education. The proposal—backed by a bipartisan group of female senators—met with tepid reaction in much of the country. However, we already know that separate but equal rarely winds up fair.

Title IX of the Education Amendments of 1972 prohibits sexual discrimination in schools that receive federal funding in order to assure that girls and boys get equal resources both in the classroom and on the athletic field. But as girls have narrowed the achievement gap—even outpacing boys in some areas—political opposition to single-sex education has dwindled. Democratic senators such as Hillary Clinton, D-NY, and Barbara Mikulski, D-MD, joined Republicans such as Kay Bailey Hutchison of Texas in calling for greater options. The Bush administration believed that loosening the regulations would give teachers, parents, and kids a broader choice in education. The National Coalition of Girls' Schools states: "This is no experiment. Single-sex schooling is a time-tested means of helping today's children become tomorrow's leaders, and we applaud efforts to make this option available to all families."

How can we reduce sexism and promote gender equity in our classrooms? A gender-fair curriculum, claims Gretchen Wilbur, quoted in the AAUW report *How Schools Shortchange Girls,* would:

- Acknowledge and affirm variation among students.
- Be inclusive of all students.
- Present accurate information.
- Affirm differences in values.

❖ Investigating the Achievement Gap

No one thought much about achievement gaps until the end of the twentieth century. Prior to 1950, all White children were encouraged to attend school and to do their best. Black American children attended separate schools which were assumed to be good enough compared to those attended by White children. Immigration with the influx of Latinos and Asians and its impact on the public schools was yet to come.

Toward the middle of the century, however, concerned activists began to question whether the schools provided for Black children really were "separate, but equal." A number of lawsuits were filed in an endeavor to permit Black children to attend the same schools that White children did. Grouped together, these cases were heard by the Supreme Court as *Brown v. Board of Education.* The court's decision in 1954 that separate schools were not equal for a number of reasons changed the public schools forever, but the change that was so slow in coming, is still on-going.

Following this important Civil Rights decision, which literally outlawed segregated schools, the expectation was that all children would have an equitable education, and therefore, they would learn more. And African American children did make noticeable gains in achievement in the 1970s and 1980s after they were able to attend better schools with better qualified teachers.

Then came the development of education research and an emphasis on testing. As education researchers began studying students' achievement at state and national levels as part of accountability efforts, it was natural that someone would compare the achievement levels of different groups of students. Gaps between students of different genders were noted, particularly in specific subject areas. And, despite the gains noted earlier, children of color, namely, African American students, failed to achieve as highly as did non-Hispanic White students. This disparity in achievement was also observed for children from low-income homes compared to those from families that were relatively well-to-do.

According to the records of the National Assessment of Educational Progress, there remains a serious achievement gap between African American, Latino, and American Indian children and their White, non-Hispanic, peers. All minority children, particularly those who live in poverty conditions, are at risk. However, Asian American children do not represent a concern as a group because they appear to have done very well. We separate Asian American students into distinct ethnic groups in order to identify the differences in school performance among them.

Thus, we come to the recognition of what has become a major concern: The Achievement Gap, which is defined by Dr. Joseph Johnson, Ohio Department of Education, as follows:

> An achievement gap exists when groups of students with relatively equal ability don't achieve in school at the same levels—in fact, one group often far exceeds the achievement of the other. There are gaps between girls and boys, gaps between poor and wealthy students, and gaps between urban and suburban students, just to name a few. But the most glaring gap, nationally and locally, is between races: African-Americans, Latinos, and Whites.

The data are plentiful to substantiate the presence of this gap. It occurs in any community that includes a diversity of students, that is, every school in the United States.

Comparing the Achievement of White Students and Students of Color

Testing has now been done extensively over a period of years. How does the achievement of different students compare? Although it is of interest, we are not discussing gender gaps at this time. When educators discuss the achievement gap today, the chief concern is determining why there is such a disparity between the achievement of students of color and White, non-Hispanic children in general.

Although the National Assessment of Educational Progress (NAEP) notes that progress was made in narrowing the gap between Whites and students of color, this progress appeared virtually to stop after the mid-1980s. The U.S. Department of Education reports, for example, that in 2003, 39 percent of White students scored at the proficient level or beyond on fourth-grade reading examinations, while just 12 percent of Black students and 14 percent of Latino children attained proficient scores.

Similarly, 42 percent of White youngsters scored at a proficient level in mathematics compared to the achievement of only 10 percent of Black students and 15 percent of Latinos.

This gap shows up early as children enter school. The National Black Caucus of State Legislators, for example, reported in 2001 that only 16 percent of Black kindergarten children can be expected to earn a bachelor's degree in college compared to 30 percent of White children who will graduate from college. Furthermore, the U.S. Department of Education provided data in 2000 revealing that both Black and Latino kindergarteners already trail their White peers on tests of general knowledge as well as reading and mathematics readiness skills.

These data represent just the tip of the iceberg, so to speak. Students who are far behind in achievement at the elementary school level, as indicated by the testing results cited, continue to fall further behind as they move through middle school and into high school. This effect is noted in the grades they earn for coursework and in all standardized test scores in later years. It also affects the kinds of courses they choose to take in high school and in student drop-out rates before completing high school. Obviously, students who are lagging behind in the K–12 schools are less likely to enter college to prepare for valuable lifetime careers.

These data expose a serious problem for the schools and for society in general. Polls conducted by Phi Delta Kappa and Gallup in 2003 indicate that the public is strongly behind efforts to close this achievement gap. Although many people feel that this problem is highly complex, going beyond teaching in the public schools, more than 50 percent of Americans think that the schools must make an effort to alleviate this disparity between what children of diverse races and ethnic groups can achieve. Therefore, we need to work toward identifying possible causes of the Achievement Gap and then endeavor to provide solutions to this serious societal problem.

Identifying Causes of the Achievement Gap

What causes this achievement gap? Many people are happy to provide simplistic answers: The schools are failing their job. Black American children are less intelligent than children of White parentage. We don't spend enough money on education. Studies show, however, that the causes for this persistent achievement gap are far more complex than any single answer would indicate. Research tells us that there are numerous factors involved in creating this achievement gap. A 2003 report from the Educational Testing Service (ETS), for example, identifies fourteen societal and education factors that are relevant to the study of what causes this gap. As the author of the report, Paul Barton, notes:

> The results are unambiguous. In all 14 correlates of achievement, there were gaps between the minority and majority student populations. Eleven of those also showed clear gaps between students from low-income families and higher income families. The gaps in student achievement mirror inequalities in those aspects of school, early life, and home circumstances that research has linked to achievement.

> Sharon Robinson, President of ETS's Educational Policy Leadership Institute, states: "This research shows that the achievement gap is not only about what goes on once kids get into the classroom; it's also about what happens to them before and after school."

The Northwest Regional Educational Laboratory in San Francisco, California, has also researched the achievement gap, making an effort to address the problems involved. They summarize the essential causes along more general lines, as follows:

- Family involvement
- Cultural differences
- Expectations
- Grouping arrangements
- English language acquisition

Let's examine these topics in more detail. How does each of these factors affect the achievement of children in school?

Family Influences and Involvement

Children of color who often come from families in the lower socioeconomic ranges particularly need the schools to provide the best possible learning opportunities. Unfortunately, their neighborhood schools tend to offer less in terms of resources, the quality of instruction, and a demanding curriculum. Nor are the teachers in these schools especially well-prepared to meet the needs of culturally diverse students.

Moreover, the children's families are not prepared to supplement what the schools fail to offer. Commonly, both parents work hard to make a living for the family. They usually don't have high levels of educational achievement themselves, and their homes are not filled with books or other reading material. Although television is present in almost all homes, it does not provide the source of enrichment that it might.

These parents may also feel uncomfortable dealing with teachers and hesitate to enter the school itself. They are seldom in a position to help their children learn, for example, guiding their performance of homework. The home probably does not provide the best environment for studying. Children who live in such homes enter school with experiential backgrounds that may not match academic assumptions, a factor that affects their ability to perform well on standardized tests.

Cultural Differences

Many students of color have trouble fitting into the school culture. African American students, for example, tend to be more interactive in a social setting than are their White peers. Teachers are often ill-prepared to build on the abilities of these children, seeing them as disruptive compared to White children. Nor are teachers apt to allow for the variety of learning styles present in a classroom with children from diverse backgrounds.

Expectations

Research also reveals that teachers' expectations of how children will perform in school often influences students' actual performance. Teachers who are not experienced and/or well-informed may have stereotyped ideas about what children can be expected to do. They may, for example, assume that African American, American Indian, or Latino children, particularly those from poorer homes, will not succeed to a high degree. On the other hand, they will expect that White children from middle-class homes will do rather well. The students, not surprisingly, tend to perform as expected.

Grouping Arrangements

There is a question whether grouping according to ability levels and/or tracking might be a detriment to the achievement level of children from minority groups. There is also the consideration of whether the same methods and materials can or should be used for all students in a class. Again, teachers commonly are not well-prepared to deal with the many problems they face in teaching a class of such diverse learners.

English Language Acquisition

Since most instruction in U.S. schools is conducted in English, the level and quality of students' ability to speak and write English is another important factor influencing their achievement levels. Here, again, the home is also involved as many students use languages other than English at home. Even African American students, who would most likely speak English at home, may lack an extensive vocabulary and fluency in educated English.

The controversy about bilingual education also continues. Many educators still regard knowledge of a second or third language as a handicap rather than an asset. And few teachers are equipped to teach bilingually. Thus, the increasing number of Latino native speakers of Spanish, for example, are at a disadvantage in our schools. So also are other immigrant children from homes that speak languages other than English.

Here, then, are major factors that impede high levels of achievement of large groups of students who attend our public schools. Overcoming the achievement gap that has been clearly identified is a challenge for our schools and for the public in general, raising numerous questions:

- Do we care enough to try to alleviate this gap?
- What difference does it make to the welfare of our country?
- What should or can we do to improve the achievement of minority children?

Narrowing/Closing the Achievement Gap

Americans have never hesitated to rise to any challenge that faces the populace. A review of Civil Rights protests and activism for social justice over the years makes that clear. We cannot afford to ignore this serious flaw in the education of children in the United States that exists today. As has often been stated, "Our children are our future." If we truly believe that, we must move quickly to assure that all children are fully educated in order to achieve to their fullest potential. We need to enable all of them to perform as well-educated adult citizens who can make wise decisions for the good of our country and for the world.

As teachers, we must participate actively in this endeavor. We all need to address the complex problem that we have identified as we work together to seek solutions. Educators and legislators across the country are endeavoring to narrow the achievement gap with the intent of eventually closing it completely. Let's examine some of these efforts, for example:

- Evaluating Assessment Methods in Education
- No Child Left Behind Legislation
- Communities and Schools Working Together

Evaluating Assessment Methods in Education

Before we accept the results of any bank of tests used to assess the achievement of students in the schools, we need to examine the tests to determine the efficacy of each test, its reliability and validity. Is there bias in the test items, for example? How is the test administered? In other words, just how is achievement in school measured? We might, for example, consider the following:

- How are all kindergarten students assessed?
- Why should we be concerned about it?
- Are examination writers operating from a deficit model?
- Does the exam emphasize the strengths of each child?

As we plan for assessment of children who are entering our schools, we may run into a number of potential problems, for example:

- Evangeline H. Stafanakis questions whether we are seeking to identify the strengths of young immigrant students as we assess them for placement in the school system. In testing non-English speakers, she notes that 85 percent of the children are referred to special education classes. It may take a child six years to get out of special education once that placement is made. This could be quite a handicap for a bright child who immigrates from Latvia, Venezuela, or Iran.

- The Boston School District has been using an Early Screening Test Instrument (ESTI) which was developed based on 700 middle-class children from Rhode Island. No minorities were included in the sample as the test was developed. The reliability and validity of the test was last checked in 1972.
- In discussing the results of testing, examiners typically suggest that any deficit is in the child. Research tells us that educators must "look not only at what is 'wrong' with the child but also what is 'wrong' about what *they* know about language and culture, as well as the learning environment itself (the school, the classroom, or the curriculum)."
- Understanding the difference, not the deficit, is the true role of education assessment.

Contrast the deficit model with a sociocultural approach that assumes each child is a unique example of difference and complexity. Consider how we might assess students' knowledge of language following this model.

We know, for example, that children learn language in real-life situations. Therefore, we would expect them to display different knowledge and language uses depending on the social contexts in which they are learning and living. We would operate following these three premises:

- Bilingualism is a cognitive asset that enhances thinking and learning.
- Assume that sociocultural factors affect learning, and the context, or learning environment, is the key to understanding language use.
- Language proficiency and individual learning abilities should be assessed in context and over time.

Improving Methods of Assessment.   We know enough about teaching and learning, including testing, to know that how, where, and by whom a test is administered makes a difference. Therefore, we need to look carefully at the interaction between the teacher who is administering an examination and the student who is being tested. It is essential, for example, that all tests be administered in a child's preferred language. For this purpose, we will often need to bring in qualified speakers of English and the other language in question. We also need to clarify the purposes, formats, and processes associated with assessment of diverse learners. Testing processes need to be equitable in all respects.

Tips for Assessing Language-Minority Students: A Sociocultural Approach

- Assess your own knowledge, then research the child's language and culture.
- Assess the language demands of the classroom.
- Probe for the child's individual strengths.
- Gather data on the child by monitoring his or her daily interactions in various groups within the classroom (and at home).

Although admittedly it requires more time than paper and pencil screening, the most accurate and fair assessment of a child's abilities is made by portfolio assessment, which involves the following components:

- Observation of play behavior by two or three teachers and/or other personnel.
- Observation of group interaction using a formal checklist.
- A preschool screening or testing instrument.
- A parent questionnaire and follow-up interview.
- Research on the child's culture of origin.

In addition to such data collected, we need to consider the many other factors that may affect the assessment process and the child's performance in school, for example:

- Health and nutrition.
- Parents' education.
- Language spoken in the home.
- Socioeconomic status of family.

At all times with assessment processes, we must bear clearly in mind that our goal should always be to find the best in all children who attend our schools.

No Child Left Behind Legislation

Passed in 2001, the No Child Left Behind (NCLB) Act represents federal legislation designed to alleviate the achievement gap that we have been discussing. The act aims to improve education for all students. It appears to be a very positive effort, but as we will see, there is growing controversy regarding the implementation of this act.

This legislation was strongly supported by President George W. Bush, who stated:

These historic reforms will improve our public schools by creating an environment where every child can learn through real accountability, unprecedented flexibility for states and school districts, greater local control, more options for parents, and more funding for what works.

The U.S. Department of Education has published a full set of transparencies online to support a presentation about the NCLB legislation, from which we draw the following description of what this act entails. For example, the four guiding principles of the NCLB Act include:

- Accountability for student performance.
- Focus on what works.
- Reduce bureaucracy and increase flexibility.
- Empower parents.

To achieve these four guiding principles, the NCLB Act calls for:

- Annual testing of all public school students in reading and math, grades 3–8 and high school, by the 2005–06 school year.
- Annual report cards on school performance for parents, voters, and taxpayers.
- Ensuring that every child reads by the third grade.
- A highly qualified teacher in every public school classroom by 2005.

The need for accountability, the first guiding principle, is based on the following reasons:

- A significant gap exists between disadvantaged students and their more affluent peers, despite billions in federal spending since 1965.
- 60 percent of poor fourth graders cannot read at a basic level.
- U.S. students lag behind their international peers in key subjects.
- Past federal education policy has lacked focus and has never insisted on results.

The NCLB also calls for the establishment of standards to provide a "Road Map to Reform." The standards are expected to "provide guideposts for academic achievement, clearly telling teachers, students, and parents where they are going." The challenge is "to establish clear expectations of what students should know and be able to do for schools, teachers, and students." The solution is "to require each state to establish its own standards in the core content areas of reading, math, and science."

The emphasis on what really works based on education research can be illustrated by "What Works in Reading Instruction," which is based on a report of the National Reading Panel, *Teaching Children to Read*. For example, this report identifies five essential components of reading instruction, as follows:

- Phonemic awareness
- Phonics
- Fluency
- Vocabulary
- Comprehension

As you review this overview of what the NCLB Act entails, it is likely that you will find little to object to in terms of its intent. On the surface it sounds good. However, as schools began implementing the requirements expected of every school district in the fifty states, as spelled out in the NCLB Act, problems arose. Many educators have spoken out against aspects of this legislation. We, for example, question the stated expectations for the preparation of teachers like yourselves, who remain a crucial element in alleviating the achievement gap.

Controversy Regarding Implementation of This Legislation.   In 2002, Gene Carter, Executive Director of the Association for Supervision and Curriculum Development, an influential professional group of educators at the K–12 levels, spoke out:

> Education policies such as No Child Left Behind demonstrate Americans' conviction that all children are entitled to a quality education. It is not enough, however, to give students the academic knowledge to be successful workers. We also need to import the skills and understandings necessary for young people to participate actively in a democratic society. The broader notions of citizenship and service are too often lost in the quagmire of nationally mandated testing, sanctions, and incentives focused on core academic subjects, such as math and reading.

The first real analysis and evaluation of this legislation appeared in 2003 under the title *No Child Left Behind? The Politics and Practice of School Accountability,* edited by

Paul E. Peterson and Martin R. West and published by the Brookings Institution Press. These authors examine the law's origins and the political and social forces that have shaped it. They also comment on some possible effects of its implementation and the legislation's impact on American education.

Available online is a 170-page report, *Failing Our Children: How No Child Left Behind Undermines Quality and Equity in Education, and an Accountability Model that Supports School Improvement*, prepared by the National Center for Fair and Open Testing, or FairTest (www.fairtest.org). It criticizes implementation of NCLB based on:

- Requirements for identifying schools in need are flawed.
- Heavy reliance on standardized tests.
- Requirements lead to a narrowed curriculum.
- Lack of adequate funding to provide for welfare of children.
- Intensive teaching to the test.
- Intensification of problems for poor and minority students.

Published in 2003, this report by what is termed a "watchdog group" concludes that NCLB is aggravating rather than "solving the real problems that cause many children to be left behind."

In 2004, Margaret DeLacy, board member of the Oregon Association for Talented and Gifted Students, wrote in *Education Week* (June 23) that talented and gifted students are actually victims of the NCLB Act. She argues that the special needs of bright students are largely forgotten in our eagerness to improve the learning of those in the lowest quartile.

She questions, furthermore, using the report from the National Research Council because it did not include experts on education of the gifted. This report ignored significant research, recommending instead instructional strategies that have long been discarded. For example, bright students do not benefit from being in mixed-ability groups of learners, as do some of the lowest achievers. Rather than moving ahead at an appropriate pace for them, the talented kids spend time reviewing material intended to meet standards that they have already met. No wonder they are bored, often depressed, and vulnerable to attempted suicide. Few teachers are adequately prepared to engage the gifted students in extending their learning, although these students do need supportive instruction in order to progress appropriately.

Superintendent of Schools in Brandon, Vermont, William J. Mathis, also writing in *Education Week* (April 21, 2004), notes the lack of federal funding provided for carrying out the added requirements of NCLB. In a time of decreased funding for schools in most states, the federal government is imposing further demands on schools without providing appropriate funding to support these additional costs. A number of states are rebelling against these mandates, which they are unable to carry out. As Mathis points out: "Assuming that schools can simply buy an inexpensive and 'proven' teaching program runs counter to the dismal record of 'one size fits all' reforms." He notes, furthermore:

> Among those who say the No Child Left Behind Act is adequately funded, the most troubling shortcoming of their analyses is the lack of attention they give to children's needs. A poor, hungry, and abused child does not learn arithmetic simply because we improve the teaching methods. These studies also ignore the huge and increasing inequities in wealth and educational spending between our poorer and richer schools.

In addition, as a number of experts have noted, No Child Left Behind is unrealistic because it requires a rate of improvement that is far too demanding for most schools to accomplish. It is especially scary because our knowledge is so weak. It tries to force educators to produce results akin to medicine's development during the past century, which would be a truly rapid pace.

Community and Schools Working Together

Many elements make a difference in the effort to alleviate this achievement gap that affects us all. Wendy Schwartz prepared an excellent summary, published in *ERIC Digest,* of what each of the following components need to contribute:

State and School District

Development and implementation of shared education goals
Development and implementation of rigorous standards that provide a basis for strong curriculum, practice, and performance
Development of accountability standards
Dissemination of research-based instructional programs
Provision of resources needed for successful student learning
Provision of opportunities to share findings across levels

Early Childhood Initiatives

Provision of high-quality preschool programs to promote readiness
Provision of parent education and social services
Provision of family literacy programs

School Climate

Expectation that all students can succeed, assistance in doing so
Giving students a sense of efficacy and drive toward excellence
Individualized assessments to determine potential, appropriate placement
Recognition of diverse cultures as part of mainstream leading to success
Safe, orderly school; clear code of conduct enforced

School Organization

Full desegregation of all school activities
Smaller classes, particularly in early grades
Equitable grouping of students of color at all levels

Teaching and Learning

Increased teaching time on reading, math, and other basic skills
Challenging curriculum and instructional strategies
Provision of learning resources—teachers, library books, technology, texts
Magnet schools and special programs to promote student interest
Individualized learning supports, tutoring, extra classes
Professionals as mentors and models
In-depth, appropriate assessments for individual support as needed

School Management

Experienced, well-qualified teachers, accountable for student performance
Able administrators providing pedagogical leadership, accountability
Professional development for new curricula, including multiculturalism
Standards applied to curriculum and instruction, assessment, and teaching
Data collection to compare performance and to guide decision making

Family Supports

Encourage parents to have high expectations for children
Encourage parent participation in school events
Provision of education, health, and social services for families

Community Involvement

School culture that values learning and achievement
Provision of libraries, museums and other cultural institutions
Provision of support services, that is, health, adult education, finance
Active school partnerships to support families
Leisure activities with academic focus

Education Research

A number of education researchers have noted the need to expand the goals and objectives for education in the twenty-first century to include more than simple basic literacy and computational skills. Particularly in this age of terrorism and given the world leadership position that the United States must assume, they stress the need for students to understand the requirements of involvement in a democracy, including fighting for the freedom that we expect to have in our country.

The National Assessment of Educational Progress notes, for example:

- Disturbing gaps in students' civic knowledge.
- Young people less involved in civic life, 57 percent totally disengaged—fifteen- to twenty-five-year-olds.

A recent PEW study emphasizes the following needs:

- Improving instruction in history and civics.
- Engaging students in opportunities for service learning.
- Building and nurturing a school culture that provides opportunities to practice being an engaged citizen.

Experimental Efforts in the Schools

Most educators are aware of the need to improve education with the intent of helping all students achieve at the highest possible level. School district personnel are experimenting with a variety of strategies that have yet to be fully studied, including:

- Reducing class sizes, for example, reduction of enrollment in grades 1–3 to twenty children per classroom.

- Creating smaller schools, for example, within high schools.
- Expanding early childhood education, for example, full-day kindergartens.
- Raising academic standards, for example, increasing graduation requirements.
- Improving the quality of teacher education, for example, increasing multicultural education coursework and experience.
- Improving the quality of teaching in low socioeconomic neighborhoods, for example, offering pay incentives to teachers in urban schools.

Although such efforts promise to improve the quality of schooling offered all children, they do not address the totality of concerns related to the achievement gap. Education researchers need to continue examining causes of this gap in an effort to improve the learning of students of color.

Helping Families Help Their Children

Some aspects of this problem related directly to the family may be largely beyond the scope of the school, for example:

- Socioeconomic status of the family.
- Education level achieved by parents.
- Language spoken in the home.
- Parental involvement with the schools.

On the other hand, the schools and the community can make an effort to alleviate negative consequences of such influences.

Schools and community members can offer further support for all parents and children by increasing library facilities. Not only do libraries provide books and other literacy materials, but they also offer story hours for children and parents and assistance with choosing suitable books to share. They may offer multicultural programs that include local parents and children who share their culture with the community. As community centers, they can present support for parents, for example, literacy instruction or English language classes.

Teachers need to learn ways of reaching out to parents of the diverse children in their classrooms with the intent of breaking down barriers between the home and school. They can, for example, entice parents into the classrooms to observe what their child experiences in school by having a Party for Parents at which the children share what they are doing and serve light refreshments they have made. Messages to the home describing periodically what each student has achieved can be written in whatever language is appropriate. Students can be included in parent conferences which are nonthreatening and friendly.

Schools can offer such programs as Reading Is Fundamental, which provides books for children. The local PTA or Home and School Club might support Book Fairs or activities that give books to children, perhaps as holiday gifts. Getting books into all homes could well be an objective for the organization.

Workshops for parents might focus on learning English in a sociable setting. Others might focus on providing information about any important topic, for example, Recommended Foods for Children, Information about Good Health for All of Us, or Free Fun for Families.

The teachers in a single school should brainstorm possible ways to reach out to parents. They might include selected parents in a planning group as they could contribute considerable insight into what is entailed in implementing such an outreach program.

Considering What Works in Education

In the beginning of 2004, Karin Chenoweth wrote in her syndicated column for the *Washington Post:*

> We adults are supposed to be teaching children BUT do we know what works? We must understand education in order to revolutionize it! We need to know what methods work for which kids under what circumstances.

We might well begin this study by identifying questions to which we need to know possible answers, for example: What is the best way to ensure that ESL students learn English efficiently, as well as the other academic subjects?

Students in the United States are not performing as well as students in many other countries, according to worldwide testing. This situation will not be improved without the input and considerable effort from all persons concerned: K–12 teachers, parents, other community members, legislators, and teacher educators. Such efforts require time and money, but the rewards will be worth it.

CONNECTIONS

In this chapter we have explored socioeconomic factors that impede the education of our students even in early childhood and the efforts to support the education of young children, such as Head Start. We also examined possible ways to engage teenagers in the "joy of learning," how we can help teens who are judged "at risk," and how we can provide gender-fair education for all.

Then, we investigated the Achievement Gap that has been identified between students of color and non-Hispanic White students in the United States. Now that this gap has been identified, we also need to determine the multiple causes that produce the gap and to seek strategies that will gradually narrow the gap and ultimately close it. Solving this problem in education is essential to the well-being of our entire country.

Finally, we examined the No Child Left Behind Legislation and its effects on schooling in the United States. We summarized ways to work with parents and the community, and we stressed the need for further research in education to determine what works.

GETTING INVOLVED

Expanding Your Reflective Teaching Portfolio

1. Write several paragraphs that you could use to introduce a group of parents to the Achievement Gap and its implications for their children's schooling. Include at least one paragraph that outlines what they, as parents, can do to help their children learn successfully.

2. How would you define a well-qualified teacher? What more do you need to know to become a well-qualified teacher? What do you need to know to help alleviate the Achievement Gap for the diverse students that you will teach?

Working with Your Cooperative Learning Group

Imagine yourselves as teachers in an urban school where many of the children come from poor homes.

1. Discuss how you can:
- Support the self-esteem of a shy young girl who has been abused.
- Help several ten-year-old African American boys who are slow readers.
- Deal with bullying that you observe on the playground.

2. Discuss methods you might use to establish rapport with the parents of the children you teach. How would you communicate with these parents? Share your ideas with the larger group.

3. Research the following topics on the Internet:
- Rosenwald Schools (historically Black schools funded by Julius Rosenwald to improve the education of African American children).
- "Black, White, and Brown: Latino School Desegregation Efforts in the Pre- and Post-*Brown v. Board of Education* Era" (see www.maldef.org).

Search for information on any other relevant topic that interests your group. Share your findings with the class.

EXPLORING FURTHER

William Ayers. *Teaching Toward Freedom: Moral Commitment and Ethical Action in the Classroom.* Beacon Press, 2004. Teacher encourages teaching that has meaning for children as well as for the teacher.

Jean Baker. *How Homophobia Hurts Children.* Harrington Park Press, 2002.

Prudence L. Carter. *Keepin' It Real: School Success beyond Black and White.* Oxford University Press, 2005.

Stephen Jay Gould. *The Mismeasure of Man.* Norton, 1981.

Richard Herrenstein and Charles Murray. *The Bell Curve: Intelligence and Class Structure in American Life.* Free Press, 1994.

Deborah Meier and George Wood, eds. *Many Children Left Behind.* Beacon Press, 2004.

Sam Swope. *I Am a Pencil: A Teacher, His Kids, and Their World of Stories.* Holt, 2004. A children's literature author relates his experiences with immigrant urban elementary school students as he engages them in writing.

CHAPTER 12

Continuing Your Professional Development

> ### *The teacher gives not of his wisdom, but rather of his faith and lovingness.*
>
> ~ KAHLIL GIBRAN, *The Prophet*

Here we go into the final chapter of *Multicultural Teaching*. Before you close your books, however, we have a few more things to say. (Will this journey never end?)

No one can tell you exactly which route to follow. Nor is there a simple formula, a medicine you can take, to suddenly make you a *culturally competent teacher*. You have only just begun a journey that will last a lifetime, a journey that will require your complete allegiance, your unqualified devotion. But we have confidence in you. We know you will not falter. The multicultural world will change around you, yet you will continue on your exploratory journey. It's a challenge, and it will be exciting.

In the quotation above, the prophet Kahlil Gibran encourages us to share our love as well as our wisdom as we work with children in the classroom. This may make all the difference to a child who is experiencing loneliness and confusion as he or she moves out into the wider world. Each teacher does make a difference!

❖ Increasing Your Multicultural Competency

No one size fits all. There will be no other teacher exactly like you, and there will be no other group of youngsters like those you face each year in your classrooms. So, above all, you must remain flexible, ready to meet the needs of each student, similar, but different. Look into their eyes! Hear their voices! Share yourself with your students.

We know that it is not possible to educate yourself about every culture that exists in this complex world. It is possible, however, to be open to diversity, to recognize the uniqueness of our American multiculture. Seek out new cultures and new ideas and feel free to explore them. Invite people to tell you their stories.

Your students will be your greatest resource. They will be glad to share with you if they sense that you are genuinely interested. Ask them. Listen to them. Be a role model as you recognize each student as an individual, thus boosting each one's self-esteem. Encourage the growth of empathy among members of the group, again serving as a role model. Share the pleasure that comes from helping others. Even if you introduce a topic in the same way each year, the results will always be different.

Let students guide the way. They will help you discover new aspects of a study you couldn't plan for, because you didn't realize they were there. Offer them choices, the chance to decide what to study next, for example. Thus, the teaching/learning process will be ever fresh and exciting.

Everyone can be engaged in this multicultural journey as we try to get along together with our neighbors, the diverse people who share decision making across our nation, and those folks who face similar problems in countries around the globe. The path may not be smooth, but there is a giant surge toward guaranteeing peace and freedom for all, a greater sense of responsibility, of interdependence. As the heroic Polish freedom fighter Lech Walesa once said:

> Everyone wants a voice in human freedom—the freedom to express our individuality in work and life. That's a fire burning inside all of us.

So, we do our bit. We try to keep informed. We strive to consider the issues that arise. We endeavor to move forward in this journey toward multicultural understanding and harmony. Consider the difference you can make in your part of this world that is growing ever smaller with the advent of new technologies.

❖ Reading Multicultural Literature

As you have no doubt noticed, the media, particularly television and the newspapers, are full of multicultural happenings every day—editorials, articles, even the comics comment on local, national, and worldwide culture clashes. What happens in the Congo concerns us. The welfare of people in Myanmar (Burma) grieves us. We share the fears of the Afghanis.

Consider a few specific avenues that you, as a teacher, can follow as you work toward achieving and maintaining multicultural competency.

Forming a Teachers' Book Club

Sometimes it helps to talk with other people. Invite a group of teachers to form a book club with the express purpose of exploring multicultural literature. As new books appear, you can select one to read each month, meeting at a scheduled time and place, to share your impressions. You may choose to follow a theme, for example, reading about childhood in different countries, or you may decide to read the work of a single author, for example, Toni Morrison or Katherine Paterson.

You may pick an older book, perhaps one that many of you missed: *The Grapes of Wrath* or *I Know Why the Caged Bird Sings.* Or a group of middle school or high school teachers might choose to read a novel that you could study with your students or add to the current reading list that you compile for the students.

The following novels are engaging for both teenage and adult readers. Thus, you will achieve two goals as you share interesting multicultural literature that (1) not only informs your own thinking but also (2) provides exciting literature to share with future groups of students in your classroom.

Sherman Alexie. *The Absolutely True Story of a Part/Time Indian.* An engaging story of Indian life by an outstanding storyteller.

Oscar Higuelos. *Dark Dude.* Atheneum, 2008. Features a Cuban teenager in New York City. Unusually light-skinned, Rico is referred to by his friends as a "dark dude," the term used by persons of color for someone who is light. Rico runs away to Janesville, Wisconsin, where he encounters the Hispanic/White conflict, rather than the racism against Blacks in New York.

Khaled Hosseini. *The Kite Runner.* Childhood in Kabul, describes two boys whose fortunes are divided by turmoil in Afghanistan.

Tracy Kidder. *Mountains Beyond Mountains: The Quest of Paul Farmer, A Man Who Would Cure the World.* Profiles MacArthur "genius-grant" winner and humanitarian Farmer, an infectious disease specialist whose work in countries such as Russia and Haiti is inspiring to those who want to combat global poverty.

Ron Koertge. *Strays.* Reveals the inner worlds of three foster teenage boys during the turmoil of adolescence, lack of roots, and the need to construct an identity from scratch.

Toni Morrison. *Mercy.* Knopf, 2008. Set in America in the seventeenth century, *Mercy* is the story of Jacob, an Anglo-Dutch trader, who develops a profitable farm, marries Rebekka, but too soon dies of pox. It is also the story of "three unmastered women"—Florens, who narrates the story, Rebekka, and Lina, a former American Indian slave.

Julie Orringer. *How to Breathe under Water.* Nine short stories, several about girls acquainted with tragedy, and young women on the verge of self-discovery.

Miriam Toews. *The Flying Troutmans.* Counterpoint, 2008. Describes a fractured family living in Canada: Hattie, rising to her suicidal sister's need, arrives to keep her niece and nephew from being placed in foster homes. The tale revolves around a trip to California to locate the kids' father. The road trip offers a comparison with the film *Little Miss Sunshine.*

Reading Stories of Real Teachers Working with Diverse Students — Insight into the Problems Teachers Face

Are you concerned about actually facing a classroom full of students? Are you a young White teacher having doubts about your ability to work with students of color? At this time you might find it very helpful to read some of the books that have been published about real teachers who worked successfully with children who came from cultures very different from their own.

Sylvia Ashton-Warner was one of the first, writing about her work with Maori children in New Zealand. Later, Herbert Kohl wrote of teaching in urban schools in Boston and New York City. More recently, a Pulitzer-prize-winning author, Tracy Kidder, wrote an engaging case study, speaking for Mrs. Zajac, a teacher in Holyoke, Massachusetts, who worked with fifth graders, half of whom were Puerto Rican. All of these teachers' stories are interesting; all are inspiring. Following are more detailed descriptions of the books that relate their experiences. Look for them in your local independent book store.

Sylvia Ashton Warner: Teaching Maori Children in New Zealand

Sylvia Ashton Warner writes of her work with Maori children in an amazing book, *Teacher* (1963, 1986), which American teachers quite literally gobbled up. She introduces us to organic reading instruction as she helps children in her infant school make the "bridge from the known to the unknown; from a native culture to a new; and, universally speaking, from the inner man out."

She describes her work with 5-year-olds. Based on a "key vocabulary," words that she draws from each child first thing every morning, words that have personal dynamic meaning, the children begin to read. Each child has his or her own pile of cards bearing words printed by the teacher. They read their cards, read them again, and read them again. They draw pictures to go with their word captions, and gradually they create their own books which they can read. As this teacher says:

> It may sound hard, but it's the easiest way I have ever begun reading. There's no driving to it. I don't teach at all. There is no work to put up on the blackboard, no charts to make and no force to marshal the children into a teachable and attentive group. The teaching is done among themselves, mixed up with all the natural concomitants of relationship. I just make sure of my cards nearby and my big black crayon and look forward to the game with myself of seeing how nearly I hit the mark. And the revelation of character is a thing that no one can ever find boring.

Teacher was first published in 1963, years after this enthusiastic young teacher worked with the Maoris. After her death in 1984, the book was reissued in 1986 with a foreword by Maxine Hong Kingston. Sylvia Ashton Warner also wrote a best-selling novel, *Spinster* (1968), among other less known works.

Vivian Gussin Paley: A Jewish White Kindergarten Teacher Works with Diverse Children

Vivian Paley has taught kindergarten for many years in the Midwest, and she has written a number of books about what she, as a teacher-researcher, has learned about teaching young children. All of them have something to offer our work with multicultural education. In *You Can't Say, "You Can't Play"* (1982), for example, she teaches children how to get along together. In *The Kindness of Children* (1986) she focuses on teaching children how and why to be kind to one another. In *White Teacher* (2004), which we will discuss in more detail here, she provides insight into her own concerns about a White Jewish teacher's ability to guide the learning of Black youngsters.

In *White Teacher,* a panel of Black parents is invited for the first time to discuss their children's learning experiences with the faculty in a midwestern school. Not uneducated, the parents speak frankly revealing their perception of the prejudice and unfairness that they observe in the school where Vivian Paley teaches kindergarten. The teachers in this relatively liberal school are surprised and somewhat defensive. But this incident leads Vivian to begin taking notes about her interaction with the Black students (about one-third of the class) in her room. She asks herself:

> Do I respond to each child in a similar manner?
> Am I fair to the Black children?

Vivian Paley introduces us to the children she teaches through describing pertinent events that she observes—friendships, free discussion about such ideas as skin color, sharing favorite family songs, inviting parents to bring a family food to share in the classroom, and so on. And, a blessing for this liberal teacher comes in the form of a talented, older student teacher who happens to be Black. Together, they work to assist the learning of the children in the room.

As a teacher-researcher, Vivian Paley is eager to investigate the hidden curriculum and to discover something of her own identity in the process. As she observes what is happening in her classroom, she comes to the following conclusion:

> The Black child is Every Child. There is no activity useful only for the Black child; there is no manner of speaking or unique approach or special environment required only for Black children. There are only certain words and actions that cause all of us to cover up, and there are other words and actions that help us reveal ourselves to one another. The challenge in teaching is to find a way of communicating to each child the idea that his or her special quality is understood, is valued, and can be talked about. It is not easy, because we are influenced by the fears and prejudices, apprehensions and expectations, which have become a carefully hidden part of every one of us.

Thus, Vivian Paley ends the forward to the study of her teaching in her own classroom. This philosophy, we might add, reflects a key understanding that we presented in the introductory chapters of *Multicultural Teaching*. Teaching *multiculturally* means enabling every child to reach his or her greatest potential using whatever methods and materials are most appropriate.

Herbert Kohl: Teaching Sixth Grade in Harlem

Herbert Kohl describes his exhausting first days as a beginning teacher working with (not teaching) 36 sixth-grade Black children in Harlem. The classroom is ugly; he has no books. His chief goal in those first days is to remain in control, moving methodically through his lesson plan—reading, arithmetic, social studies. One young girl inquires plaintively:

"You like it here, Mr. Kohl?"

I looked up into a lovely sad face.

"What do you mean?"

"I mean do you like it here, Mr. Kohl, what are you teaching us for?"

After several miserable days plugging through the inadequate books that finally arrive, interspersed with periods of chaos, this Harvard graduate begins to "see" the kids as individuals. At last he comes to this momentous conclusion:

> I am convinced that the teacher must be an observer of his class as well as a member of it. He must look at the children, discover how they relate to each other and the room around them. There must be enough free time and activity for the teacher to discover the children's human preferences. Observing children at play and mischief is an invaluable source of knowledge about them—about leaders and groups, fear, courage, warmth, isolation.

He notes, furthermore, that never in his year of teacher training did he hear anyone talk about how to observe children or even suggest that this might be valuable. With that self-enlightment, the doors open for Kohl and his students as they talk about what is important in their lives and write stories of events that are real. Many of these stories are reproduced in Kohl's book *36 Children,* which was published in 1967. This book shocked the American public with its honest revelation of one teacher's endeavors to set children free from the traditional controlled inadequate education that was commonly offered in urban ghetto schools. Herbert Kohl followed this first book with others as he continued to endeavor to improve the education of children in poor urban areas.

Tracy Kidder: A Case Study of a Fifth-Grade Teacher in Holyoke, Massachusetts

Skilled author Tracy Kidder was once a teacher of high school English, but it is not his own teaching that he chooses to write about. Rather, he relates the story of Chris Zajac's year with a troupe of fifth graders who live in the poorest section of one of our smaller industrial cities. Clearly, Kidder has observed and listened with understanding in order to produce his publication, *Among Schoolchildren,* published in 1989. Although he changed the names of the children and the student teacher, this case study describes the work of a real teacher with all her doubts as she attempts to help individual pupils, half of whom are Puerto Rican.

We come to know to know Clarence, for example, "a small, lithe, brown-skinned boy with large eyes and deep dimples." Clarence makes frequent journeys to the pencil sharpener, taking "the longest possible route around the room, walking heel-to-toe and brushing the back of one leg within the shin of the other at every step—a cheerful little dance across the blue carpet, around the perimeter of desks, and along the back wall, passing under the American flag, which didn't quite brush his head."

Clarence's cumulative record (*cume file*) is as thick as the Boston phone book, but Chris is not interested in reading it. She keeps him after school, which only punishes her because Clarence refuses to write. As he leaves the classroom after the second detention, he calls back, "I hate Mrs. Zajac!" and Chris is left with her feelings of guilt. But Mrs. Zajac doesn't give up.

We come to know Chris Zajac intimately, sharing her innermost thoughts, her reluctance to let the student teacher take over "her" classroom, her worries about what will happen to Judith, a bright child who has great potential, and, of course, Clarence, who is still angry at the end of the year. The dialogue is real; the situations typical of poor urban schools, the interactions with principal and other teachers, human. It's nonfiction, but it reads like a novel punctuated with humor and pathos.

Through *Among Schoolchildren* we also come to know Tracy Kidder, a Pulitzer Prize–winning author. You may be interested in exploring his other works: *The Road to Yuba City* (1989), *The Soul of a New Machine* (1999), and *House* (2002).

E. R. Braithwaite: Teaching Teenagers in London's Lower East Side

Born in Dutch Guiana, Rick Braithwaite is well-educated and ready to step forward into a career, but no one wants to hire a Black man. Finally, because the schools are desperate for teachers, and Rick does make a good impression, he is hired by a principal who espouses an interesting child-centered philosophy of education.

Rick is horrified at the crude language the students use in and out of the classroom, but he really doesn't know what to do about it. He asks the other teachers, but they don't have an answer. Troubled, he ponders for days over the problem.

> Looking back, I realized that in fact I passed through three phases in my relationship with them. The first was the "silent" treatment, and during that time, for my first few weeks, they would do any task I set them without question or protest, but equally without interest or enthusiasm; and if their interest was not required on the task in front of them, they would sit and stare at me with that same careful, patient attention a birdwatcher devotes to the rare feathered visitor.
>
> Gradually, they moved on to the second and more annoying phase of their campaign, the "noisy" treatment. . . . During a lesson, especially one in which it was necessary for me to read or speak to them, someone would lift the lid of a desk and then let it fall with a loud bang; the culprit would merely sit and look at me with wide innocent eyes as if it were an accident.

Then comes the turning point, a nasty incident in which the students burn a soiled sanitary napkin in the fireplace, filling the classroom with noxious smoke. When he discovers what they have done, he tears into the girls about their sluttish behavior and filthy language. To his surprise, "they took it!" On the next morning, he spells out what was to be the third phase:

> My business here is to teach you, and I shall do my best to make my teaching as interesting as possible. If at any time I say anything you do not understand or with which you do not agree, I would be pleased if you would let me know. Most of you will be leaving school within six months or so; that means in a short while you will be embarked on the very adult business of earning a living. Bearing that in mind, I have decided that from now on you will be treated, not as children, but as young men and women, by me and by each other.

Much to their amazement, he announces that girls in the class were to be addressed as "Miss," the boys were to be called by their last names, and he is to be addressed as "Sir."

In his first film, Sidney Poitier played the role of this Negro (the acceptable term at that time) teacher in a secondary school in the outskirts of London's East End based on Braithwaite's book, *To Sir, with Love* (Pyramid, 1959).

Evan Hunter: Teaching English in a New York City: Trade School (Fiction)

Rick Dadier wants very much to be a teacher. Following a stint in the U.S. Navy, he applies for a teaching job in New York City. Both he and his wife are delighted when he is hired, even though he lands his first job as an English teacher in a large vocational high school. Although he assumes that the kids at North Manual Trades High School will be tough, Rick feels sure that he can handle them. Facing his homeroom class, all male juniors, for the first time, he reminds himself of the advice other teachers have given him: "Start out tough; you can always ease up later."

In this novel (later made into a film) we follow Rick through his first semester working with five classes of reluctant learners. As a beginning teacher, he has much to learn, and these rough city boys are happy to give him a few lessons. His first lesson is the result of his rescuing a sexy young female teacher from rape in a stairwell. Righteously, Rick marches the would-be rapist to the principal who "throws the book at him," seeing that he ends up in jail. The fellow's buddies resent such treatment and, blaming Rick, they gang up on him and another teacher one night to give them a severe beating.

Rick talks with other experienced teachers, but they are not much help, so he bungles along, grateful when the principal enters the room because then there are no discipline problems, and he can teach. However, he soon realizes that there is something other than a lack of discipline to fight at North Manual Trades. He discovers that the kids simply do not want to learn.

Rick does have happier experiences, for example, putting on a Christmas program that proves highly successful thanks largely to an enthusiastic Black student whom Rick befriends. The highpoint comes, however, when he reads the allegory "The Fifty-first Dragon" aloud to a class. Much to Rick's surprise, the response to this "story within a story" is exhilarating! All the students want to hear that dragon story!

LouAnne Johnson: Teaching High School English in a Special Program

A former Marine, Miss Johnson is 35 when she first faces a class of smart-alecky city high school students who really don't want to be in school. Presented as snapshots, the chapters in the book cover four years of teaching, as follows:

1. Intern, teaching two sophomore English classes, one accelerated.
2. New "Academy Program": two periods sophomore English; two periods Non-English Proficient (NEP) students, grades 9–12 mixed.

3–4. Teaching and counseling three levels in Academy; Program Director.

The Academy program is a "school within a school." Students remain with the same class and teacher for three years which encourages bonding. As Ms. Johnson writes: "It is this bonding that is the key to the success of the Academy model programs. When classes are small enough to allow individual student-teacher interaction, a minor miracle occurs: teachers teach and students learn."

One clever ploy Ms. Johnson uses is sending unsealed letters home to parents with a student. When the student reads it, he or she is amazed to find that the letter is very complimentary. Ms. Johnson never lies, but she seldom addresses academic achievement. Rather she says something to the effect "that I enjoyed having the child in my class, or was pleased to have the chance to be his or her teacher for some reason—the student's wit or charming personality . . . courteous behavior, impeccable dress, and so on. . . . Mostly I simply praised the student as a person." A few students are unimpressed, but most visibly change their perception of themselves.

Another method she uses is to let NEP students choose their own vocabulary words to learn each week. In her book, she shares funny mistakes such as the time she writes *horse* on the board for a student and leaves out the *s.* You'll laugh at how she manages to extricate herself from answering the student who askes, "What does that spell, teacher?"

Again, we observe a teacher who genuinely cares about what happens to the "tough" Hispanic boys who are in her classes or the smart girls who don't see themselves as *smart* until she manages to convince them that they really do have what it takes to succeed.

Originally published under the title *My Posse Don't Do Homework* (St. Martins, 1992), this book was made into a film starring Michelle Pfeiffer called *Dangerous Minds.*

Frank McCourt: Teaching High School English in New York City

Moving from position to position, Frank McCourt finally lands at Stuyvesant High School, one of the most prestigious schools in New York City. These stories about his teaching are hilarious, especially when viewed through the eyes of the more conventional English teachers in the school. Whoever heard of singalongs featuring recipe ingredients as lyrics, accompanied by the various musical instruments the students can supply, in an English classroom? What English teacher ever asks students to write "An Excuse Note from Adam or Eve to God?"

McCourt struggles to find his way in the classroom, spending his evenings drinking with writers and dreaming of one day putting his own story into a book. This short memoir displays his unparalleled ability to tell a great story as, five days a week, five periods per day, he works to gain the attention and respect of unruly, hormonally charged or indifferent adolescent students.

He asks himself as a teacher, "Who am I to try to teach writing to these students when I have never done it myself?" After much pondering, he decides to retire. As he writes:

> It was time to retire, live on the teacher's pension that was less than princely. I'll catch up on the books I missed in the last thirty years. I'll spend hours at the Forty-second Street Library, the place I love most in New York, walk the streets, have a beer at the Lion's Head, talk to Deacy, Duggan, Hamill, learn the guitar and a hundred songs to go with it, take my daughter, Maggie, for dinner in the Village, scribble in my notebooks. Something might come.
>
> I'll get by.

Teacher Man: *A Memoir* (Scribner, 2005) is the third volume in a kind of trilogy that begins with Pulitzer Prize-winning *Angela's Ashes,* in which McCourt relates the tale of his poverty-stricken childhood in Limerick, Ireland. That book was followed by *'Tis,* which shares the glorious stories of Frank's early years as an immigrant in New York City. In *Teacher Man,* he tells us how he learns to be a high school English teacher.

Mike Rose: A Teacher Studies How K–12 Teachers Teach

Mike Rose, an educator who is concerned about the welfare of learners of all ages, wants to do something to improve the education we offer students across the nation in our schools. He wrote an award-winning book, *Lives on the Boundary,* in which he talks first about his own life as an inner city kid struggling to succeed in school. Later, as a teacher, he meets diverse

IDEAS IN ACTION!

Laws of Life and the Power of Storytelling

The question faced by understanding educators is: "How do we help disadvantaged youths remain resilient and hopeful while the long-term efforts of school reform proceed around them?" Psychologist James Pennebaker and philanthropist Sir John Templeton knew that research showed "that people facing chronic difficulties in their lives . . . benefit greatly from telling stories about their experiences and feelings."

Templeton also believed that young people in our culture are influenced in so many different ways that "they have trouble establishing a coherent set of guiding principles for living." Yet, he felt sure that youngsters were "getting positive messages from the caring adults around them and just needed a vehicle for tuning in to their own deepest understandings." In response, he created the "Laws of Life Essay Program."

His idea builds on the healing and uplifting power of storytelling. The John Templeton Foundation has funded a worldwide program of Laws of Life essay writing (www.Laws-of-Life.org). Students reflect on their lives and begin writing their stories in narrative essays, a process that expands the students' sense of possibilities. In the United States this program has largely been undertaken in more affluent high schools.

Recently, however, Plainfield, New Jersey, an urban school district with a student population that is almost entirely African American or Latino, with the social and health-related problems that often accompany poverty, adapted the Laws of Life program to fit their needs. They focused on fifth- and eighth-grade students in order to affect students before they enter high school.

Students discussed what was important in their lives with classmates and their families. Then, they began writing their Laws of Life essays, touching on such themes as love, relationships, respect, responsibility, kindness, courage, and so on. One student wrote:

> Laws of Life are rules that I live my life by. . . . I think loving others is the most important of them. A person must have love in his or her life. Love makes a person feel important.

The district involved high school students and community members in judging the essays using a previously established rubric for evaluation. All essays were acknowledged, with prizes for outstanding ones awarded at banquets planned by the communities.

This successful program "illustrates how urban youths, so often the object of remediation and subjected to the pedagogy of poverty, can have their learning energized by reflection and inspiration." (Reported by Prof. Maurice Elias in *Education Week,* Dec. 10, 2008.)

Here is a program worth adapting to your school and community needs. It can be developed by a committee of teachers, high school students, and community members along the lines described above.

students who are ill-prepared to cope with the teaching/learning process offered in the schools. Labeled "remedial" or "illiterate," they remain at the bottom of the ranks in school. Mike is concerned about these *lost students,* who never have a real chance to become educated.

Following this exposé of conditions in the public schools, Mike Rose decides to study what can possibly happen in schools when superior teachers are given an opportunity to apply creative methods to overcome the pitfalls that stymy many teachers. He seeks out teachers who are recommended as outstanding, observing in their classrooms, interviewing both teacher and students, taking extensive notes. Examining the full range of education at K–12 levels, he visits school districts in every state over a period of four years. His publication, *Possible Lives: The Promise of Public Education in America* (Houghton Mifflin, 1995), shows the reader just what really is possible when top quality teachers go to work with a group of students in a classroom. As he comments:

> Classrooms are powerful places. . . . Some of the most significant encounters of my late adolescence and adulthood took place in classrooms, and it was in classrooms that I appropriated powerful bodies of knowledge and methods of inquiry. As I moved from student to teacher, I came of age in these rooms, realizing things about my own abilities and limits . . . the interplay of understanding and uncertainty that defines teaching, the sheer hard human work of it. I have been privy to remarkable moments, spent untold hours with people—from elementary school children to adults in literacy programs—as they acquired knowledge and new skills, played with ideas and struggled to understand, reached tentatively across divides, felt the grounded satisfaction of achievement, raged against history, and moved toward clarity and resolve.
>
> A democracy, I believe, cannot leave the conditions for such experience to chance. . . . A society that defines itself as free and open is obligated to create and sustain the public space for this kind of education to occur across the full broad sweep of its citizenry.

❖ Reflecting on Your Competency at This Time

Do you remember the assessment survey you completed at the beginning of this course? You filed it in your portfolio months ago when you were just beginning on your journey toward achieving multicultural competency. Turn now to page 39 where this assessment results appears in *Multicultural Teaching*. It is appropriate to take this survey again now that you have finished this course.

After you have completed this assessment a second time, turn to the assessment stored in your portfolio at the beginning of this course. Compare the answers you gave on the two forms.

- How have you progressed?
- What changes do you observe in your thinking about multicultural education?

Planning for the Future

Based on the results of your assessment above, begin thinking about what you might do to continue moving yourself ahead on this journey toward multicultural competency. Make a list of things you can do. Consider the following:

- Subscribe to a publication (or find one at the library or with a website) that represents a specific identity group or ethnic group's interests and concerns (News from Native California).
- Volunteer to work with a community organization (Boys and Girls Clubs) or educational program (teaching adults literacy).
- Find a local resource/oranization working toward social justice that you can consult regularly to keep you up-to-date on planned political action (Peace Now).
- Join a professional organization with a journal (or listserv) that interests you (National Council of Teachers of Mathematics, National Association for Multicultural Education).

Writing Your Story

You are just beginning to create your story as a teacher. Perhaps the stories we have introduced in this section will inspire you to relate the tale of your teaching adventures to share with others . . . You might keep a journal with this in mind, addressing questions such as the following:

- Where do you want to be as a teacher five years from now?
- What have you read recently that influenced your thinking?

CONNECTIONS

As a result of the mobility within our society, the student mix in most classrooms in K–12 schools throughout the United States has changed perceptibly in the past twenty to thirty years. Increasingly, even rural and small-town classrooms in the Midwest more closely reflect the diversity of the total population in the United States. Frequently, the cultural roots of the teacher and the children she or he teaches are very different. Therefore, all teachers must know how to provide an equitable education for students from a wide variety of cultural backgrounds. Moreover, teachers must lead the way in promoting multiculturalism at the local and state levels.

GETTING INVOLVED

Expanding Your Reflective Teaching Portfolio

1. Review your Reflective Teaching Portfolio to see how your thinking has evolved during this course. Observe the kinds of comments you made as you completed each chapter's focus. Write a one-page summary of your preparation as a multicultural teacher. Answer some of these questions as you write:
   - How has your thinking changed from the beginning of this course to the end?
   - What ideas do you think will be most helpful to you as a classroom teacher?

- What do you plan to do now to make sure that you continue to grow as an outstanding teacher of multicultural concepts and understandings?

2. Prepare to share your portfolio with your instructor. Mark those items that you would especially like him or her to read or to be aware of. Naturally, you will select those things in which you take most pride, or which show the most growth.

Working with Your Cooperative Learning Group

1. In your CLG plan to interview local educators to identify one exemplary practice related to multicultural education in your area. Write a review of this idea or program and attempt to obtain newspaper coverage for this outstanding instructional practice.
2. Write a letter together to the editor of your local newspaper, pointing out the accomplishments of a specific group in your community.

EXPLORING FURTHER

Judith M. Blohm and Terri Lapinsky. *Kids Like Me: Voices of the Immigrant Experience.* Intercultural Press, 2006.

Barbara Feinberg. *Welcome to Lizard Motel: Children, Stories, and the Mystery of Making Things Up.* Beacon, 2004.

Maxine Greene. *Releasing the Imagination: Essays on Education, the Arts, and Social Change.* Jossey-Bass, 2000.

Deborah Meier, Theodore P. Sizer, and Nancy F. Sizer, eds. *Keeping School: Letters to Families from Principals of Two Small Schools.* Beacon, 2004. Principals write to families about four themes: authority, community, learning, and standards.

An Afterword

Now we have come full circle with you in our study of multicultural education and our focus on *Multicultural Teaching*. We have shared our model focusing on *Esteem, Empathy*, and *Equity* and its implications for instruction in all classrooms. As authors, we know that our words will never be heard by all the students in K–12 classrooms. We cannot reach each child for whom these words are truly intended.

We must trust you as teachers to be our emmissaries, to go forth into the schools as teachers dedicated toward making a difference in the lives of children. We trust you to establish a classroom climate in which all children have a sense of belonging. And we trust you to smile at those diverse faces, even though some may scowl in return.

Furthermore, we hope you will address children with respect and caring and get to know each one as an individual who needs you desperately as an adult guide and advocate at this crucial stage of their lives. Keep in mind the words of the famous educator, John Dewey, who wrote in 1902:

Education enables all individuals to come into full possession of all their powers.

That, then, is our expectation for you and for our schools. You are one of the educators who will make it possible for children to reach their fullest potential. What you do in one year with a single child may make the difference between success and failure in achieving this goal.

What you do also in speaking out about curriculum development and how teachers can collaborate to make our schools outstanding is essential.

Go forth with aim and purpose. We wish you well.

We are always glad to hear from our readers who have ideas to share. Contact us at *Tiedtp@aol.com* or *irist@cwo.com*.

~ Pamela and Iris Tiedt

Appendix A: Recommended Authors of Literature on Multicultural Themes

❖ A Library to Build On for K–12 Classrooms

The following highly selective list represents an ideal foundation for you to begin educating yourself about the wealth of multicultural literature available and to begin collecting your own library of multicultural trade books. Represented here are well-known authors who have worked in many different genres, such as fiction, informational books, biography, folklore, bilingual books, and poetry, including many award-winning titles.

These books would be appropriate for students of any racial, ethnic, or linguistic group because they provide a base for discussing multicultural principles of diversity, inclusion, and tolerance in a variety of settings. Schools with primarily African American, Native American, or Hispanic populations, for example, could expand on this list, adding more titles that reflect the specific historical and cultural experiences of those groups.

The list is divided into three sections, (1) Picture Books, (2) Books for Independent Readers, and (3) Young Adult Readers. Under Picture Books are included titles that can be read aloud to preschoolers, read independently at the primary level, used as discussion starters with intermediate students, serve as resources for studies in the middle school, and support critical reading strategies in high school classes. Books for Independent Readers and the Books for Young Adult Readers can be read aloud, shared with the whole class, or discussed in small groups composed of students with diverse reading abilities. They provide models of quality writing and can be used as reference materials.

Every author listed below has produced a body of quality literature so that you can expect to discover additional excellent titles written by them under more than one category.

Picture Books

Francisco Alarcón. *Iguanas in the Snow and Other Winter Poems.*

Rudolfo Anaya. *Maya's Children*

Monica Brown. *My Name Is Gabito: The Life of Gabriel García Márquez.*

Debbie Holsclaw Birdseye. *Under Our Skin: Kids Talk about Race.*

Tonya Bolden. *G. W. Carver.*

Eve Bunting. *How Many Days to America?*

Sandra Cisneros. *Hairs/Pelitos.*

Lucille Clifton. *Some of the Days of Everett Anderson.*

Lulu Delacre. *Golden Tales: Myths, Legends and Folktales from Latin America.*

Arthur Dorros. *Abuela.*

Mem Fox. *Wilfrid Gordon McDonald Partridge.*

Carmen Lomas Garza. *In My Family/En Mi Familia.*

Paul Goble. *Beyond the Ridge.*

Eloise Greenfield. *Honey I Love, and Other Poems.*

Francisco Jimenez. *La Mariposa.*

Tony Johnston. *Angel City.*

Kathleen Krull. *Harvesting Hope.*

Gerald McDermott. *Arrow to the Sun.*

Pat Mora. *Tomas and the Library Lady.*

Yuyi Morales. *Just a Minute.*

Toni Morrison. *The Big Box.*

Christopher Myers. *Wings.*

Gloria Pinkney. *Back Home.*

Patricia Polacco. *Pink and Say.*

Faith Ringgold. *Tar Beach.*

Allen Say. *Grandfather's Journey.*

John Steptoe. *Stevie.*

Amy Tan. *The Chinese Siamese Cat.*

Alice Walker. *Finding the Green Stone.*

Jeanette Winter. *Follow the Drinking Gourd.*

Ed Young. *Sadako.*

Books for Independent Readers

Alma Flor Ada. *Under the Royal Palms: A Childhood in Cuba.*

Christopher Paul Curtis. *Bud, Not Buddy.*

Louise Erdrich. *The Birchbark House.*

Candace Fleming. *The Lincolns.*

Russell Freedman. *Eleanor Roosevelt.*

Jean Craighead George. *Julie of the Wolves.*

Nikki Giovanni. *The Sun Is So Quiet.*

Rosa Guy. *The Friends.*

Virginia Hamilton. *The People Could Fly: American Black Folktales.*

June Jordan. *Who Look at Me?*

Julius Lester. *To Be a Slave.*

Lois Lowry. *The Giver.*

Victor Martinez. *Parrot in the Oven.*

Patricia and Frederick McKissack. *Red-Tail Angels: The Story of the Tuskegee Airmen of World War II.*

Walter Dean Myers. *Now Is Your Time! The African-American Struggle for Freedom.*

Phyllis Reynolds Naylor. *Roxie and the Hooligans.*

Naomi Shihab Nye. *Habibi.*

Andrea Davis Pinkney. *Let It Shine: Stories of Black Women Freedom Fighters.*

Pam Munoz Ryan. *Esperanza Rising.*

Cynthia Rylant. *Missing May.*

Uri Shulevitz. *How I Learned Geography.*

Gary Soto. *Baseball in April.*

Jerry Spinelli. *Milkweed.*

Mildred D. Taylor. *Roll of Thunder, Hear My Cry.*

Joyce Carol Thomas. *Bright Shadow.*

Laurence Yep. *Dragonwings.*

Jane Yolen. *Not One Damsel in Distress: World Folktales for Strong Girls.*

Valerie Zenatti. *A Bottle in the Gaza Sea.*

Young Adult Books

Maya Angelou. *I Know Why the Caged Bird Sings.*

Joseph Bruchac. *March Toward the Thunder.*

Christopher Paul Curtis. *Elijah of Buxton.*

Sharon Draper. *Copper Sun.*

Angela Johnson. *Looking for Red.*

Donna Jo Napoli. *Zel.*

Gary Paulsen. *Nightjohn.*

Louis Sachar. *Holes.*

Yoshiko Uchida. *Journey to Topaz.*

Carole Boston Weatherford. *Becoming Billie Holiday.*

Gloria Whelan. *Homeless Bird.*

Jacqueline Woodson. *From the Notebooks of Melanin Sun.*

Appendix B: Recommended Films

Seeing people's stories on film allows us the opportunity to enter another person's life and experience the world through different eyes. The following films include both fiction and documentary and are particularly suited to illustrate the diverse nature of childhood and adolescence in communities around the world. As part of your coursework, you might organize a Multicultural Film Festival, calling it "Focusing on Children Around the World," and select films from this list to present at your school or to the community, followed by a discussion.

FILM	COUNTRY
Born into Brothels	India
Tsotsi	South Africa
City of God	Brazil
To Be and to Have	France
Ciao Professore	Italy
Mad Hot Ballroom	United States
Rabbit Proof Fence (historical)	Australia
The Story of the Weeping Camel	Mongolia
The Story of the Yellow Dog	Mongolia
Lost Boys of Sudan	Sudanese refugees in United States
Quinceanera	United States
400 Blows (historical)	France
Angela's Ashes (historical)	Ireland
Salaam Bombay	India
War Dance	Uganda
Whale Rider	New Zealand
My Life in Pink	France
Children of Heaven	Iran
Osama	Afghanistan
The Color of Paradise	Iran
The King of Masks	China
Smoke Signals (Native Americans on reservation)	United States

FILM	**COUNTRY**
God Grew Tired of Us	Sudan/United States
Baran	Iraq
Au Revoir Les Enfants (historical)	France
Monsieur Ibrahim	France
Spring Summer Fall Winter Spring	South Korea
Pelle the Conqueror (historical)	Sweden
Boys Don't Cry	United States
The Way Home	South Korea
The Same Moon (La Misma Luna)	Mexico to United States
The Clay Bird	Bangladesh
The Apu trilogy (historical)	India

Professional Bibliography

The following is a selective list of significant works in the field of multicultural education. We include all the writings that have informed the ideas presented in this book, both in terms of theory and of practice. We also include works by provocative authors who have made major contributions to the development of multicultural thinking, people we judge you should know about. These references will supplement the chapter resource list *(Exploring Further),* intended to stimulate classroom discussion, by directing interested students toward more extensive investigation of related topics.

Adger, Carolyn, Catherine Snow, and Donna Christian, eds. *What Teachers Need to Know about Language.* Center for Applied Linguistics, 2002.

Albrecht, G. L. et al, eds. *Handbook of Disability Studies.* Sage, 2001.

Anyon, Jean. *Radical Possibilities: Public Policy, Urban Education, and a New Social Movement.* Routledge, 2005.

Apple, Michael W. *Identity and Curriculum.* 3rd ed. Routledge, 2004.

August, D. and Timothy Shanahan, eds. *Developing Literacy in Second Language Learners: Report of the Naational Literacy Panel on Language Minority Youth and Children.* Erlbaum, 2006.

Banks, James A. and Cherry McGee Banks, eds. *Multicultural Education: Issues and Perspectives.* 4th ed. Wiley, 2003.

Banks, James A. and Cherry McGee Banks, eds. *Handbook of Research on Multicultural Education.* 2nd ed. Jossey-Bass, 2004.

Banks, James A., et al. *Diversity within Unity: Essential Principles for Teaching and Learning in a Multicultural Society.* Center for Multicultural Education, University of Washington, 2001.

Beykont, Zeynep, ed. *The Power of Culture: Teaching across Language Differences.* Harvard Education Publishing, 2002.

Bigelow, Bill, et al., eds. *Rethinking Our Classrooms: Teaching for Equity and Justice.* Vols. 1 and 11. Rethinking Schools, 1994.

Books, Sue, ed. *Invisible Children in the Society and Its Schools.* 3rd ed. Erlbaum, 2007.

Bothelo, Maria Jose and Masha Kabakow Rudman. *Mirrors, Windows, and Doors: Critical Multicultural Analysis of Children's Literature.* Erlbaum, 2008.

Bowles, Samuel and Herbert Gintis. *Schooling in Capitalist America: Educational Reform and the Contradictions of Economic Life.* Basic Books, 1976.

Cazden, Courtney. *Classroom Discourse. The Language of Teaching and Learning.* Heinemann, 2001.

Center for Applied Linguistics. *Guiding Principles for Dual Language Education.* CAL, 2005.

Compton-Lilly, Catherine. *Confronting Racism, Poverty, and Power: Classroom Strategies to Change the World.* Heinemann, 2004.

Crawford, James. *Educating English Learners: Language Diversity in the Classroom.* Los Angeles Bilingual Educational Services, 2004.

Crystal, David. *Cambridge Encyclopedia of the English Language.* 3rd edition. Cambridge University Press, 2006.

Cummins, James. *Language, Power, and Pedagogy: Bilingual Children in the Crossfire.* Multilingual Matters, 2000.

Darling-Hammond, Linda and John Bransford, eds. *Preparing Teachers for a Changing World: What Teachers Should Learn and Be Able to Do.* Jossey-Bass, 2005.

Delpit, Lisa. *Other People's Children.* The New Press, 1995.

Delpit, Lisa and T. Perry, eds. *The Real Ebonics Debate: Power, Language, and the Education of African-American Children.* Beacon, 1998.

Delpit, Lisa and Joanne Kilgour Doudy, eds. *The Skin That We Speak: Thoughts on Language and Culture in the Classroom.* New Press, 2002.

Derman-Sparks, Louise and Patricia Ramsey. *What If All the Kids Are White? Anti-Bias Multicultural Education with Young Children and Families.* Teachers College Press, 2006.

Fine, Michelle, et al., eds. *Off-White: Readings in Power, Privilege, and Resistance.* Routledge, 2004.

Freire, Paulo. *Pedagogy of the Opressed.* Continuum, 1970.

Garcia, Eugene E. *Teaching and Learning in Two Languages: Bilingualism and Schooling in the United States.* Teachers College Press, 2005.

Gay, Geneva. *Culturally Responsive Teaching: Theory, Research, and Practice.* Teachers College Press, 2000.

Gay, Lesbian, Straight Education Network. *National School Climate Survey.* GLSEN, 2005.

Genesee, Fred, et al., eds. *Educating English Language Learners: A Synthesis of Research Evidence.* Cambridge University Press, 2006.

Genishi, Celia and Ann Haas Dyson. *Children, Language, and Literacy: Diverse Learners in Diverse Times.* Teachers College Press, 2009.

Gibson, Margaret and John U. Ogbu. *Minority Status and Schooling.* Garland, 1991.

Giroux, Henry A. *Theory and Resistance in Education: A Pedagogy for the Opposition.* Bergen & Garvey, 1983.

Gonzalez, J., ed. *Encyclopedia of Bilingual Education.* Sage, 2008.

Gonzalez, Norma E., Luis Moll and Cathy Amanti, eds. *Funds of Knowledge: Theorizing Practices in Households and Classrooms.* Erlbaum, 2005.

Harry, Beth and Janette Klingner. *Why Are So Many Minority Students in Special Education? Understanding Race and Disability in Schools.* Teachers College Press, 2006.

Heath, Shirley Brice. *Ways with Words.* Cambridge University Press, 1996.

Howard, Elizabeth R., Donna Christian and Fred Genesee. *The Development of Bilingualism and Biliteracy from Grade 3 to 5: A Summary of Findings from the CAL/CREDE Study of Two-Way Immersion Education.* Center for Research on Education, Diversity, and Excellence, University of California Santa Cruz, 2004.

Howard, Gary. *We Can't Teach What We Don't Know: White Teachers in Multiracial Schools.* 2nd ed. Teachers College Press, 2006.

Igoa, Cristina. *The Inner World of the Immigrant Child.* St. Martins Press, 1995.

Jacob, Evelyn and Cathie Jordan, eds. *Minority Education: Anthropological Perspectives.* Ablex, 1993.

Katz, Michael B. *Class, Bureaucracy, and the Schools: The Illusion of Educational Change in America.* Praeger, 1975.

Kosciw, J. G. *The 2003 National School Climate Survey: The School Related Experiences of Our Nation's Lesbian, Gay, Bisexual, and Transgender Youth.* GLSEN, 2003.

Kozol, Jonathan. *Savage Inequalities: Children in America's Schools.* Harper, 1991.

Ladson-Billings, Gloria. *The Dreamkeepers—Successful Teachers of African-American Children.* Jossey-Bass, 1994.

Longmore, P. K. *Why I Burned My Book and Other Essays on Disability.* Temple University Press, 2003.

McDermott, Ray P. "Social Relations as Contexts for Learning in School." In *Harvard Educational Review* May, 1977.

Michie, Gregory. *See You When We Get There: Teaching for Change in Urban Schools.* Teachers College Press, 2005.

Nieto, Sonia. *Affirming Diversity: The Sociopolitical Context of Multicultural Education.* Allyn & Bacon, 2004.

Oakes, Jeanne. *Keeping Track: How Schools Structure Inequality.* 2nd ed. Yale University Press, 2005.

Padden, Carol and T. Humphries. *Deaf in America: Voices from a Culture.* Harvard University Press, 1988.

Pang, Victoria. *Multicultural Education: A Caring-centered, Reflective Approach.* McGraw-Hill, 2005.

Philips, Susan. *The Invisible Culture: Communication in the Classroom and Community in the Warm Springs Indian Reservation.* Waveland Press, 1993.

Portes, P. *Dismantling Educational Inequality: A Cultural-Historical Approach to Closing the Achievement Gap.* Peter Lang, 2005.

Rist, Ray C. "Student Social Class and Teacher Expectations: The Self-Fulfilling Prophecy in Ghetto Education." In *Challenging the Myths: The Schools, the Blacks, and the Poor.* Reprint series no. 5. Harvard Educational Review, 1971.

Rosenthal, Robert and Lenore Jacobson. *Pygmalion in the Classroom.* Holt, Rinehart, and Winston, 1968.

Sleeter, Christine and Carl Grant. *Making Choices for Multicultural Education: Five Approaches to Race, Class, and Gender.* Wiley, 2007.

Smitherman, Geneva. *Talkin' that Talk: Language, Culture, and Education in African America.* Routledge, 2000.

Spring, Joel. *Deculturalization and the Struggle for Equality: A Brief History of the Education of Dominated Cultures in the United States.* 5th ed. McGraw-Hill, 2006.

Tatum, Beverly. *Why Are All the Black Kids Sitting Together in the Cafeteria? And Other Conversations about Race.* Basic Books, 1997.

Taylor, Denny and Catherine Dorsey-Gaines. *Growing Up Literate: Learning from Inner-City Families.* Heinemann, 1988.

Yaghmaian, B. *Embracing the Infidel: Stories of Muslim Migrants on the Journey West.* Delta, 2006.

Index